American Judicial Proceedings First Printed Before 1801

American Judicial Proceedings First Printed Before 1801

An Analytical Bibliography

Compiled by
WILFRED J. RITZ

GREENWOOD PRESS
Westport, Connecticut • London, England

Library of Congress Cataloging in Publication Data

Ritz, Wilfred J.
American judicial proceedings first printed before 1801.

Includes bibliographical references and index.
1. Law reports, digests, etc.—United States—Bibliography. I. Title.
KF3.R57 1984 016.34973 83-18605
ISBN 0-313-24057-4 (lib. bdg.) 016.3473

Library of Congress Catalog Card Number: 83-18605
ISBN: 0-313-24057-4

First published in 1984

Greenwood Press
A division of Congressional Information Service, Inc.
88 Post Road West, Westport, Connecticut 06881

Printed in the United States of America

10 9 8 7 6 5 4 3 2 1

To the Library Staffs and Others
Who Helped Make This Book Possible

Contents

Introduction

I. OBJECTIVES

For the period before 1801, this bibliography lists every printed item (except those found in newspapers) that report on an actual judicial proceeding within the territory of the United States, as it existed in 1801; rules of court applicable to those proceedings; all judicial proceedings in England relating to the English colonies within that territory; and all American reprintings of reports of English and European judicial proceedings.

The term "judicial proceeding" defies precise definition. It includes, however, every proceeding that today would be considered "judicial," as well as those before 1801 which, if modern conceptions are extended back to that period, would also be viewed as judicial proceedings, whether or not they were so considered at the time.

This is the first and only comprehensive bibliography of American judicial proceedings before 1801. Present-day standard legal bibliographies limit their coverage to law reports. Since the first American law report was not published until 1789, this means such bibliographies ignore the pre-1789 period as though there had been no American judicial activity during the first 182 years of the American existence. Inasmuch as there are available somewhat comparable bibliographies for statutes and for legal treatises, this bibliography fills a gap now existing in legal and historical scholarly literature.

This bibliography is analytical in that it is organized chronologically, by geographical location, and by subject.

It is easy to obtain from it a complete list of the titles of everything previously printed about American judicial proceedings for any date before 1801. One can find what would have been in "a hypothetically complete" law library of judicial proceedings when the

Constitution was drafted in 1787, or with the addition of a few more titles, when the First Congress met in 1789 to form the federal government.

In the same way, a list can be developed easily for any jurisdiction, and for several definable legal subjects, such as grand jury charges and impeachments. But as to many modern subject areas, the pre-1801 materials do not lend themselves so readily to classification and organization. For this reason, and also because of problems arising out of using duplicate classifications, it is more difficult to obtain from this bibliography a list of titles on modern-day subject areas, such as admiralty, chancery, criminal law, property, and the like. For this purpose, there is no alternative to examining the table of contents and the body of the bibliography. The Index of Main Entries should be useful, however, in finding some particular trial in which the searcher is interested.

The bibliography also lists, without purporting to be comprehensive, significant reprints and secondary materials relating to the pre-1801 judicial proceedings covered.

The Index of Parallel Entries converts the sixty-six bibliographical sources listed in section III of this Introduction into a like number of indexes. If the user finds an imprint or subject listed in any of these sources, this Index of Parallel Entries shows whether it is also included herein. If it is, the user is given access, not only to the imprint, but to related materials as well.

Making decisions as to inclusion and exclusion of both primary and secondary materials is difficult. For instance, 3.05(1) deals with Anne Hutchinson and the Antinomian controversy. For this proceeding there are a number of primary sources, each of diminishing relevancy, and the secondary sources are seemingly legion. "There is scarcely a book about seventeenth century New England that fails to touch on the Antinomian Controversy."[1]

An enumeration of the objectives of this bibliography may help to clarify what is covered and how it is organized. The objectives are:

1. To list every imprint published in America or England before 1801 that relates to or is relevant to a specific judicial proceeding, which took place within the present United States or was of some peculiar interest to its inhabitants.

2. To indicate the extent of contemporary interest, as shown by the number of editions issued and the extent and location of reprintings.

3. To indicate American interest in English and European trials by showing the extent of American printings and reprintings of reports first published in England.

---

1. David D. Hall, The Antinomian Controversy, 1636-1638: A Documentary History 441 (Middletown, Connecticut 1968).

4. To shed light on both the contemporary interest in and the availability and accessibility of each publication. For example, judging by the number and widespread distribution of extant copies, the report of the Rhode Island case of Trevett against Weeden [1.03(6)] was a 1787 "best-seller." By comparison, there was only a modest amount of interest in 1793 in the U.S. Supreme Court decision in Chisholm v. Georgia, [2.04(2)(f)], the case that led to the Eleventh Amendment.

5. To be informative by virtue of its organization.

6. To be easy to use.

7. To provide a guide to the location of original imprints and accessible photoreproductions and reprints.

8. To aid further research by listing the most significant secondary sources.

No single format or organization can be best for attaining all of these objectives. I have chosen an organizational structure and a numbering system similar to that used in a modern statutory code. At the same time I have made an effort to meet the needs of persons other than lawyers. Without losing sight of my own objectives--which were both legal and historical--the bibliography is designed for ease of use by anyone interested in the subject matter. Yet I hope that it will fully serve the specialized needs of the lawyer, the historian, and the librarian as well. I have given primary emphasis to the objective of providing an easy guide to finding all the printed materials relating to particular judicial proceedings in each American jurisdiction, cumulative as of any particular year. The other objectives have been subordinated to this one.

II. DESCRIPTION OF THE BIBLIOGRAPHY

Lawyers already know how to find law reports in law libraries without bothering with card catalogues, in which law reports are barely catalogued anyway. Scholars using large libraries, other than those specializing in legal materials, know that they must use card catalogues or other finding aids to locate almost anything.

Almost all of the American law reports and the books, pamphlets, broadsides, and so forth, that are listed in this bibliography can be found in two sources: Charles Evans, American Bibliography, and Roger P. Bristol, Supplement to Evans' American Bibliography. These works are referred to herein simply as Evans and Bristol.

Evans is a fourteen-volume bibliography, published between 1903 and 1959, covering all American imprints issued from the beginning of American printing in 1638 through 1800. The first twelve volumes were prepared by Evans himself, the thirteenth by Clifford K. Shipton, and the fourteenth--an index--by Bristol. The basic arrangement is chronological, with an alphabetical listing for each year by library cataloguing rules, that is, by author. When there is no determinable personal author, the listing is under the name of a government or a governmental agency; when there is no ascertainable author, as so defined, the listing is by title. Each imprint in Evans is numbered consecutively, the total being 39,162.

Bristol is a one-volume work published in 1970. It covers imprints that are not found in Evans, although published in the same pre-1801 period. The entry numbers in Bristol total 11,262. A forum for "Additions and Corrections to Evans and to Bristol's Supplement Thereto" is provided on a current, but only occasional, basis in the Proceedings of the American Antiquarian Society.

In 1954 the American Antiquarian Society, under Shipton's leadership, in association with the Readex Microprint Corporation, undertook in the Early American Imprints Project to reproduce the full text of every available imprint, except serials, listed in Evans and Bristol. The microprinting for the Project was completed before Bristol finished his work, so that it has a cut-off date that excludes some 1,200 imprints to be found in Bristol. Thus, with a few exceptions the American imprints listed in this bibliography can be found reproduced in microprint.

Although not an additional source, mention should also be made of the National Index of American Imprints Through 1800: The Short-Title Evans, prepared by Clifford K. Shipton and James E. Mooney, and published as a two-volume work in 1969. This is an alphabetical listing of the headings (with some variations) used in Evans and Bristol. It contains a partial list of libraries that own sets of Early American Imprints Project microcards.

English imprints for the period before 1701 are to be found in Donald G. Wing, Short-Title Catalogue. . . 1641-1700, published in three volumes in New York between 1943-51. A second edition, revised and enlarged, is being issued. This source is cited hereafter as Wing. In 1982, A Bibliography of Eighteenth-Century Legal Literature was published in England. This work has its own peculiar classification system. It was published too recently to have been used in the preparation of this work, but it has been used for checking purposes, and one entry is based on it. Otherwise the eighteenth-century English imprints included herein were found in a variety of sources.

Each of these fine bibliographical works, and others I have used, were designed to accomplish particular purposes. When I used them for a different purpose, I naturally ran into some difficulties.[2] But my difficulties do not diminish at all my respect and admiration for the skill and dedication with which these professionals accomplished their objectives.

---

2. A note describing some of the problems I encountered in using these and other bibliographic sources may be useful. Generally, the bibliographic sources mentioned list each imprint separately and

The bibliography is based largely on the information contained in the titles of the imprints listed, and not on an analysis of the full text. In preparing the material, the title information has sometimes been supplemented from the full text or from other reliable sources.

This bibliography is not in and of itself a study of pre-1801 American law, but it should be useful to anyone studying any aspect of the subject, perhaps as much for showing what was not printed during the period as for showing what was printed.

A. Coverage

This bibliography undertakes to list every law report, trial, or separate event of judicial significance occurring in or relating to what was the United States in 1801, and for which there was something printed prior to that date (other than a newspaper account).

---

only once, perhaps with a note containing additional comment. Cross-references are seldom used. Short-Title Evans, however, enters "all anonymous items under title and again under the author if known, except in the case of a few well-known works which ran to many editions" (p. vi).

The Short-Title Evans uses the alphabet as the basic organizing device, alphabetizing by library cataloguing rules. But headings such as "Gt. Brit. Laws, Statutes, etc." are "chronologized" by the addition to the heading of the year of publication.

To locate a "known" imprint in Evans or Bristol, it is almost necessary to know the year of publication, and then for that year to look under likely subject headings. Chronological arrangement thereby limits the area of search. The Short-Title Evans, in spite of its title as a "National Index," is not easy to use as an initial finding aid, except for works by some known "personal" authors. One quickly runs into problems even trying to find something that might seem to be easily identifiable. It is usually easier and quicker first to use Evans or Bristol as an "index" to find the subject heading under which the imprint will usually--but not always--be indexed in the Short-Title Evans.

Library card cataloguing and bibliographical listings differ in one major respect. It is possible in bibliographies of "date-oriented" materials to use a chronological arrangement so as to reduce the area of search. This is not done with library card catalogues or with the Short-Title Evans, so one can never be certain whether an item simply is not there or whether one has not looked under the right headings.

But when one looks for something without having a "known" imprint in mind, there is seldom any alternative to searching the whole bibliography, whether Evans, Bristol or any other, with the help of what little aid is given by chronological arrangement, subject headings, subject-matter indexes, and whatever other finding aids are provided.

The first American law reports in the modern sense were not published until 1789, and only a handful appeared before 1801. Before that date there were few if any neutral or unbiased materials published. What did get into print in one way or another was usually written to promote political, religious, or similar ends. Among the separate events of judicial significance that are included here are the dying confessions and last words of criminals and the sermons preached upon their executions. Obviously, these materials are at the very periphery of what can be considered legal materials. Their inclusion serves to show the very limited range of the judicial materials that were printed in the seventeenth and eighteenth centuries.

B. Exclusions

Major categories of printed materials that have been excluded are listed below, along with some comments on the considerations involved. (Full text of the short-titles used are to be found in section III of this Introduction.)

1. Charters, Constitutions, Session Laws, and Statutory Compilations. The full text of colonial charters and pre-1801 state constitutions are to be found in the collections prepared by Thorpe[3] and Swindler.[4]

Keitt has published a guide to bibliographies of statutory materials.[5] The Library of Congress and the University of North Carolina have microfilmed early state records, all of which are listed in a Guide.[6] Checklists, a loose-leaf publication prepared by Pimsleur for the American Association of Law Libraries, lists session laws and statutory compilations.[7] While both the Guide and Checklists are very useful, neither is wholly satisfactory either as to comprehensiveness or detail.

---

3. Francis Newton Thorpe, The Federal and State Constitutions, Colonial Charters, and Other Organic Laws of the States, Territories, and Colonies Now or Heretofore Forming the United States of America, 7 vol. (Washington, D.C. 1909).

4. William F. Swindler, Sources and Documents of United States Constitutions, 10 vol. (Dobbs Ferry, New York 1974-79).

5. Lawrence Keitt, An Annotated Bibliography of Bibliographies of Statutory Materials of the United States (Cambridge 1934).

6. William Sumner Jenkins and Lillian A. Hamrick, A Guide to the Microfilm Collection of Early State Records (Washington, D.C. 1950); Supplement (Washington, D.C. 1951).

7. Meira G. Pimsleur, Checklists of Basic American Legal Publications (AALL Publications Series No. 4 Littleton, Colorado).

2. Legislative Proceedings. While legislative proceedings as set forth in journals and reports are excluded, a legislative proceeding in the nature of a judicial proceeding is included if a separate imprint was published regarding the matter. Thus, impeachments are included [Chapter 7]. Similarly, Daniel Fowle's Case [1.02(11)] is included. But the somewhat similar case of Alexander McDougall is excluded, there being no imprint, as distinguished from a newspaper account or a legislative journal entry, published about it before 1801. The attempted expulsion of Matthew Lyon from the House of Representatives [Evans 34,757-60] is excluded, but materials relating to Lyon's trial for sedition are included [2.03(9)].

3. Executive Materials. Speeches of governors [Evans 3,813 and 3,818] and proclamations offering rewards for the apprehension of persons charged with crimes [Evans 5,045] are excluded.

4. Legal Treatises. All treatises listed by James are excluded.[8] For imprints not included in James, the test of inclusion has been whether the subject matter relates to a specific judicial proceeding. When the contents are a general discussion of a subject, I have considered it more in the nature of a treatise such as those listed by James, and have excluded it.[9]

Parrish's bibliography of Law Books 1760-1840[10] is an unclassified listing of "law books," which has been used as a bibliographical source. The Parrish bibliography may be found useful in locating materials of a legal nature that are difficult to classify.

5. Newspaper Accounts. Although I have occasionally included significant news accounts that add to the fullness of the eighteenth-century printed record, I did not systematically search newspapers for accounts of judicial proceedings. Since newspapers are not viewed as permanent repositories of legal information and are not filed and kept

---

8. Eldon Revare James, "A List of Legal Treatises Printed in the British Colonies and the American States Before 1801," Harvard Legal Essays 159-211 (Cambridge 1934).

9. Even so, some of my decisions as to inclusion or exclusion may be found debatable by users of this bibliography. For example, John Hale, A Modest Enquiry Into the Nature of Witchcraft and How Persons Guilty of that Crime may be Convicted [Evans 1,050], published at Boston in 1702, has been excluded, on the ground that it is more in the nature of a treatise than a report on the Salem witchcraft trials [1.02(1)]. However, the 1788 New York reprint of Francis Buller, An Introduction to the Law Relative to Trials at Nisi Prius [Evans 20,987], is included [8.05(2)]. Perhaps a sufficient reason is that James did not include this work in his list of Treatises.

10. Jenni Parrish, "Law Books and Legal Publishing in America, 1760-1840," 72 Law Library Journal 355 (1979). Of the 565 numbered entries, eight are for pre-1801 trial and law reports, as defined in this bibliography.

for that purpose, their exclusion can be justified on theoretical grounds. While clippings may be kept, an unindexed newspaper is of little use to the legal profession.

Newspapers, of course, contain much valuable information, and some pre-1801 newspaper accounts have been published in the law reports and so brought into the mainstream of law reporting. Francis Wharton did this in State Trials.[11] These newspaper accounts were further legitimatized as law reports near the end of the nineteenth century, when West Publishing Company reprinted them in Federal Cases,[12] a major law report publishing venture, but in this process the humble newspaper origins became even further obscured.

Admittedly, the general exclusion of newspaper accounts leads to some apparently incongruous results. For example, the now well-known 1793 trial in Philadelphia of Gideon Henfield is excluded. There appears to have been no separate imprint issued before 1801 relating to this case, although there were newspaper accounts concerning the trial. It was not until 1849, when Wharton published a report on the case[13] based largely on notes he found in the papers of counsel as well as the newspaper accounts, that the case became well publicized. By way of contrast, this bibliography does list United States v. Brigstock [2.03(14)], a case that is virtually unknown today, but for which there is an imprint, although the purpose of the printing is far from clear.

---

11. Francis Wharton, State Trials of the United States During the Administrations of Washington and Adams (Philadelphia 1849).

12. The full title sets forth the coverage: The Federal Cases Comprising Cases Argued and Determined in the Circuit and District Courts of the United States from the Earliest Times to the Beginning of the Federal Reporter, Arranged Alphabetically by the Titles of the Cases, and Numbered Consecutively (St. Paul 1894-98). This is a set of thirty books. It constitutes this commercial lawbook publisher's link to the past. Federal Cases plus Federal Reporter, begun in 1890, and the subsequent series of West reporters provide complete (or nearly so) coverage of the published reports of decisions in the lower federal courts from 1789 to date. The series is designed to continue indefinitely into the future. There always have been many unpublished decisions, and today many opinions are printed for limited distribution, stamped "Not for Publication," and are not available in any published series of law reports. The alphabetical arrangement of Federal Cases introduces a discordant note into the otherwise almost universal chronological development of major series of law reports, as well as submerging the identity of the sources from which the cases are drawn. Information as to sources is to a limited extent found in explanatory footnotes and cross-reference tables. Similarly, the consecutive numbering of the cases introduces a complicating note into the customary system of citation.

13. Wharton, State Trials, above note 11, 49, Federal Case No. 6,360.

This incongruity calls for no apology. It may be thatEthe present view of the 1793 significance of Henfield's Case is largely the product of Wharton's 1849 report. Similarly, Brigstock may have involved something considered important in 1800 that is now being overlooked. In any event, the reasons why no separate imprint regarding Henfield was ever published, while there is one in Brigstock, merits study.

Another example can be found in grand jury charges. Some seem to have been published in newspapers and nowhere else.[14] Others were published only as separate imprints, and still others both in newspapers and separately [Chapter 4.00].[15] Obviously a thorough study of grand jury charges requires the researcher to go beyond those listed in this bibliography.

It would be disingenuous, though, not to point out that there is a single overriding reason for excluding newspaper accounts. The task of collecting and organizing them presents huge difficulties (certainly for an individual) and it is questionable whether the anticipated result would justify the effort, unless the effort was directed toward an objective different from that of simply collecting all newspaper accounts relating to judicial proceedings.

The few newspaper accounts listed are those that help to round out the picture of a specific judicial proceeding, or even of a topic, as Section 2.04, which covers decisions of the United States Supreme Court. Entry 2.04(1)(a) is the newspaper report for the 1791 decision in West v. Barnes, the first reported decision of the Supreme Court. The full report of this decision, at least since the eighteenth century, has never been reprinted and still can be found only in eighteenth-century newspapers.

Newspaper supplements and extras are included as separate imprints if they were so listed in the bibliographical sources I have used. For the period after 1700, Bristol included newspaper supplements and extras "if numbered." But Edwin Wolf, II, of The Library Company of Philadelphia has observed that "hundreds of numbered supplements and extras of, for example, the Pennsylvania Gazette were omitted by Bristol."[16]

6. Magazines. Eighteenth-century magazines were intended as repositories of information, as well as to serve current informational

---

14. The grand jury charge of Justice James Iredell delivered in the Middle circuit, held for the District of Virginia, at Richmond, on May 22, 1797, is published in The Virginia Gazette and General Advertiser, issue of May 24, 1797. No contemporary separate imprint is known.

15. Inasmuch as newspaper printings are not included in this bibliography, this is an inference and not demonstrated by the materials included.

16. Edwin Wolf, II, "Book Review," 65 Papers of the Bibliographical Society of America 186, 187 (1971).

interests. This intended permanency, when compared with newspapers, justifies a distinction in their handling. Even so, the titles of eighteenth-century magazines and the bibliographical descriptions of their contents give no suggestion that they contain anything of legal value. I have not searched magazines, with the exception of American Museum and Columbian Magazine, for items about legal proceedings. Whether or not these two magazines are unique in their reporting of some legal proceedings, the beginnings of American law reporting are to be found in their pages. Francis Hopkinson and Alexander Dallas, two of America's first three law reporters, both were associated with the American Museum as editors, and Dallas also contributed to the Columbian Magazine.

7. Church Proceedings. In the early American period religious and secular affairs were often so merged that it is difficult to distinguish sharply between a religious or church controversy and a judicial proceeding. The witchcraft trials of Salem were judicial proceedings. Some proceedings involving Quakers are not so clearly judicial, but they have been included. Proceedings involving the dismissal of pastors are difficult to classify. The case of Ebenezer White in Connecticut in 1764 [Evans 9,871] has been excluded, since the proceedings appear to have taken place within the framework of the church. Publications relating to differences in dogma, as distingushed from some type of a proceeding, are more obvious exclusions.

8. Miscellany Relating to Courts and Judges. Judges' commissions (Bristol B3,837); letters addressed to judges (Evans 1,960, 9,809, 9,810, and 9,811); letters and speeches by judges (Bristol B9,562); judicial sales (Bristol B5,535, B6,157, B6,759, B7,386, B7,797); judicial regulations (Bristol B7,346 and B10,038 - tavern charges; Ford 2,047 - innoculation hospitals); judicial notices (Bristol B3,359 - granting liquor licenses; Rink 118 - setting prices that keepers of public houses can charge for liquors and other articles; Rink 460 - setting rates for innkeepers); notices of jail breaks and wanted persons (Bristol B7,647, and B7,884, B10,902; Rink 515).

9. Sermons and Eulogies. Sermons upon opening of court (Evans 6,605, 12,785, 24,372); sermons on some theme actually or figuratively relating to the law, as King Jehoshaphat's Charge to the Judges (Evans 3,469 and 7,618); devotions for persons about to be executed, as The Convict's Visitor (Evans 23,776). However, printed sermons relating to the executions of actual persons are included in Chapters 5 and 6.

10. General Narratives About Criminals and Crimes. General narratives about criminals and crimes (Evans 2,814, 10,042, 19,401, 23,334, 25,849, 26,695), including those of which no imprints are known to exist (Evans 23,211, 30,635) and whose contents thus cannot be determined.

11. Printed Legal Forms. The problems involved in listing printed forms in bibliographies are discussed generally by Shipton and Mooney in the introduction to the Short-Title Evans and by Bristol in the introduction to the Supplement. Shipton says that "any large manuscript collection of the eighteenth century contains . . . such

ephemera which have never been recorded in any bibliography,"[17] and accordingly he did not for the most part reproduce forms in the Early American Imprints Project. Bristol included all types of printing before 1700, but for the period 1700 to 1800 he excluded "Legal forms (e.g., deeds, indentures). . . unless date and printer are printed in the text."[18] These decisions were made from a bibliographical rather than a historical point of view. Legal historians have not paid sufficient attention to the distinction between printed and manuscript materials to have developed any point of view.

To what extent American lawyers used printed forms before 1801 is simply not known. Such forms do occasionally turn up in court records. Two printed legal forms are reproduced in the Adams Papers.[19] They occasionally are to be found in historical collections and are then recorded by bibliographers. Rink lists three bond forms in a checklist of 566 Delaware imprints.[20] Wolf says there are scores of printed forms in the collections of the Historical Society of Pennsylvania and the Library Company of Philadelphia, and probably in other older manuscript collections as well, but that they have never been segregated.[21]

12. Flyers. Printed handbills (Bristol B6,301 - Public Sale of Land; Bristol B10,808 - Opening of Conveyancer's Office).

13. Nonlegal Imprints With Legal Terms in the Titles. Such legal terms as case, complaint, plea, proceeding, or dispute are sometimes used in the title of imprints that do not relate in any way to a judicial proceeding (Evans 6,548, 8,224, 17,561, 18,392, 38,687; Bristol B11,234).

14. Miscellaneous. Election contests (Evans 24,421); boundary disputes (Bristol B3,854); Vermont's claim to statehood (Evans 16,722, 17,452); and entries erroneously listed as American imprints (Evans 294 - Inditement of the D. of York (1680), a London publication.)

---

17. Short-Title Evans at vii.

18. Bristol at x.

19. L. Kinvin Wroth and Hiller B. Zobel, eds., 1 The Legal Papers of John Adams illustrations 3 and 8 (Cambridge 1965).

20. Evald Rink, Printing in Delaware 1761-1800 (1969). Entries 79 and 80 were probably printed in 1774 and 411 probably in 1796. Number 79 has a blank for the name of the obligee, Number 80 prints a merchant's name, and Number 411 prints the name of the High Sheriff.

21. Wolf, "Book Review," above note 16, at 186.

C. Organization

The bibliography is organized into eleven chapters on the basis of subject matter. Each state and the United States is given a number. The original thirteen states are numbered geographically (North to South), new states on the basis of dates of admission, and the United States arbitrarily.

Within each chapter, the materials are classified according to the state in which the judicial event took place, rather than by the state where the work was published. Listings for each state are chronological by date of publication. Where there has been more than one publication pertaining to a particular judicial event, all imprints relating to the event are grouped and listed in order of publication, to the extent ascertainable, with the full text of the title given for each significantly different title.

Imprints relating to the United States are handled somewhat differently than those for the states. Chapter 2 is in effect an elaboration of what would otherwise be Chapter 1.20. The classification 8.20 is used for a special purpose. Inasmuch as all United States printings and reprintings of foreign trials were printed in particular states, 8.20 lists items that were printed or reprinted in more than one state. To locate for a single state all of the reprintings of English and French trials, both the entries for that state and for 8.20 should be examined.

The most troublesome problem of organization arises out of the question of whether one is dealing with imprints or cases. The question seldom arises for the materials printed before 1787. Until 1787 nearly every imprint related to a separate and distinct judicial proceeding. The result, therefore, is the same whether the listings are conceived of as being of separate imprints or of separate judicial proceedings. Soon after 1801 law reports became the conventional form used for publishing information about judicial proceedings, with each law report covering a number of cases. No one would think of listing separately each case in a modern law report. However, reports of individual trials, generally criminal trials, quite frequently have been published separately, and then are treated as a special category of law reports--trial reports.

The period from 1787 to 1801, however, was one of transition--rapid transition--in which the method of publication changed. The organization and contents of this bibliography reflect this transition. It is not wholly oriented either toward the listing of separate judicial proceedings or toward the listing of separate imprints.

To the extent that there were law reports before 1801, I have listed them as principal entries only once and do not show the individual cases reported. I have defined a "law report" as an imprint listed in modern authoritative legal bibliographies.[22] If such a

22. Miles O. Price and Harry Bitner, Effective Legal Research (New York 1953); Charles C. Soule, The Lawyer's Reference Manual of Law Books and Citations (Boston 1883).

legal bibliography lists an imprint as a law report, I have treated it similarly. But if the imprint is not shown, then I have not only made it a principal entry, but have also shown the individual cases reported. Whenever there is a separate imprint of a case, even if the case is also reported in a law report, I have made the imprint a principal entry, and have shown by a cross-reference where it is also to be found in a law report. This frequently occurs with cases reported by Dallas.

The effect of this treatment is to bring into greater prominence the beginnings of American law reporting, that is, the publication of short items in American Museum and Columbian Magazine and the publication in newspapers and pamphlets of reports of individual cases such as West v. Barnes and Chisholm v. Georgia. In this respect, consistency of treatment of the materials listed is subordinated to coverage of materials not to be found listed in modern legal bibliographies. The emphasis is on the significance of the materials covered in the period of first publication and not on their significance at the present time.

Bibliographies tend to follow library cataloguing practices. This one does so only to a limited extent. It neither replicates a library card catalogue nor provides model entries for card catalogues.[23] The emphasis in the Cataloguing Rules[24] is on providing, through the use of main and added entries, a number of access points that make it possible to find imprints. By definition, each entry in this bibliography relates to a particular judicial proceeding, and so the emphasis is on placing it in context--that is, listing it with all printed materials relating to the same proceeding.[25] The bibliography also

23. The close relationship between bibliographical undertakings and library card cataloguing is clearly evident in the introduction to the Short-Title Evans, which describes how the non-cataloguing target cards of the Early American Imprints Project were metamorphosed into library cataloguing cards.

24. Michael Gorman and Paul W. Winkler, Anglo-American Cataloguing Rules (2d ed. Chicago 1978).

25. In this bibliography, the Duane indictment is listed under Entry 2.03(10)--that is, as a judicial proceeding in a United States Circuit Court, along with all the other printed materials relating to the same proceeding, including citations to the Duane case as reported in the law reports. Cataloguing Rules uses the Duane indictment to illustrate the cataloguing of an "Indictment." Under Rule 21.36C4 the Main Entry is under the name of the defendant, William Duane, with an Added Entry for the court in which he was indicted. Actually, an indictment as such is of little legal significance, it being just one of the many things involved in criminal proceedings in the first instance, a subject already covered by Cataloguing Rule 21.36C1.

seeks to emphasize the legal significance of the imprint within the context of a particular judicial proceeding.[26]

D. Entries

The basic criterion for inclusion in this bibliography is that the work be a pre-1801 imprint. But these imprints are of two types. Some relate to a single judicial proceeding; others are law reports, or of that nature, and report on two or more cases. For the former type of imprint, this bibliography is a listing of individual cases. For the latter type, it is a listing of imprints, and not of individual cases. To this extent, the work is a fruit basket, combining apples and oranges, that is, individual cases and law reports.

When a judicial proceeding has been recorded in both a separate imprint and a law report, an entry is made for the individual case, which is then cross-referenced to the law report. Cross-references also are used to lead the researcher to later reprintings of a particular case.

Only one Main Entry is made for each imprint, and that is made in what appears to be the most appropriate chapter. All other entries for this same imprint are cross-referenced to the one Main Entry. It should be noted, however, that modern views of "appropriateness" may differ from those of the eighteenth century. The name of Dallas today immediately brings to mind the United States Supreme Court and the United States Reports. But in the eighteenth century, Dallas was

---

26. In this bibliography, Judge Paterson's charge to the petit jury in Van Horne's Lessee v. Dorrance is listed as part of Entry 2.03(6)--that is, as a judicial proceeding in a United States Circuit Court. This entry shows that the charge was first printed in 1795, then reported in 1798 in 2 Dallas, which is a law report found in every law library, and then reprinted in 1801 under a slightly different title. Cataloguing Rules uses the charge to illustrate cataloguing of charges to juries under Rule 21.36C5. The Main Entry is made under the name of the court (unlike for indictments where it is under the name of the defendant), with Added Entries under Dorrance, Van Horne, and Paterson.

The Cataloguing Rules lumps together charges to petit or trial juries and the quite different charges to grand juries. Charges to petit juries are simply a part of the criminal trial in the first instance, and adequately covered by Cataloguing Rule 21.36C1. On the other hand there appears to be no Cataloguing Rule that can be applied to grand jury charges. The seemingly applicable Rules, 21.36C1 and 21.36C5, call for cataloguing by the name of the defendant. Inasmuch as it is the grand jury that "makes" defendants by charging persons with crime, there are no defendants at the time the grand jury is charged.

reporting the decisions of courts sitting in Pennsylvania, of which the United States Supreme Court happened to be one for a short period of time. Dallas is treated here as being primarily a reporter of Pennsylvania judicial proceedings, not of the U.S. Supreme Court, and the Main Entry for Dallas is 1.07, not 2.04.

Entries are listed chronologically by date of publication after they have been placed topically and geographically. The only feasible way of ordering the early law reports, which include cases from several different years, is by date of publication. Imprints relating to individual judicial proceedings are arranged the same way. Moreover, this bibliography is premised on the theory that the fact of printing of judicial proceedings has had a legal significance in the development of law that is independent of the substance of the judicial proceedings. Therefore, even if it were feasible to arrange the materials by the date of cases, it would still be done by date of publication.

This bibliography is organized by use of a numbering system similar to those used in legislative codes, whereby the number of each entry shows where it fits into the overall picture.[27] Consequently, some familiarity with the overall arrangement of the bibliography, as in the case of a legislative code, is almost as essential as knowing the alphabet when one uses a dictionary.

The whole bibliography and the chapters are comparable to one title and the chapters of a legislative code. Within each chapter, the imprints are arranged in the manner of sections and subsections. Each full entry, or section, consists of:

1. Entry and Classification Number
2. Heading
3. Title of Imprint
4. Pagination and Size
5. List of Repositories
6. Bibliographic References
7. Evans and Other Ghosts
8. Post-1801 Publications
9. Notes

---

27. This numbering system may very well be easier to understand through its visualization in the example given in the text than by verbal description. The word "entry" is used both to describe the judicial event and the imprints relating to that event, some of which, following a legislative code model, are more accurately described as subentries.

1. *Entry and Classification Number*. For each imprint a single number is both an entry number and a classification number. The imprint may be either a law report containing a number of cases or an imprint relating only to a single judicial proceeding.

This number shows first the subject matter and the jurisdiction of the event (the state or United States). If there has been a series of editions or printings, this number also places the imprint in the series. Thus the New York reprinting by John Holt in 1770 of *A Brief Narrative of the Case and Trial of John Peter Zenger* has 1.05(9)(b)(5) as the entry and classification number. The schematic outline below shows what each part of this number means.

1.05(9)(b.5)

1.	Chapter (Trial and Law Reports of the States)
.05	State (New York)
(9)	Ninth New York entry in this Chapter
(b.	Second publication in series of at least two
.5)	Fifth printing, or fourth reprinting, of this title.

2. *Heading*. The headings, like the entry numbers, are brief informational statements. They do not follow cataloguing rules or the headings used in any other bibliographical source. Where possible, identification is modelled on the style of case names used in law reports, as, for example, *Fletcher v. Vassall* [1.02(10)]. However, no Procrustean measures have been taken to follow this style.

All headings include the first and fourth elements listed below. Unless otherwise shown by the Entry Number, and if the information is available, an effort has also been made to include the second and third elements as well. The information given is:

1. Identification of the Entry;
2. Subject of the Proceeding;
3. Court; and
4. Date of First Significant Publication (If different, other relevant dates are also shown).

3. *Title of Imprint*. For most imprints a complete verbatim description of the title page is given, omitting only mottos, quotations, and similar material having no direct bearing on the subject matter. Dates in Arabic or Roman are given as on the title pages. In a few

instances, where the title is excessively wordy and verbatim transcription of a part only is sufficient for exact identification, some of the title may be omitted. The text of broadsides, as distinguished from their titles and printing data, is omitted. Omissions are shown by ellipses. When I have had to rely on a bibliographical source alone, without being able to examine the imprint itself, the information given is the edited version as set forth in the source.

The full text of the title of an imprint is given only once, usually the first time it is referred to. This is the Main Entry. The titles for subsequent editions and reprintings are given only to the extent that they vary from the first edition.

It is of course impractical to reproduce, except by facsimile, the type styles and sizes and the physical arrangement of the text of a title page. The entries undertake to do no more than convey a visual impression of the title, catching as it were, the spirit if not the letter of the original.

I made all the original transcriptions, mostly from the microcards of the Early American Imprints Project. When a microcard was not available, an effort has been made to check the entry against an original imprint or a photocopy.

The primary objective of this bibliography is identification, not bibliographic description, but the descriptions I have given should be fully sufficient for most purposes.

The need to identify precisely each imprint was a starting point for compiling a list of repositories. One cannot ask a library what unrecorded or unreported imprints it may have without having precise descriptions that make possible the separation of those previously located from the newly discovered.

4. <u>Pagination and Size</u>. The number of pages and size of the publication, where available, are given following the text of the title page at the right-hand margin. These data are taken from what appear to be the most up-to-date bibliographical sources, but no effort has been made either to check or reconcile the sources. The number of pages is the total, however numbered, shown in the source or independently counted and should be considered an approximation rather than an exact figure; similarly, sizes are as given in the bibliographical source. I have not done any measuring.

5. <u>List of Repositories</u>. There are three reasons for including the library repositories having copies of the imprints. It provides information for present-day researchers on the availability and accessibility of each imprint. Secondly, an indication of the number of copies now in existence and their present locations may be useful information, when properly interpreted. It must not be uncritically regarded as directly indicative of past popularity or distribution. Yet the substantial number of pamphlets relating to Jonathan Robbins [Entry 2.03(11)], which even this imperfect census shows have been preserved in libraries throughout the country, must have some legal and historical significance when compared with the almost total loss

of the much more important, or so it would now seem, Cadwalader Pamphlet [Entry 2.03(2)]. Thirdly, this listing is an acknowledgment of the debt owed to the many libraries assisting in the preparation of the bibliography.

This list of repositories for each imprint is a composite of information. It is based on reports from libraries that checked this bibliography in the course of its development, on library responses to specific inquiries, on library locations as shown in other carefully developed bibliographical sources, and on my personal knowledge.

For American imprints, a library location marked with an asterisk shows that the Early American Imprints Project microcard reproduced this library's copy. This imprint will always have either an Evans number or the microprint number shown in both Bristol and in the Short-Title Evans. There is no comparable photoreproduction of English imprints. However, University Microfilms is in the process of microfilming selected English books from Wing's Short-Title Catalogue.[28]

Generally, I have not listed library holdings of photocopies. However, they are listed for certain rare imprints, as well as when the Early American Imprints Project microcard reproduces such a copy.

No effort has been made to supplement the listings with those found in the National Union Catalog[29] or the Union List of Serials,[30] nor to reconcile the listings with either of those sources.

6. Bibliographical References. A listing of bibliographical references follows the list of repositories. For American imprints the first is either the Evans number, a number taken from Bristol, or

---

28. Wing Microform Cataloguing Project of University Microfilms International, Ann Arbor, Michigan 48106, is microfilming Early English Books 1641-1700; Selected from Donald Wing's Short-Title Catalogue. Access is provided through a Cross Index based on the Wing entry numbers.

29. When this project began, the first volume of the National Union Catalog - Pre-1956 Imprints had not yet been published.

30. Information on library holdings of American Museum and Columbian Magazine is available in 1 Union List of Serials in Libraries in the United States and Canada (3d ed. 1965). The libraries shown in this bibliography as having these magazines are only those specifically reporting them. The Union List of Serials expressly excludes "Law Reports and Digests" from its coverage.

a Shaw-Shoemaker number.[31] The Evans number is the same as the microprint or mp. number used by the Early American Imprints Project. For numbers derived from Bristol, the first number is the mp. number, which is then followed by the Bristol number, or if there is no mp. number then by the Bristol number alone.[32]

A very few American imprints are listed for which there is no Evans or Bristol number. These entries are based on what I consider reliable information reported to me. In some instances, such as the imperfect Cadwalader pamphlet [Entry 2.03(2)], the earlier existence of the imprint can be documented.

The next bibliographical reference is the Sabin Number, derived from Joseph Sabin, Bibliotheca Americana, a twenty-nine volume set of books published between 1868 and 1936.[33] Other bibliographical references follow in alphabetical order, in accordance with the abbreviated forms shown in the next section. Where the bibliographical work referred to did not use entry numbers, the references are to pages, with an additional reference to the number of the entry on the page if needed for clarity.

In addition to the Sabin and Shaw-Shoemaker numbers for works printed after 1801, references are given to the entry numbers in the

---

31. Ralph R. Shaw and Richard H. Shoemaker, American Bibliography. This twenty-two-volume series has a separate volume for each of the years 1801 through 1819, and three volumes of finding aids, all published between 1958 and 1966. For each year the arrangement is alphabetical by author, and if none then by title. All are consecutively numbered from 1 through 50,192. This series is also being microprinted by the Early American Imprints Project, which identifies the entries with an "S" number.

32. As has already been noted, there are about 1,200 more Bristol numbers than there are mp. numbers. The Bristol numbers run from B1 through B11,262 and the mp. numbers from 36,1963 through 49,197. It is much easier to use Bristol to find an imprint and so to find both the mp. number and the Bristol number, than it is to use the Short-Title Evans to find the mp. number. Similarly, given an mp. number, it is often easier to look at the microcard to find the heading under which it is likely to be listed in the Short-Title Evans, than it is to find it in the first instance in the Short-Title Evans.

33. Sabin, like Evans, starts with earliest American printings but has no single cut-off date, which date depends instead on the date of publication. The arrangement of the 106,413 numbered entries is alphabetical, under headings based on the then contemporary practice. In order to make Sabin easier to use, John Edgar Molnar published in 1974 a three-volume Author-Title Index to Joseph Sabin's Dictionary of Books Relating to America. While this has been helpful in locating entries in Sabin, my Sabin references may not be complete.

later comprehensive bibliographies of American imprints, now extending through 1833.[34]

7. Evans and Other Ghosts. Ghosts are bibliographical entries for what are, in fact, nonexistent imprints. The information provided is from the Early American Imprints Project, as shown on the microcards.

8. Post-1800 Entries. Entries for imprints through 1819 on Shaw-Shoemaker microcards are presented in the same form and with the same completeness as though they had been published before 1801.

Post-1800 reprintings of pre-1801 imprints, and post-1800 commentaries on the judicial events included in the bibliography, were researched in the course of my effort to locate all pre-1801 imprints. A listing of post-1800 reprints may be useful to some researchers who do not have access to originals or photoreproductions. Ordinarily I have not treated a photoreproduction as a post-1800 reprinting, but an exception has been made for the Photostat Americana Series of the Massachusetts Historical Society, a project in and of itself of some significance. My inclusion of post-1800 commentary is intended to serve merely as a starting point for further research, and no claims are made about the completeness of this bibliographical information. For most of the judicial events recorded here there has been little commentary and it is particularly for these that the listing of post-1800 materials may be useful.

Generally, only the first post-1800 edition or reprinting of a pre-1801 imprint is shown. I have not attempted to list all the later editions and reprintings.

9. Notes. These notes contain additional information, thought to be worthwhile, which does not fit into the standardized entries described above.

E. Citations

The form of citation used generally follows that in Legal Papers of John Adams, published by Harvard University Press. The editors of this work say:

---

34. Richard H. Shoemaker. A Checklist of American Imprints. There is one volume for each year, 1820 through 1829, all published between 1964 and 1971, and supplemented by a one-volume Title Index and a two-volume Author Index and Corrections, prepared by M. Frances Cooper and published in 1972-73. Shoemaker is independently numbered, the numbers running from 1 through 41,633. The series has been continued for 1830 by Gayle Cooper, and for 1831-1833 by Scott Bruntjen and Carol Bruntjen, all volumes being published between 1973 and 1979. This series is also independently numbered, with the last entry for 1833 numbered 22,795. The two series for the period after 1819 are not at the present being microprinted.

> "Since so much of the material cited is legal in nature, the editors decided to render virtually all citations in the basic legal form--volume number preceding the name of the author or work and page numbers following, without punctuation or abbreviation for the word 'page.' The basic guide to citation form has been the Harvard Law Review's Uniform System of Citation (the 'Blue Book'), with certain variations to permit the adding of supplementary bibliographical information."[35]

I have put all citations in basic legal form--and not just works "cited often enough to merit a standard short-title form."[36] In order to avoid unintelligible abbreviations, I have eliminated all of them, except for those that are very much in current use, departing in this respect from both legal and nonlegal practice. In the interest of providing the most informative citations possible, I have also felt free to depart from other standard practices.

All dates given in connection with imprints, whether of law reports or any other works, are to the dates of publication, elaborated upon when appropriate to show the date of the decision. The customary form of legal case citation uses the date of the decision, ignoring completely the date of publication of the report in which the decision appears. In listing a law report, legal bibliographies and law catalogues give the period or dates covered by the decisions reported, ignoring the date of publication of the report itself. The issuance of different editions is generally ignored because the content of every edition is presumably the same. This assumption is not always valid. There are no satisfactory sources for finding the date of first publication of an American law report, or for finding information about subsequent editions. To the extent that these law reports are listed herein, a modest beginning is made on providing this type of information for American law reports.

III. BIBLIOGRAPHIC SOURCES AND SHORT TITLES

Adams Controversy	Adams, Thomas R. The American Controversy: A Bibliographical Study of the British Pamphlets About the American Disputes, 1764-1783 (Providence 1980).
Adams Independence	Adams, Thomas R. American Independence: The Growth of an Idea: A Bibliographical Study of the American Political Pamphlets Printed Between 1764 and 1776 Dealing with the Dispute Between Great Britain and Her Colonies (Providence 1965).

---

35. 1 Legal Papers, above note 19, xxxvii.

36. Id. at cxxv.

Alden	Alden, John E. Rhode Island Imprints, 1727-1800 (New York 1949).
Baer	Baer, Elizabeth. Seventeenth Century Maryland: A Bibliography (Baltimore 1949).
Bristol	Bristol, Roger P. Supplement to Evans' American Bibliography (Charlottesville 1970).
Bristol Additions	Additions and Corrections to Evans and to Bristol's Supplement Thereto, 82 Proceedings of the American Antiquarian Society 46-53 (1972); 83 Id. 261-73 (1974); 87 Id. 409-15 (1978); 88 Id. 102-14 (1978).
Church	Cole, G. W. Catalogue of Books Relating to the Discovery and Early History of North and South America, 5 vol. (New York 1907).
Clayton-Torrence	Clayton-Torrence, William. Trial Bibliography of Colonial Virginia (Richmond 1908-10).
Cooley	Cooley, Elizabeth F. Vermont Imprints Before 1800 (Montpelier 1937).
Cotton Mather	Holmes, Thomas James. Cotton Mather: A Bibliography of His Works, 3 vol. (Cambridge 1940).
Evans	Evans, Charles. American Bibliography, 14 vol. (Worcester 1903-59).
Fisher	Fisher, Samuel H. The Publications of Thomas Collier, Printer 1784-1808 (Litchfield, Connecticut 1933).
Ford	Ford, Worthington C. Broadsides, Ballads, &c. Printed in Massachusetts, 1639-1800 (Boston 1922).
Ford Briefs	Ford, Paul Leicester. "List of some Briefs in Appeal Causes tried before the Lords Commissioners of Appeals of Prize Causes of His Majesty's Privy Council which relate to America, 1736-1758," 5 Proceedings of the Massachusetts Historical Society, Second Series 85-101 (Boston 1890).
Gaines	Gaines, Pierce W. William Cobbett and the United States 1792-1835 (Worcester 1971).
Garrett	Garrett, John W. "Seventeenth Century Books Relating to Maryland," 34 Maryland Historical Magazine 1-39 (March 1939).
Hildeburn	Hildeburn, Charles R. A Century of Printing. The Issues of the Press in Pennsylvania 1685-1784. 2 Vol. (Philadelphia 1885-86).
Hill	Hill, Frank P. American Plays (Stanford 1934).

Humphrey	Humphrey, Constance H. "Check-list of New Jersey Imprints to the End of the Revolution," 24 The Papers of the Bibliographical Society of America 43-133 (Chicago 1930).
Humphrey Appendix	Humphrey, Constance. "Appendix, A Partial List of New Jersey Official Publications Not Printed in New Jersey," 24 The Papers of the Bibliographical Society of America 134-49 (Chicago 1930).
Huntington	Waters, Willard O. American Imprints, 1648-1797, in the Huntington Library (Cambridge 1933).
Increase Mather	Holmes, Thomas James. Increase Mather: A Bibliography of his Works, 2 Vol. (Cleveland 1931).
Kentucky Imprints	McMurtrie, Douglas C. and Albert H. Allen. American Imprints Inventory, No. 5 and No. 6. Check List of Kentucky Imprints 1787-1810 (Louisville 1939).
McCorison	McCorison, Marcus A. Vermont Imprints 1778-1820 (Worcester 1963).
McDade	McDade, Thomas M. The Annals of Murder (Norman 1961).
McMurtrie North Carolina	McMurtie, Douglas C. Eighteenth Century North Carolina Imprints, 1749-1800 (Chapel Hill 1938).
Metzger	Metzger, Ethel. Supplement to Hildeburn's Century of Printing 1685-1775 (Thesis, School of Library Service, Columbia University 1930).
Minick	Minick, A. Rachel. A History of Printing in Maryland, 1791-1800, with a Bibliography of Works Printed in the State During the Period (Baltimore 1949).
Morgan	Morgan, Richard Parker. A Preliminary Bibliography of South Carolina Imprints, 1731-1800 (Clemson, South Carolina 1965?).
Morsch	Morsch, Lucile M. American Imprints Inventory. No. 9. Check List of New Jersey Imprints 1784-1800 (Baltimore 1939).
Mosimann	Mosimann, Jeanne D. A check list of Charleston, South Carolina Imprints from 1731 to 1799, with a Historical Introduction. (M.S.L.S. Thesis, Catholic University 1951).
mp. (also cited as <u>Short-Title Evans</u> in text)	Shipton, Clifford K. and James E. Mooney. National index of American Imprints Through 1800: The Short-Title Evans, 2 vol. (Worcester 1969).
New London	Johnson, Hazel A. A Checklist of New London, Connecticut, Imprints 1709-1800 (Charlottesville 1979).

New York Public	Stark, Lewis M., and Maud D. Cole. The New York Public Library, Checklist of Additions to Evans' American Bibliography in the Rare Book Division of the New York Public Library (New York 1960).
NUC	The National Union Catalog - Pre-1956 Imprints, 685 vol. (1968-1980).
Parrish	Parrish, Jenni. "Law Books and Legal Publishing in America, 1760-1840," 72 Law Library Journal 355-452 (Summer 1979).
Pearl	Pearl, Morris Leonard. William Cobbett. A Bibliographical Account of His Life and Times (London 1953).
Porter	Porter, Dorothy B. "Early American Negro Writings: A Bibliographical Study," 39 The Papers of the Bibliographical Society of America 192-268 (1945).
Rink	Rink, Evald. Printings in Delaware 1761-1800 (Wilmington 1969)
Rosenbach	Rosenbach, A. W. S. American Jewish Bibliography (Baltimore 1926).
RPJCB 4th	Bibliotheca Americana Catalogue of the John Carter Brown Library in Brown University: Books Printed 1675-1700 (Providence 1973).
Rutherfurd	Rutherfurd, Livingston. John Zenger, His Press, His Trial and a Bibliography of Zenger Imprints (New York 1904).
Sabin	Sabin, Joseph. Bibliotheca Americana, 29 vol. (New York 1868-1936).
Shaw-Shoemaker	Shaw, Ralph R., and Richard H. Shoemaker. American Bibliography, a Preliminary Checklist for 1801-1819, 19 vol. (New York 1958-63).
Shoemaker	A Checklist of American Imprints for 1820-1833, 14 vol. (Shoemaker, Cooper, and Bruntjen, Compilers, New York 1964-1979).
Short-Title Evans	See mp. above.
Sowerby	Sowerby, E. Millicent. Catalogue of the Library of Thomas Jefferson, 5 vol. (Washington, D.C. 1952-59).
Stoddard	Stoddard, Roger E. A Catalogue of Books and Pamphlets Unrecorded in Oscar Wegelin's Early American Poetry, 1650-1820 (Providence 1969).
Swem	Swem, E. G. A Bibliography of Virginia, Parts 1 and 2 (1915-17).

Tapley	Tapley, Harriet Silvester. Salem Imprints 1768-1825 (Salem 1927).
Thornton Official	Thornton, Mary Lindsay. Official Publications of the Colony and State of North Carolina 1749-1939: A Bibliography (Chapel Hill 1939).
Thornton Unofficial	Thornton, Mary Lindsay. A Bibliography of North Carolina 1589-1956 (Chapel Hill 1958).
Tinker	Tinker, Edward Laroque. "Francois Xavier Martin and Jean Leclerc," 39 New York Public Library Bulletin 675-97 (September 1935).
Trumbull	Trumbull, James H. List of Books Printed in Connecticut, 1709-1800 (Hartford 1904).
Trumbull 2d	Bates, Albert Carlos. Supplementary List of Books Printed in Connecticut 1709-1800 (Nos. 1,742 through 2,820) (Hartford 1938).
Trumbull 3d	Bates, Albert Carlos. Second Supplementary List of Books Printed in Connecticut 1709-1800 (Nos. 2,821 through 2,903) (Hartford 1947).
Turnbull	Turnbull, Robert J. 1 Bibliography of South Carolina, 1563-1814 (Charlottesville 1956).
Vail	Vail, R. W. G. The Voice of the Old Frontier (New York 1949).
Vail Patriotic Pair	Vail, R. W. G. "Patriotic Pair of Peripatetic Printers," Essays Honoring Lawrence W. Wroth 391-422 (Portland, Maine 1951).
VCRP	Virginia Colonial Records Project, Virginia State Library (Richmond).
Weeks	Weeks, S. B. The Press of North Carolina in the Eighteenth Century (Brooklyn 1891).
Whittemore	Whittemore, Caroline. A Checklist of New Hampshire Imprints 1756-1790 (Thesis, School of Library Service, Columbia University 1929).
Wegelin	Wegelin, Oscar. Early American Poetry (2d ed. New York 1930).
Wheeler	Wheeler, Joseph T. Maryland Press, 1777-1790 (Baltimore 1938).
Wing	Wing, Donald. Short-Title Catalogue of Books Printed in England, Scotland, Ireland, Wales, and British America and of English Books Printed in other Countries 1641-1700, 3 vol. (New York 1945-51).

Winship — Winship, George Parker. Rhode Island Imprints. A List of Books. Pamphlets, Newspapers and Broadsides Printed at Newport, Providence, Warren, Rhode Island Between 1727 and 1800 (Providence 1915).

Winslow — Winslow, Ola Elizabeth. American Broadside Verse from Imprints of the 17th and 18th Centuries (New Haven 1930) (Library Symbol in parenthesis indicates imprint reproduced in Winslow.)

IV. LIBRARY LOCATIONS AND LIBRARY SYMBOLS

The symbols for libraries are based on the symbols used in the National Union Catalog issued by the Library of Congress. The letter "L" added to a university symbol designates the Law Library.

These library symbols are based on several conventions. Each state, as well as Canada and Great Britain, is given an abbreviation. That abbreviation standing alone designates the State Library, as M for the Massachusetts State Library, and Vi for the Virginia State Library. The state abbreviation plus a library abbreviation is used to designate some libraries for which there is no chance of confusion, as MHi for the Massachusetts Historical Society and ViHi for the Virginia Historical Society; and the state abbreviation plus a university abbreviation is used to designate state universities, as NcU for the University of North Carolina and ViU for the University of Virginia. The state abbreviation plus a library abbreviation is used to designate other well-known libraries, as MH for Harvard University and NjP for Princetown University.

Other than use of these conventions the library symbol is constructed from a state abbreviation, a city abbreviation, an institution abbreviation, and perhaps a more specific library abbreviation, as NNB for the library of the Association of the Bar of the City of New York and ViLxW-L for the Law Library of Washington and Lee University.

Libraries designated with one asterisk checked the complete preliminary mimeographed draft of this bibliography. Libraries designated with two asterisks responded to a specific inquiry. Where no asterisk precedes the library symbol, the attribution of a copy of an imprint to that library is based upon some bibliographical source (listed under bibliographical sources) and was not independently verified by the library.

Inasmuch as new entries were added after the libraries checked the preliminary draft or responded to specific inquiries, and new library locations were added as revealed by new bibliographical sources, errors in the list of library repositories are not the fault of the library but are attributable to the way in which the bibliography was developed and to errors in the compilation. Moreover, library holdings may have changed since this information was compiled.

Key to Library Symbols

**AU-L	University of Alabama School of Law, University, Alabama
**Ar-U	University of Arkansas, Fayetteville, Arkansas
**Ar-U-L	University of Arkansas School of Law, Fayetteville, Arkansas
**AzU-L	University of Arizona College of Law, Tucson, Arizona
BBB-N	Bevan-Naish Library, Birmingham, England
BCT	Trinity College, Cambridge, England
BCU	Cambridge University, Cambridge, England
BDT	Trinity College, Dublin, Ireland
BEN	National Library of Scotland (Advocates'), Edinburgh, Scotland
BENew	New College, Edinburgh, Scotland
BEU	University of Edinburgh, Edinburgh, Scotland
BGH	Hunterian Museum, Glasgow, Scotland
BGU	Glasgow University, Glasgow, Scotland
BLC	Congregational Library, London, England
BLF	Friends Library, London, England
**BLM	British Museum, London, England
BLPro	Public Record Office, London, England
BLS	Sion College, London, England
BLU	University of London, London, England
BLW	Dr. Williams Library, London, England
BMR	John Rylands Library, Manchester, England
BOB	Bodleian Library, Oxford, England
*CLL	Los Angeles County Law Library, Los Angeles, California
**CLU	University of California, Los Angeles, California
**CLU-C	William Andrews Clark Memorial Library, University of California, Los Angeles, California
*CLU-L	University of California School of Law, Los Angeles, California
**CLSU-L	University of Southern California School of Law, Los Angeles, California
**CSfH	University of California, Hastings College of Law, San Francisco, California
**CSfU-L	University of San Francisco Law School, San Francisco, California
*CSmH	Henry E. Huntington Library and Art Gallery, San Marino, California
**CStclU-L	University of Santa Clara School of Law, Santa Clara, California
CSt	Stanford University, Stanford, California
**CSt-L	Stanford University Law School, Stanford, California
**CU	University of California, Berkeley, California
*CaOOA	Public Archives of Canada, Ottawa, Ontario
*CoU-L	University of Colorado School of Law, Boulder, Colorado

Ct	Connecticut State Library, Hartford, Connecticut
*CtHT	Trinity College, Hartford, Connecticut
*CtHT-W	Watkinson Library, Trinity College, Hartford, Connecticut
*CtHi	Connecticut Historical Society, Hartford, Connecticut
**CtMW	Wesleyan University, Middletown, Connecticut
CtNlC	Connecticut College Library, New London, Connecticut
**CtSoP	Pequot Library, Southport, Connecticut
**CtU-L	University of Connecticut School of Law, Hartford, Connecticut
CtY	Yale University, New Haven, Connecticut
**DCU-L	Catholic University of America School of Law, Washington, D.C.
*DGU	Georgetown University Libraries (except Law Center), Washington D.C.
**DGW-L	George Washington University Law School, Washington, D.C.
*DLC	Library of Congress, Washington, D.C.
*DUSC	United States Supreme Court Library, Washington, D.C.
DeHi	Historical Society of Delaware, Wilmington, Delaware
*DeWint	Henry Francis DuPont Winterthur Museum, Winterthur, Delaware
**FU-L	University of Florida College of Law, Gainesville, Florida
*GU	University of Georgia Libraries, Athens, Georgia
**IC	Chicago Public Library, Chicago, Illinois
*ICABF	American Bar Foundation, Chicago, Illinois
ICN	Newberry Library, Chicago, Illinois
*ICU-L	University of Chicago Law School, Chicago, Illinois
**IEN-L	Northwestern University School of Law, Chicago, Illinois
**IdU-L	University of Idaho College of Law, Moscow, Idaho
**InNd-L	Notre Dame Law School, Notre Dame, Indiana
**InU	Indiana University, Bloomington, Indiana
**InU-L	Indiana University School of Law, Bloomington, Indiana
**InValU	Valparaiso University School of Law, Valparaiso, Indiana
*KBB	Baker University, Baldwin City, Kansas
**KTW-L	Washburn University School of Law, Topeka, Kansas
*KWi	Wichita City Library, Wichita, Kansas
**KyLoU-L	University of Louisville School of Law, Louisville, Kentucky
**KyU-L	University of Kentucky College of Law, Lexington, Kentucky
LNT	Tulane University of Louisiana, New Orleans, Louisiana
**LNT-L	Tulane University of Louisiana School of Law, New Orleans, Louisiana

*LU	Louisiana State University, Baton Rouge, Louisiana
*LU-L	Louisiana State University Law School, Baton Rouge, Louisiana
*M	Massachusetts State Library, Boston, Massachusetts
**MAJ	Jones Library, Amherest, Massachusetts
*MB	Boston Public Library, Boston, Massachusetts
*MBAt	Boston Athenaeum, Boston, Massachusetts
**MBC	Congregational Library, Boston, Massachusetts
MBev	Public Library, Beverly, Massachusetts
**MBS	Social Law Library, Boston Massachusetts
*MBU	Boston University, Boston, Massachusetts
MBU-L	Boston University Law School, Boston, Massachusetts
MDeeP	Pocumtuck Valley Memorial Association, Deerfield, Massachusetts
MH	Harvard University, Cambridge, Massachusetts
**MH-AH	Andover-Harvard Theological Seminary Library, Cambridge, Massachusetts
**MH-BA	Harvard University Graduate School of Business Administration, Cambridge, Massachusetts
*MH-L	Harvard University Law School, Cambridge, Massachusetts
*MHi	Massachusetts Historical Society, Boston, Massachusetts
MLy	Lynn Public Library, Lynn, Massachusetts
**MSa	Salem Public Library, Salem, Massachusetts
*MSaE	Essex Institute, Salem, Massachusetts
**MTaHi	Old Colony Historical Society, Taunton, Massachusetts
*MWA	American Antiquarian Society, Worcester, Massachusetts
**MWC	Clark University, Worcester, Massachusetts
**MWa	Warren Free Library, Warren, Massachusetts
**MWelC	Wellesley College, Wellesley, Massachusetts
MWHi	Worcester Historical Society, Worcester, Massachusetts
*MWiW	Williams College, Williamstown, Massachusetts
*MWiW-C	Chapin Library, Williams College, Williamstown, Massachusetts
*MdBB	Baltimore Bar Library, Baltimore, Maryland
*MdBE	Enoch Pratt Free Library, Baltimore, Maryland
*MdBP	Peabody Institute, Baltimore, Maryland
*MdBJ-G	John Work Garrett Library, John Hopkins University, Baltimore, Maryland
*Me-L	Maine State Law Library, Augusta, Maine
**MeB	Bowdoin College, Brunswick, Maine
MeBa	Bangor Public Library, Bangor, Maine
**MeHi	Maine Historical Society, Portland, Maine
*MeU-L	University of Maine Law School, Portland, Maine
MiD-B	Burton Historical Collection, Detroit Public Library, Detroit, Michigan
*MiDW-L	Wayne State University Law School, Detroit, Michigan
*MiU-C	William L. Clements Library, University of Michigan, Ann Arbor, Michigan
*MiU-L	University of Michigan Law School, Ann Arbor, Michigan

*MoSW	Washington University, St. Louis, Missouri
*MoSW-L	Washington University School of Law, St. Louis, Missouri
*MoU-L	University of Missouri School of Law, Columbia, Missouri
*MsU-L	University of Mississippi School of Law, University, Mississippi
**MtU-L	University of Montana School of Law, Missoula, Montana
N	New York State Library, Albany, New York
*N-L	New York State Law Library, Albany, New York
NBuG	Grosvenor Reference Division, Buffalo and Erie County Public Library, Buffalo, New York
**NCH	Hamilton College, Clinton, New York
*NCooHi	New York State Historical Association, Cooperstown, New York
*NHi	New York Historical Society, New York, New York
**NIC	Cornell University, Ithaca, New York
*NIC-L	Cornell University Law School, Ithaca, New York
*NN	New York Public Library, New York, New York
*NNB	Association of the Bar of the City of New York, New York, New York
*NNC-L	Columbia University Law School, New York, New York
NNLI	New York Law Institute Library, New York, New York
**NNM	American Museum of Natural History, New York, New York
*NNPM	Pierpoint Morgan Library, New York, New York
**NNS	New York Society, New York, New York
**NNStJ-L	St. John's University School of Law, Brooklyn, New York
*NNU-L	New York University Law School, New York, New York
*NNUT	Union Theological Seminary, New York, New York
*NPV	Vassar College, Poughkeepsie, New York
NSchU	Union College, Schenectady, New York
NSm	Smithtown Public Library, Smithtown, New York
*NSyU-L	Syracuse University College of Law, Syracuse, New York
*NbO	Omaha Public Library, Omaha, Nebraska
*NcAsS	Sondly Reference Library, Asheville, North Carolina
*NcD	Duke University, Durham, North Carolina
*NcD-L	Duke University Law School, Durham, North Carolina
*NcU	University of North Carolina, Chapel Hill, North Carolina
NhD	Dartmouth College, Hanover, New Hampshire
*NhHi	New Hampshire Historical Society, Concord, New Hampshire
*Nj	New Jersey State Library, Archives and History, Trenton, New Jersey
*NjHi	New Jersey Historical Society, Newark, New Jersey
*NjP	Princeton University, Princeton, New Jersey
*NjPera-B	Board of Proprieters, Perth Amboy, New Jersey
NjPT	Princeton Theological Seminary, Princeton, New Jersey
*NjR	Rutgers University, New Brunswick, New Jersey

OC-L	Cincinnati Law Library, Cincinnati, Ohio
**OCU	University of Cincinnati, Cincinnati, Ohio
*OCU-L	University of Cincinnati College of Law, Cincinnati, Ohio
*OU-L	Ohio State University College of Law, Columbus, Ohio
*OkTU-L	University of Tulsa Law School, Tulsa, Oklahoma
*OrU-L	University of Oregon Law School, Eugene, Oregon
*P	Pennsylvania State Library, Harrisburg, Pennsylvania
*P-L	Pennsylvania State Law Library, Harrisburg, Pennsylvania
*PBL	Lehigh College, Bethlehem, Pennsylvania
*PCarlD	Dickinson College, Carlisle, Pennsylvania
**PCH	Haverford College, Haverford, Pennsylvania
*PHi	Historical Society of Pennsylvania, Philadelphia, Pennsylvania
**PMA	Allegheny College, Meadville, Pennsylvania
*PP	Free Library of Philadelphia, Philadelphia, Pennsylvania
**PPAmP	American Philosophical Society, Philadelphia, Pennsylvania
PPB	Philadelphia Bar Association (Law Library Company of Philadelphia), Philadelphia, Pennsylvania
*PPL	Library Company of Philadelphia, Philadelphia, Pennsylvania
*PPPrHi	Presbyterian Historical Society Library, Philadelphia, Pennsylvania
PPRF	Rosenbach Foundation, Philadelphia, Pennsylvania
*PPT-L	Temple University Law School, Philadelphia, Pennsylvania
*PSC-Hi	Friends Historical Library, Swarthmore College, Swarthmore, Pennsylvania
*PU	University of Pennsylvania, Philadelphia, Pennsylvania
*PU-L	University of Pennsylvania Law School, Philadelphia, Pennsylvania
**PV-L	Villanova University School of Law, Villanova, Pennsylvania
*R	State Library, Providence, Rhode Island
*R-L	State Law Library, Providence, Rhode Island
*RHi	Rhode Island Historical Society, Providence, Rhode Island
**RNHi	Newport Historical Society, Newport, Rhode Island
*RNR	Redwood Library and Athenaeum, Newport, Rhode Island
**RP	Providence Public Library, Providence, Rhode Island
**RPA	Providence Athenaeum, Providence, Rhode Island
*RPB	Brown University, Providence, Rhode Island
*RPJCB	John Carter Brown Library, Brown University, Providence, Rhode Island
*ScC	Charleston Library Society, Charleston, South Carolina
**TNJ	Vanderbilt University, Nashville, Tennessee
**TNJ-L	Vanderbilt University Law School, Nashville, Tennessee
**TU	University of Tennessee, Knoxville, Tennessee
**TU-L	University of Tennessee College of Law, Knoxville, Tennessee

**TxDaM-L	Southern Methodist University School of Law, Dallas, Texas
*TxU	University of Texas, Austin, Texas
*TxU-L	University of Texas School of Law, Austin, Texas
*Vi	Virginia State Library, Richmond, Virginia
*ViHi	Virginia Historical Society, Richmond, Virginia
*ViLxW	Washington and Lee University, Lexington, Virginia
*ViLxW-L	Washington and Lee University School of Law, Lexington, Virginia
**ViRU-L	University of Richmond, T. C. Williams School of Law, Richmond, Virginia
*ViU	University of Virginia (including Law School), Charlottesville, Virginia
*ViW	College of William and Mary (including Law School), Williamsburg, Virginia
*ViWC	Colonial Williamsburg, Williamsburg, Virginia
*ViWI	Institute of Early American History and Culture, Williamsburg, Virginia
*Vt	Vermont State Library, Montpelier, Vermont
*VtBennM	Bennington Museum, Bennington, Vermont
*VtHi	Vermont Historical Society, Middlebury, Vermont
**VtMiM	Middlebury College, Middlebury, Vermont
VtMiS	Sheldon Museum, Middlebury, Vermont
*VtU	University of Vermont, Burlington, Vermont
*WHi	State Historical Society of Wisconsin, Madison, Wisconsin
*WaU-L	University of Washington School of Law, Seattle, Washington
**WvU-L	West Virginia University College of Law, Morgantown, West Virginia

V. HISTORY AND ACKNOWLEDGMENTS

The initial encouragement to undertake the preparation of this bibliography came from the late Mark DeWolfe Howe, Professor of Law at the Law School of Harvard University. Professor Howe was also instrumental in my receiving a small Ames Foundation supporting grant for the project.

I began research in 1961, with the assistance of David Gibson, working under a Robert E. Lee Research Grant from Washington and Lee University. Our first task was to search through the fourteen volumes of Evans, American Bibliography. Later, other bibliographical sources at Washington and Lee were examined.

A preliminary typewritten draft of 278 distinct entries was completed on December 1, 1963. The late Philip A. Putnam, then Assistant Librarian, Harvard Law School, very kindly checked this draft against the holdings of the Harvard Law Library, both for its accuracy and to provide additional entries. The same type of check was made by the late Joseph Andrews, Reference Librarian, Association of the Bar of the City of New York. On the basis of this checking, I prepared a partial revision of the typewritten draft prepared in late 1964, which was checked against the holdings of the American Antiquarian Society by Marcus A. McCorison, Librarian.

Meanwhile, I was able to engage the interest of the Library of Congress, through Walter H. Zeydel, Chief American-British Law Division. In early 1964, Lewis C. Coffin, Law Librarian, agreed to check the typewritten draft against the Library's holdings. The checking was done by James W. Elder, Reference Assistant, American-British Law Division.

On the basis of these checks and the additional information received from the libraries involved, a revised draft was prepared, more or less in the present form. This draft was sent to each library shown by some bibliographical source to have a copy of one or more of the pre-1801 imprints listed, requesting its assistance in checking the bibliography. The response was excellent. In spite of the fact that the bibliography was not an alphabetical listing by author, which would have facilitated checking against card catalogues, almost all of the libraries returned the draft within a reasonable length of time, fully checked against their holding and with additions and many useful comments. Questions raised by the libraries were resolved by correspondence and frequently by procuring photocopies of title pages.

When the late John Cook Wyllie, Librarian, University of Virginia, was asked to check the bibliography against its holdings, he readily and graciously agreed to do so. As a result, Donald R. Haynes, Virginia State Librarian, then a Reference Assistant at the University of Virginia, thoroughly checked the bibliography against the University's holdings, both those in the Alderman Library and at the Law School, and provided many photocopies of title pages.

When I learned that the late Roger P. Bristol, at the University of Virginia, was preparing a Supplement to Evans, his assistance was also solicited. It was readily given, and thereafter the materials being developed by Bristol were examined for additional imprints, library holdings, and so on, and Mr. Bristol was very helpful in clearing up many questions.

During the development of the bibliography extensive use was made of the libraries at the University of Virginia, both the Alderman and the Law Library. All checking against the microprint cards of the Early American Imprints Project was done at the Alderman Library in Charlottesville. Extensive use was also made of the large collection of bibliographical source materials at the Alderman Library. William H. Runge, then the Curator of Rare Books, and Frances Farmer, Law Librarian, now retired, were always most helpful. The same can also be said of all members of their staffs.

Through the courtesy of the late Louis Piacenza, Law Librarian, UCLA, then president of the American Association of Law Libraries, a notice was carried in the AALL President's Newsletter calling attention to this bibliography in process and inviting requests for the preliminary draft. In response, a number of libraries requested copies for use in checking against their own holdings.

A two-page checklist of traditional law reports was prepared and sent to all law schools that had not already checked the bibliography requesting information on their holdings of pre-1801 law reports. Most responded to the request.

As must be evident from what I have said thus far, the staffs of many libraries have been helpful in developing this bibliography. In the list that follows, I have made an effort to acknowledge by name all those not already named who kindly undertook to check in whole or in substantial part the preliminary draft of the bibliography against their holdings. It has not been possible to acknowledge by name, however, the many persons who responded to specific requests for information. The amount of work involved in this checking, of course, depended in large part on the size of the library's holdings. The name of the library itself thus gives a measure of my indebtedness to its staff, whether listed by name or not. Additionally, I am grateful for assistance to Stanley N. Katz, at the time of his services to me an Assistant Professor at Harvard Law School and now Professor at Princeton, for assistance with the Zenger imprints, and to Thomas R. Adams, Librarian, John Carter Brown Library, for assistance with the Boston Massacre imprints.

Last but not least are the obligations I owe to my own institution and its staff. Washington and Lee has assisted with financial backing through a series of Robert E. Lee Research Grants for student assistance and John M. Glenn grants for summer travel and research. The staff of the University Library, under Librarians Henry S. Coleman and Maurice D. Leach, have always been most helpful. Law Librarians Louise Moore, Peyton Neale, and Sally Wiant, as well as all the members of the staff, have always been of great assistance. The difficult typing of the manuscript has been excellently done: the first draft by Mrs. Anna Claytor; and the final draft including the tedious tables and indexes by Mrs. Linda Carter. Other members of the Word Processing Center have also been most helpful.

LIST OF ADDITIONAL ACKNOWLEDGMENTS

CLL	William B. Stern, Foreign Law Librarian
CSmH	Lyle H. Wright, Head of Reference Department
CaOOA	W. Kayle Lamb, Dominion Archivist and National Librarian
CoU-L	Roy M. Mersky, Law Librarian; and Oscar J. Miller, Professor of Law and Law Librarian
CtHT, CtHT-W	Marian Clarke, Curator, Watkinson Library
DGU	Samuel T. Waters, Assistant Librarian; and Lawrence C. Chamberlain
DUSC	Helen Newman, Librarian
DeWint	Frank H. Sommer, Head of Libraries

GU	W. P. Kellam, Director of Libraries
ICU-L	Frances H. Hall, Law Reference Librarian
KBB	Mary McCormick, Librarian
KWi	Fred A. Rockwell, Librarian
LU, LU-L	Kate Wallach, Law Librarian
M	I. Albert Matkov, State Librarian
MB	John Alden, Keeper of Rare Books
MBAt	Walter Muir Whitehill, Director and Librarian; and Margaret Hackett, Reference Librarian
MBU	Howard B. Gotlieb, Head of Reference and of Special Collections
MBU-L	Charles S. Connolly, Librarian
MHi	John D. Cushing, Librarian; and Mr. Wheeler
MSaE	David R. Proper, Librarian
MWiW	W.E. Wright, Librarian
MWiW-C	H. Richard Archer, Custodian
MdBB	Samuel M. Briggin, Librarian
MdBE	Eve Davis, Head, Civics & Sociology Department
MdBP	Clayton E. Rhodes, Acting Librarian
MdBJ-G	Elizabeth Baer, Librarian
Me-L	Edith L. Hary, Law Librarian
MeU-L	Donald L. Garbrecht, Librarian; and L. Kinvin Wroth, Associate Professor of Law
MiU-C	Howard H. Peckham, Director; and Joyce Bonk, Catalog Librarian
MiU-L	Beverley J. Pooley, Assistant to the Director
MoSW, MoSW-L	Jean Ashman, Law Librarian
MoU-L	George E. Skinner, Law Librarian
N-L	Ernest H. Breuer, State Law Librarian
NCooHi	Paul Z. DuBois, Librarian
NHi	James J. Heslin, Director
NIC-L	Harry Bitner, Law Librarian
NN	Lewis M. Stark, Chief, Rare Book Division; and Maud Cole, First Assistant
NNC-L	Gersten Rappaport, Reference Librarian
NNPM	Herbert Cahoon, Chief, Reference Department
NNU-L	Edward J. Bander, Assistant Librarian; and Robert Sperry, Reference Librarian
NNUT	John Young, Reference Librarian
NSyU-L	Peter E. Herzog, Law Librarian
NbO	Catherine Beal, Supervisor, Adult Services
NcAsS	Ida L. Padelford, General Reference Librarian; and E. Richard Cole, Sondley Reference Librarian
NcD	John P. Waggoner, Jr., Assistant Librarian
NcD-L	Marianna Long, Law Librarian
NcU	Harry Bergholz, Chief Bibliographer
NhHi	John Lindenbusch, Manuscripts Librarian
Nj	Herta Prager, Head, Bureau of Law and Legislative Reference
NjHi	Edith O. May, Librarian
NjP	William S. Dix, Librarian; and Earle E. Coleman, Curator of Rare Books and Special Collections
NjR	Donald A. Sinclair, Curator of Special Collections
OCU-L	William Jeffrey, Jr., Professor of Law and Law Librarian
OU-L	Kathleen G. Farmann, Assistant Director of Research Services

OkTuL	Marianna Grotefend, Assistant Law Librarian
OrU-L	Lois I. Baker, Law Librarian
P, P-L	Elizabeth H. Poe, Law Librarian; and Joyce M. Arnold, Reference Librarian, Law
PBL	James D. Mack, Librarian; and Georgia E. Raynor, Head Cataloger
PCarlD	Charles Coleman Sellers, Librarian
PHi	Henry Cadwalader, Executive Director, and R. N. Williams, II, Director
PP	Albert C. Gerould, Chief, Central Public Depts.; Ellen Shaffer, Rare Books Librarian; and Howell J. Heaney, Bibliographer
PPAmP	Gertrude D. Hess, Associate Librarian
PPL	Edwin Wolf, II, Librarian
PPPrHi	William B. Miller, Assistant Secretary
PPT-L	Erwin C. Surrency, Law Librarian
PSC-Hi	Dorothy G. Harris, Associate Director
PU	Neda M. Westlake, Curator, Rare Book Collection
PU-L	Morris L. Cohen, Biddle Law Librarian; and Paul Gay, Assistant Librarian
R	Elliott E. Andrews, State Librarian
R-L	Clarence H. Shoren, Librarian
RHi	Clarkson A. Collins, III, Librarian
RNR	Donald T. Gibbs, Librarian
RPB	Christine D. Hathaway, Special Collections Librarian
ScC	Virginia Rugheimer, Librarian
TxU, TxU-L	Roy M. Mersky, Professor of Law and Director of Research
Vi	William J. Van Schreeven, State Archivist
ViHi	Virginius C. Hall, Jr., Curator of Rare Books; and E. Lee Shepard, Assistant Curator of Manuscripts
ViW	James A. Servies, Librarian
Vt	Lawrence J. Turgeon, State Librarian
VtBennM	Allen D. Hill, Genealogical Consultant
VtHi	David D. Warden, Assistant to the Librarian and Museum Director
VtU	T. D. Seymour Bassett, Curator Wilbur Collection
WHi	Ben H. Wilcox, Librarian
WaU-L	Marian G. Gallagher, Law Librarian

My thanks, also, to the others I have inadvertently overlooked and to those of whose names I have no record.

BIBLIOGRAPHY

1.00

Trial and Law Reports of the States

1.02 <u>Massachusetts</u>

(1) Salem Witchcraft Trials, 1692

(a) A Brief and True Narrative of some Remarkable Passages Relating to sundry Persons Afflicted by Witchcraft at Salem Village: Which happened from the Nineteenth of March to the Fifth of April, 1692. Collected by Deodat Lawson. Boston, Printed for Benjamin Harris and are to be sold at his Shop, over against the Old Meeting House. 1692. 10 p. 12mo.

MHi*

Evans 613 Sabin 39,442 Wing L-702

(a.2) Massachusetts Historical Society, Photostat Americana, 2d Series, No. 3 (Boston 1936).

(b) Christ's Fidelity The only Shield Against Satans Malignity. Asserted in a Sermon Delivered at Salem Village, the 24th of March, 1692. Being Lecture-day there, and a time of Publick Examination, of some Suspected for Witchcraft. By Deodat Lawson, formerly Preacher of the Gospel there . . . . Boston Printed, by B. Harris, & Sold by Nicholas Buttolph, next to Guttridg's Coffee-House. 1693. 86 p. 16mo.

CSMH, MHi, MWA*, ViU

Evans 643 Sabin 39,443 Wing L-703

(b.2) Christ's Fidelity . . . a Sermon Deliver'd . . . . By Deodat Lawson, Minister of the

Gospel . . . next to Guttridgs Coffee-House.
1693. 96 p. 8vo.

Sabin 39,443

(b.3) The Second Edition. Printed at Boston in New-England, and Reprinted in London, by R. Tookey, for the Author; and are to be sold by T. Parkhurst, at the Bible and Three Crowns in Cheapside; and J. Lawrence, at the Angel in the Poultrey. 1704.
132 p. 12mo.

Sabin 39,443

(c) The Wonders of the Invisible World. Observations as well Historical as Theological, upon the Nature, the Number, and the Operations of the Devils . . . . By Cotton Mather. Boston: Printed and Sold by Benjamin Harris for Sam. Phillips. 1693. Published by the Special Command of His Excellency, the Governour of the Province of the Massashusetts-Bay in New-England. 216 p. 8vo.

BLM, BOB, CSmH, DLC, MB(2), MHi, MSaE, MWA*, NN, RPJCB, ViU

Evans 657 Sabin 46,603 Church 733
Cotton Mather 454-A Wing M-1172

(c.2) Boston, Printed, and Sold by Benjamin Harris, 1693.
216 p. 8vo.

MH, MWA, RPJCB

Cotton Mather 454-A² RPJCB 4th at 271
Wing M-1173

(d) The Wonders of the Invisible World: Being An Account of the Tryals of Several Witches, Lately Executed in New-England: And of several remarkable Curiosities therein Occurring . . . . By Cotton Mather. Published by the Special Command of his Excellency the Govenour of the Province of the Massachusetts-Bay in New-England. Printed first, at Bostun [sic] in New-England; and Reprinted at London, for John Dunton, at the Raven in the Poultry. 1693. 102 p. 4to.

BCU, BGU, BLM, BMR, CSmH, DLC, MB, MWA, MWiW-C, MiU-C, MiU-L, NN(3, 2 imp.), NjP, P, PHi, PP, PPL, RPJCB, ViU, ViW

Sabin 46,604 Church 734 Cotton Mather 454-B
RPJCB 4th at 271 Wing M-1174

(d.2) The Second Edition. Printed first at Boston in New England, and reprinted at London, for John Dunton, at the Raven in the Poultrey. 1693. 62 p. 4 to.

BOB, CSmH, Ct, ICN, MB, MH, MHi, MWiW-C, NN, RPJCB

Sabin 46,605 Cotton Mather 454-C
RPJCB 4th at 271 Wing M-1175

(d.3) The Third Edition. Printed first at Boston in New England, and reprinted at London, for John Dunton, at the Raven in the Poultrey. 1693. 64 p. 4to.

BCU, BEN, BLM, BOB, CSmH, DLC, MBS, MH, NN, ViU

Sabin 46,606 Cotton Mather 454-D Wing W-1176

Evans Ghost 35,047 (New London 1,371)

(e) A Further Account of the Tryals of the New-England Witches, With the Observations Of a Person who was upon the Place several Days when the suspe led Witches were first taken into Examination. To which is added, Cases of Conscience Concerning Witchcrafts and Evil Spirits personating men. Written at the request of the ministers of New-England. By Increase Mather, President of Harvard Colledge. Licensed and entred according to order. London: Printed for J. Dunton, at the Raven in the Poultrey, 1693. Of whom may be had the Third Edition of Mr. Cotton Mather's First Account of the Tryals of the New-England Witches, Printed on the same size with this Last Account, that they may bind up together. 58 p. 4to.

BEU, BLM, BLS, BOB CSmH, Ct, CtY, DLC, MBC, MBS, MSaE, MWA, MWelC, MiU-C, NHi, NIC, NN, PP, PPL, RPJCB, ViU

Sabin 46,687 Church 736 Increase Mather 22-B
RPJCB 4th at 268 and 272 Wing M-1213

(f) A true account of the Tryals, Examinations, Confessions, Condemnations, and Executions of divers Witches, at Salem, in New-England, for Their Bewitching Sundry People and Cattel to Death, and doing other great Mischiefs, to the Ruine of many People about them. With the Strange Circumstances that attended their Enchantments: And Their Conversation with Devils, and other Infernal Spirits. In a Letter to a Friend in London. Licensed according to Order. London, Printed for J. Conyers, in Holbourn. [1693] 8 p. 4to.

NN, RPJCB

Sabin 46,563 Cotton Mather between 410 and 411
RPJCB 4th at 278

Note This is called a bookseller's fraud by George H. Moore, "Notes on the Bibliography of Witchcraft in Massachusetts," 5 American Antiquarian Society,

Proceedings, New Series 256-57 (Worcester 1889). This conclusion is endorsed by Thomas James Holmes in the cited Mather bibliographical entry.

(g) More Wonders of the Invisible World: Or, The Wonders of the Invisible World, Display'd in Five Parts . . . . Collected by Robert Calef, Merchant, of Boston in New-England. Licensed and Entred according to Order. London: Printed for Nath. Hillar, at the Princes-Arms, in Leaden-Hall-street, over against St. Mary-Ax, and Joseph Collyer, at the Golden-Bible, on London-Bridge. 1700. 166 p. 4to.

BCU, BGU, BLC, BLM, BOB, CSmH, CLU-C, CtHT-W, DLC, ICU, MB, MHi, MWiW-C, MiU-C, NN(2, 1 imp.), NNPM, PBL, PPL, RPJCB, ViU

Sabin 9,926 Cotton Mather 15-A RPJCB 4th at 407
Sowerby 451 Wing C-288

(g.2) Printed in London in the year 1700. Reprinted in Salem, Massachusetts, 1796, by William Carlton. Sold at Cushing & Carlton's Book-Store, at the Bible and Heart, Essex-Street. 320 p. 12mo.

CtHT-W, DLC, MB, MBAt, MH, MHi, MSaE, MWA*, MiU-C, NHi, NN, RPJCB, ViU, WHi

Evans 30,149 Sabin 9,927 Tapley at 361 and 363

(g.3) Printed in London, A.D. 1700. Re-printed in Salem, by John D. and T. C. Cushing, Jr. for Cushing and Appleton. 1823.

Sabin, 9,927 Shoemaker 12,046 Tapley at 472

(g.4) Reprinted at Boston in A New Edition by T. Bedlington. 1828.

Sabin, 9,927

(h) "Copy of a MS. Letter giving a full and candid account of the delusion called Witchcraft, which prevailed in New-England; and of the judicial trials and execution at Salem, in the county of Essex, for that pretended crime, in 1692. Written by Thomas Brattle, F.R.S. and communicated to the Society by Thomas Brattle, Esq. of Cambridge," [5] Collections of the Massachusetts Historical Society for the Year M,DCC,XCVIII. [61-80] Printed at Samuel Hall, No. 53, Cornhill, Boston, 1798. 292 p. 8vo.

BLM, CSmH, DLC, MB, MBAt, MSaE, MWA*, MWiW, MdBP, NN, PBL, PHi, PPAmP, RPB, TxU, ViU, ViW, WHi

Evans 34,082

(h.2) Reprinted by John H. Eastburn, 1835.

(i) "Trials For Witchcraft before the Special Court Of Oyer And Terminer, Salem, Massachusetts, 1692," 1 Peleg W. Chandler, ed., American Criminal Trials 65-140 (Boston 1841).

Sabin 11,868

(j) Samuel P. Fowler, An Account of the Life, Character, &c., of the Rev. Samuel Parris, of Salem Village, and of his connection with the Witchcraft Delusion of 1692 (Salem 1857)

Sabin 25,320

(k) Samuel P. Fowler, ed., Salem witchcraft, comprising More Wonders of the Invisible World. Collected by Robert Calef; and Wonders of the Invisible World, by Cotton Mather; together with notes and explanation (Salem 1861).

Sabin 75,736

(k.2) [The Same] (1865).

Sabin 75,736

(l) John Russell Smith, ed., The wonders of the invisible world . . . . By Cotton Mather, D.D. To which is added a farther account of the tryals of the New-England witches. By Increase Mather, D.D. President of Harvard College (Library of Old Authors. London 1862).

Sabin 46,607

(m) Records of Salem Witchcraft, Copied from the Original Documents (Woodward's Historical Series Nos. I-II. Roxbury, Mass. 1864).

Sabin 68,405

(n) S. G. Drake, ed., The Witchcraft Delusion in New England (Woodward's Historical Series Nos. V-VII. Roxbury, Mass. 1866).

Sabin 20,884

(o) Charles W. Upham, Salem Witchcraft with an Account of Salem Village, and A History of Opinions on Witchcraft and Kindred Subjects, 2 vols. (Boston 1867).

Sabin 98,039n.

(p) Samuel G. Drake, ed., Annals of Witchcraft in New England, and elsewhere in the United States, from their First Settlement (Woodward Historical Series No. VIII. Boston 1869).

Sabin 20,867

(q) J. Wingate Thornton, "Communication," 27 New England Historical & Genealogical Register 55 (Boston 1873).

(r) "Appendix A: The Examination of Abigail Hobbs," The Diaries of Benjamin Lynde and of Benjamin Lynde, Jr., With an Appendix 211-16 (Boston 1880).

(s) "Witch-trials in Salem in 1692, history of witchcraft in Massachusetts and the Act of 1711," 1 Massachusetts Historical Society, Proceedings, 2d Series 65-70, 99-118, 339-58 (Boston 1885).

(t) George H. Moore, "Notes on the Bibliography of Witchcraft in Massachusetts," 5 American Antiquarian Society, Proceedings, New Series 245-73 (Worcester 1889).

(u) Winfield S. Nevins, Witchcraft in Salem Village in 1692, together with some account of other witchcraft prosecutions in New England and elsewhere (Salem 1892).

(v) George Lyman Kittredge, "Ch. XVIII: Witchcraft and the Puritans," Witchcraft in Old and New England 329-73 (Cambridge 1929). Reprinted from American Antiquarian Society, Proceedings (Worcester 1907).

(w) George Lincoln Burr, ed., Narratives of the Witchcraft Cases 1648-1706 (Original Narratives of Early American History New York 1914).

(x) John D. Lawson, ed., "The Trials of Bridget Bishop and George Burroughs for Witchcraft, Salem, Massachusetts, 1692," 1 American State Trials 514-30 (St. Louis 1914).

(y) David Levin, ed., What happened in Salem? Documents pertaining to the 17th-century witchcraft trials (New York 1952).

(z) Frank W. Grinnell, "Obscuring American History: Reversing the Salem Witchcraft Convictions," 43 American Bar Association Journal 997-99 (Chicago 1957).

(aa) Kai T. Erikson, Wayward Puritans: A Study in the Sociology of Deviance (New York 1966).

(bb) Sanford J. Fox, Science and Justice: The Massachusetts Witchcraft Trials (Baltimore 1968).

(cc) Chadwick Hansen, Witchcraft at Salem (New York 1969).

(dd) Marion L. Starkey, Devil in Massachusetts: A Modern Enquiry into the Salem Witch Trials (New York 1949).

(ee) Paul Boyer and Stephen Nissenbaum, eds., Salem-Village Witchcraft: A Documentary Record of Local Conflict in Colonial New England (Belmont, Cal. 1972).

(ff) Paul Boyer and Stephen Nissenbaum, Salem Possessed: The Social Origins of Witchcraft (Cambridge 1974).

(gg) Paul Boyer and Stephen Nissenbaum, eds., The Salem Witchcraft Papers: Verbatim Transcripts of the Legal Documents of the Salem Witchcraft Outbreak of 1692, 3 vols. (New York 1977).

(2) Maule's Trial for Slander and Blasphemy, 1695

(a) Truth held Forth and Maintained According to the Testimony of the holy Prophets, Christ and his Apostles recorded in the holy Scriptures. With some Account of the Judgments of the Lord lately inflicted upon New-England by Witch craft, To which is added, Something concerning the Fall of Adam, his state in the Fall, and way of Restoration to God again, with many other weighty things, necessary for People to weigh and consider. Written in true Love to the Souls of my Neighbours, and all Men, which includeth that Love to them, as to my self, by Thomas Maule. Printed in the Year 1695. 276 p. 4to.

BLF(2), MH*, MSaE, RPJCB, ViU

Evans 730 Sabin 46,935 RPJCB 4th p. 315
Wing M-1354

(b) New-England Pesecutors Mauld With their own Weapons. Giving some Account of the bloody Laws made at Boston against the Kings Subjects that dissented from their way of Worship. Together with a brief Account of the Imprisonment and Tryal of Thomas Maule of Salem, for publishing a Book, entituled, Truth held forth and maintained, &c. By Theo. Philathes. [New York: Printed by William Bradford. 1697]. 66 p. 4to.

BLF(2), CSmH, MH, MHi, MSaE, NHi, NN(imp.), PHC, RPJCB*, ViU

Evans 801 Sabin 46,934 Church 767
RPJCB 4th p. 352 Wing M-1353

(c) Peleg W. Chandler, ed., "Trial of Thomas Maule before the Superior Court of Judicature, for a Slanderous Publication and Blasphemy, Salem, Massachusetts, 1696," 1 American Criminal Trials 141-49 (Boston 1841).

Sabin 11,868

(d) John D. Lawson, ed., "The Trial of Thomas Maule for Slander and Blasphemy, Massachusetts, 1696" 5 American State Trials 85-89 (St. Louis 1916).

(e) Matt Bushnell Jones, "Thomas Maule, the Salem Quaker, and Free Speech in Massachusetts Bay, with Bibliographical Notes," 72 Essex Institute Historical Collections 1-42 (Salem 1936).

(3) Quelch's Trial for Piracy, 1704

(a) Faithful Warnings to prevent Fearful Judgments. Uttered in a brief Discourse, Occasioned, by a Tragical Spectacle, in a Number of Miserables Under a Sentence of Death for Piracy. At Boston in N.E. Jun. 22 1704 [By Cotton Mather] Boston, Printed & Sold by Timothy Green, at the North End of the Town. 1704. 48 p. 8vo.

MHi*
Evans 1,175 Cotton Mather 125

(b) An Account of the Behaviour and last Dying Speeches Of the Six Pirates, that were Executed on Charles River, Boston side, on Fryday June 30th 1704. Viz. Capt. John Quelch, John Lambert, Christopher Scudamore, John Miller, Erasmus Peterson and Peter Roach . . . . [Colophon] Printed for and Sold by Nicholas Boone, at his Shop near the Old Meeting-House in Boston, 1704.

2 p. 28.5 x 17.5 cm.

MHi, MiU-C, NHi, NN, NcAsS

mp. 39,402 Bristol B251 Ford 265
New York Public 53

Note Microcard not issued as of July 6, 1982.

(b.2) George Francis Dow and John Henry Edmonds, The Pirates of the New England Coast 1630-1730, Appendix III 376-78 (Marine Research Society, Salem 1923).

(c) The Arraignment, Tryal and Condemnation of Capt. John Quelch, and others of his Company &c. For sundry Piracies, Robberies and Murder committed upon the Subjects of the King of Portugal, Her Majesties Allie, on the Coast of Brasil, &c. Who upon full Evidence were found Guilty, at the Court-House in Boston, on the 13th. of June 1704. With the Arguments of the Queen's Council, and Council for the Prisoners, upon the Act for the more effectual Suppression of Piracy. With an account of the Ages of the several Prisoners, and the Places where they were Born. Printed for and Sold by Nicholas Boone, 1704.

No copy located (advertised by this title at the end of (b) above. Church 826, below (c.2), incorrectly locates copy in BLM.)

Sabin 67,085

(c.2) The Arraignment, Tryal, and Condemnation, Capt. John Quelch, and Others of his Company, &c. For Sundry Piracies, Robberies, and Murder, Committed upon the Subjects of the King of Portugal, Her Majesty's Allie, on the Coast of Brasil, &c. Who Upon full Evidence, were found Guilty, at the Court-House in Boston, on the Thirteenth of June, 1704. By Virtue of a Commission, grounded upon the Act of the Eleventh and Twelfth Years of King William. For the more effectual Suppression of Piracy. With the Arguments of the Queen's Council, and Council for the Prisoners upon the said Act. Perused By his Excellency Joseph Dudley, Esq; Captain-General and Commander in Chief in and over Her Majesty's Province of the Massachusetts-Bay, in New-England, in America, &c. To which are also added, some Papers that were produc'd at the Tryal abovesaid. With An Account of the Ages of the several Prisoners, and the Places where they were Born. London: Printed for Ben. Bragg in Avemary-Lane 1705. (Price One Shilling.)

CSmH, DLC, MB, MH-L, MHi, NN
Sabin 67,086 Church 826

(c.2.a) Massachusetts Historical Society, Photostat Americana, 2d Series, No. 37 (Boston 1937).

(d) "Case No: 56. The Trial and Condemnation of Capt. John Quelch, and others of his Company, &c. for sundry Piracies, Robberies, and Murder, committed upon the Subjects of the King of Portugal, Her Majesty's Ally, on the Coast of Brasil, &c. at the Court-House in Boston, on the 13th of June, 1704," A Collection of State-Trials and Proceedings, upon High-Treason, and other Crimes and Misdemeanours, from The Reign of King Edward VI. to the Present Time. The Eighth Volume. With an Alphabetical Table to the Two Supplemental Volumes. [columns 205-18] London: Printed for Benj. Motte, and C. Bathurst, at the Middle-Temple-Gate; and Tho. Wooton, at the Queen's Head and Three Daggers, over-against St. Dunstan's Church, in Fleet-street. MDCCXXXV.

DLC, NcAsS, ViU

(d.2) "Case No. LV," The Fourth Edition . . . . To which is prefixed, A New Preface, By Francis Hargrave, Esquire. Volume the Eighth. [205-19] London: Printed by T. Wright, Essex-Street, Strand; For . . . . And Sold by G. Kearsly, No. 46, near Sergeant's-Inn, Fleet-Street. MDCCLXXVIII.

Note The report of Quelch's trial in State Trials was one of the authorities relied upon by John Adams in his representation of the defendant in Rex v. Nickerson. L. Kinvin Wroth and Hiller B. Zobel, eds., 2 Legal Papers of John Adams 335 at 344 (Cambridge 1965).

(d.3) Thomas B. Howell, "Case No. 436," 14 Complete Collection of State Trials 1067-96 (London 1816).

(e) John D. Lawson, ed., "The Trial of Captain John Quelch and others for Piracy, Boston, Massachusetts, 1704" 5 American State Trials 330-59 (St. Louis, 1916).

(f) Abner C. Goodell, Jr., "Capt. John Quelch, the Pirate," 3 Colonial Society of Massachusetts Publications, Transactions 1895-97 71-77 (Boston 1900).

(g) George Francis Dow and John Henry Edmonds, "Ch. VII: John Quelch and his Crew who were Hanged in Boston and their Gold Distributed," The Pirates of the New England Coast 1630-1730 99-115 (Marine Research Society, Salem 1923).

(4) Eight Pirates, Special Court of Admiralty, 1717

(a) Instructions to the Living, from the Condition of the Dead. A Brief Relation of Remarkables in the Shipwreck of above One Hundred Pirates, Who were Cast away in the Ship Whido, on the Coast of New-England, April 26, 1717. And in the Death of Six, who after a Fair Trial at Boston, were Convicted & Condemned, Octob. 22. And Executed, Novemb. 15. 1717. With some Account of the Discourse had with them on the way to their Execution. And a Sermon Preached on their Occasion. [By Cotton Mather] Boston, Printed by John Allen, for Nicholas Boone, at the Sign of the Bible in Cornhill. 1717. 64 p. 8vo.

MHI*

Evans 1,901 Sabin 46,369 2 Cotton Mather 185

(a.2) Massachusetts Historical Society. Photostat Americana, 2d Series, No. 134 (Boston 1941).

(b) The Trials of Eight Persons Indited for Piracy &c. Of whom Two were acquitted, and the rest found Guilty. At a Justiciary Court of Admiralty Assembled and Held in Boston within His Majesty's Province of the Massachusetts-Bay in New-England, on the 18th of October 1717 and by several Adjournments continued to the 30th. Pursuant to His Majesty's Commission and Instructions, founded on the Act of Parliament Made in the 11th. & 12th of King William IIId. Intituled, An Act for the more effectual Suppression of Piracy. With an Appendix, Containing the Substance of their Confessions given before his Excellency the Governour, when they were first brought to Boston, and committed to Goal. Boston: Printed by B. Green, for John Edwards, and Sold at his Shop in King's Street. 1718. 27 p. fol.

MHi*, RPJCB

Evans 2,003 Sabin 96,954

(b.2) Massachusetts Historical Society, Photostat Americana, No. 132 (Boston 1939).

(c) "Of Capt. Bellamy," A General History of the Robberies and Murders of the most notorious Pyrates, and also Their Policies, Discipline and Government . . . . Vol. II. By Capt. Charles Johnson, Author of Vol. I. [217-27] London: Printed for, and Sold by T. Woodward, at the Half-moon, over against St. Dunstan's Church, Fleet-street. [1728]

PHi, PP

Note There are many editions, of both this Volume II and of Volume I, below 3.12(1)(b). The work is probably the single most important source for the voluminous writings on piracy, and Johnson has been translated into other languages as well as being reprinted in English. For other editions, both pre-1801 and later, see Philip Gosse, _A Bibliography of the Works of Capt. Charles Johnson_ (London 1927).

There is no known Captain Charles Johnson who could have been the author of this work. Since 1931-32 it has been generally thought that Daniel Defoe was the author, writing under a pseudonym. John Robert Moore, _Defoe in the Pillory and Other Studies_ 126-88 (Bloomington, Indiana 1939). There still appears to be no direct evidence of Defoe's authorship, but rather the conclusion is based on a comparison of this work with "Defoe's previously accepted writings" and other facts known about his life and the period. _Id_. at 126. Consequently the work is now accepted into the body of Defoe's writings. John Robert Moore, A Checklist of the Writings of Daniel Defoe (2d ed. Hamden, Connecticut 1971).

A recent useful edition is Daniel Defoe, A General History of the Pyrates (Manuel Schonhorn, ed., Columbia, South Carolina 1972). Schonhorn points out that "less than a dozen of the more than 500 works now attributed to Defoe carried his name on the title page." Id. at xxii. Since Defoe wrote both fact and fiction it is impossible to tell from his works where one ends and the other begins. What little testing of this work, against creditable sources has been done, leaves much to be desired. It should always be remembered that it is by the same author as wrote, The Shortest Way with the Dissenters and Robinson Crusoe, works that were similarly not labeled as either fact or fiction.

The first volume of the first edition was published in 1724, followed by a second edition in the same year, and by third and fourth editions in 1726. The first edition of Volume II was published in 1728. The fourth edition of Volume I and the first edition of Volume II are "usually regarded as the complete fourth edition of the History, but they are often mistakenly assigned to the same year (1726)." Moore, above, Checklist No. 458. It is this "fourth edition" that is reprinted by Schonhorn.

(d) George Francis Dow and John Henry Edmonds, "Ch. VIII: Samuel Bellamy, whose Ship was Wrecked at Wellfleet and 144 Drowned," The Pirates of the New England Coast 1630-1730 116-31 (Marine Research Society, Salem 1923).

(5) Matson v. Thomas, Trespass and Ejectment, Superiour Court, 1720

(a) To the Honourable the Judges of the Superiour Court for the Counties of Plymouth, Barnstable and Dukes County. Nathaniel Matson, Plantiff, [vs.] Nathaniel Thomas, Esq; Defendant. In a Plea of Trespass and Ejectment . . . . [Signed Isaac Little, Attorney for the Plaintiff] [Colophon] Boston: Printed by S. Kneeland, at the lower End of Queen-Street. 1720. 32 p. 4to.

DLC (not located), MB, MHi*

Evans 2,150

(b) To the Honourable His Majesty's Justices of the Superiour Court of Judicature, for the Counties of Plymouth, Barnstable, &c. Nathanael Matson is Plaintiff, [vs.] Nathanael Thomas, Defendant. In the Original of this

Suit. Arguments for the Defendant, on a Special Verdict in this Cause in Answer to the Plaintiffs Reasons and Arguments. . . . [Signed John Valentine. Boston: 1720] 20 p. 4to.

MWA*

Evans 2,151 Sabin 46,875

(6) Five Pirates, Court of Admiralty, 1726

(a) The Trials of Five Persons for Piracy, Felony, and Robbery, Who were found Guilty and Condemned, at a Court of Admiralty for the Trial of Piracies, Felonies and Robberies, committed on the High Seas, Held at the Court-House in Boston, within His Majesty's Province of the Massachusetts-Bay in New-England, on Tuesday the Fourth Day of October, Anno Domini, 1726. Pursuant to His Majesty's Royal Commission, founded on An Act of Parliament made in the Eleventh and Twelfth Years of the Reign of King William the Third Entituled, An Act for the more effectual Suppression of Piracy; And Made Perpetual by an Act of the Sixth Year of the Reign of our Sovereign Lord King George. Boston: Printed by T. Fleet, for S. Gerrish, at the lower End of Cornhill. 1726. 34 p. 4to.

MHi, MSaE, MWA*, RPJCB(imp.)

Evans 2,818 Sabin 96,955

Note A copy was in the library of William Pyncheon in 1789. Harriet Silvester Tapley, Salem Imprints 1768-1825 285-87 (Salem 1927).

(a.2) Massachusetts Historical Society, Photostat Americana, 2d Series, No. 39 (Boston 1937).

(b) George Francis Dow and John Henry Edmonds, "Ch. XX: Pirate Life and Death," The Pirates of the New England Coast 1630-1730 353-69 (Marine Research Society, Salem 1923).

(7) Sixteen Pirates, Court of Admiralty, 1726

(a) The Tryals of Sixteen Persons for Piracy, &c. Four of which were found Guilty, And the rest Acquitted. At a Special Court of Admiralty for the Tryal of Pirates, Held at Boston within the Province of the Massachusetts-Bay in New-England, on Monday the Fourth Day of July, Anno Dom. 1726. Pursuant to His Majesty's Commission, Founded on an Act of Parliament, made in the Eleventh and Twelfth Years of the Reign of King William the Third, Intitled; An Act for the more Effectual Suppression of Piracy. And made Perpetual by an Act of the

Sixth of King George. Boston: Printed for and Sold by Joseph Edwards, at the Corner Shop on the North-side of the Town-House, 1726. 25 p. 4to.

KWi, MHi, MWA*, NN

Evans 2,819 Sabin 96,957

(a.2) Massachusetts Historical Society, Photostat Americana, 2d Series, No. 75 (Boston 1939).

(b) The Vial poured out upon the Sea. A Remarkable Relation Of certain Pirates Brought unto a Tragical and Untimely End. Some Conferences with them, after their Condemnation. Their Behaviour at their Execution And A Sermon Preached on that Occasion. . . . [By Cotton Mather] Boston: Printed by T. Fleet, for N. Belknap, and sold at his Shop near Scarlet's Wharf. 1726. 53 p. 8vo.

BLM, DLC, MBAt, MHi*

Evans 2,799 Sabin 46,577 Cotton Mather 426

(c) It is a fearful thing to fall into the Hands of the Living God. A Sermon Preached to some miserable Pirates July 10. 1726. On the Lord's day, before their Execution. By Benjamin Colman, Pastor of a Church in Boston. To which is added some Account of said Pirates . . . . Boston, N.E. Printed for John Phillips and Thomas Hancock, and Sold at their Shops. 1726. 43 p. 8vo.

CtY, DLC, KWi, MB, MBAt, MHi, MWA*, MiU-C, NHi, NcU, RPJCB

Evans 2,737 Sabin 14,494 McDade 308

(d) "Of Captain William Fly, And his crew," A General History of the Robberies and Murders of the most notorious Pyrates. . . Vol. II. By Capt. Charles Johnson . . . [228-39], above 1.02(4)(c).

(e) George Francis Dow and John Henry Edmonds, "Ch. XVIII: William Fly, who was Hanged in Chaines on Nix's Mate," The Pirates of the New England Coast 1630-1730 (Marine Research Society, Salem 1923).

(8) Crosby v. Wyman, 1735

(a) A Copy of a Case between Joseph Crosby of Worcester in the County of Worcester, Sadler, Plantiff [sic]; and Jacob Wyman of Woburn in the County of Middlesex, Trader, Defendant. [Boston 1735] 11 p. 4to.

MB (Copy not located although on shelf December 1, 1964)

Evans 3,893 Sabin 17,642

(9) Gerrish v. Barrell, Commercial Shipping Dispute, 1751

(a) The State of Gerrish and Barrell's Accounts and Disputes Deliver'd Mr. Robert Sanderson and Mr. Nathaniel Bethune, June 1751. [By John Barrell] Boston: Printed and Sold by D. Fowle in Queen-Street, next to the Prison. 1751. 47 p. 8vo.

MBAt, MHi, MWA*, RPJCB

Evans 6,635 Sabin 3,599

(10) Fletcher v. Vassall, Defamation, Superiour Court, 1753

(a) The State of the Action Brought by William Fletcher against William Vassall, For Defaming him: Tried In the Superiour Court at Boston, August Term, A.D. 1752. And Now Pending by Appeal to His Majesty in Council. Boston: Printed in the Year, 1753. 43 p. 4to.

BLM (Add. Ms. 36,217, f. 48), DLC, MH-L, MHi, MWA*

Evans 7,001 Sabin 24,744

(b) To the King's most Excellent Majesty in Council, Sheweth, The Humble Petition and Appeal of Wm. Vassall. 11 p. Ms.

BLM (Add. Ms. 36,217, f. 70)

(c) New England. William Vassall, Appellant. William Fletcher, of Boston in the Province of the Massachusetts Bay in New England, Merchant, Respondent. The Respondent's Case. 3 p.

BLM (Add. Ms. 36,217, f. 46)

(d) Hugh F. Bell, "James Otis's First Big Case--Fletcher v. Vassall," 25 Boston Bar Journal 7-19 (1981).

(11) Fowle's Case of Contempt, House of Representatives, 1755

(a) A Total Eclipse of Liberty: Being a true and faithful Account of the Arraignment, and Examination of Daniel Fowle before the Honourable House of Representatives of the Province of the Massachusetts-Bay in New-England, Octob. 24th, 1754. Barely on Suspicion of his being concern'd in Printing and Publishing a Pamphlet, intitled, The Monster of Monsters. Also, his Imprisonment and Sufferings in a Stinking Stone Goal, without the Liberty of Pen, Ink or Paper, and not allowed to see his nearest Friends, nor to write a Line to his Wife; with many other Incidents and Aggravations; which shews it to be Monstrous Treatment. Written by Himself . . . . Boston, Printed [by Daniel Fowle] in the year 1755. 32 p. 12 mo.

CSmH, CtHT-W, DLC, MB, MBAt, MHi, MSaE, MWA*, MiU-C, NN(2, 1 imp.), RPJCB

Evans 7,418 Sabin 25,296

<u>Note</u> No Boston 1775 reprint, as reported in Evans 7,418, is known.

(a.2) 40 <u>Magazine of History</u> (No. 2, Extra No. 158) 5-34 (Tarrytown, New York 1930).

(b) Extract from the Journal of the Honble House of Representatives, of His Majesty's Province of the Massachusetts-Bay, in New-England, Begun and held at Boston, in the County of Suffolk, on Wednesday the 28th day of May, Annoque Domini, 1755. Relating to the Imprisonment of Daniel Fowle and Royall Tyler. Veneris 30. Die Maii, A.D. 1755 . . . . [Printed by Daniel Fowle, Boston 1755] 14 p. 12 mo.

MWA*

Evans 7,481 Sabin 45,730

(c) An Appendix To the late Total Eclipse of Liberty. Being some Thoughts on the End and Design of Civil Government; also the inherent Power of the People asserted and maintained; that it is not given up to their Representatives; this confirm'd and acknowledged by Kings or Emperors, and prov'd from Scripture and reason. . . . Boston: Printed 1756. 24 p. 12mo.

MB, MBAt, MWA*, NN, RPJCB

Evans 7,664

(c.2) 40 <u>Magazine of History</u> (No. 2, Extra No. 158) 35-55 (Tarrytown, New York 1930).

(12) Proprietors Holding under Lake & Clark v. Proprietors from Plymouth-Colony, 1757

(a) The Proprietors holding under Lake & Clark, Plaintiffs, Against Proprietors from Plymouth-Colony, Defendants. Plaintiffs State of the Case. . . . [Boston? 1757?) 7 p. 33 cm.

MWA*

mp. 40,928 Bristol B1,912

(b) The Award and final Determination Of the Referees respecting the Claims of the Proprietors of the Kenebeck Purchase from the late Colony of New-Plymouth, and the Company holding under Clark and Lake, relative to the

Lands on each Side Kenebeck River . . . . Attest, Samuel Winthrop, cler. [Boston 1757] Broadside fol.

MHi, MWA*, PHC

Evans 7,837 Ford 1,074

(c) Statement of the Kennebeck Claims, by the committee appointed by a Resolve of the General Court of the 28th of October, A.D. 1783, On the Subject of unappropriated Lands in the County of Lincoln And, among other Things, to ascertain the Extent and Authenticity of private Claims to Lands in that County. Boston: Printed by Adams and Nourse, Printers to the General Court. M,DCC,LXXXVI. 29 p. 4to.

MWA*, RPJCB

Evans 19,794 Sabin 37,384

(13) Gardiner v. Flagg, Commercial Dispute, Referees, 1767

(a) Dr. Gardiner Versus James Flagg, Merchant. Boston: Printed in the Year 1767. 28 p. 8vo.

MBAt(imp.), MH, MHi, MWA*

Evans 10,623 Sabin 26,630a

(b) To the Public. . . . [Boston 1767?] 18 p. 12mo.

MBAt, MWA*, NN, RPJCB

Evans 10,627

(c) To Messieurs Edward Payne & Henderson Inches. . . . [Boston 1767] 14 p. 8vo.

MBAt, MH, MHi, MWA*

Evans 10,626 Sabin 26,630a

Note Short-Title Evans gives conjectural date of 1769.

(d) A short Vindication of the Conduct of the Referees in the Case of Gardiner versus Flagg, against the unjust Aspersions contained in two anonymous Pamphlets lately published and handed about. . . . [Boston 1767] 22 p. 8vo.

DLC, MHi, MH-L, MWA*, NN, RPJCB

Evans 10,614 Sabin 26,630a

(e) A full Answer to the Pamphlet intitled 'a short Vindication of the Conduct of the Referees in the Case of Gardiner versus Flagg,' &c. . . . [Boston 1767]
44 p. 8vo.

MBAt, MH, MHi, MWA*, RPJCB

Evans 10,624 Sabin 26,630a

(f) Messieurs Payne & Inches. In the Evening Post of March 5th . . . . [Colophon] Boston, March 15, 1770. 8 p. 20 cm.

BOB, MWA*

mp. 42,147 Bristol B3,243

Evans Ghosts 10,622 and 10,625

(14) Gardner v. Starbuck, Land Dispute, Committee, 1770

(a) A Copy of a Relation, Or Substance of the Pleas made Use of by two Parties claiming a Right in Half a Share of Land on the Island of Nantucket, viz. Demandents. Grafton Gardner, Ebenezer Calef, Uriah Gardner, Hezekiah Gardner, Barzillai Folger, Jonathan Gardner, William Russel, Samuel Bunker, Thomas Gardner. Respondents. Thomas Starbuck, Tristram Starbuck, Samuel Starbuck, Joseph Macy, jun'r, Jethro Starbuck, Jethro Barnard, Richard Coffin. And also the Determination of a Committee chose by the Parties to decide the Controversy, viz. Stephen Hopkins, Moses Brown, William Redwood, Thomas Steere, Benjamin Arnold, and Edward Shove. [Newport] Printed [by Solomon Southwick] in the Year 1770. 16 p. 4to.

MHi, MWA*

Evans 11,614 Sabin 32,964, and 51,572 Alden 438

(15) Boston Massacre, Murder, Superior Court of Judicature, 1770

(a) A particular Account of the most barbarous and Horrid Massacre: Committed in King-Street, Boston, on Monday, March 5, 1770, by the Soldiery quartered in said Town. [Boston? 1770] Broadside 55 x 39 cm.

MH, MHi(imp.), MWA*(imp.), RPJCB

mp. 42,145 Bristol B3,241 New York Public 444

(a.2) Typis Johannes Boyle, [Boston] MDCCLXX.
Broadside 55 x 39 cm.

PPL*

mp. 42,146 Bristol B3,242

Note The text above is taken from Bristol. The imprint reproduced on the microcard is mutilated, and reproduces only the title set forth in (a) above, but ending with an exclamation mark instead of a period.

(b) The Fruits of Arbitrary Power, or the Bloody Massacre, perpetrated in King Street Boston, on March 5th 1770, in which Messrs. Saml. Gray: Saml. Maverick. James Caldwell. Crispus Attucks. Patrick Carr were killed. Six others wounded two of them mortally . . . . [Engraving by Henry Pelham, Boston 1770]

MWA

(b.2) Clarence S. Brigham, Paul Revere's Engravings, Plate 13 and pp. 41-44 (Worcester 1954).

(c) The Bloody Massacre perpetrated in King Street Boston on March 5th 1770 by a party of the 29th Regt . . . . Engrav'd Printed & Sold by Paul Revere Boston [1770]
Broadside 28.5 x 24 cm. and 26.5 x 23 cm.

CSmH, CtHi, CtY, DLC, DeWint, MB, MH, MHi, MSaE, MWA (composite), MWiW-C, NN, NHi, PP

mp. 42,161 Bristol B3,257 Church 1081A

Note See d.2 for additional locations.

(c.2) Clarence S. Brigham, Paul Revere's Engravings, Plate 14 and pp. 44-45, 56-57 (Worcester 1954).

(d) The Bloody Massacre perpetrated in King Street Boston on March 5th 1770 by a party of ye 29th Regt . . . . Jona Mulliken Newbury Port sculp. Broadside

DeWint, MH, MWA, PP

Note See d.2 for additional locations.

(d.2) Clarence S. Brigham, Paul Revere's Engravings, Plate 15 and p. 45 (Worcester 1954).

(e) An Account of a late Military Massacre at Boston, or the Consequences of Quartering Troops in a populous well-regulated Town, taken from the Boston Gazette, of March 12, 1770. . . . [Edes & Gill, Boston 1770]
Broadside 50 x 40 cm.

NHi*, ViU

mp. 42,050 Bristol B3,156 New York Public 424

(e.2) An Account of a late Military Massacre at Boston, or the Consequences of Quartering Troops in a populous Town. . . . [John Holt, New York 1770] 2 p. fol.

MB*

Evans 11,543 Ford 1,510 McDade 119

(e.3) New-York Historical Society. Annual Report for the Year 1930 frontispiece (New York 1931).

(e.4) Clarence S. Brigham, Paul Revere's Engravings, Plate 16 and p. 46 (Worcester 1954).

(e.5) The American Heritage History of the Thirteen Colonies 354 (1967).

(e.6) Mason I. Lowance, Jr., and Georgia B. Bumgardner, eds., Massachusetts Broadsides of the American Revolution 31 (Amherst 1976).

(f) On the Death of Five young Men who was Murthered, March 5th 1770. By the 29th Regiment. . . . [Boston? 1770] Broadside 32 x 14 cm.

NHi*

mp. 42,143 Bristol B3,239 New York Public 443
Winslow 22 (MHi photostat)

(f.2) 56 Massachusetts Historical Society Proceedings 268 (Boston 1923).

(g) A Poem, In Memory of the (never to be forgotten) Fifth of March, 1770 . . . . Printed and sold next to the Writing-School, in Queen-Street. [Boston 1770] Broadside 33.5 x 20.5 cm.

MHi*

mp. 42,156 Bristol B3,251 New York Public 445

(g.2) Massachusetts Broadsides, above 1.02(15) (e.6), 29.

(h) A Verse Occasioned by the Late Horrid Massacre in King-Street. You True Sons of Liberty . . . . (Boston 1770) Broadside 35 x 21 cm.

MHi (photostat)

mp. 42,179 Bristol B3,280

Note Microcard not issued as of July 6, 1982.

(i) A Short Narrative of The horrid Massacre in Boston, Perpetrated In the Evening of the Fifth Day of March, 1770. By Soldiers of the XXIXth Regiment; which with The XIVth Regiment Were then Quartered there: with some observations on the State Of Things prior to that Catastrophe. [By James Bowdoin] Printed by Order of the Town of Boston, And Sold by Edes and Gill, in Queen-Street, And T. & J. Fleet, in Cornhill, 1770.
116 p. 8vo.

MBAt

Bristol B3,150 Adams Controversy 70-5a
Adams Independence 75a

(i.2) [The Same] 119 p. 8vo.

CSmH*, CtHW-T, DLC, ICN, MB, MBAt, MBS, MH, MWA, MeB, MiU-C, NHi, NNC-L, NNU-L, PHi, PP, RPJCB, ViU

Evans 11,580 Sabin 6,739 and 80,668
Adams Controversy 70-5b
Adams Independence 75b [Evans 11,581] Church 1,076
McDade 120n

(i.3) [The Same] (For American Distribution.)
136 p. 8vo.

BLM, CSmH, CtHT-W, CtSoP, CtY(2), DLC(2), InU, MB, MHi, MSaE, MWA*, MWiW-C, MeB, MiU-C, NHi, NjP, PHi, PPL(2), RHi

Evans 11,581 Bristol B3,149
Adams Independence 75c, 75d Church 1,077
McDade 120 Huntington 297

(i.4) [The Same] To which is added an Appendix containing the several Depositions . . . . Boston, Printed, by Order of the Town, by Messrs. Edes and Gill; and Re-printed for W. Bingley, in Newgate-Street, London. MDCCLXX.
121 p. 8vo.

BLM(3), CSmH, CtY, DLC, InU, MB, MBAt, MH, MHi, MWA, MWiW-C, MiU-C, PPAmP, RPJCB, ViU

Sabin 6,740, 80,671 Adams Controversy 70-5c
Adams Independence 75f Church 1,078

(i.5) [The Same as (i.4) except "Messrs" misspelled "Messirs" and reprinted in Boston, 1770]
121 p. 8vo.

CSmH, CtY, DLC, MB, MBAt, MH

Bristol B3,151 Sabin 6,740
Adams Independence 75e

(i.6) Printed by Order of the Town of Boston: London, Re-printed for E. and C. Dilly, in the Poultry; and J. Almon, in Piccadilly. M.DCC.LXX. 166 p. 8vo.

BLM, CSmH, DLC, InU, ME, MH, MHi, MWA, MWiW-C, MiU-C, NN(3), NjHi, PPAmP, RPJCB

Sabin 6,740, 80,672 Adams Controversy 70-5d
Adams Independence 75g

(i.6.a) "No. 15. A Short Narrative of the Horrid Massacre in Boston," 4 A Collection of Tracts, On The Subjects of Taxing The British Colonies in America, and Regulating Their Trade. In Four Volumes. London: Printed for J. Almon, opposite Burlington-House, Piccadilly, MDCCLXXIII. Price One Guinea.

BLM, CtY, DLC, MH, RPJCB

Adams Controversy 73-1
Adams Independence 75g note

(i.7) [The Same Abridged] A Letter from the Town of Boston to C. Lucas, Esq. inclosing a Narrative of the Massacre perpetrated there March 5, 1770, by the Soldiers of the 29th Regiment, &c. Printed by Order of the Town of Boston, And Dublin Reprinted. By Tho. Ewing . . . . [1770?] 56 p. 8vo.

DLC, MH, MiU-C, RPJCB

Sabin 6,736 and 40,348 (improved title)
Adams Independence 75h

(i.8) Boston. 1840.

Sabin 6,740

(i.9) New York: re-published with Notes and Illustrations by John Doggett, Jr. 1849.

Sabin 6,740 and 80,673

(i.10) Reprinted in Kidder, below 1.02(15)(11), at 29-113.

Evans Ghost 11,582 (Hildeburn 2,592)

(j) Additional Observations To A Short Narrative of the Horrid Massacre in Boston, perpetrated In the Evening of the 5th of March 1770. Printed by Order of the Town of Boston. M DCC LXX. [London: Reprinted for E. and C. Dilly, 1770] 12 p. 8vo.

BLM, CSmH, CtY, DLC* ICN, InU, MB, MH, MHi, MWA, MWiW-C, MiU-C, NN(imp.), NNC-L, PPAmP, PPL, RPJCB, ViU

Evans 11,583 Sabin 6,741 Adams Controversy 70-4
Adams Independence 75i McDade 121

(j.2) Reprinted in Kidder, below 1.02(15)(11), at 114-22.

(k) A fair Account of the late Unhappy Disturbance At Boston in New England; Extracted From the Depositions that have been made concerning it by Persons of all Parties. With an Appendix, Containing Some Affidavits and other Evidences relating to this Affair, not mentioned in the Narrative of it that has been published at Boston. [By Francis Maseres] London: Printed for B. White, in Fleet-street. M DCC LXX 59 p. 8vo.

BLM, CtY, DLC, MB, MBAt, MH, MWA, MWiW-C, MiU-C, NNC-L, RPJCB

Sabin 6,735 Adams Controversy 70-11
Adams Independence 77

(l) Proceedings Of His Majesty's Council of the Province of Massachusetts-Bay, relative to The Deposition of Andrew Oliver, Esq, Secretary of the said Province, Concerning what passed in Council in Consequence of the unhappy Affair of the 5th of March 1770. Boston, New-England: Printed by Edes and Gill, Printers to the Honorable House of Representatives. MDCCLXX. 35 p. fol.

CSmH, CtY, DLC, MB, MBAt, MH, MHi, MWA*, MiU-C, NN, RPJCB

Evans 11,737 Sabin 45,940 Adams Independence 80
Church 1,080

(m) Innocent Blood Crying to God from the Streets of Boston. A Sermon occasioned by the Horrid Murder of Messieurs Samuel Gray, Samuel Maverick, James Caldwell, and Crispus Attucks, with Patrick Carr, since dead and Christopher Monk, judged irrecoverable, and several others badly wounded, by a Party of Troops under the Command of Captain Preston: On the Fifth of March, 1770. And Preached the Lord's Day following: By John Lathrop, A.M. Pastor of the Second Church in

Boston . . . . London: Printed by E. and C. Dilly, in the Poultrey and J. Almon, in Piccadilly. M.DCC.LXX
22 p. 8vo.

CSmH, MBAt, MH, NN

Sabin 39,184 Adams Controversy 70-15
Adams Independence 79a

(m.2) London, Printed. Boston: Re-Printed and Sold by Edes and Gill, Opposite the New Court-House in Queen-Street. M,DCC,LXXI.
21 p. 8vo.

CtY, DLC, InU, MB, MBAt, MH, MHi, MWA*, NHi, NN, NjHi, NjP, RPJCB, ViU

Evans 12,094 Sabin 39,184
Adams Independence 79b

(n) The Trial of William Wemms, James Hartegan, William M'Cauley, Hugh White, Matthew Killroy, William Warren, John Carrol, and Hugh Montgomery, Soldiers in his Majesty's 29th Regiment of Foot, for the Murder of Crispus Attucks, Samuel Gray, Samuel Maverick, James Caldwell, and Patrick Carr, on Monday-Evening, the 5th of March, 1770, at the Superior Court of Judicature, Court of Assize, and general Goal Delivery, held at Boston. The 27th day of November, 1770, by Adjournment. Before the Hon. Benjamin Lynde, John Cushing, Peter Oliver, and Edmund Trowbridge, Esquires, Justices of said court. Published by Permission of the Court. Taken in Short-Hand by John Hodgson. Boston: Printed by J. Fleeming, and sold at his Printing-Office, nearly opposite the White-horse Tavern in Newbury-street. M,DCC,LXX. 217 p. 4to.

CSmH, CtY, DLC, MB, MBAt, MH, MH-L, MHi, MWA*, MeB(2), NN, NNPM, NNU-L, PHi, PP, PPAmP, PPL, RPB, RPJCB, ViU

Evans 11,683 Sabin 32,362 and 96,951
Adams Controversy 70-29a Adams Independence 84a
McDade 122 Parrish 232

(n.2) Boston Printed, London Reprinted for T. Evans . . . . [1771?] 216 p. 8vo.

MH, MiU-C

Sabin 32,362 and 96,951 Adams Controversy 70-29b
Adams Independence 84b

(n.3) The Trial of the British Soldiers, Of The 29th Regiment Of Foot, for the Murder of Crispus Attucks, Samuel Gray, Samuel Maverick,

James Caldwell, and Patrick Carr, On Monday Evening, March 5, 1770, before the Honorable Benjamin Lynde, John Cushing, Peter Oliver, And Edmund Trowbridge, Esquires, Justices Of The Superior Court Of Judicature, Court of Assize, And General Gaol Delivery, Held At Boston, By Adjournment, November 27, 1770. Boston: Printed And Published By Belcher & Armstrong, No. 70, State Street, 1807. 120 p.

CSmH, DLC, ICN, MWA*, NN, RPB

Sabin 96,946 McDade 122n
Shaw-Shoemaker 13,739

(n.4) "Trials of Certain British Soldiers before the Superior Court of Judicature, for the murder of Crispus Attucks and Others. Boston 1770," 1 Peleg W. Chandler, ed., <u>American Criminal Trials</u> 301-418 (1841).

Sabin 11,868

(n.5) Boston: Published by William Emmons. 1824.
Sabin 96,946 McDade 122n Shoemaker 18,239

(n.6) Frederick Kidder, <u>History of the Boston Massacre, March 5, 1770; Consisting of the Narrative of the Town, and Trial of the Soldiers: and a Historical Introduction, Containing Unpublished Documents of John Adams, and Explanatory Notes</u> 123-285 (Albany 1870).

Sabin 37,712

(n.7) L. Kinvin Wroth and Hiller B. Zobel, eds., 3 <u>Legal Papers of John Adams</u> (Cambridge 1965).

(o) By the Honorable Thomas Hutchinson, Esq: . . . . A Proclamation. Whereas a Paper was this Morning found posted upon the Door of the Town-House in Boston, wrote in a feigned Hand, tending to inflame the Minds of the People against the Judges of the Superior Court now sitting in Boston . . . . [offering a reward for discovery of author or authors]. Dated, December 13, 1770. Broadside

Ford 1,535

(p) An Oration Delivered April 2d, 1771. At the Request Of The Inhabitants of the Town Of Boston; to commemorate the bloody Tragedy of the Fifth of March, 1770. By James Lovell, A.M. . . . . Boston: Printed by Edes and Gill, by the Order of the Town of Boston. 1771. 19 p. 4to.

CSmH, CtHi, CtY, DLC, ICN, InU, MB, MBAt, MH, MHi, MWA*, MWiW-C, MdBP, MiU-C, NHi, NN, NNC-L, PHi, PP, PPL, PPRF, RPJCB, ViU

Evans 12,099 Sabin 42,374 Adams Independence 85
Church 1,086

(q) "An account of the Trial of Captain Preston, at Boston, in New-England," The Annual Register, or a View of the History, Politics, and Literature, For the Year 1770 [218-19] London: Printed for J. Dodsley, in Pall-Mall, 1771.

Note There were subsequent editions. See e.g., (q.2) below.

(q.2) "Case No. 63," L. Kinvin Wroth and Hiller B. Zobel, eds. 3 Legal Papers of John Adams 87 (Cambridge 1965)

Note Reprints from 5th edition, London 1794.

(r) An Oration Delivered March 5th, 1772. at the Request of the Inhabitants of the Town of Boston; to Commemorate the bloody Tragedy of the Fifth of March, 1770. By Dr. Joseph Warren . . . . Boston: Printed by Edes and Gill, by Order of the Town of Boston, 1772. 18 p. 4to.

BLM, CtY, DLC, MB, MBAt, MH, MHi, MWA*, MdBP, NN, PHi, PPRF, RPB, RPJCB, ViU

Evans 12,600 Sabin 101,477 Adams Independence 88a

(r.2) [Second Edition] 18 p. 4to.

CSmH, CtY, DLC, MB, MHi, MiU-C, RPJCB*, ViU, WHi

Evans 12,601 Sabin 101,477
Adams Independence 88b Church 1,094

Note Brackets in original.

(s) The Poem which the Committee of the town of Boston had voted unanimously to be published with the late oration; with Observations relating thereto; together with some very pertinent Extracts from an ingenious Composition never yet published. [By James Allen] Boston: Printed and Sold by E. Russell, at his Printing-Office, near Dr. Gardiner's in Marlborough-Street. M,DCC,LXXII. 30 p. 4 to.

CSmH, DLC, MB, MBAt, MH, MSaE, MWA*, MiU-C, PPL, RPB

Evans 12,301 Sabin 833 and 6,738 Wegelin 2

(t) An Oration, delivered March 5th, 1773. at the Request Of The Inhabitants of the Town of Boston; to Commemorate the bloody Tragedy of the Fifth of March, 1770. By Dr. Benjamin Church . . . . Boston: Printed and Sold at the New Printing-Office [J. Greenleaf], in Hanover-Street near Concert-Hall. M,DCC,LXXIII 20 p. 4to.

BLM, CSmH, CtHi, CtY, MB, MBAt, MH, MHi, MWA*, MiU-C, NN, PHi, RPJCB, ViU

Evans 12,721 and 12,722 (defective copy) Sabin 12,983
Adams Independence 94a

(t.2) [The Third Edition, Corrected by the Author.] Boston. Printed by Edes and Gill, in Queen-Street. M,DCC,LXIII. 18 p. 4to.

CSmH, CtHi, CtY, DLC, ICN, InU, MB, MBAt, MH, MHi, MWA*, MWiW-C, MdBJ-G, MiU-C, NN(imp.), NcD, NjHi, PHi, PPL, PPRF, RPJCB

Evans 12,723 Sabin 12,983
Adams Independence 94b Church 1.095
Huntington 327

(t.3) The Fourth Edition. Boston: Printed by J. Greenleaf, and Sold at his Printing-Office, in Hanover-Street near Concert-Hall. 1773. 20 p. 4to.

CtHi, CtY, MHi, MWA, MiU-C, NHi, PP, RPJCB*

Evans 12,724 Sabin 12,983
Adams Independence 94c

(t.4) The Fourth Edition. Salem, Re-printed by Samuel and Ebenezer Hall, in the main Street. 1773. 16 p. 4to.

MHi, MSaE, MWA*, MiU-C, NHi, ViU

mp. 42,426 Bristol B3,545
Adams Independence 94d Tapley p. 313

(t.5) 47 Magazine of History (No. 2, Extra No. 186) 5-18 and 48 Id. (No. 4, Extra No. 192) 3-14 (Tarrytown, New York 1933 and 1934).

(u) An Oration; delivered March 5, 1774, at the Request of the Inhabitants of the Town of Boston: to commemorate the Bloody Tragedy of the Fifth of March 1770. By The Honorable John Hancock, Esq; . . . . Boston: Printed by Edes and Gill, in Queen-Street. M,DCC,LXXIV. 20 p. 4to.

BLM, CSmH, CtHi, CtY, DLC, MB, MBAt, MH, MHi, MWA*, MWiW-C, MiU-C, NN, NjHi, PHi, PP, PPL, RPJCB, ViU

Evans 13,314 Sabin 30,177 Adams Controversy 74-35a Adams Independence 117a Church 1,104

(u.2) Newport: Rhode-Island. Re-printed and Sold by S. Southwick, in Queen-Street. 1774. 19 p.

CSmH, CU, CtHi, CtY, DLC, ICN, MWA*, MdHi, NHi, RHi, RNHi, RNR, RP(imp.), RPJCB

Evans 13,317 Sabin 30,177
Adams Independence 117c Alden 542
Winship p. 30

(u.3) [The Second Edition.] Boston: Printed by Edes and Gill, in Queen Street, M,DCC,LXXIV. 20 p. 4to.

CtHi, CtY, DLC, MH, MHi, NN*, PPL, PPRF, RPJCB, ViU

Evans 13,315 Sabin 30,177
Adams Independence 117b

Note Brackets in original.

(u.4) New-Haven: Re-Printed by Thomas and Samuel Green. M,DCC,LXXIV. 15 p. 8vo.

CSmH, CtHi, CtY, DLC, MWA*, MiU-C, RPJCB

Evans 13,316 Sabin 30,177
Adams Independence 117d

(u.5) London: Printed for J. Miller, No. 6 in the Old Bailey, 1774

No copy located.

Adams Controversy 74-35b

(u.6) Philadelphia: Printed by J. Douglass M'Dougall, in Chesnut-Street. M,DCC,LXXV. 23 p. 8vo.

DLC, NN*, PHi, PPAmP

Evans 14,097 Adams Independence 117e
Hildeburn 3,217

(v) An Oration; delivered March Sixth, 1775. at the Request of the Inhabitants of the Town of Boston: to Commemorate the bloody Tragedy of the Fifth of March 1770. By Dr.

Joseph Warren . . . . Boston: Printed by Messieurs Edes and Gill in Queen-street, and by Joseph Greenleaf in Union-street, near the Market. M,DCC,LXXV.
23 p. 4to.

BLM, CSmH, CtY, DLC, MB, MH, MHi, MWA*, MiU-C, NN, NNC-L, PHi, PP, PPL, PPRF, RPB, RPJCB, ViU

Evans 14,608 Sabin 101,478 Adams Independence 201a Church 1,126

(v.2) New York: Printed by John Anderson, at Beekman's Slip. [1775] 16 p. 8vo.

CSmH, MBAt, MHi, MiU-C, NHi, NN*

Evans 14,609 Sabin 101,478
Adams Independence 201c Huntington 392

(v.3) Newport, Rhode Island: Reprinted and Sold by S. Southwick in Queen Street, 1775. 22 p. 8vo.

CtY, DLC, InU, MB, MH, MHi, MTaHi, MWA*, NCH, NHi, NN, NNPM. RHi, RNHi, RP, RPB(imp.), RPJCB, ViU

Evans 14,610 Sabin 101,478
Adams Independence 201b Alden 630
Winship p. 32

(w) An Oration delivered March Fifteenth, 1775. at the Request of a Number of the Inhabitants of the Town of Boston. By Dr. Thomas Bolton . . . . [Boston] Printed in the year M,DCC,LXXV. 9 p. 8vo.

CSmH, MBAt, NHi, PHi, RPJCB*

Evans 13,840 Sabin 6,249 Adams Independence 153

Note This is a burlesque oration, ridiculing the patriots, and particularly Warren's 1775 oration, 1.05(15)(v).

(x) Some Strictures upon the Sacred Story recorded in the Book of Esther, shewing The Power and Oppression of State Ministers tending to the Ruin and Destruction of God's People: - And the remarkable Interpositions of Divine Providence, In Favour of the Oppressed; in a Discourse, delivered at Newbury-Port, North Meeting-House, March 8th, 1775. In Commemoration of the Massacre at Boston, March the Fifth, 1770. By Oliver Noble, M.A. And Pastor of a Church in Newbury. Preached at the Request of a Number of Respectable Gentlemen of said Town; and now Published at the General Desire of the Hearers . . . . Newbury-Port, New-England: Printed by E. Lunt and H. W. Tinges. MDCCLXXV. 32 p. 8vo.

DLC, MBAt, MWA*, NN, NNC-L, RPJCB, ViU

Evans 14,352 Sabin 55,387

(y) Considerations On The Commencement Of The Civil War In America; Addressed to the People of England, &c. by an American. Embellished with an elegant Engraving, exhibiting an exact Representation, of the inhuman and horrid Massacre, exercised without Distinction of Age, Sex, or Condition . . . . London: Printed for J. Williams' (No. 39) Fleet-Street; and may be had of all other Booksellers; and at the Pamphlet Shops at the Royal-Exchange. 1775 [Price One Shilling.] 46 p. 8vo.

MBAt

Sabin 15,977 Adams Controversy 75-33

Note Brackets in original.

(y.2) Clarence S. Brigham, Paul Revere's Engravings, Plate 21 and p. 54-55 (Worcester 1954).

(z) An Oration Delivered at Watertown, March 5, 1776. To Commemorate The Bloody Massacre at Boston: Perpetrated March 5, 1770. By Peter Thacher, A.M. . . . Watertown: Printed and Sold by Benjamin Edes, on the Bridge, M,DCC,LXXVI. 15 p. 8vo.

BLM, CSmH, CtHi, CtY, DLC, InU, MB, MH, MHi, MWA*, MiU-C, NN, NjHi, PHi, PP, PPRF, RPJCB, ViU

Evans 15,101 Sabin 95,172 Adams Independence 229 Church 1,140

(aa) An Oration, delivered March 5th, 1777, at the Request of the Inhabitants of the Town of Boston; to Commemorate the Bloody Tragedy of the Fifth of March, 1770. By Benjamin Hichborn, Esq; . . . . Boston: Printed by Edes and Gill. M,DCC,LXXVII. 18 p. 4to.

CSmH, DLC, MB, MBAt, MHi, MWA*, NN, NNC-L, PP, ViU

Evans 15,363 Sabin 31,689 Church 1,145

(bb) An Oration, delivered March 5th, 1778, at The Request of the Inhabitants of the Town of Boston: to Commemorate the Bloody Tragedy of the Fifth of March, 1770. By Jonathan Williams Austin, Esq; . . . . Boston; Printed by B. Edes, and T. & J. Fleet. M,DCC,LXXVIII. 14 p. 4to.

BLM, CSmH, MBAt, MHi, MWA*, NN, PPL, RPJCB, ViU

Evans 15,725 Sabin 2,417 Church 1,148

(cc) A Discourse, Preached on March the Fifth, 1778. By John Lathrop, A.M. Pastor of the second Church in Boston. Published at the Request of the Hearers. Together with some Marginal Notes. Boston: Printed and Sold by Draper and Folsom at their Printing-Office, near the Lamb Tavern, Newberry-Street. M,DCC,LXXVIII. 24 p. 8vo.

MWA*

Evans 15,866 Sabin 39,180

(dd) An Oration, delivered March 5th, 1779, at the Request of the Inhabitants of the Town of Boston; to Commemorate the Bloody Tragedy of the Fifth of March, 1770. By William Tudor, Esquire . . . . Boston: Printed by Edes & Gill, in Court-Street. M,DCC,LXXIX. 23 p. 4to.

BLM, CSmH, MHi, MWA*, NN, PP, ViU

Evans 16,550 Sabin 97,404 Church 1,160

(ee) An Oration, delivered March 6, 1780. at the Request of the Inhabitants of the Town of Boston; To Commemorate the Bloody Tragedy of the Fifth of March, 1770. By Mr. Jonathan Mason, Jun. . . . . Boston: Printed by John Gill, in Court-Street. M DCC LXXX. 23 p. 4to.

BLM, CSmH, MBAt, MHi, MWA*, ViU

Evans 16,836 Sabin 45,468 Church 1,175

(ff) An Oration Delivered March 5th 1781 At The Request of the Inhabitants Of The Town of Boston, To Commemorate the Bloody Tragedy Of The Fifth of March 1770. By Thomas Dawes, Junr. . . . Boston: Printed by Thomas and John Fleet. M,DCC,LXXXI. 23 p. 4to.

BLM, CSmH, MH, MHi, MWA*, NN, NNC-L, RPJCB, ViU

Evans 17,132, Sabin 18,923 Church 1,181

(gg) An Oration Delivered March 5th, 1782. At The Request of the Inhabitants of the Town of Boston; To Commemorate the bloody Tragedy of the Fifth of March, 1770. By George Richards Minot. . . . Boston: Printed by B. Edes and Sons, By Order of the Town of Boston. 1782. 15 p. 4to.

BLM, CSmH, MHi, MWA*, PP, RPJCB, ViU

Evans 17,606 Sabin 49,325 Church 1,190

(hh) An Oration, delivered March 5th, 1783. At the Request of the Inhabitants of the Town of Boston; to Commemorate the Bloody Tragedy of the Fifth of March, 1770. By Doctor Thomas Welsh . . . . Boston: (Commonweatlh of Massachusetts) Printed by John Gill, in Court-Street. 18 p. 4to.

CSmH, MWA*, NN, PP, RPJCB, ViU

Evans 18,302 Sabin 102,617 Church 1,200

(ii) Orations Delivered at the Request of the Inhabitants of the Town of Boston, to Commemorate the Evening of the Fifth of March, 1770; When a number of Citizens were killed by a party of British troops, quartered among them, in a time of Peace. Boston, Printed by Peter Edes, in State-Street. [1785] 200 p. 16mo.

CLU, CSmH, DLC, MB, MHi, MSaE, MWA*, MdBJ-G, MiU-C, NHi, NN(3), NNC-L, RPJCB

Evans 18,977 (includes 18,955) Sabin 6,737 and 6,738 Wegelin 3

(ii.2) Second Edition. Boston: Published By Wm. T. Clap, No. 88, Fish Street, Greenough, Stebbins and Hunt, Printers. 1807. 198 p.

CSmH, CtSoP, DLC, MB, MHi, MSaE, MWA*, MiU-C, NN, NNUT, NjR, RPB

Shaw-Shoemaker 12,301 and 13,295 Sabin 6,737

(ii.3) Hezekiah Niles, ed., _Principles and Acts of the Revolution_ 1-59 (Baltimore 1822).

Sabin 55,312 Shoemaker 9,718

(ii.3.a) Hezekiah Niles, ed., _Centennial Offering Republication of the Principles and Acts of the Revolution in America_ 490, 17-19 (Samuel V. Niles Revision. New York 1876).

(jj) Thomas Hutchinson, 3 _History of the Colony and Province of Massachusetts-Bay_ 194-204, 235ff (London 1828).

Sabin 34,081

(jj.2) [The Same] 194-201, 203, 235-37 (Lawrence Shaw Mayo, ed., Cambridge 1936).

(kk) Peleg W. Chandler, ed., "Trials of certain British soldiers before the Superior Court of Judicature for the murder of Crispus Attucks and others, Boston, 1770," 1 _American Criminal Trials_ 301-418 (Boston 1841).

Sabin 11,868

(ll) Frederick Kidder, History of the Boston Massacre, March 5, 1770 (Albany 1870).

Sabin 37,712

(mm) "Appendix F. Letter of Andrew Oliver, Jr., to Benjamin Lynde. Boston 6 March 1770; Appendix G. A Portion of the Charge Delivered by Judge Lynde at the Trial of the Soldiers who fired on the Mob March 5, 1770," The Diaries of Benjamin Lynde and of Benjamin Lynde Jr., with an Appendix 228-30 (Boston 1880).

(nn) John D. Lawson, ed., "The Trial of William Wemms and Seven Other British Soldiers for the Murder of Crispus Attucks, Samuel Gray, Samuel Maverick, James Caldwell and Patrick Carr, Boston, Massachusetts, 1770" 10 American State Trials 415-511 (St. Louis 1918).

(oo) Randolph G. Adams, "New Light on the Boston Massacre," 47 American Antiquarian Society Proceedings, New Series, 259-354 (Worcester 1938).

(pp) 3 L. Kinvin Wroth and Hiller B. Zobel, eds., Legal Papers of John Adams (Cambridge 1965).

(qq) Hiller B. Zobel, The Boston Massacre (New York 1969).

(16) Star Chamber, 1770

(a) Charles-Town, July 28, 1770. On Friday last was opened a Star-Chamber Court, held by Virtue of a Commission lately received from Governor Bernard, . . . [Signed] Timothy Free, Secretary. [Boston, 1770]
Broadside fol.

DLC*, PHC

Evans 11,597

(17) Richardson's Enlargement after Conviction of Murder, 1772.

(a) The Life, and Humble Confession, of Richardson, The informer. . . . [Boston? 1770? 1772?]
Broadside 30 x 18 cm.

PHi*

mp. 42,373 Bristol B3,486 Ford 1,630
Winslow 45 (PHi)

(a.2) [The Same] William R. Cutter, Broadside Regarding Ebenezer Richardson the Informer, Found in the Library of the Historical Society of Pennsylvania at Philadelphia. (n.p. 1847?)

(b) A Monumental Inscription on the Fifth of March. Together with a few Lines On the Enlargement of Ebenezer Richardson, Convicted of Murder . . . . [Boston 1772]
Broadside 11" x 18"

MHi*, MWA, NN, PHC

Evans 12,302 Ford 1,606 Winslow 46 (MHi)

(b.2) Justin Winsor, 6 Narrative and Critical History of America 89 (Boston and New York 1887).

(b.3) Clarence S. Brigham, Paul Revere's Engravings, Plate 18 and p. 50 (Worcester 1954).

(b.4) L. Kinvin Wroth and Hiller B. Zobel, 2 Legal Papers of John Adams, facing 293 (Cambridge 1965).

(b.5) Massachusetts Broadsides, above 1.02(15) (e.6), 35.

(c) Upon the Enlargement of the infamous Ebenezer Richardson, Convicted of wilful-murder. [Salem? 1772] Broadside
MHi, MSaE (No copy available for reproduction)

mp. 42,377 Bristol B3,495 Ford 1,632

(d) "Case No. 59: Rex v. Richardson 1770-1772," L. Kinvin Wroth and Hiller B. Zobel, eds., 2 Legal Papers of John Adams 396-430 (Cambridge 1965).

(18) Oliver's Case, Impeachment, Superior Court, 1774

(a) Suffolk, ss. At the Superior Court, &c. August 1774. Whereas the Honourable Peter Oliver, Esq; Chief Justice of this Court, stands charged and impeached of divers High Crimes and Misdemeanors, . . . [Boston 1774]
Broadside 4to.

MHi*, MWA, PHC

Evans 13,426

(19) Complaint of Treason, Inferior Court of Common Pleas, 1780

(a) To the honorable the justices of the Inferior Court of Common Pleas holden at [Boston] . . . on the first Tuesday of [July] Anno Domino, One Thousand seven Hundred and Eighty Be it remembered, That complains . . . that said since the nineteenth Day of April, Anno Domini, One Thousand seven Hundred and Seventy-five, viz. on the twentieth Day of the same April, being an Inhabitant and Member of the late Province, now State of Massachusetts-Bay, levied War, and conspired to levy

War against the Government and People of this Province, Colony and State; . . . . [Boston 1780] Broadside

MHI

Mp, 43,899 (reproduces wrong imprint) Bristol B5,189
Ford 2,274

(20) Anonymous 1786 Case Respecting Transfer of Certificates, 1788

(a) Law Case, respecting the transfer of certificates, tried at Falmouth in Massachusetts, July 1786, 4 American Museum [July 1788], below 1.07(15)(a).

(21) Foster's Case, Supreme Judicial Court, 1790?

(a) Commonwealth of Massachusetts. Essex ss. At the Supreme Judicial Court . . . holden at Ipswich . . . the sixteenth day of said month . . . 1789 . . . Daniel Foster . . . [1790?] Broadside

MSaE (No copy available for reproduction)

mp. 45,906 Bristol B7,412 Ford 2,531

(22) Maine Court Records for 1640-1649, 1792

(a) "Extracts from the Records of the Province of Maine," Collections of the Massachusetts Historical Society for the Year 1792. Volume I. [101-04] Printed at the Apollo Press in Boston, By Belknap and Hall. MDCCXCII
292 p. 8vo.

CLU, CSmH, DLC, MB, MH, MHi, MSaE, MWA*, MiU-C, NN, PBL, PHi, PPAmP, RPB, RPJCB, TxU, ViU

Evans 24,530 Sabin 45,852

(a.2) Re-printed by Munroe & Francis, Court-Street. Printers to the Historical Society (Boston 1806).

Sabin 45,852

(23) Hill's Trial for Heresy, Church of Christ, 1793

(a) The Trial of Jeremiah Hill, Esq. for Heresy, before the Church of Christ in Biddeford. [Maine] May 2, 1793. [Portland: Printed by Benjamin Titcomb, junior. 1793]
24 p. 12mo.

MBAt, MH, MHi, MSaE, MWA*, RPJCB

Evans 25,603 Sabin 31,842

(24) Massachusetts 1795-97 Law Cases, 1798

(a) "Seven Law Cases," [5] Collections of the Massachusetts Historical Society, for the year M,DCC,XCVIII 45-52, above 1.02(1)(h).

(25) Boardman's Court Martial, 1798

(a) Division Orders [of the 2d Division, Massachusetts Militia, concerning court martial of Capt. Abel Boardman, Lt. David Wells and Capt. Ithamar Emerson, issued by Maj. General Stephen Abbot]. Salem, Mar. 1, 1798. . . . [Salem: Printed by Thomas C. Cushing 1798] Broadside

MSaE, NHi*, PHC

Evans 34,080 Tapley pp. 364 and 366

1.03 Rhode Island

(1) Trials of Thirty-Six Persons for Piracy, Admiralty, 1723

(a) Tryals Of Thirty-Six Persons for Piracy. Twenty-Eight of them upon full Evidence were found Guilty, and the Rest Acquitted. At a Court of Admiralty for Tryal of Pirates, Held at Newport within His Majesties Colony of Rhode-Island and Providence-Planations in America, on the Tenth, Eleventh, and Twelfth Days of July, AnnoDom 1723. Pursuant to His Majesties Commission, Founded on an Act of Parliament, made in the Eleventh & Twelfth Years of King William the Third, Entituled, An Act for the more Effectual Suppression of Piracy. And made perpetual by an Act of the Sixth of King George. Boston: Printed and Sold by Samuel Kneeland, in Queen-street, below the Prison. 1723. 14 p. 22.5 cm.

RHi*

mp. 39,785 Bristol B648 Evans 2,409

New York Public 130

Note Evans 2,409 described "An Account of the Pirates . . . ," which according to Short-Title Evans was derived from "Adv. Boston News-Letter, July 25, 1723."

(a.2) Massachusetts Historical Society, Photostat Americana, 2d Series, No. 79 (Boston 1939).

(b) Useful Remarks. An Essay upon Remarkables in the Way of wicked Men. A Sermon on the Tragical End unto which the Way of Twenty-Six Pirates brought them; At New Port on Rhode-Island, July 19, 1723. With an Account of their Speeches, Letters & Actions, before their Execution [By Cotton Mather . . . New-London: Printed and Sold by T. Green, 1723. 47 p. 8vo.

BOB, CtHi, MWA*, RPJCB

Evans 2,451 Cotton Mather 417 Trumbull 2d 2,698

(b.2) Massachusetts Historical Society, Photostat Americana, 2d Series, No. 56 (Boston 1938).

(c) An Account of the Pirates, with divers of their Speeches, Letters, &c. And a Poem Made by One of them: Who were Executed at Newport, on Rhode-Island, July 19th, 1723. [Newport?] Re-printed in the year 1769. 16 p. 8vo.

DLC*, RNHi

Evans 11,129 Alden 404 Wegelin 473 Winship p. 23

(d) George Francis Dow and John Henry Edmonds, "Ch. XVI: Charles Harris who was Hanged at Newport with Twenty-Five of his Crew," _The Pirates of the New England Coast 1630-1730_ 288-309 (Marine Research Society, Salem 1923).

(2) Macsparran v. Torrey, Ministry Land, 1739

(a) A brief Representation of the Case depending between the Rev. Dr. McSparran, Plaintiff, and the Rev. Mr. Torrey, Defendant, relating to the ministry Land and Narranganset. . . . July 1739. [Newport? Printed by Ann Franklin? 1739 or Boston 1739]
Broadside 30.5 x 20.5 cm.

MHi, PHC, RPJCB*

mp. 40,177 Bristol B1,064 Sabin 96,298 Alden 53
New York Public 188

(b) A Brief Representation Of the Case depending between the Rev. Doctor Macsparran, and Mr. Torrey, Relating to the Ministerial Land in Narraganset. In a Letter from a Gentleman in Newport, to his Friend in Boston . . . . I am, Sir, Your humble Servant, A.B. Newport, August 29th, 1739 [Newport? Ann Franklin? 1739] 2 p.

CtHi, NHi, PHC, RPJCB*

mp. 40,156 Bristol B1,041 Sabin 96,298n Alden 48

New York Public 187

Note _Bristol_ uses heading "B.A." _Short-Title Evans_ uses heading "A Brief Representation."

(c) An Answer to a Printed Letter said to be wrote from a Gentleman in Newport to his Friend in Boston Aug. 27; Pretending to find Fault with a Brief Representation of the Case between Dr. McSparran Plaintiff and Mr. Torrey Defendant, relating to the Ministry Land in South Kingstown, Narrangansett, which was dated July 1739. . . [By Thomas Prince?] [Boston? 1739] 10 p. fol.

MB, NN*, RHi, RNHi(imp.)

Evans 4,379 Sabin 43,663 and 65,578 Alden 51

(d) "Judge Auchmuty's Opinion of the Naraganset Ministerial Land [signed and dated: Robt Auchmuty Boston, 21st May 1735]," 5 Collections of the Connecticut Historical Society 462-67 (Hartford 1896).

(e) See also 10.03(2)

(3) Gardner v. Maylem, Debt Dispute, 1742

(a) A short Narrative of the unjust Proceedings of Mr. George Gardner of Newport Distiller, against Ann Maylem Widow and Administratrix to the Estate of John Maylem late of Newport Distiller Deceased. [Newport: Printed by Ann Franklin, 1742?] Broadside 31.5 x 21.5 cm.

MHi*

mp. 40,280 Bristol B1,180 Alden 64

New York Public 204

(4) Debts, Old Tenor, 1763

(a) A Letter to the Common People of the Colony of Rhode-Island; concerning the unjust Designs and actual Attempts, of a Number of Misers, and Money Jobbers (particularly such of that Character as are in Place and Power,) to compel all the Old Tenor Debtors in this Colony to pay near three Times as much as they owe. By T. R. Cooper. Providence: Printed for the Author, by William Goddard. 1763. 4 p. 4to.

DLC, RHi*, RPJCB

Evans, 9,494 Alden 283 Winship p. 19

(a.2) Massachusetts Historical Society, Americana No. 97 (Boston 1923).

(5) Brown's Case, Deposition, 1767

(a) I Levi Whipple, of Cranston . . . depose and say, That I heard Elisha Brown . . . Deposition, April 13th, 1767, before me, Samuel Chace . . . [Providence, Printed

by Sarah Goddard and Company. 1767]
Broadside 16 x 21.5 cm.

RPJCB*

mp. 41,778 Bristol B2,827 Alden 379
Winship p. 22

(6) Trevett v. Weeden, Refusing Paper Bills, Superior Court, 1787

(a) The Case, Trevett against Weeden: On information and Complaint, for refusing Paper Bills in Payment for Butcher's Meat, in Market, at Par with Specie. Tried before the Honourable Superior Court, in the County of Newport, September Term, 1786. Also, The Case of the Judges of said Court, Before the Honourable General Assembly, at Providence, October Session, 1786, on Citation, for dismissing said Complaint. Wherein the Rights of the People to Trial by Jury, &c. are stated and maintained, and the Legislative, Judiciary and Executive Powers of Government examined and defined. By James M. Varnum, esq; Major-General of the State of Rhode-Island, &c. Counselor at Law, and Member of Congress for said State. Providence: Printed by John Carter, 1787. 64 p. 4to.

BLM, CLL, CSmH, CaOOa, Ct, CtHT-W, CtMW, CtSoP, CtY, DLC(4), ICN, M, MB, MBAt, MH, MH-L, MHi, MWA*, MiU-C, NHi, NIC-L, NN(2), NNB, NNC-L, NNU-L, NcD, NcD-L, NjP, P, PHi(2), PP, PPAmP, PPB, PPL, PU-L, R, RHi, R-L, RNHi(4), RNR, RP, RPA, RPB, RPJCB, RPL, ScC, ViW, WHi

Evans 20,825 Sabin 98,638 Alden 1,105
Sowerby 2,018 Winship p. 52

Note On June 3, 1790, David Howell sent to Thomas Jefferson "a Packet of pamphlets. I pray you to send them to the several Gentlemen whose names are written on them." 16 Papers of Thomas Jefferson 451, 452 (Princeton 1961). On June 15, 1790, Jefferson sent a copy to George Washington. 16 Id. 511.

(b) Peleg W. Chandler, ed., "Proceedings of the General Assembly of Rhode Island, against the Judges of the Superior Court of Judicature, for their judgment in the case of Trevett against Weeden, on information and complaint for refusing paper bills for butcher's meat. Rhode Island, 1786," 2 American Criminal Trials 267-350 (Boston 1844).

Sabin 11,868

(c) John Winslow, The trial of the Rhode Island judges. An Episode touching currency and constitutional law (Brooklyn 1887).

(d) John D. Lawson, ed., "The Action of John Trevett Against John Weeden for Refusing Paper Money, Rhode Island, 1786. The Proceedings of the General Assembly of Rhode Island Against the Judges of the Supreme Court for Their Judgment in the Case of Trevett Against Weeden, Newport, Rhode Island, 1786," 4 American State Trials 548-99 (St. Louis 1915).

(7) Lawsuits Relative to Property Held for Pious Uses, 1795

(a) A Narrative of the Rise, Progress & Issue of the Late Law-Suits, relative to Property held and devoted to Pious Uses, in the First Precinct in Rehoboth: containing the Substance of the Records which shew for whose Use and Benefit the Property was originally intended; together with some Observations on certain constitutional Principles, which respect the Support of Public Worship, and the equal Protection and Establishment of all regular Denominations of Christians. By James Ellis, A.M. Attorney at Law. Warren, (Rhode-Island): Printed by Nathaniel Phillips. M,DCC,XCV
76 p. 12mo.

BLM, MBAt, MH, MWA*, NN, NNUT, RHi, RPJCB

Evans 28,622 Sabin 22,316a Winship p. 65

1.04 Connecticut

(1) Norwich Whippings in 1725, Justice's Court, 1726.

(a) The Proclamation of the honourable Joseph Jenks, Dep. Governour, Answered; and the proceedings of a Justice's Court, Held at Norwich, July 26, 1725, therein Refer'd to, vindicated. Printed for the Author [Joseph Backus]: Sold at Several of the Booksellers Shops in Boston, and N. London. [Timothy Green] 1726 34 p. 8vo.

MWA*

Evans 2,726 Trumbull 299

(b) A few words respecting the sufferings of those eight persons That were so cruelly whipt at Norwich, by the Sentence and Command of Joseph Backus, July 26. 1725. being All namd, Page 3. in his Book published to vindicate himself in that rash Act. Printed, 1726.

MWA*(imp.)

Evans 2,606 at [36]-38(imp.) Trumbull 372

<u>Note</u> This is the last 3 pages, although incomplete of an imprint, whose title-page is missing, but is given by <u>Short-Title Evans</u> as "An Answer of Confutation upon the Articles of the Confession of Faith." It is attributed to John Bolles and stated to have been printed by James Franklin at Newport in 1731. The Contents of this imprint at [vi] and the pagination show that "A few words" was printed as a part of it, but the title-page of "A few words" is suggestive that it was first printed separately in 1726.

(2) Simson v. <u>St. Joseph</u> and <u>St. Helena</u>, Court of Vice-Admiralty, 1752

(a) Colony of Connecticut, Court of Vice-Admiralty. At a Court of Vice-Admiralty held for the said Colony at the Town of New-London, on Saturday the thirtieth day of December, in the twenty sixth year of the reign of our sovereign Lord George the second, by the grace of God of Great Britain, France, and Ireland, King, Defender of the Faith, &c. and in the year of our Lord one thousand seven hundred and fifty two; before the Honourable Lewis Morris, Esq; Commissary and Judge of the said court. John Simson against the snow St. Joseph and St. Helena, and lading. [New-London: Printed by Timothy Green, 1752] 35 p. fol.

MBAt (No Copy Located)

Evans 6,832 Sabin 81,390 New London 566
Trumbull 2d 1,990

(3) Brown's Land Claim, 1765

(a) The Claim or Title of Mr. James Brown, to A certain Tract or Gore of Land (It being the Westermost Part of the Lands granted, by the General Assembly of the Colony of Connecticut, to the Proprietors of New-Fairfield,) Stated and Vindicated, &c. New Haven: Printed by B. Mecom. M,DCC,LXV 32 p. 8vo.

CtY*, NHi

Evans 9,920 Sabin 8,497 Trumbull 401

(4) Babcock v. Stanton, Commercial Shipping Dispute, 1777

(a) A Brief Historical View, Of the several Cases and Trials that have subsisted between Mr. Adam Babcock, Merchant, at New-Haven, in the Colony of Connecticut, and Phineas Stanton, Junior, of Stonington, in said Colony, With the Substance of the most essential Paragraphs in the Evidences used in said Trials; and some Remarks on the whole.---Wrote for the Perusal of the Friends of Justice and Liberty. By Phineas Stanton, Father of the said Phineas Stanton, Junior . . . . Norwich: Printed by John Trumbull, for the Author. M,DCC, LXXVII. 168 p. 8vo.

CtHi*, CtHT-W, NHi

mp. 43,376 Bristol B4,605 (cf. Evans 14,655, no copy located) Sabin 90,433 Trumbull 1,409

(5) Kirby's Reports, 1785-1788 Cases, Superior Court and Supreme Court of Errors, 1789

(a) Reports of Cases adjudged in the Superior Court of the State of Connecticut. From the Year 1785, to May 1788; with some Determinations in the Supreme Court of Errors. By Ephraim Kirby, Esquire. Litchfield: Printed by Collier & Adam. M,DCC,LXXXIX. 493 p. 8vo.

ArU-L, AzU-L, CLU-L, CtU-L, DCU-L, DGW-L, DLC, InU-L, KTW-L MBAt, MH-L, MWA*, MdBBar, MiU-L, NIC-L, NN, NNB, NNC-L (3, 1 with ms. notes), NNStJ-L, NcD-L, NjP, OU-L, P-L, PU-L, PV-L, TNJ-L, TxDaM-L, TxU, TxU-L

Evans 21,914 Fisher 15 Trumbull 941

Note The Litchfield Weekly Monitor issue of April 13, 1789, advertised Kirby's Reports as "Just Published," and offered them at $3.00. Samuel H. Fisher, The Publications of Thomas Collier, Printer 1784-1808 14 (Litchfield 1933). See also Frederick C. Hicks, Materials and Methods of Legal Research 132 n. 4 (Rochester 1942). Hicks gives credit to Elizabeth Forgeus of the Yale Law Library for the date of publication, reporting also that a known copy was inscribed with the name of an advance subscriber, Nathaniel Minor, and dated April 2, 1789.

Jefferson appointed Kirby judge of the newly organized territory of New Orleans, but he died October 2, 1804 on the way to assume the post. Before leaving he sold his law books to Seth P. Beers. After his death, his widow delivered the library to Beers, with a list of the books being delivered. It contained one copy of Kirby's Reports.

A copy was in George Washington's library. A Catalogue of the Washington Collection in the Boston Athenaeum (Appleton P. C. Griffin, compiler and annotator 1897).

(a.2) [The Same] Waterbury, Conn. 1898.

(6) Root's Reports, 1774-1793 Cases, Superior Court and Supreme Court of Errors, 1798

(a) Reports of Cases adjudged in the Superior Court and Supreme Court of Errors, from July A.D. 1789 to June A.D. 1793; with a Variety of Cases Anterior to that Period. Prefaced with Observations upon the Government and Laws of Connecticut. To which is subjoined sundry law points adjudged, and rules of practice adopted in the Superior Court. By Jesse Root, A Judge of the Superior Court. Vol. I. Hartford: Printed by Hudson and Goodwin. 1798. 640 p. 8vo.

AzU-L, CLU-L, CSmH, CtU-L, DCU-L, DGW-L, DLC, KTW-L, MBAt, MH-L, MWA*, MdBB, MiU-L, NIC-L, NNB, NNC-L, NNStJ-L, NcD-L, NjP, OU-L, P-L, PU-L, PV-L, TxDaM-L

Evans 34,485 Sabin 73,132 Trumbull 1,312

(a.2) [The Same] Waterbury, Conn. 1898.

1.05 New York

(1) Leisler's Trial for High Treason, 1691

(a) A Modest and Impartial Narrative Of Several Grievances and Great Oppressions That the Peaceable and most Considerable Inhabitants of Their Majesties Province of New-York in America Lye Under, By the Extravagent and Arbitrary Proceedings of Jacob Leysler and his Accomplices. Printed at New-York, and Re-printed at London 1690.

BLM

Note: Andrews, below (a.3), at 320 note 1 says that this pamphlet could not have been printed in New York in 1689 or 1690, as at that time there was no printing-press in the province. The date of publication may be 1691 New Style.

(a.2) Edmund B. O'Callaghan, ed., 3 Documents Relative to the Colonial History of the State of New York 665-84 (Albany 1853).

(a.3) Charles M. Andrews, ed., Narratives of the Insurrections 314-54 (New York 1915).

(b) . . . By His Excellency the Governor and Council, and House of Representatives for the Province of New-York . . . April 17, 1691 Resolved Upon further Consideration of the Petition presented to this House by many of the Freeholders and the Inhabitants within this City and Province, Nemine Contraditcente, that Jacob Leisler, Samuel Edsall and divers others, aiding,

Assisting, and Abetting him, in Dissolving the Convention that was convened at the City of New-York . . . .
Broadside 35 x 44.5 cm.

MHi (photostat)*

mp. 39,293 Bristol B139

(c) A Letter From A Gentleman of the City of New-York To Another, Concerning the Troubles which happen'd in That Province in the Time of the late Happy Revolution. Printed and Sold by William Bradford at the Sign of the Bible in New-York, 1698.

NN* (composite copy)

Evans 823

(c.2) Edmund Bailey O'Callaghan, ed., 2 Documentary History of New York 425-35 (Albany 1849).

(c.3) Charles M. Andrews, ed., Narratives of the Insurrections 355-72 (New York 1915).

(d) Loyalty Vindicated from the Reflections of a Virulent Pamphlet called [A Letter from a Gentleman of New York, concerning the troubles which happened in that Province, in the time of the late happy Revolution] wherein the Libellous Author falsely scandalises those Loyal Gentlemen, who couragiously [sic] threw off the absolute Slavery that Province then lay under: and Declar'd for His present Majesty, the Protestant Religion, and the English Law . . . . [Boston: Printed by S. Green and J. Allen. 1698] 28 p. 4to.

NHi*

Evans 824

Note First brackets are in original.

(d.2) [1] Collections of the New York Historical Society 365-94 (New York 1868).

(d.3) Charles M. Andrews, ed., Narratives of the Insurrections 373-401 (New York 1915).

(e) Peleg W. Chandler, ed., "Trial of Jacob Leisler Before a Special Court of Oyer and Terminer, for High Treason," 1 American Criminal Trials 255-66 (Boston 1841).

(f) John D. Lawson, ed., "The Trial of Jacob Leisler For High Treason. New York City, 1691," 10 American State Trials 512-17 (St. Louis 1918).

(g) Lawrence H. Leder, "Records of the Trials of Jacob Leisler and His Associates," 36 New York Historical Society Quarterly 431-57 (1952).

(h) Paul M. Hamlin and Charles E. Baker, eds., "Supreme Court of Judicature of the Province of New York 1691-1704," 78-80 Collections of the New-York Historical Society for the Year 1945-47 passim (New York 1959).

(2) Bayard's Trial for High Treason, 1702

(a) A Narrative of the Treatment Coll. Bayard received From the Time that Sentence was passed against him to the Time of his giving that Petition which the Lieut. Governor & Council caused to be printed and published in justification of their Proceedings against him . . . . [New York: Printed by William Bradford. 1702]
6 p. fol.

BLPro*, DLC, NHi

Evans 1,079

(a.2) Massachusetts Historical Society, Photostat Americana, 2d Series, No. 102. (Boston 1940).

(b) An Account of the Illegal Prosecution and Tryal of Coll. Nicholas Bayard, In the Province of New-York, For Supposed High-Treason, in the Year 170 1/2. Collected from several Memorials taken by divers Persons privately, the Commissioners having strictly prohibited the taking of the tryal in open Court. Printed and Sold by William Bradford, at the Sign of the Bible in New-York. MDCCII. 48 p. fol.

BLM, CSmH, MH, NHi, NN*, N, PHi, PPL

Evans 1,038 Sabin 4.034 Church 802

(c) New York Edition known only from London Reprint. See (c.2) below.

Evans 1,102 Sabin 4,033

(c.2) An Account of the Commitment, Arraignment, Tryal and Condemnation of Nicholas Bayard Esq; for High Treason, in Endeavouring to subvert the Government of the Province of New York in America, by his signing and procuring others to sign Scandalous Libels, call'd Petitions or Addresses to his Late Majesty King William, the Parliament of England, and the Lord Cornbury now Governour of that Province. Before William Atwood Esq; Abraham De Peyster Esq; and Robert Walters Esq;

Appointed by a Special Commission Justices of Oyer and Terminer at the City of New York, February 19. 1701. Collected from several Memorials taken by divers Persons privately, the Commissioners having strictly prohibited the taking of the Tryal in open Court. Together with a true Copy of the Libels or Addresses themselves. Printed at New York by Order of his Excellency the Lord Cornbury, and reprinted at London, 1703. 32 p. sm. fol.

DLC, MH-L, MiU-C, N, NHi, NN, NNC-L, NNPM, RPJCB

Sabin 53,436 Church 809

(d) "An Act declaring the Illegality of the Proceedings against Coll. Nicholas Bayard and Alder-man John Hutchins for pretended High-Treason, and for Reversing and making Null and Void the said Judgments, and all Proceedings thereon," Acts passed the 2d Sessions of the General Assembly, Beginning the 13 Day of April, 1703. Ano Regni Regina Anna, Anglia, Scotia, Francia & Hibernia, Secondo. [210-11] [New York 1703]
26 p. [numbered 203-28 fol.]

PHi*

Evans 1,137

Note Evans 1,138 is a separate printing of this Act, but no copy of such a separate has been found.

(e) "The Prosecution and Tryal of Col. Nicholas Bayard, in the Province of New-York, for High-Treason, Anno 1701/2," A Compleat Collection of State-Tryals, and Proceedings upon Impeachments for High Treason, and other Crimes and Misdemeanours; from the Reign of King Henry the Fourth, to The End of the Reign of Queen Anne. The Fourth Volume. With an Exact Alphabetical Table to the Whole. [552-73] London: Printed for Timothy Goodwin, against St. Dunstan's Church in Fleet-Street; John Walthoe in the Middle-Temple Cloysters; Benj. Tooke at the Middle-Temple Gate in Fleet-Street; John Darby in Bartholomew Close; Jacob Tonson against Katherine-Street in the Strand; and John Walthoe Jun. against the Royal-Exchange in Cornhill. M.DCC.XIX.

DLC, ViU

Sowerby 1,951

(e.2) "CLXIX. The Trial of Colonal Nicholas Bayard, in the Province of New York, for High-Treason, Febr. the 19th, 1701/2, 14 Will. III," [419-36, 441-45].

MB

(e.3) "CLXII. The Trial of Colonel Nicholas Bayard in the Province of New-York, for High-Treason, February the 19th, 1701-2, 14 Will. III," [419-39] The Fourth Edition . . . To which is prefixed. A New Preface, by Francis Hargrave, Esquire. Volume the Fifth. London: Printed by T. Wright, Essex Street, Strand; For . . . And Sold by G. Kearsly, No 46, near Serjeant's-Inn, Fleet-Street. MDCCLXXVII.

ViU

(e.4) Thomas B. Howell, ed., "Case No. 421," 14 A Complete Collection of State Trials 471-516 (London 1816).

(f) Peleg W. Chandler, ed., "Trial of Nicholas Bayard before a Special Court of Oyer and Terminer, for High Treason, 1702," 1 American Criminal Trials 267-300 (Boston 1841).

Sabin 11,868

(g) John D. Lawson, ed., "The Trial of Nicholas Bayard for High Treason, New York City, 1702," 10 American State Trials 518-39 (St. Louis 1918).

Note See also 3.05(1).

(3) Makemie's Imprisonment and Prosecution, 1707

(a) A Narrative Of a New and Unusual American Imprisonment Of Two Presbyterian Ministers: And Prosecution of Mr. Francis Makemie One of them, for Preaching one Sermon at the City of New-York. By a Learner of Law, and Lover of Liberty. Printed for the Publisher. [Boston?] 1707. 51 p. 4to.

DLC, MB, MSaE(imp.), MWA*, NN

Evans 1,300 Sabin 44,079

(a.2) A Narrative of the Imprisonment of two Non-Conformist Ministers [F. Makemie and J. Hampton] and prosecution or trial of one of them, for preaching a sermon in . . . New York. Boston in New-England reprinted London, 1708. 8vo.

BLM

(a.3) New-York: Re-printed and Sold by H. Gaine, at the Printing-Office between the Fly and Meal-Markets. 1755.

DLC, MWA*, NHi, NN, PHi, PPL

Evans 7,455 Sabin 44,080

(a.4) 4 Peter Force, Tracts No. 4 (Washington, D.C. 1846).

(4) Writ of Superior Court, 1717

(a) A Writ issu'd out from the Supream Court at New-York to the Justices, Vestry-men and Church-Wardens of the Precinct of Jamaica on Nassau-Island, in haec Verba . . . . [New York? 1717?] 7 p. 32 cm.

NHi*

mp. 39,668 Bristol B528

(5) Palmer v. van Cortland, Land Dispute, 1727

(a) Obadiah Palmer, Nehemiah Palmer, Sylvanus Palmer, Solomon Palmer, Josiah Quenby. Tho. Townsend, Richard Cornwall and Henry Cock, Complainants Against Jacobus van Cortland & Adolph Philipse, Defendants, In Cancellaria Novae Eborac . . . . [New York: Printed by William Bradford 1727] 58 p. fol.

MH-L, MWA*, NHi

Evans 2,940 Sabin 58,366

(6) De Medina v. Het, Commercial Shipping Dispute, Cancelloria, 1728

(a) The Decree In the Case of Solomon De Medina, Mosesson and Company, Merchants in London, and Roderigo Pacheco, Jacob De Lara, and Manual de Costa, Bearers of their Orders, Complainants Against Rene Het, and the Executors of Andrew Fresneau, Deceased, Defendants, in Cancellaria Nova-Eborac. Printed and Sold by William Bradford in New-York, 1728. 46 p. fol.

MWA*, NHi, NN(2), PHi

Evans 3,019 Sabin 47,349

(b) Ship Victory, 1736, below 10.05(1). Related case?

(7) Trusdell v. Harison, for Illegal Imprisonment, Mayor's Court, 1733

(a) New-York Mayor's Court. William Trusdell against Francis Harison, Esq. For arresting, imprisoning and keeping the plaintiff ten weeks in prison, at the suit of Joseph Weldon, without authority. [New York: William Bradford 1733] Broadside 30 x 18 cm.

PPRF (No copy located)

mp. 40,033 Bristol B916 New York Public 176

(a.2) See below 1.05(8)(1).

(8) Rip Van Dam's Plea to Jurisdiction, Supream Court, 1733

(a) The Arguments of the Council for the Defendant, In Support of A Plea to the Jurisdiction, Pleaded to a Bill filed in a Course of Equity, At the Suit of The Attorney General, Complainant, Against Rip Van Dam, Defendant, in the Supream Court of New-York. New York: Printed by John Peter Zenger, M,DCC,XXXIII.
63 p. fol.

BLPro, NN*, RPJCB(imp.)

Evans 3,727 Sabin 98,429 Rutherfurd p. 145, No. 5

(b) The Proceedings of Rip Van Dam, Esq; in order for obtaining Equal Justice of His Excellency William Cosby, Esq; [Colophon] New York: Printed, and Sold by John Peter Zenger, where also is to be sold, The Argument of Van Dam's Council in Support of his Plea to the Jurisdiction of the Supream Court of New-York. MDCCXXXIII. [pages numbered 53-63]

NHi, NN*, PPL

Evans 3,727 (Described as Half-title) Sabin 98,430
Rutherfurd p. 146, No. 1

(c) Farther proceedings concerning the Case of Rip Van Dam, Esqr. at the Suit of the Attorney General being for the Use of his Excellency Coll. Cosby Governour of the Province, in the Equity Side of the Exchequer. [New York 1734] [pages numbered 65-80 (sic for 68)]

NN*

Evans 3,845 Sabin 98,431 Rutherfurd p. 147, No. 1

(d) Heads of Articles of Complaint, made by Rip Van Dam, Esq; on Thursday the 30th of May, 1734. to the Committee of Grievances appointed by the General Assembly for the Province of New-York; reduced to Writing by order of the said Committee; who also ordered, that a copy thereof be served on the Chairman, and Mr. Justice Phillipse. [New York 1734] [pages numbered 69-71]

NN*

Evans 3,846 Sabin 98,432 Rutherfurd p. 151, No. 3

(e) To All to whom these Presents shall come or may any Way concern: Rip van Dam sendeth greeting . . . . [New York: Printed by John Peter Zenger. 1736] [pages numbered 69-73]

NN*

Evans 4,093 Sabin 98,433 Rutherfurd p. 154, No. 3
Evans Ghost 4,092

(f) The Opinion and Argument of the Chief Justice of the Province of New-York, concerning the Jurisdiction of the supream Court of the said Province, to determine Causes in a Course of Equity . . . . [Colophon] New-York, Printed and sold by John Peter Zenger, in Smith Street. 1733. 15 p. fol.

BLPro*, DLC

Evans 3,700 Rutherfurd p. 148, No. 1

(f.2) The Second Edition Corrected and Amended. [Colophon] New-York, Printed and sold by John Peter Zenger, in Smith Street, 1733. 15 p. fol.

BLPro*, CtY, N?, NN

Evans 3,701 Sabin 50,849
Rutherfurd p. 148, No. 2

(f.2.b) Massachusetts Historical Society, Americana No. 241 (Boston 1929).

(f.3) The Second [sic Third] Edition Corrected . . . . [Colophon] New-York, Printed and Sold by J. Peter Zenger, 1733. 15 p. fol.

BLPro*, NN

Evans 3,702 Rutherfurd p. 148, No. 3

(f.3.b) Massachusetts Historical Society, Americana No. 233 (Boston 1929).

(f.4) The Second Edition Corrected, 55 New Jersey Historical Society Proceedings 87-116 (1937).

(g) The Report of the Committee of His Majesty's Council, To whom it was Referred, To Examine and make Enquiry, touching a Letter found in the House of Mr. Alexander in New-York, on Friday the First Day of February, 1733/4. In Order To make the fullest Discovery concerning the Author of the same. New-York, Printed and Sold by William Bradford, 1734. 11 p.fol.

NjHi*, PHi, PPL

Evans 3,816 Sabin 730

(h) To his Excellency William Cosby, Esq; Capt. General and Governor in Chief of the Provinces of New-York, New-Jersey, and the Territories thereon depending in America, Vice-Admiral of the same, and Colonel in his Majesty's Army, &c. The humble Address of the General Assembly of the Colony of New York . . . . [Colophon] Printed and Sold by William Bradford in New-York, 1734.
2 p. fol.

BLPro*

Evans 3,817

(i) Heads of Articles of Complaint by Rip Vandam, Esq; against His Excellency William Cosby, Esq; Governor of New-York, &c. To which is prefixed, Mr. Vandam's Letter sent to His Excellency with a Copy of those Articles. As also A Letter from some of the Gentlemen of the Council of New-York, to his Grace and the Duke of Newcastle, one of His Majesty's principal Secretaries of State, in Answer to the several Articles of Complaint. And A Reply to those Answers of the Gentlemen of the Council . . . . Boston: Printed in the year 1734. [Boston printing questioned]

CSmH, N, NN*, RPJCB

Evans 3,847 Sabin 98,435 Rutherfurd p. 151, No. 3

(j) Mr. Smith's Opinion Humbly Offered to the General Assembly of the Colony of New-York, One [sic] the Seventh of June, 1734. At their request. Occasion'd by sundry Petitions of the Inhabitants of the City of New-York, Westchester County & Queens-County, to the said General Assembly, praying an Establishment of Courts of Justice within the said Colony by Act of the Legislature. Published at the Request of the said General Assembly . . . . Printed and Sold by William Bradford in the City of New-York, 1734. 45 p.fol.

CSmH, NHi, NN*

Evans 3,834 Sabin 84,556

Note A copy was in the library of Joseph Murray, New York lawyer, c 1694-1757. Paul M. Hamlin, Legal Education in Colonial New York 177, 179 (New York 1939).

(k) Mr. Murray's Opinion Relating to the Courts of Justice In the Colony of New York; Delivered to the General Assembly of the said Colony, at their Request, the 12th of June, 1734 . . . . [New York: Printed by William Bradford. 1734] 44 p. [37-44 incorrectly paginated] fol.

Evans 3,799 Sabin 51,530

Note A copy was in the library of Joseph Murray, New York lawyer, c 1694-1757. See above note, 1.05(8)(j).

(l) The Vindication. Of James Alexander, One of His Majesty's Council for the Province of New-York, And Of William Smith, Attorney at Law, From the Matters charged and suggested against them in two Pamphlets lately published. The One A Paper addressed to the Mayor, Aldermen and Commonalty of the City of New-York, by the Honourable Francis Harrison, Esq; one of His Majestys Council, for the Province of New-York. The Other A Report of the Committee of His Majesty's Council, to whom it was referred to examine and make Inquiry touching a Letter found in the House of Mr. Alexander, in New-York on Fryday the 1st of February, 1732-3 in order to make the fullest Discovery concerning the Author of the same. To which is Added A Supplement Containing A brief Account of the case of William Trusdell, Plaintiff, Against the Honourable Francis Harison, Esq; Defendant, For Arresting and Imprisoning the Plaintiff and Keeping him 9 Weeks in Prison at the Suit of Joseph Weldon, without the Assent, Consent, or Knowledge of the same Joseph Weldon. Which Cause was tried in the Supream Court of New-York, on the 19th of April, 1734. wherein the Jury found for the Plaintiff Trusdell £ 150. Damages, and Costs of Suit. Printed by John Peter Zenger, and to be sold by him at his House in Broad Street, near the upper End of the long Bridge, in New-York, 1733. [Error for 1734] Price 1 s. 22 p. fol.

NN*, NjHi, PPL

Evans 3,848 Sabin 84,588, 731, 30,380
Rutherfurd p. 148, No. 5

(m) The case of Lewis Morris, Esq; late Chief Justice of the Province of New York, who was removed from the said office by H. E. William Cosby, Governor of said Province. London. 1735. Signed J. Willes. 8 p. fol.

N, NN(2, 1 imp.), NjHi

Sabin 50,847

(n) New-York, April 26th, 1736. Sir; Whereas on the 10th Day of March last, immediately upon the death of His Excellency William Cosby, Esq; . . . [New-York: Printed by John Peter Zenger. 1736] Broadside fol.

NN*, PHC

Evans 4,091 Sabin 98,436 Rutherfurd p. 154, No. 2

(o) Copy of a Letter from Rip Van Dam, Esq; to the several Members of that General Assembly of New-York, that stood adjourned to the last Tuesday of March, 1736 . . . . 4 p. [numbered 11-13] fol.

NN*

Evans 4,090 Sabin 98,434 Rutherfurd p. 154, No. 5

(p) A Letter To one of the Members of the late General Assembly . . . [Colophon] Printed by John Peter Zenger. 1736. 2 p.fol.

MWA*, NN

Evans 4,030 Rutherfurd p. 154, No. 4

(q) By the Honourable George Clark, Esq; President of His Majesty's Council and Commander in Chief of the Province of New-York, A Proclamation, whereas Rip Van Dam, Esq; . . . . Printed by William Bradford, Printer to the Kings most excellent Majesty for the Province of New York, 1736. Broadside fol.

BLPro, N, PHC (No copy located)

Evans 4,052 Sabin 98,436

(r) Stanley N. Katz, Newcastle's New York: Anglo-American Politics, 1732-1753 (Cambridge 1968).

(s) Joseph H. Smith and Leo Kershkowitz, "Courts of Equity in the Province of New York: The Cosby Controversy, 1732-1736," 16 American Journal of Legal History 1-50 (1972).

(9) Zenger's Trial for Libel, Supreme Court of Judicature, 1735

(a) The Complaint of James Alexander and William Smith to the Committee of the General Assembly of the Colony of New York, &c . . . . [New York: Printed by John Peter Zenger, 1735]

CSmH, DLC, MH-L, MWiW-C, MiU-C, MiU-L, N, NHi, NN*, NNC-L, NNFed, NNPM, NjHi, NjP, NjR, PP, PPL, RPJCB

Evans 3,864 Sabin 84,554 (revised 729)
Rutherfurd p. 153, No. 1

(b) A brief Narrative of the Case and Tryal of John Peter Zenger, Printer of the New-York weekly Journal.

[Colophon] New-York, Printed and sold by John Peter Zenger. MDCCXXXVI
40 p. [pages 15-40 incorrectly paginated] fol.

CLU-L, DLC, MBAt, NHi, NN*, NNU-L, PPL

Evans 4,107 Sabin 106,304
Rutherfurd p. 155, No. 2, and p. 249, No. 1

(b.2) [Colophon] Boston: Printed and Sold by Thomas Fleet, at the Heart and Crown in Cornhill, 1738. 48 p. 4to.

BLM, DLC, MB, MBAt, MH-L, MHi, MWA*, N, NHi, NN, NjP, P, PP, RPJCB

Evans 4,330 Sabin 106,305
Rutherfurd, p. 250, No. 1

(b.3) [English edition printed by J. Wilford? 1738?] 32 p. 4to.

MH-L

Rutherfurd p. 251, No. 3

(b.4) New-York Printed: Lancaster Re-printed, and Sold by W. Dunlap, at the New Printing-Office, in Queen-Street, 1756. 39 p. fol.

CSmH, DLC(imp.), MWA*, NN, PHi, PPAmP, PPL

Evans 7,824 Sabin 106,310 Church 1,016
Hildeburn 1,483 Rutherfurd p. 252, No. 2

(b.5) New-York: Re-printed, by John Holt, at the Exchange. 1770. 55 p. 4to.

CSmH, CtHi(imp.), CtY, DLC, MH-L, MHi, MSaE, MWA*, MiU-C, NHi, NN, NNC-L, PPL, RPJCB

Evans 11,952 Sabin 106,312
Rutherfurd p. 253, No. 1

(b.6) Reprinted and Sold at the Bible and Heart, Cornhill, Boston, MDCCXCIX. 48 p. 8vo.

DLC, ICN, MB, MBAt, MHi, MWA*, N, NHi, NN, NNC-L, RPJCB

Evans 36,749 Sabin 106,314
Rutherfurd p. 253, No. 3

(b.7) Livingston Rutherfurd, John Peter Zenger His Press, His Trial and A Bibliography of Zenger Imprints. Also A Reprint of the First Edition of the Trial, 171-246 (New York 1904).

(b.8) Frank Luther Mott, ed., Zenger's Own Story. (Vol. 2, Oldtime Comments on Journalism, Columbia, Missouri 1954).

(b.9) Vincent Buranelli, The Trial of Peter Zenger. (1957). (edited version.)

(b.10) Stanley Nider Katz, ed., A Brief Narrative of the Case and Trial of John Peter Zenger, Printer of the New York Journal (Cambridge 1963).

(c) Remarks on Zenger's Tryal, Taken out of the Barbados Gazette's. For the Benefit of the Students in Law, and others in North America . . . . [By Jonathan Blenman. Philadelphia: Printed by Andrew Bradford. 1737] 71 p. fol.

NHi, NN, PHi*, PPAmP, PPL

Evans 4,118 Hildeburn 551 Rutherfurd, p. 249, No. 2

(c.2) The Pennsylvania Gazette. Nos. 466, 467, 468, and 469. Philadelphia: Printed by B. Franklin, Post Master, at the New Printing-Office near the Market. 1737 [Reply written by James Alexander] fol.

Evans 4,185 Rutherfurd p. 249, No. 2n

(c.3) Caribbeana. Containing Letters and Dissertations, Together with Poetical Essays, On various Subjects and Occasions; Chiefly wrote by several Hands in the West-Indies. And some of them to Gentlemen residing there. Now collected together in Two Volumes. Wherein are also comprised, divers Papers relating to Trade, Government, and Laws in general; but more especially, to those of the British Sugar-Colonies, and of Barbados in particular: As Likewise the Characters of the most eminent Men that have died, of late Years, in that Island. To which are added in an Appendix, Some Pieces never before Published. Vol. II. [198-273] London: Printed for T. Osborne, in Gray's-Inn; J. Clarke, at the Royal Exchange; S. Austin, in St. Paul's Church-Yard; G. Hawkins, at Temple-Bar; R. Dodsley, in Pall-Mall, and W. Lewis in Covent-Garden. M,DCC,XLI.
Rutherfurd p. 254, No. 1

(c.4) Barbados, Printed: New-York, Re-printed by H. Gaine, Bookseller and Stationer, at the Bible and Crown, in Hanover-Square, 1770.
60 p. 12mo.

DLC*

Evans 11,573

Evans Ghosts 4,119 and 4,120.

(d) The Tryal of John Peter Zenger, Of New-York, Printer, Who was lately Try'd and Acquitted for Printing and Publishing a Libel against the Government. With the Pleadings and Arguments on both Sides . . . . London: Printed for J. Wilford, behind the Chapter-House, St. Paul's Church-Yard. 1738. 34 p. 4to.

CLL, CSmH, MH-L, MWiW-C, NN, NNC-L, NNFed, NjP

Sabin 106,307 (see also 106,306) Rutherfurd p. 250, No. 2

(d.2) The Second Edition.

BLM, CSmH, DLC, MiU-C, NN(3, 1 imp.), NNC-L, PHi, PP, PPL, RPJCB, ViU

Sabin 106,307 Rutherfurd p. 250, No. 3

(d.3) The Third Edition.

NHi, NN, RPJCB

Sabin 106,307 Rutherfurd p. 250, No. 4

(d.4) The Fourth Edition.

BLM, MB, MBAt, MdBP, NN, NNC-L, P, PHi, WHi

Sabin 106,307 Rutherfurd p. 251, No. 1

(d.5) Dublin: Printed by and for J. Jones in Clarendon Street, opposite to Coppinger's-Lane, 1738.

CSmH, PU

(d.6) The Trial of John Peter Zenger, of New-York, Printer; Who was tried and acquitted for printing and publishing a Libel against the Governor and Council. With the Pleadings and Arguments on both Sides. [n.p. n.d.] 64 p.

MH-L

(d.7) The Case and Tryal of John Peter Zenger, of New-York, Printer, Who was lately tryed and acquitted for Printing and Publishing a Libel against the Government. With The Pleadings and Arguments on both Sides . . . . London: Printed for J. Wilford, behind the Chapter-

House, St. Paul's Church-Yard, 1750. [Price a British Sixpence.] 60 p. 8vo.

DLC, MH-L, NN, NNC-L, NNFed, NjP, PP, PPL

Sabin 106,308 Rutherfurd p. 251, No. 4

Note Brackets in original.

(d.8) The Trial of John Peter Zenger . . . . London: Printed for P. Brown, in Fleet-Street, MDCCLII. (Price One Shilling and Sixpence.) 76 p. 8vo.

BLM, DLC, MH, MH-L, MHi, MWA, N, NHi, NN, NNB, NNC-L, NNU-L, PP, PPL, RPJCB

Sabin 106,309 Rutherfurd p. 252, No. 1

(d.9) London: Printed for J. Almon, opposite Burlington-House, Piccadilly. MDCCLXV. 60 p. 8vo.

CLL, CLU, CSmH, DLC, MB, MBAt, MH, MH-L, MWA, MdBP (2 copies - 1 with bookplate of Charles Carroll), MoU-L, NHi, NN, NNB, NNC-L, NNPM, NNU-L, NjR, PP, PPL, PU, RPJCB, ViU, ViW

Sabin 106,311 Rutherfurd p. 252, No. 3

(d.10) The Trial of John Peter Zenger, Of New-York, Printer; For A Libel Against the Government, On The Fourth of August, MDCCXXV. Inscribed To The Honorable T. Erskine . . . . London: Printed for Flexney, Holbourn, Davies, Russell-Street; Merril, Cambridge; and Eddowes, Shrewsburg. 1784. 64 p. 8vo.

NN, PPL

Sabin 106,313 Rutherfurd p. 253, No. 2

(d.11) Sutro Branch California State Library, (Occasional Papers English Series No. 7. 1940) [Reproduces d.9 above.]

(e) Remarks On The Trial of John-Peter Zenger, Printer of the New-York Weekly Journal, Who was lately Try'd and Acquitted for Printing and Publishing Two Libels Against the Government of the Province. London: Printed for J. Roberts in Warwick-Lane. MDCCXXXVIII. (Price One Shilling.) 32 p. 4to.

DLC, MiU-C, NN(3), NNC-L, NNPM, NNU-L, PHi, PP, PU-L, ViU

Sabin 106,314n Rutherfurd p. 251, No. 2

(f) "Case No. XXII. The Trial of John Peter Zenger, of New-York, Printer, for printing and publishing a Libel against the Government; before the Honourable James de Lancey, Esq; Chief Justice of the Province of New-York, and the Honourable Frederick Phillipse, Esq; second Judge; at New-York, on August 4th, 1735., [Cols. 275-98] XXIII. Remarks on the Trial of John Peter Zenger, Printer of the New-York Weekly Journal, who was lately tried and acquitted, for printing and publishing two Libels against the Government of that Province," [Cols. 299-315] A Complete Collection of State-Trials, and Proceedings for High-Treason, and other Crimes and Misdemeanours; the Fourth Edition; commencing with The Eleventh Year of the Reign of King Richard II and ending with The Sixteenth Year of the Reign of King George III. With Two Alphabetical Tables to the whole. To which is prefixed, A New Preface, By Francis Hargrave, Esquire. Volume the Ninth. London: Printed by T. Wright, Essex-Street, Strand; For . . . And Sold by G. Kearsly, No. 46, near Serjeant's-Inn, Fleet-Street. MDCCLXXVIII.

ViU

(g) Thomas B. Howell, ed., "Case No. 490," 17 A Complete Collection of State Trials 675-764 (London 1816).

Rutherfurd p. 254, No. 2

(h) Peleg W. Chandler, ed., "Trial of John Peter Zenger before the Supreme Court of New York, For Two libels On The Government, 1735," 1 American Criminal Trials 151-209 (Boston 1841).

Sabin 11,868

(i) John D. Lawson, ed., "The Trial Of John Peter Zenger, For Libel, New York City, 1735," 16 American State Trials 1-39 (St. Louis 1928).

(j) Walker Lewis, "The Right to Complain: The Trial of John Peter Zenger," 46 American Bar Association Journal 27 (1960).

(k) Leonard W. Levy, "Did the Zenger Case Really Matter?: Freedom of Press in Colonial New York," 17 William and Mary Quarterly (3d Series) 35-50 (1969).

(l) Leonard W. Levy, Legacy of Suppression (Cambridge 1960).

(m) John Peter Zenger (n.d. Zenger Memorial New York)

(n) Paul Finkelman, "Ch. 1: The Zenger Case: Prototype of a Political Trial," American Political Trials 21-42 (Michal R. Belknap, ed. Westport, Connecticut 1981).

(10) Slave Conspiracy, Supream Court, 1741

(a) The Defense of John Ury, Made before the Supream Court in New-York, at his Tryal for being concerned in the late Negro-Conspiracy. [Philadelphia, B. Franklin, 1741] 2 p. 24 cm.

MWA*

mp. 40,262 Bristol B1,159

(b) The Dying Speech of John Ury, Who was executed at New-York, on Saturday the 29th of August, 1741, for being concerned in the Negro-Conspiracy. [Philadelphia 1741) 2 p.

MWA*

mp. 40,263 Bristol B1,159

(c) A Journal of the Proceedings in The Detection of the Conspiracy Formed by some White People, in Conjunction with Negro and other Slaves, for Burning the City of New-York in America, And Murdering the Inhabitants. Which Conspiracy was partly put in Execution, by Burning His Majesty's House in Fort George, within the said City, on Wednesday the Eighteenth of March, 1741, and setting Fire to several Dwelling and other Houses there, within a few Days succeeding. And by another Attempt made in Prosecution of the same infernal Scheme, by putting Fire between two other Dwelling-Houses within the said City, on the Fifteenth day of February, 1742; which was accidentally and timely discovered and extinguished. Containing, I. A Narrative of the Trials, Condemnations, Executions, and Behaviour of the several Criminals, at the Gallows and Stake, with their Speeches and Confessions; with Notes, Observations and Reflections occasionally interspersed throughout the whole. II. An Appendix, wherein is set forth some additional Evidence concerning the said Conspiracy and Conspirators, which has come to Light since their Trials and Executions. III. Lists of the several Persons (Whites and Blacks) committed on Account of the Conspiracy; and of the several Criminals executed; and of those transported, with the Places whereto. By the Recorder of the City of New York [Daniel Horsmanden] . . . . New York: Printed by James Parker, at the New Printing-Office. 1744. 234 p. 4to.

BLM, CSmH, CtSo-P, DLC, MB, MH, MWA*, MWiW-C, MdBP, MiU-C, N, NHi, NN, NNPM, NNS, NjP, PBL, PPAmP, PPL, PU, RPJCB, ViU

Evans 5,413 Sabin 33,058 Church 951

Note William Munford, Virginia lawyer and law reporter, had a copy. "A List of my Books taken this 10th day of Octr 1802." Manuscript in Duke University Library, Durham, North Carolina.

(d) A journal of the proceedings in the detection of the conspiracy formed by some white people, in conjunction with Negro and other slaves, for burning the city of . . . . By the Recorder of the City of New York. Printed at New-York: London: Reprinted and sold by John Clarke. 1747. 440 p. 8vo.

CSmH, NHi, NN

Sabin 33,059

(e) The New-York Conspiracy, or a History Of The Negro Plot, with the Journal Of The Proceedings against the Conspirators At New-York In The Years 1741-2. Together with Several Interesting Tables . . . . By Daniel Horsmanden, Esq. New York: Southwick & Pelsue . . . . 1810. 385 p.

CSmH, MBAt, MH, MSaE, MWA*, MdBP, MoU-L, NHi, NN, NNC-L, NcD, NjHi, NjP, PPL, TxU, WHi

Shaw-Shoemaker 20,384 Sabin 33,060

(e.2) The New York Conspiracy By Daniel Horsmanden. With an Introduction by Thomas J. Davis (Boston 1971).

(f) Peleg W. Chandler, ed., "Trials of certain Negroes and others before the Supreme Court of New York, for a conspiracy to burn the city and murder the inhabitants, 1741," 1 American Criminal Trials 211-54 (Boston 1841).

Sabin 11,868

(g) William B. Wedgwood, ed., The Negro conspiracy in the city of New York, in 1741 (New York 1851).

Sabin 33,061

(h) The trial of John Ury "for being an ecclesiastical person . . ." (Philadelphia 1899).

(i) John D. Lawson, ed., "The Trial of John Ury for inciting Negroes to Crime and for being a Romish Priest, New York, 1741," 1 American State Trials 114-31 (St. Louis 1914).

(j) Ferenc M. Szasz, "The New-York Slave Revolt of 1741: A Re-Examination," 48 New York History 215-30 (1967).

(k) Thomas J. Davis, "The New York Slave Conspiracy of 1741 as Black Protest," 54 Journal of Negro History 17-30 (1971).

(11) Forsey v. Cunningham, Assault, Battery and Wounding, Supreme Court of Judicature, 1764

(a) The Report of an Action of Assault, Battery and Wounding, Tried in the Supreme Court of Judicature For the Province of New-York, In the Term of October 1764, Between Thomas Forsey, Plaintiff, and Waddel Cunningham, Defendant. New York: Printed by John Holt, in the year 1764. 20 p. 4to.

CSmH, DLC, MBAt, MWA*, MWiW-C, NHi, NN, NNB, NNC-L, PHi

Evans 9,660 Sabin 25,124

(a.2) [The Same] 72 p.

CSmH, DLC, MWA*, MiU-L, NN, NNB, PPAmP

mp. 41,438 Bristol B2,464 Huntington 252

Evans Ghost 10,190

Note The title page and first part of the contents are the same as in (a), but in addition it reports proceedings, of an appeal to the Council, the latest being under date of February 6, 1765. Johnson, below (c), cites Evans 9,660 and its ghost 10,190, but not mp. 41,428. However, it appears that he had access to and was using an imprint with more pages than Evans 9,660, but seemingly fewer pages than mp. 41,438. He cites pages 32-56 and the date Jan. 11, 1765, whereas mp. 41,438 reports on events through February 6, 1765.

(b) The Conduct of Cadwallader Colden, Esquire, Late Lieutenant-Governor of New-York: relating to the Judges Commissions, Appeals to the King, and the Stamp-Duty. [London] Printed in the Year MDCCLXII. 70 p. 8vo.

MH, MWA*, RPJCB

Evans 10,582 (microcard) as New York imprint)
Adams Independence 48a
Sabin 14,276 (describes Adams Controversy 67-4

(b.2) [New York reprint 1767] 58 p. 8vo.

RPJCB

Evans 10,582 Adams Controversy 67-4 note
Adams Independence 48b

Note This imprint does not refer specifically to Forsey v. Cunningham, but it appears to have been issued as a consequence of that, and perhaps related, cases.

(b.3) Edmund B. O'Callaghan, ed., 7 Documents Relative to the Colonial History of the State of New York (Albany 1856).

(b.4) "The Colden Letterbooks," 9 Collections of the New-York Historical Society for the Year 1876 passim (New York 1877); "The Letters and Papers of Cadwallader Colden," 55 Id. for the Year 1922 and 56 Id. for the Year 1923 passim (New York 1923).

(c) Milton M. Klein, "Prelude to Revolution in New York: Jury Trials and Judicial Tenure," 17 William and Mary Quarterly (3d Series) 439, 453-62 (1960).

(d) Herbert Alan Johnson, "George Harrison's Protest: New Light on Forsey versus Cunningham," 50 New York History 61-82 (1969).

Note In the debate on December 8, 1787, in the Pennsylvania Convention, the comments of John Smilie, a delegate from Fayette County and a leading anti-federal were noted by Jasper Yeates:

> "The Appellate Jurisdiction is borrowed from the Civil Law and Will exclude Trials by Jury for giving a false Verdict.
>
> "Writ of Attain lies against a Jury for giving a false Verdict.
>
> "Case of Forcy v. Cunningham at New York in 1764.--Appeal from the general Verdict of a Jury assessing Damages in the Case of a Trespass and Assault to the Governor and Council refused in the Supreme Court by the Judges."

R. Carter Pittman, "Jasper Yeates's Notes on the Pennsylvania Ratifying Convention, 1787, 22 William and Mary Quarterly (3d Series) 301, 311-12 (1965).

(12) Lydius's Land Titles, 1764

(a) Some Reflections on the Disputes between New York, New Hampshire, and Col. John Henry Lydius Of Albany . . . . To these Reflections are added, Some Rules of Law fit to be observed in purchasing Land, &c. [by Philodicaios (Thomas Young)] New-Haven: Printed and Sold by Benjamin Mecom. 1764. 23 p. 8vo.

CSmH, DLC, MB, NHi(2), NN*, RPJCB, VtU-W

Evans 9,889 Sabin 42,758 Trumbull 1,405

(13) Oudenarde's Imprisonment, 1766

(a) An Expostulatory Letter To The Honourable Daniel Horsmanden, Esq, Concerning the unnecessary and cruel Imprisonment of Henry Oudenarde, Late Merchant in the City of New-York. New-York: Printed MCCDLXVI. 16 p. 8vo.

CSmH, RPJCB

Evans 10,437 Huntington 272

(b) Seven Letters to the Honourable Daniel Horsmanden, Esq; Concerning the unnecessary and cruel Imprisonment of Hendrick Oudenaarde, Late Merchant in the City of New-York. New-York: Printed MCCDLXVI. 16 p. 8vo.

CSmH*, RPJCB

Evans 10,438 Sabin 57,903 Huntington 273

(14) Rutgers v. Waddington, Constitutional Law, Mayor's Court, 1784

(a) Arguments and Judgment of the Mayor's Court of the City of New-York, In a Cause between Elizabeth Rutgers and Joshua Waddington. New-York: Printed by Samuel Loudon. M,DCC,LXXXIV. 47 p. 8vo.

DLC, MH-L, MdBJ-G, MiU-C, NHi, NN*, NjP, P, PHi, RPJCB

Evans 18,773 Sabin 74,432

<u>Note</u> James Duane of New York sent George Washington a copy. Washington acknowledged receipt of the copy in a letter from Mount Vernon, dated April 10, 1785, in which he wrote: ". . . I thank you for the Arguments and judgment of the Mayor's Court of the City of New York in the Cause betwn. Elizabeth Rutgers and Joshua Waddington. I have read them with all the attention I could give the subject, and though I pretend not to be a competent judge of the Law of Nations, or the principle and policy of the Statute upon which the Action was found; yet I must confess, that reason seems very much in favor of the opinion given by the Court, and my judgment yields a hearty assent to it." 28 Writings of Washington 123-24 (John C. Fitzpatrick, ed., 1938). This copy remained in Washington's Library. See above note 1.04(5).

(a.2) Julius Goebel, Jr., ed., 1 <u>Law Practice of Alexander Hamilton, Documents and Commentary</u> 393-419 (New York 1964).

(b) An Address from the Committee Appointed at Mrs. Vandewater's on the 13th Day of September, 1784. To the People of the State of New-York. New-York: Printed by Shepard Kollock, opposite the Coffee-House. M,DCC, LXXIV. [Signed by Melancthon Smith and eight others. Defendant's side of the case.] 16 p. 8vo.

MWA*, MiU-C, NHi, NN

Evans 18,320 Sabin 53,473

(b.2) Loudon's New-York Packet. November 4, 1784. New-York: Printed a d published, every Monday and Thursday, by Samuel Loudon, No. 5, Water-Street. 1784. fol.

Evans 18,560

(c) <u>The case of Elizabeth Rutgers versus Joshua Waddington . . . With an Historical Introduction by Henry B. Dawson</u>. (Morrisania, New York 1866).

Sabin 74,433

(d) Richard B. Morris, ed., <u>Select Cases of the Mayor's Court of New York City, 1674-1784</u> 57-59, 302-27 (Washington, D.C. 1935).

(e) Louis Ottenberg, "Alexander Hamilton's First Court Case: Elizabeth Rutgers v. Joshua Waddington," 41 <u>New York Historical Society Quarterly</u> 423-39 (1957).

(f) Julius Goebel, Jr., ed., "Ch. 3: The Trespass Act--The Rutgers Test Case," 1 <u>Law Practice of Alexander Hamilton, Documents and Commentary</u> 282-543 (New York 1964).

(15) Assault on Livingston, 1785

(a) The attack made on Mr. B. Livingston in the evening of the 5th of October, instant, I consider one of the most unfortunate incidents of my life, as it happened during my controversy with him, and while I was preparing a vindication of my character for the press, against his publication of the 3d inst. . . . Abraham L. Smith . . . . [New York 1785] Broadside 17 x 13 cm.

MHi*

mp. 44,793 Bristol B6,171 Evans 19,246 (no copy located)

(16) Morhouse's Trial for Forgery, 1789

(a) The First Trial of A. Morhouse, for Forgery. Written by Himself. New-York 1789. 24 p.

CSmH*, NHi

Evans 21,976 Sabin 96,907

(b) The Writings of a Pretended Prophet, (In six letters,) Who assumed the title of faithful servant of Jesus Christ, officially commissioned by Almighty God, to demand and receive of Abraham Morehouse, Esq. two thousand pounds, with terrible denunciations in case of refusal. To which is added, His Recantation: Or Four Letters written by him during his Confinement. Rutland: Printed for Samuel Williams, August 1796.

No copy located

Evans 30,821 McCorison 418

(b.2) Bennington: Printed By Collier & Stockwell. 1802.

MWA*, VtU-W

Shaw-Shoemaker 3,598 McCorison 671

(b.3) Second Vermont Edition. Juyy [sic] 1816. [Rutland? Fay & Davison] 12 p.

DLC, MWA*, MnU, NN, Vt, VtHi, VtMiS, VtU-W, WHi

Shaw-Shoemaker 39,883 McCorison 1,891

(17) Anonymous 1787 Common Pleas Case, 1790

(a) A Review of the Laws of the United States 1787, below 3.20(1).

(18) Morris's Title to New York Land, 1791

(a) Brief of the Titles of Robert Morris, Esquire, to a tract of country in the county of Ontario, in the State of New-York, One of the United States of America. Extracted from authentic Documents, by Miers Fisher, Counselor at Law, In The Supreme Court Of The United States. To which is added A Schedule, containing authentic Copies of the principal Acts and Resolves of the General Congress of the United States, and of the Legislatures of the States of Massachusetts and New-York, and of other Deeds and Evidences of Title, cited in the Brief, for the satisfaction of those who who may wish to see them at full Length. Philadelphia: Printed by Benj. Franklin Bache in Market between Third and Fourth Streets. [1791] 47 p. 4to.

MBAt*, NN, PPAmP

Evans 23,376

Note The Minutes of the Supreme Court of the United States record that on February 7, 1791, the first day of February Term, "Miers Fisher Esqr. having been proposed by the said Attorney General [Edmund Randolph] of the United States for Admission as a Counsellor of this Court he is affirmed agreably to the Order thereof and is admitted to practice accordingly." "The Minutes of the Supreme Court of the United States 1789-1806, Edited by Erwin C. Surrency," 5 American Journal of Legal History 67, 75 (1961).

(19) Bedlow's Trial for Rape, Court of Oyer and Terminer, 1793

(a) Report of the Trial of Henry Bedlow, For Committing A Rape On Lanah Sawyer. And arguments of the counsel on each side. At a Court of Oyer and Terminer, and Gaol Delivery for the City and County of New York, held 8th October, 1893 . . . . Impartially taken by a Gentleman of the Profession. [William Wyche] New-York: Printed according to Act of Congress. M,DCC,XCIII. 62 p. 16mo.

MWA*

Evans 26,513 Sabin 69,914

(20) Price's Trial for Rape, Court of Oyer and Terminer, 1797

(a) The Trial of Nathaniel Price, For Committing a Rape on the Body of Unice Williamson, A Child between 10 and 11 Years of Age. At Brooklyn in King's County, in May 1797. This Cause which had much excited the public Attention, was tried at a Court of Oyer and Terminer, held by the Hon. Judge Hobart, At Flat-Bush Court-House, on the 29th of August 1797. New York: Printed for Elijah Weedg. (with Copy Right) (Price Six-Pence) [1797] 8 p. 8vo.

NHi*

Evans 32,712 Sabin 65,442

(21) Young's Trial for Murder, 1797

(a) The Trial of John Young for the Murder of Robert Barwick, One of the Deputy Sheriffs. New York: Taken by means of shorthand, for the benefit of the citizens of New-York, by William Green, 1797. [New York? 1797] 16 p. 16mo.

NIC-L(imp.)

Bristol B9,952

(b) Conversation & Conduct, of the late unfortunate John Young, who was executed for the Murder of Robert Barwick, (deputy sheriff,) From the time of receiving Sentence of Death, to that of his Execution. By Christopher Flanagan, Preacher of the Gospel. Who frequently Visited him, during that Period . . . . New York, printed by T. Kirk, two doors from the Tea-Water Pump. 1797. (Copy Right Secured.) Price Six-Pence.
8 p. 8vo.

MWA*, NHi, NN

Evans 32,133 Sabin 24,664 McDade 1,123

(c) Narrative of the Life, Last Dying Speech & Confession of John Young, Condemned to be executed this Day for the Murder of Robert Barwick, one of the Deputy Sheriffs . . . . [Price Six-Pence.] [New York 1797]
8 p. 21cm.

NHi*

Evans 33,255 Sabin 106,080 McDade 1,124

<u>Note</u> First brackets in original.

(d) The Ghost of John Young The Homicide, Who was Executed the 17th of August last, For the Murder of Robert Barwick, a Sherif's officer. The following Monody is written with a View of rescuing his Memory from Obloquy, and shewing his inconsistent sanguinary Laws are, in a Country which boasts of her Freedom and Happiness. By Mrs. Faugeres. [Price six pence.] [New-York 1797]
6 p. 8vo.

RPB*

Evans 32,116 McDade 1,125 Wegelin 136

<u>Note</u> First Brackets in original.

(22) Le Guen v. Gouverneur and Kemble, Court for the Trial of Impeachments and the Correction of Errors, 1797-1800

(a) Special Verdict, in the Case of Lewis Le Guen and Isaac Gouverneur & Peter Kemble, in the Supreme Court of the State of New-York. 1797. New-York: Printed at the Argus Office. 61 p. 8vo.

DLC, MB, MWA*, NHi, NNC-L, PHi, PP

Evans 32,369 Sabin 39,877n.

(b) State of the case and argument on the part of Gouverneur and Kemble, in their controversy with Louis Le Guen. 1797. New-York, Printed at the Argus Office 1797.
99 p. 20 cm.

NNC-L

Bristol B10,027

(c) Court for the Correction of Errors. Gouverneur and Kemble, vs. Louis Le Guen. Reasons assigned by Mr. Chief Justice Lansing, and Mr. Justice Benson, for their judgment, in the Court below. Albany, Printed by Charles R. and George Webster. [1798] 19 p. 19 cm.

NNC-L

Bristol B10,431

(d) In the Court for the Trial of Impeachments, and the Correction of Errors, by Appeal from the Court of Chancery. Case on the Part of the Appellant. [New York? 1798?] 13 p. 21 cm.

NHi, NNU-L

Bristol B11,094 (dates as 1800?)

(e) Court for the Trial of Impeachments and the Correction of Errors: Isaac Gouverneur and Peter Kemble, Appellants; and Louis LeGuen, Respondent: Case, on the Part of Louis LeGuen, the Respondent. Printed by Charles R. & George Webster. [Albany 1798] 25 p.

MWA* (two different settings reproduced), N

mp. 48,502 Bristol B10,432

Note Bristol uses heading "New York. Court for the Trial . . ." Short-Title Evans uses heading "Le Guen, Louis, respondent."

(f) Report of the Case in the Court of Errors, for the State of New-York, Between Isaac Gouverneur and Peter Kemble, Plaintiffs in Error, and Louis LeGuen, Defendant in Error. Albany: Printed by Charles R. & George Webster. At theie Bookstore, in the White House, corner of State and Pearl-Streets.--1798. 135 p. 8vo.

CSmH, DLC, MBAt, MWA*, NHi, NN, NNB(2), NNU-L, NcD-L

Evans 34,220 Sabin 28,147 and 39,877

(g) Court for the Trial Of Impeachments, and the Correction Of Errors. Isaac Gouverneur & Peter Kemble, Respondents, ads. Louis Le Guen, Appellant. Case on the part of Gouverneur & Kemble, the Respondents. New York: Printed by George Forman, No. 64, Water-Street. 1800. 32 p. 8vo.

N*

Evans 38,080

(h) See also Le Guen v. Gouverneur and Kemble, 1 Johnson Cases 436 below 1.05(29)(b).

(i) Julius Goebel, Jr., ed., 2 Law Practice of Alexander Hamilton 48-164 (New York 1969).

(23) Baker's Trial for Seduction, 1798

(a) The Hypocrite Unmask'd. Trial and Conviction of John Baker, A Methodist Teacher, of this City, for Seducing Miss Ann Burns, Under a Promise of Marriage. Held before the Hon. Judge Kent, at the City-Hall, on Friday Aug. 18, 1798. With the Pleadings of the Counsel On both Sides. In which is introduced a Specimen of Methodistical Orthography. To which is added Judge Kent's Excellent Charge to the Jury. [New York 1798] 8 p. 8vo.

RPJCB*

Evans 33,360 Sabin 96,819

(24) Le Roy v. Servis, Court for the Trial of Impeachments and the Correction of Errors, 1798

(a) In the Court for the Trial of Impeachments and the Correction of Errors. Peter Servis and others, Respondents, Ads. Herman Le Roy, William Bayard, and Gerrit Boon, Appellants. Case of the Respondents . . . . [Signed] Edward Livingston, Solicitor for Respondents, Richard Harrison, of Counsel. T. Greenleaf, Printer. [New York] Broadside 34 x 21 cm.

NHi*

mp. 45,929 Bristol B7,434 (dates as 1790?)

(b) Julius Goebel, Jr., and Joseph H. Smith, eds., 4 Law Practice of Alexander Hamilton 44-45 (New York 1980).

(25) Land Disputes, 1799

(a) The Honest Landlord, Truth Swearing Judge, and the Real Genuine Patent Republican; Or, the Patriot of '75, Whig of '76, and Soldier of '77 . . . . [Lansingburgh? 1799?] Broadside 40 x 32 cm.

MWA*

mp. 48,882 Bristol B10,810

(26) James's Case, Lien on Property for Debt, 1799

(a) The Case of Robert James, with the Particulars of his Trial, Observations, and Depositions, Taken Since. New-York: Printed for the author 1799. 26 p.

DLC*

mp. 48,898 Bristol B10,825

(27) Weeks's Trial for Murder, Court of Oyer and Terminer, 1800

(a) Report of the Trial of Levi Weeks, On an Indictment for the Murder of Gulielma Sands, on Monday the thirty-first day of March, and Tuesday the first day of April, 1800. Taken in short hand by the clerk of the court. New-York: Printed by John Furman, and sold at his blank, stamp and stationary shop, opposite the City-Hall. 1800. 98 p. 8vo.

CtHi, DLC, MB, MH, MH-L, MWA*, N, NIC-L, NHi, NN(2, 1 imp.), NNS, NNU-L, PP

Evans 38,372 Sabin 102,461 McDade 1,073

(a.2) Julius Goebel, Jr., ed., 1 Law Practice of Alexander Hamilton, Documents and Commentary 704-74 (New York 1964).

(b) A Brief Narrative of the Trial for the Bloody and Mysterious Murder of the Unfortunate Young Woman, in the Famous Manhattan Well. Taken in short hand by a Gentleman of the Bar. [David Longworth] [New York? 1800] 16 p. 8vo.

MH, MH-L, N, NHi*

Evans 37,039 Sabin 7,882 McDade 1,071

(c) An Impartial Account of the Trial of Mr. Levi Weeks for the Supposed Murder of Miss Julianna Elmore Sands. At a court held in the City of New-York, March 31, 1800. By James Hardie, A.M. New York: Printed and Sold by M. M'Farlane, No. 29 Gold-Street. 1800. 41 p. 8vo.

DLC*, NHi, P-L(imp.)

Evans 37,576 Sabin 102,461 McDade 1,072

(d) Edward S. Gould, "The Manhattan Well Murder," 44 Harper's Magazine 924-28 (May 1872).

(e) Henry Cabot Lodge, "An American Myth," 98 The Outlook 952-59 (August 26, 1911).

(f) John D. Lawson, ed., "The Trial of Levi Weeks for the Murder of Gulielma Sands, New York City, 1800," 1 American State Trials 1-40 (St. Louis 1918).

(g) Julius Goebel, Jr., ed., "The Manhattan Well Mystery: People v. Weeks," 1 Law Practice of Alexander Hamilton, Documents and Commentary 693-774 (New York 1964).

(28) Croucher's Trial for Rape, Court of Oyer and Terminer, 1800

(a) Report of the Trial of Richard D. Croucher, on an indictment for a Rape on Margaret Miller; on Tuesday, the 8th day of July, 1800. Taken in Short Hand. New York: Printed by George Forman, No. 64, Water-Street and Sold by the respective Booksellers in this city. 28 p. 8vo.

CtHi, DLC, MH-L*, MdBB, NHi, NN*, NNS, NNU-L (imp.) PP

Evans 38,373 Sabin 96,856

(29) Five New York Cases, Court for the Trial of Impeachments and the Correction of Errors 1800. [No title page other than that of first case. Title page of each case the same, except for designation of parties. Paging continuous. Index on last page.] 317 p. 8vo.

(a) [Arnold and Ramsey v. United Insurance Co.] Court for the Trial of Impeachments, and the Correction of Errors. George Arnold & Charles Ramsay Plaintiffs vs. The United Insurance Company, in the City of New York, Defendants. Case on the part of Arnold and Ramsay, Plaintiffs in error. New York: Printed by John Furman, at his Blank and Stationary Shop, opposite City Hall. 1800. [Duguet v. Rhinelander] . . . Philip Urbin Duguet, versus Frederick Rhinelander & Others. Case on the part of Duguet, plaintiff in error . . . . [Goix v. Low] . . . Nicholas Goix, versus Nicholas Low, President of the United Insurance Company in the City of New-York. Case on the part of Nicholas Goix, Plaintiff in error . . . . [Livingston v. Rogers] . . . John R. Livingston versus William Rogers. Case on the part of John R. Livingston. Plaintiff in error . . . . [Ludlow v. Gracie] . . . Daniel Ludlow & Gulian Ludlow, versus Archibald Gracie. Case on the part of D. and G. Ludlow, plaintiffs in error . . . .

DLC, N, NNB, PPB

Evans 38,079 (No copy located) Sabin 96,813

(b) Reports of Cases Adjudged in the Supreme Court of Judicature of the State of New-York; . . . together with cases determined in the Court For The Correction of Errors, during that period. By William Johnson, [Volumes I, II, and III] [Arnold and Ramsey v. The United Insurance Co. is reported in Volume I at 363; Duguet v. Rhinelander is reported in Volume II at 476; Goix v. Low is reported in Volume II at 480; Livingston

v. Rogers is reported in Volume II at 488; but Ludlow v. Gracie is not reported in Johnson.] New-York. Printed and published by Issac [sic] Riley; 1808

NNLI*

Shaw-Shoemaker 15,759

(c) Goix v. Low, 1801. Court for the trial of impeachments and correction of errors; between Nicholas Low, Defendant in error, and Nicholas Goix, Plaintiff in error. Case on the part of the defendant in error. Albany: Printed by Charles R. and George Webster 1801.

DLC, N

(d) Goix v. Low, 1802. Special Verdict, In Error. Nicholas Goix, Versus Nicholas Low, President of the United Insurance Company. Albany: Printed By Whiting And Leavenworth. M,VIII,II 15 p.

N-L*, NNB

Shaw-Shoemaker 2,785

(e) Julius Goebel, Jr., ed., "Ch. IV: Maritime Affairs," 2 Law Practice of Alexander Hamilton, Documents and Commentary 645-46 (Arnold and Ramsey); 649-50 (Duguet); 423 and 615-20 (Goix); and 770 (Ludlow) (New York 1969)

(30) Gilchrist v. Armstrong and Barnewall, Court for the Trial of Impeachments and the Correction of Errors, 1800

(a) In the Court for the Trial of Impeachments and the Correction Of Errors. Robert Gilchrist, William Armstrong & Geo. Barnewall. Case, on the part of the defendant in error. New York: Printed at the Law Press, Washington's Head, No. 84, Maiden Lane, 1800. 11 p. 8vo.

N*

Evans 38,083

(b) See also Armstrong and Barnwell v. Gilchrist, 2 Johnson's Cases 424, above 1.05(29)(b).

1.06 New Jersey

(1) Lutherland's Trial for Murder, 1692

(a) Blood Will Out, or, an Example of Justice in the Tryal, Condemnation, Confession and Execution of Thomas Lutherland, Who Barbarously Murthered the Body of John Clark of Philadelphia, And was Executed at Salem in West-Jersey the 23d of February 1691/2. Philadelphia, Printed and Sold by Will Bradford, 1692. 21 p. 4to.

NN*

Evans 588 Sabin 42,737 (Lutherland) and 88,270 (Southerland) Hildeburn 32 McDade 640

(a.2) Rex et Regina vs. Lutherland. A facsimile reprint with introduction and comments by Joseph S. Sickler (Woodstown, New Jersey 1948).

(2) Billing v. Jenings, 1699

(a) The Case Put & Decided by George Fox, George Whitehead, Stephen Crisp, and other the most Antient & Eminent Quakers between Edward Billing on the one part, and some West-Jersians, headed by Samuell Jenings On the other Part, In an Award Relating to the Government of their Province, . . . With some Reflections or the Sensless Opposition of these Men against the present Governour, and their daring Audatiousness in their presumptous asserting an Authority here over the Parliament of England. . . . [By Daniel Leeds. New York: Printed by William Bradford 1699] 16 p. 4to.

NjHi*

Evans 822 Wing C-1200

(a.2) Facsimile Reprint by Collins Printing House, Philadelphia 1880.

(b) Truth Rescued from forgery and falshood, being An Answer to a late Scurrilous piece Entituled The Case Put And Decided &c. Which Stole into the World without any known Authors named affixed thereto, And renders it the more like it's Father, Who was a Lyer and Murtherer from the beginning. Samuel Jenings. Printed at Philadelphia By Reynier Jansen. 1699. 31 p. 4to.

PHi*

Evans 865 Hildeburn 70 Wing J-557

(b.2) Reprint by Collins Printing House, Philadelphia 1881.

(3) Sonman's Perjury Case, 1709

(a) To his Excellency John Lord Lovelace, Barron of Hurly, Captain General and Governour in Chief of the Provinces of New-Jersey, New-York, and Territories depending thereon in America, and Vice Admiral of the same. The Answer of Peter Sonmans, To an Address presented to your Excellency, by the House of Representatives, dated March 17, 1708 . . . . [Colophon] Printed by William Bradford, at the Sign of the Bible in New-York, 1709. 26 p.

BOB*

Evans 1,431 Sabin 86,960

(4) Dunstar's Estate, Court of Chancery, 1740

(a) Perth-Amboy, January 21st 1739-40. Whereas in a Cause depending in the Court of Chancery of New-Jersey at the Suit of the Creditors and Legatees of Charles Dunstar deceased, against Michael Kearney, and James Alexander, his Executors . . . [Signed] Michael Kearney, James Alexander. Executors. New-York, Printed by John Peter Zenger, where Advertisements are taken in [1740] Broadside 33 x 21 cm. (Printer's Proof?)

NHi*

mp. 40,208 Bristol B1,098

(5) Stair and Others, Proprietors v. Bond and Others, Clinker Lot Right Men, Bill in Chancery, 1746

(a) A Brief Vindication of The Purchassors Against the Propritors in a Christian Manner. [By Griffin Jenkins] New-York. Printed, by J. Zenger, jun. 1745.6 48 p. 4to.

BLPro, CSmH, NN*

Evans 5,792 Sabin 7,919 Church 954
Rutherfurd p. 166, No. 5

(a.2) William A. Whitehead, ed., 6 _Documents Relating to the Colonial History of the State of New Jersey_ 266-92 (6 New Jersey Archives, 1st Series Newark 1882).

Note This printing has a note, "Mr. Alexander, in the title page of the original copy, wrote 'Pages 17, 18 & 19 Sum all thats any way to the purpose, one of these [pamphlets] could not be got to send to Mr. Penn in June last possibly it may Entertain him to See it.' --Ed."

(b) A Bill in the Chancery of New-Jersey, At the Suit of John Earl of Stair, and others, Proprietors of the Eastern-Division of New-Jersey; against Benjamin Bond, and some other Persons of Elizabeth-Town, distinguished by the name of the Clinker Lot Right Men. With Three large Maps, done from Copper-Plates. To which is added; The Publications of The Council of Proprietors of East New-Jersey, and Mr.

Nevill's Speeches to the General Assembly, concerning The Riots committed in New-Jersey, and The Pretences of the Rioters, and their Seducers. These Papers will give a better Light into the History and Constitution of New-Jersey, than any Thing hitherto published, the Matters whereof have been chiefly collected from Records. Published by Subscription: Printed by James Parker, in New-York, 1747; and a few copies are to be Sold by him, and Benjamin Franklin, in Philadelphia; Price bound, and Maps coloured, Three Pounds; plain and stitcht only, Fifty Shillings, Proclamation Money. 164 p. fol. [3 maps]

BLM, CSmH, DLC, MH, MH-L, MiU-C, MWA*, NHi, NN, NNB, NNC-L, Nj, NjP, NjHi, NJPera-B, NjR, PHi(2), PPAmP, PPL

Evans 6,021, 6,022, 6,023, 6,024 (Evans microcard 6,021 reproduces the complete publication, stating that there are no known separates.) mp. 40,421 Bristol B1,353 (erroneously shows NjR to have only 124 pages)

Sabin 5,378 Church 961 Humphrey Appendix 33

Note William Samuel Johnson of Connecticut and New York had a copy in his library. Johnson Collection shelflist, Law Library of Columbia University, New York City.

(c) An Answer to the Council of Proprietor's two Publications; Sett forth at Perth-Amboy the 25th of March 1746, and the 25th of March 1747. As also some Observations on Mr. Nevil's Speech to the House of Assembly, in Relation to a Petition presented to the House of Assembly, met at Trentown in the Province of New-Jersey in May, 1746 . . . . [Colophon] New-York: Printed and Sold by the Widow Catharine Zenger, at the PrintingOffice in Stone-street 1747. 13 p. fol.

CSmH, MiU-C, NN*, NjHi, PHi, RPJCB

Evans 5,901 Sabin 53,067 Rutherfurd p. 167, No. 2

(d) An Answer to a Bill in the Chancery of New-Jersey, At the Suit of John Earl of Stair, and others, commonly called Proprietors of the Eastern Division of New-Jersey, Against Benjamin Bond, and others claiming under the original Proprietors and Associates of Elizabeth-Town. To which is added; Nothing either of The Publications of The Council of Proprietors of East New-Jersey, or of the Pretences of the Rioters, and their Seducers; Except so far As the Persons meant by Rioters, Pretend Title Against The Parties to the above Answer; But A great Deal of the Controversy, though Much Less Of the History and Constitution of New-Jersey, than the said Bill . . . . Published by Subscription. New-York: Printed and sold by James Parker, at the New Printing-Office in Beaver-Street. 1752. 48 p. fol.

CSmH, MiU-C, NHi, NN*, NjHi, PPL, RPJCB

Evans 6,808 Sabin 53,066 Church 982
Humphrey Appendix 40

(e) A Letter from a Gentleman of New-Brunswick, to his Friend in Elizabeth-Town: On the first Point in Controversy between the Proprietors and Elizabeth-Town. New Brunswick, August 31, 1752. . . . [New York 1752] 4 p. 8vo.

NN*

Evans 6,864

(f) To His Excellency Jonathan Belcher, Esq; Captain General and Governor in Chief of the Province of New-Jersey, and Territories thereon depending in America, Chancellor and Vice-Admiral in the same. The Memorial of the Council of Proprietors of the Eastern Division of New-Jersey. . . . [New York 1755] 118 p. fol.

CSmH(imp.), DLC, N, NHi, NN*, NjHi, PHi(imp.), PPRF

Evans 7,508 Sabin 53,153 Church 988
Humphrey Appendix 44 Huntington 167

Note: mp. 40,669 (PHi*) and Bristol B1,627 are derived from the imperfect PHi imprint, which has the first 12 pages.

Note William Samuel Johnson kept a reading list between 1753 and 1765. This list shows that in 1753 he read "Mr. Alexander's Bill in Chancery" and "Answer to Mr. Alexander's Bill in Chancery." George C. Groce, Jr., William Samuel Johnson 27 (1937).

(g) The case of the Proprietors of East New-Jersey, with the opinions of counsel on the same. Newark: Printed by W. Tuttle & Co. 1825. (Contains opinions of Elias Van Arsdale and James Kent.)

Sabin 53,082

(h) William A. Whitehead, 6 Documents Relating to the Colonial History of the State of New Jersey (6 New Jersey Archives, 1st Series. Newark 1882).

(6) Clarke v. Proprietors, Bill in Chancery, 1760

(a) The Bill of Complaint in the Chancery of New-Jersey, brought by Thomas Clarke, and others, against James Alexander Esq; and others, commonly called The Proprietors of East New-Jersey. Wherein The Title of the People of Elizabeth-Town, to the controverted Lands, is fully exhibited, and the objections of the pretended Proprietors, stated, and refuted. Now published from the Original filed in the Court of Chancery, in 1754, to satisfy many who are curious to know the Foundation of a private Debate of the greatest Importance in

America. Printed by William Weyman, in New-York, 1760. 20 p. fol.

CSmH, DLC, NN*, NHi

Evans 8,550 Sabin 53,075 Humphrey Appendix 60

Note In 1761, William Samuel Johnson read "Smith's Bill in Chancery in Jersey Dispute." See above note to 1.06(7). This seems to be identifiable as this imprint. See Edwin F. Hatfield, History of Elizabeth New Jersey 309 (New York 1868).

(7) Libel of Franklin, 1765

(a) The Answer of his Excellency William Franklin, Esq; Governor of His Majesty's Province of New-Jersey, to the invidious Charges of the Proprietary Party, contained in a Libel, read by Mr. James Biddle, Clerk of the Common Pleas for the County of Philadelphia, on Saturday last, and afterwards published and industriously dispersed through the Province. Burlington, New-Jersey, October 1, 1765. . . . [Philadelphia: Printed by B. Franklin and D. Hall, 1765] Broadside fol.

PU*

Evans 9,973 Sabin 25,636 Hildeburn 2,125

(8) Newark's Land Claim, 1766

(a) The Claim of the Inhabitants of the Town of Newark, in virtue of The Indian Purchase made by the first Settlers of Newark, in 1667, Stated and Considered. [by David Ogden] Woodbridge, in New-Jersey: Printed by Samuel F. Parker. M.DCC.LXVI 14 p. 8vo.

CSmH, NN, NjR, RPJCB*

Evans 10,435 Sabin 56,800 Church 1,058 Humphrey 94

(a.2) Facsimile reproduction. Publisher and date unknown.

(9) Indian Purchases and the General Proprietors of East-New-Jersey, 1767

(a) To the several Persons claiming under the Indian Purchases, called the Mountain, Horsneck and Van Gieson Purchases. [Signed by David Ogden and Dated February 20, 1767. Woodbridge: Printed by James Parker? 1767] 8 p. 8vo.

NjP*

Evans 10,720 Sabin 56,801 Humphrey 97

(10) Hunt v. Proprietors, Bill in Chancery, 1767

(a) A Bill in the Chancery of New-Jersey, At the Suit of John Hunt, against William Earl of Stirling, And Others, Proprietors of the Eastern Division of the Province of New-Jersey. Philadelphia: Printed by William Goddard, at the New Printing-Office, in Market Street. M.DCC.LXVII.
21 p. fol.

NN, NjHi, PHi*

Evans 10,654 Sabin 5,379 and 33,874 Hildeburn 2,279
Humphrey Appendix 60

(b) The Plea and Answer Of the Right Honourable William Earl of Stirling, and others, Proprietors of East New-Jersey, to John Hunt's Bill in Chancery. New York: Printed by John Holt, at the Exchange, 1770.
46 p. fol. [2 folding leaves]

NN*, NjHi, PHi, RPJCB

Evans 11,765 Sabin 91,855

(11) Bland v. Ashfield, Bill in Chancery, 1771

(a) A Bill in the Chancery of New-Jersey, At the Suit of Priscilla Bland, John Mann and Mercy his Wife; Against Redford Ashfield, and others. Printed in the Year MDCCLXXI [Burlington] 25 p. fol.

NHi, NN*, NjHi(2), NjR, PHi

Evans 12,159 mp. 42,215 Bristol B3,324

Sabin 53,542 Humphrey 110

Note Evans 12,159 is erroneously listed under the heading "New York. Chancery Court"; Short-Title Evans correctly lists under heading "New Jersey (Colony) Chancery Court, 1771"; and the microcard reproduces the NN copy. Bristol lists the same imprint under the heading "Bland, Priscilla, plaintiff" and locates copies at NHi and PHi. Short-Title Evans repeats the Bristol listing, using the same heading, but states that "No copy could be located." Neither Bristol nor Short-Title Evans show any place of publication.

(12) Smith v. Kennedy, Bill in Chancery, 1773

(a) A Bill in the Chancery of New-Jersey, at the suit of Samuel Smith, esq. one of the treasurers of New-Jersey, against Archibald Kennedy . . . Burlington, Isaac Collins, 1773.
11 p. 30.5 cm.

DLC, NN*

mp. 42,472 Bristol B3604a Humphrey 129

(13) Barclay v. Proprietors, Bill in Chancery, 1773

(a) A Bill in the Chancery of New-Jersey, at the suit of Robert Barclay, against William Earl of Stirling, And Others, Proprietors of the Eastern Division of the Province of New-Jersey. [By Elias Boudinot, Esq.] Burlington: Printed by Isaac Collins, M,DCC,LXXIII. 51 p.

CSmH, NN*, NNB, NjR, PHi, RPJCB

Evans 12,882 Sabin 53,074 Humphrey 128

(14) New Jersey Proprietors' Land Claim, 1784

(a) The Petitions and Memorials of the Proprietors of West and East-Jersey, to the Legislature of New-Jersey, together with a Map of the State of New-Jersey, and the Country adjacent: and also An Appendix Containing Extracts from several original Papers, and instruments, tending to elucidate the subject matter of the said Petitions, &c. The Whole giving a clear and comprehensive view of a dispute respecting the right of Property in a Tract of Land, containing above Four Hundred Thousand Acres in the Heart of New-Jersey, and which dispute may ultimately destroy the Title to above Four Hundred Thousand more, in different parts of the State, and which land now is, and part of it for above sixty Years past has been, possessed by thousands of industrious Freeholders. New York: Printed by Shepard Kollock, No. 156, Water-Street [1784] 74 p. 8vo.

DLC* (no copy located with map), NHi, NN, NjHi, NjP

Evans 18,640 Sabin 53,203

(a.2) Edition of 1785. 97 p. 8 vo. [1 map]

CSmH, DLC*, NHi, NN, NjR

Evans 19,126

(b) A Concise View of the Controversy between the Proprietors of East and West-Jersey: being An Explanation of the Bill presented by the Western Proprietors to the Legislature of New-Jersey; published with a Design to remove the Misrepresentations contained as well in a Pamphlet, entitled 'The Petitions and Memorials of the Proprietors of East and West-Jersey to the Legislature of New-Jersey,' as in certain Petitions, which were unfairly dispersed among the Inhabitants, a short time before the Hearing appointed by the Assembly in November, 1784. [By Richard Stockton, though usually attributed to Ebenezer Cowell] Philadelphia: Printed by Hall and Sellers. 1785. 24 p. 12mo.

NN*, NjR, RPJCB

Evans 18,976

(15) Kease's, Kinnon's, and Campbell's Trial for Burglary and Murder, Supreme Court, 1787

(a) The trial of John Kease, Patrick Kinnon and John Campbell, for burglary and murder. Before the Honorable Isaac Smith, Esquire, second justice of the Supreme Court of New Jersey. At a Court of oyer and terminer, and General gaol delivery, of the state of New Jersey for the County of Burlington, holden at the city of Burlington, on Tuesday the 18th of September, 1787, by virtue of a commission under the great seal of the state, for holding said courts, dated at Burlington the 22d day of May, 1787. Published by desire. By a person present at the trial. Philadelphia: Printed in the year 1787. 24 p. 20.5 cm.

DLC (No copy could be reproduced)

mp. 45,086 Bristol B6,510 McDade 548

(16) Bloomfield's Manumission Cases, 1775-1793 Cases, Supreme Court 1794

(a) Cases Adjudged in the Supreme Court of New-Jersey, Relative to the Manumission of Negroes, and others holden in bondage. . . . Burlington, Printed for 'The New Jersey Society For Promoting The Abolition Of Slavery,' By Isaac Neale, -- M,DCC,XCIV.

DLC, MH-L, MiU-C, NHi(2), NIC-L, NN, Nj, NjHi, NjP, NjR, PBL, PHi, PP, PPL*, RPJCB, TxDaM-L 32 p. 8vo.

Evans 27,391 Sabin 53,084 Morsch 240

(a.2) Second edition (Camden 1843).

(a.3) Photoreproduction of PBB copy (Dennis & Co., Inc., Buffalo 1940).

(17) Tatem v. Chew, Cause in Chancery, 1799

(a) Tatem, complainant. The Evidence in a Cause depending in the Court Of Chancery of the State of New-Jersey. Between William Tatem, Esquire, and others, complainants, and Jeffery Chew, and others, defendants. Taken pursuant to the rules of the said court. Trenton: Printed by Gershom Craft. 1799. 136 p. 4to. [1 folding table]

NjP*

Evans 36,396 Sabin 94,405 Morsch 453 Parrish App. 52

1.07 Pennsylvania

(1) Quakers's Trial, 1693

(a) New-England's Spirit of Persecution Transmitted to Pennsilvania; And the Pretended Quaker found Persecuting the True Christian-Quaker, in the Tryal of Peter Boss, George Keith, Thomas Budd, and William Bradford, At the Sessions held at Philadelphia the Nineth, Tenth and Twelfth Days of December, 1692. Giving an Account of the most Arbitrary Procedure of that Court. [By George Keith] Printed [by William Bradford New York or Philadelphia] in the Year 1693. 40 p. 4to.

BBB-N, BLF, BOB, DLC, MWA*, MdBJ-G, MiU-C, NN, PHI, PP, RPJCB, ViU

Evans 642 Sabin 37,203 Baer 150 Hildeburn 64
Wing K-186

(a.2) The Tryals of Peter Boss, George Keith, Thomas Budd, and William Bradford, Quakers, For several Great Misdemeanours (As was pretended by their Adversaires) before a Court of Quakers: At the Sessions held at Philadelphia, in Pennsylvania, the Ninth, Tenth, and Twelfth days of December, 1692. [By George Keith] Giving also an Account of the most Arbitrary Procedure of that Court. Licensed Octob 19th 1693. Dan Poplar. Printed first Beyond-Sea, and now Reprinted in London for Richard Baldwin in Warwick-lane. 1693. 34 p. 4to.

BCT, BCU, BGU, BLM, BOB, DLC, MdBJ-G, MiU-C, NN, NNC-L, NjP, PHC, PP, PPRF, RPJCB

Sabin 37,226 Baer 151 RPJCB 4th p. 271
Wing T,2254

(b) The Judgment Given forth by Twenty Eight Quakers Against George Keith, And his Friends, With Answers to the said Judgment, declaring those Twenty Eight Quakers to be No Christians. As Also, An Appeal (for which several were Imprisoned, &c.) by the said George Keith, &c. to the Yearly Meeting, Sept. 1692. With a Full Account of the said Yearly Meeting, Signed by Seventy Quakers. . . . Printed at Pensilvania; and now Re-printed at London, for Richard Baldwin, near the Oxford-Arms in Warwick-lane. 1694. 22 p. 20 cm.

RPJCB

Sabin 37,200 RPJCB 4th p. 287 Wing J-1,173

(c) The State of the case--betwixt the people called Quakers, in Pensilvania, &c. in America, who remain in unity; and George Keith . . . as also a just vindication of myself from the reproaches and abuses of those backsliders. By Samuel Jennings. . . . London, Printed & sold by T. Sowle, near the Meeting-house at White-hart-court in Grace-church-street, and at the Crooked billet in Holly-well-lane near Shoreditch. 1694. 84 p. 8vo.

BOB, BLF, CSmH, DLC, NN, PHi

Sabin 36,048 RPJCB 4th p. 286 Wing J-670

(d) A Further Discovery Of the Spirit of Falsehood & Persecution in Sam. Jennings, And his Party that joyned with him in Pensilvania; and some Abettors that cloak and defend him here in England: In Answer to his scandalous Book, called, The State of the Case . . . . [By George Keith] [Colophon] London: Printed for R. Levis, 1694. 52 p. 4to.

BLF, BLM, BOB, CSmH, PHi, RPJCB

Sabin 37,196 Church 744 Wing K-170

(e) Samuel W. Pennypacker, "The Proprietor vs. George Keith, William Bradford, Thomas Budd, and Peter Boss," Pennsylvania Colonial Cases 117-42. (Philadelphia 1892).

(2) Story v. Hoskins, Pennsylvania Company, 1724

(a) A Determination of the Case of Mr. Thomas Story and Mr. James Hoskins, Relating to an Affair of the Pennsylvania Company, &c. . . . [Philadelphia: Printed by S. Keimer. 1724] 3 p. fol.

PHi*

Evans 2,502 Sabin 6,106 Hildeburn 214

(a.2) London: J. Roberts, 1724.

(a.3) The Determination of the Affair betwixt Mess. Story and Hoskins, Relating to the Pennsylvania Company. [Supposed to have been written by Elias Bockett.] The Second Edition. London: Printed for T. Smith in Cornhill. 1724.

PHi(2, 1 imp.)

Sabin 6,106

(3) Register of Persons Naturalized, Supreme Court, 1743

(a) Extract aus der Registratur der Supreem-Court zu Philadelphia . . . . [Philadelphia, Joseph Crellius? 1743] 4 p. 32.5 cm.

DLC*

mp. 40,315 Bristol B1,219 Hildeburn 815

(4) Richardson's Land Title, 1755

(a) A True State of the Case of R.[ebecca] R.[ichardson] Widow [respecting a house and lot in Philadelphia]. [Signed E.F.] [Philadelphia: Printed by W. Bradford? 1755] 15 p. 16mo.

PPL*

Evans 7,414 Sabin 71,082 Hildeburn 1,442

(5) Reed v. Reid, Land Case, 1768?

(a) [No title page] Joseph Reed defendant; Ad. John Reid. Argument for the Defendant in Error. [Philadelphia: 1768?] [Relates to a dispute about a track of land called "Tenicum." The appeal is signed "Jos. Reed. Propria Persona."] 28 p. 4to.

DLC, PHi*

Evans 11,053 Sabin 68,567 Hildeburn 2,391

(6) Talbot v. Three Brigs, High Court of Errors and Appeals, 1785

(a) The Resolution of the High Court of Errors and Appeals, for the State of Pennsylvania; in the Cause of Silas Talbot, quitam, &c. Against the Commanders and Owners of the Brigs, Achilles, Patty, and Hibernia; January 14, 1785. Philadelphia: Printed by T. Bradford, in Front-street. M,DCC,LXXXV 24 p. 8vo.

DLC, MiU-C, NHi, NN*, PHi(2), PPAmP, PU-L, RPJCB

Evans 19,164 Sabin 60,582

(6a) Mary Harrison v. Joseph Galloway. Claim. . . decree [1786 Philadelphia] folio

BLM

Bibliography of Eighteenth Century Legal Literature p. 874 (Bell Project 1982).

(a.2) Hopkinson, Judgments, below 1.07(20)(a).

(a.3) 1 Dallas 95, below 1.07(26).

(a.4) 3 Hopkinson, Miscellaneous Essays 132, below 1.07 (29).

(7) Clifton's and M'Glochlin's Trials for Murder, Court of Oyer and Terminer, 1787

(a) The Trial of Alice Clifton, for the Murder of her Bastard-Child. At the Court of Oyer and Terminer and General Gaol Delivery, held at Philadelphia, on Wednesday the 18th day of April, 1787 . . . . The Trial of James M'Glochlin, for feloniously entering the dwelling house of James Bryne, in the night of the 14th of November last, at the Court and City aforesaid. . . . 16 p. 8vo.

MBAt*, MH-L, PPL

Evans 20,275 Sabin 13,697 McDade 184

(8) Trials, Court of Oyer and Terminer, 1787

(a) The Remainder of the Tryals at the late Court of Oyer and Terminer; among others that of Alice Clifton for the murder of her bastard child. Philadelphia: Printed by Eleaser Oswald: Sold at the several Book-Stores in the City. 1787.

No copy located.

Evans 20,276 Sabin 96,849

(9) Gerard v. La Coste, Court of Common Pleas, Philadelphia County, 1787

(a) [No parties named] "Interesting decision of the court of common pleas in Philadelphia," 2 The American Museum, or Repository of Ancient and Modern Fugitive Pieces. Prose and Poetical [November 1787] 469. Philadelphia: Printed by Matthew Carey. M,DCC,LXXXVII.

CtHT-W, DLC, MBAt, MWiW, MdBE, MdBP, NHi, NN, NNB, NjP, NjR, P, PBL, PHi, PPAmP, PPL, RPB, TxU, ViU, ViW

Evans 20,194

(b) Gerard v. La Coste, 1 Dallas 194, below 1.07(26).

(c) A Review of the Laws of the United States 163, below 3.20(1)

(10) Pollard v. Shaffer, Supreme Court, 1787

(a) "Law Report, in the Supreme Court of Pennsylvania. Sarah Green, and William Pollard, against The Executors of David Shaffer," 2 American Museum [November 1787] 470-74, above 1.07(9)(a).

(b) Pollard v. Shaaffer, 1 Dallas 210, below 1.07(26)

(c) A Review of the Laws of the United States 171, below 3.20(1).

(11) Stoddard v. Penhallow, Court of Common Pleas, Philadelphia County, 1787

(a) "Law case, respecting a captured vessel," 2 American Museum [December 1787] 588-89, above 1.07(9)(a).

(a.2) Second Edition. M.DDCC.XCIII.

DLC, MWA, MWiW

Evans 25,101

(b) Doane's Administrators v. Penhallow, 1 Dallas 208, below 1.07(26).

(c) A Review of the Laws of the United States 165, below 3.20(1).

(12) January v. Goodman, Court of Common Pleas, Philadelphia County, 1787

(a) "Law regulation relating to notes of hand," 2 American Museum [December 1787] 589, above 1.07(9)(a).

(a.2) Second Edition, above 1.07(11)(a.2).

(b) January Assignee v. Goodman, 1 Dallas 208, below 1.07(26).

(c) A Review of the Laws of the United States 163, below 3.20(1).

(13) Millar v. Hall, Supreme Court, 1788

(a) "The Law Budget. In the Supreme Court of Pennsylvania, January Term 1788, Millar v. Hall," 2 The Columbian Magazine, or Monthly Miscellany [January 1788] 37-38. Philadelphia: Printed for T. Seddon, W. Spotswood, C. Cist, & J. Trenchard.

CtHT-W, DLC, MBAt, MdBJ-G, NN, NjP, P, PBL, PHi, PPAmP, PPL, RPB

Evans 21,007

(b) Millar v. Hall, 1 Dallas 228, below 1.07(26).

(14) Commonwealth v. Gordon, Supreme Court, 1788

(a) "The Law Budget . . . The Commonwealth v. Gordon," 2 Columbian Magazine [January 1788] 39, above 1.07(13)(a).

(b) Respublica v. Gordon, 1 Dallas 233, below 1.07(26).

(15) Nathan v. Virginia, 1781 Case from Court of Common Pleas, Philadelphia County, 1788

(a) "Statement of a cause decided in the court of common pleas of the Commonwealth of Pennsylvania, September 1781," 4 American Museum [September 1788] 271-75, above 1.07(9)(a).

Library Locations, above 1.07(9)(a).

Evans 20,928

(b) Common Pleas, Philadelphia County, June Term, 1 Dallas note 77-80, below 1.07(26).

(16) Commonwealth v. Oswald, Contempt, Supreme Court, 1788

(a) "Law Budget. In the Supreme Court, July Term, 1788. The Commonwealth v. Oswald," 2 The Columbian Magazine, or Monthly Miscellany [September 1788] 519-25. Philadelphia: Printed for the Proprietors by W. Spotswood, Front-Street.

CtHT-W, DLC, MBAt, MdBJ-G, NN, NjP, P, PBL, PHi, PPAmP, PPL, RPB

Evans 21,007

(b) "A Summary of the Proceeding in the General Assembly of Pennsylvania, upon the Complaint of Col. Eleazer Oswald against the Justices of the Supreme Court," 2 Columbian Magazine [October 1788] 583-88, above 1.07(16)(a).

(c) The Case of the Commonwealth against Eleazer Oswald; for a Contempt of the Supreme Court of Pennsylvania. Adjudged the fourteenth day of July, 1788. With A Brief Account of the Proceedings in the General Assembly, upon the Memorial of the Defendant against three of the Justices of that Court, for the Judgment and Sentence pronounced against him. Reported by a Gentleman of the Law. Philadelphia: Printed by William Spotswood, Front-Street. M.DCC.LXXXVIII.
16 p. 8vo.

DLC, MH-L?, MWA*, NHi, NNU-L, PPL

Evans 21,363 Sabin 57,828

(d) Respublica v. Oswald, 1 Dallas 319, below 1.07(26).

(17) Poultney v. Ross, Court of Common Pleas, Philadelphia County, 1788

(a) "Law Budget. In the Common Pleas, Philadelphia, March Term, 1788, Before Shippen, President, and Others, Justices. Poultney et al. v. Ross," 2 Columbian Magazine [November 1788] 647-48, above 1.07(16)(a).

(b) Poultney et al v. Ross, 1 Dallas 28, below 1.07(26).

(18) Chapman v. Steinmetz, Supreme Court, 1788

(a) "In the Supreme Court, April Term, 1788, Chapman v. Steinmetz," 2 Columbian Magazine [November 1788] 648, above 1.07(16)(a).

(b) Chapman v. Steinmetz, 1 Dallas 261, below 1.07(26).

(19) Robertson v. Vogle, Court of Common Pleas, Philadelphia County, 1788

(a) "Law Budget. In the Common Pleas, Philadelphia County, March Term, 1788: Before Shippen, President, and Others, Justices. Robertson et al. versus Vogle," 2 Columbian Magazine [December 1788] 703-06, above 1.07(16)(a).

(b) Robertson et al. v. Vogle, 1 Dallas 252, below 1.07(26).

(20) Hopkinson's Judgements in Admiralty, 1785-1786 Cases, 1789

(a) Judgements in the Admiralty Of Pennsylvania In Four Suits brought as for Maritime Hypothecations. Also, the case of Silas Talbot, against the Briggs Achilles, Patty, and Hibernia, and of The Owners Of The Hibernia against Their Captain John Angus. With an Appendix, containing the testimony exhibited in the admiralty in those causes. The Hon. Francis Hopkinson, Judge. Philadelphia, Printed by T. Dobson and T. Lang, in Second Street. M DCC LXXXIX. 131 p. 8vo.

DLC, MH-L, MWA*, NIC-L, NNC-L, NNU-L, NcD-L, P-L, PHi, PPAmP, PU-L, TxDaM-L

Evans 22,053

(b) Cases reprinted in whole or in part in Hopkinson's Judgments in Admiralty, 1792, below 1.07(29).

(21) Marshall v. Scots Presbyterian Church, Supreme Court, 1789?

(a) Some Queries Intended to be put to the Rev. Dr. Witherspoon, and other Clergymen, on the trial in the Supreme Court of Pennsylvania, between Mr. Marshall and the Scots Presbyterian Church. . . . [Philadelphia? 1789?] 3 p.

MWA*

mp. 45,595 Bristol B7,068

(22) Camp v. Lockwood, 1788 Case from Court of Common Pleas, Philadelphia County, 1790

(a) "Law case--common pleas, Philadelphia, Dec. 7, 1788," 7 The American Museum, or Universal Magazine [January 1790] 8-11. Philadelphia: Carey, Stewart and Co. M,DCC,XC

Library locations, above 1.07(9)(a).

Evans 22,309

(b) Law case. . . [February 1790] 78-81, above 1.07(22)(a).

(c) Law case. . . [March 1790] 132-35, above 1.07(22)(a).

(d) Camp v. Lockwood, 1 Dallas 393, below 1.07(26).

(23) Bolton v. Martin, 1788 Case from Court of Common Pleas, Philadelphia County, 1790

(a) "Law case. Common pleas, Philadelphia County, June term, 1788. Bolton vs. Martin. From Dallas's reports, now in the press, and which will be published in a few days," 8 American Museum [July 1790] 4-7, above 1.07(22)(a).

Library Locations, above 1.07(9)(a).

Evans 22,310

(b) "Law case. Common pleas, Philadelphia county, June term, 1788. Bolton vs. Martin. From Dallas's reports, just published," 8 American Museum [August 1790] 87-91, above 1.07(23)(a).

(c) Bolton v. Martin, 1 Dallas 296, below 1.07(26).

(24) Caldwell v. Barclay, Court of Common Pleas, Philadelphia County, 1790

(a) "Another case of privilege. Caldwell vs. Barclay, et al.--From the same [i.e., Dallas's Reports]" 8 American Museum [August 1790] 91, above 1.07(23)(a).

(b) Caldwell v. Barclay, 1 Dallas 305 note, below 1.07(26).

(25) Anonymous 1787 Case from Philadelphia Common Pleas, 1790

(a) A Review of the Laws of the United States 162, below 3.20(1).

(26) Dallas's Reports, 1754-1789 Cases, Volume 1, Courts of Pennsylvania, 1790

(a) Reports of Cases ruled and adjudged in the Courts of Pennsylvania, before and since the Revolution: By A. J. Dallas, Esquire. . . . [Vol. 1] Philadelphia: Printed, for the Reporter, by T. Bradford. M,DCC,XC. [This is Volume 1 of the United States Reports.] 531 p. 8vo.

AzU-L, CLU-L, CSmH, DCU-L, DLC, MB, MH-L, MWA*, MdBB, MiU-L, NIC-L, NN, NNB, NNC-L, P-L, PHi, PPL, PU-L, PV-L, RPJCB, TxDaM-L, ViLxW-L, ViU

Evans 22,445 Sabin 18,313 Sowerby 2,088

(a.2) Philadelphia: Printed for the Reporter by J. Ormrod, 1799. 505 p. 8vo.

PHi

Bristol B10,758a

(a.3) Vol. I. The Second Edition, with additional notes, references, and authorities. . . . Philadelphia: Printed for P. Byrne, No. 182, Market Street. 1806. 536 p.

CLL, MB, MH-L, MWA*, NNU-L, PP, PPB, PU-L

Shaw-Shoemaker 11,130

<u>Note</u> Volume 1 of Dallas was in George Washington's library. See above note 1.04(5).

Copies of the first three volumes were in the collection of the Law Library Company of the City of Philadelphia in 1805. "Catalogue Number 31," <u>Catalogue of the Books Belonging to the Law Library Company of the City of Philadelphia</u> (1805).

(27) Commonwealth v. Purdon, Church Dispute about Pastor, 1791

(a) An Address, Delivered July 8th, 1790, to the Jury In the Case of the Commonwealth against John Purdon and others; By the Honourable Jacob Rush, Esquire, Late one of the Judges of the Supreme Court of Pennsylvania. Philadelphia: Printed by William Young, Bookseller, No. 52, Second-street, the corner of Chestnut-street. M,DCC,XCI 38 p. 8vo.

PPL*

Evans 23,748

(28) McKnight's Case of Bankruptcy, 1792

(a) The Case of Robert McKnight, A Bankrupt, Written by himself in Prison at Philadelphia, 1792. . . . [Philadelphia 1792] 24 p. 8vo.

PHi, PPL*

mp. 46,494 Bristol B8,049

(29) Hopkinson's Judgments in Admiralty, 1785-1788 Cases, 1792

(a) Judgments in Admiralty by Francis Hopkinson, Esq. Philadelphia: Printed by T. Dobson, at the Stone-House, No 41. Second Street. M,DCC,XCII. 215 p.

ICU-L

Not in Evans or Bristol

(a.2) Photoreproduction published by Dennis & Co., Inc., Buffalo, N.Y., in 1942.

(b) The Miscellaneous Essays and Occasional Writings of Frangis [sic] Hopkinson, Esq. Volume III. Philadelphia: Printed by T. Dobson, at the Stone House, No 41, Second Street, M,DCC,XCII 426 p. 8vo.

BLM, CSmH, DLC, MB, MBAt, MH-L, MWA*, MdBE, MdBP, MiU-L, MoSW-L, NHi, NN, NjP, NjR, PHi, PP, PPAmP, PPL, PU-L, RPB, ViU(3), ViW

Evans 24,407 Sabin 32,979

Note For a book review see "Impartial Review of American Publications," II (or 9) Universal Asylum and Columbian Magazine for August 1792 11-12.

3 Miscellaneous Essays has two separately-paged parts. The first part is "Judgments in Admiralty," above 1.07(29)(a). The second part is "Poems." The Judgments in Admiralty set forth above as a separate imprint almost certainly is from the same press run as the "Judgments" incorporated into Miscellaneous Essays, but it has a different title page and it does not have a Table of Contents. There is a Table of Contents in the Essays.

(c) Admiralty Decisions in the District Court Of The United States, for the Pennsylvania District, By The Hon. Richard Peters, comprising also Some Decisions In The Same Court by the late Francis Hopkinson, Esq. . . . Philadelphia: Published By William P. Farrand. Robert Carr, Printer. 1807. [The Hopkinson cases are scattered throughout the two volumes.]

DLC, MWA*, NN, NjR, RPB

Shaw-Shoemaker 13,364

(d) Reports of Cases Adjudged in the District Court of South Carolina. By the Hon. Thomas Bee, Judge of that Court. To which is added An Appendix, containing Decisions in the Admiralty Court of Pennsylvania. By the late Francis Hopkinson, Esquire. . . . (Philadelphia 1810). [Twenty-one of the Hopkinson cases reprinted at pp. 337-432.]

Sabin 87,456

(e) Federal Cases (St. Paul 1894-98). Neither Hopkinson's Judgments of 1789 nor 1792 are covered. See 1 Federal Cases xxxviii listing of reports and "unattached" footnote 16. However, the Hopkinson cases that were reprinted by Peters and Bee are reported. See Digest of Federal Cases Table of Citations for Bee and Peters.

(30) Cobbett's 1797 Trial for Libel, 1798

(a) The Democratic Judge: or the Equal Liberty of the Press, as Exhibited, Explained, and Exposed, In the Prosecution of William Cobbett, For a pretended Libel against The King of Spain and his Embassador; before Thomas M'Kean, Chief Justice of the State of Pennsylvania. By Peter Porcupine. Philadelphia: Published by William Cobbett, opposite Christ-Church. March, 1798.

102 p. 8vo.

CSmH, CtHT-W, CtY, DLC, MB, MBAt, MH, MWA*, MdBB, MDBJ-C, NN, NNUT, NjP, NjR, PHi(2), PP, PPAmP, PPL, ViU, WHi

Evans 33,523   Sabin 13,880   Gaines 37a and 37b
Pearl 31

(b) The Republican Judge: or the American Liberty of the Press, as Exhibited, Explained, and Exposed, In the Base and Partial Prosecution of William Cobbett, For a pretended Libel against The King of Spain and his Embassador, Before The Supreme Court of Pennsylvania. With an Address to the People of England. By Peter Porcupine. London: Printed for J. Wright, opposite Old Bond Street, Piccadilly. 1798.

CtY, CUL, CSmH, DLC, MBAt, MH, MH-L, MWA, MdBJ-G, MiU-C, N, NN, NjP, PPL, PU-L, RPJCB

Sabin 14,053   Gaines 39a, 39b, and 39c   Pearl 32

(b.2) Second Edition. 1798

CSmH, CtY

(b.3) Third Edition. 1798

NN, NjR, PU(imp.), RPJCB

Gaines 39d, 39e

(c) Francis Wharton, ed., "Trial of William Cobbett, for Libel. In the Supreme Court of Pennsylvania. November, 1797," <u>State Trials of the United States</u> 322-32 (Philadelphia 1849).

(d) John D. Lawson, ed., "The Trial of William Cobbett for Libel. Philadelphia, Pennsylvania, 1797," 6 <u>American State Trials</u> 675-86 (St. Louis 1916).

(31) M'Kean's Election Opinion, 1798

(a) Opinion of Chief Justice M'Kean. "The Chief justice of Pennsylvania is requested to answer the following queries, at the particular desire of the Judges of the election for the township of the Northern Liberties, the District of Southwark and the townships of Moyamensing and Passyunk." . . . Thomas M'Kean. [Philadelphia 1798]
Broadside fol.

PHi*

Evans 34,038

(32) M'Manus's Trial for Murder, Court of Oyer and Terminer, 1798

(a) A Correct Account of the Trials of Charles M'Manus, John Hauer, Elizabeth Hauer, Patrick Donagan, Francis Cox and others; At Harrisburgh -- June Oyer And Terminer, 1798. For the Murder of Francis Shitz, on the night of the 28th December, 1797, at Heidelberg Township, Dauphin County, in the Commonwealth of Pennsylvania. Containing, The Whole Evidence, and the Substance Of All The Law Arguments in those celebrated Trials. Printed at Harrisburgh, by John Wyeth. 1798. [Entered according to Law.] 165 p. 8vo.

CSmH, DLC, MBAt, MH-L, NIC-L, NN, PHi, PP, PPL*, PU-L, RPJCB

Evans 34,040 Sabin 43,564 McDade 663

Note Brackets in original.

(b) Peleg W. Chandler, ed., "Trials of John Hauer and Others, before the Court of Oyer and Terminer, for the Murder of Francis Shitz, Pennsylvania, 1798," 2 American Criminal Trials 351-74. (Boston 1844).

Sabin 11,868

(33) Dallas's Reports, Volume 2, 1781-1798 Cases, Courts of the United States and Pennsylvania Held In Philadelphia, 1798

(a) Reports of Cases ruled and adjudged in the Several Courts of the United States, and of Pennsylvania, held at the seat of the federal government. By A. J. Dallas. Vol. II . . . Philadelphia: Printed for the Reporter, at the Aurora Office. M,DCC,XCVIII. [This is Volume 2 of the United States Reports.] 505 p. 8vo.

ArU-L, AzU-L, BLM, CLU-L, CSfU-L, CSmH, DCU-L, DLC, InNd-L(2), KyLoU-L, MB, MH-L, MWA*, MdBB, MiU-L, MoU-L, NIC-L, NN, NNB, NNC-L, NcD-L, NcU-L, NjP, NjR, P-L, PPL, PU-L, PV-L, RPJCB, TxDaM-L, ViLxW-L, ViU

Evans 33,598 Sabin 18,313 Sowerby 2,088

(34) Alien Bill Rioters' Trial, 1799

(a) A Report of the Extraordinary Transactions Which Took Place At Philadelphia, In February 1799. In Consequence Of A Memorial From Certain Natives Of Ireland To Congress, Praying A Repeal Of The Alien Bill; -- containing -- An account of the Proceedings which produced the Memorial -- the Assault on the Committee at St. Mary's Church -- and the Proceedings at the Mayor's Office, upon the arrest of Memorialists. A copy of the Memorial. And, the Trial, with the names of the Jury, the Evidence at large, the Speeches of Counsel on both sides, and the Charge to the Jury. By William Duane. Philadelphia: Printed At The Office Of The Aurora. 1799. 57 p. 8vo.

DLC, PHi*, PPL, PPAmP

Evans 35,424 Sabin 21,002

(b) Minutes of examination, taken in short notes-on the trial of rioters, for a riot and assault on Wm. Duane, on the 15th May, 1799-trial 28 April, 1801 [Philadelphia? 1801?] 24 p.

DLC(2), MBAt (The only recorded copy cannot be reproduced)

Shaw-Shoemaker 935 Sabin 20,994n Sowerby 3,294

(c) Francis Wharton, ed., "Trial of Duane, Reynolds, Moore, and Cuming, for seditious riot, In the Court of Oyer and Terminer for the County of Philadelphia. Philadelphia, 1799," State Trials of the United States 345-91 (Philadelphia 1849).

(d) John D. Lawson, ed., "The Trial of William Duane, James Reynolds, Robert Moore, and Samuel Cuming for Riot, Philadelphia, Pennsylvania, 1799," 7 American State Trials 676-741 (St. Louis 1917).

(e) James Morton Smith, "Chapter XIII: William Duane, the Aurora, and the Alien and Sedition Law," Freedom's Fetters 277-306 (Ithaca 1956).

(35) Dallas's Reports, Volume 3, 1794-1799 Cases, Courts of the United States and Pennsylvania Held in Philadelphia, 1799

(a) Reports of Cases ruled and adjudged in the Several Courts of the United States, and of Pennsylvania, held at the seat of the federal Government. By A. J. Dallas. Volume III. . . . Philadelphia: printed for the Reporter, by J. Ormrod. 1799. [This is Volume 3 of the United States Reports. Volume 4 was published in 1807.]

541 p. 8vo.

ArU-L, AZU-L, BLM, CLU-L, CSfU-L, CSmH, DCU-L, InNd-L, KyLoU-L, MB, MH-L, MWA*, MdBB, MiU-L, MoU-L, NIC-L, NN, NNB, NNC-L, NcD-L, NcU-L, NjP, NjR, P-L, PU-L, PV-L, RPB, TxDaM-L, ViLxW-L, ViU

Evans 35,374 Sabin 18,313 Sowerby 2,088

(36) Addison's Reports, 1791-1799 Cases, County Courts of the Fifth Circuit and High Court of Errors of Appeals, 1800

(a) Reports Of Cases in the County Courts of the Fifth Circuit, and in the High Court of Errors & Appeals, of the State of Pennsylvania. and Charges to Grand Juries of those County Courts. By Alexander Addison, President Of The Courts Of Common Pleas Of The Fifth Circuit Of The State Of Pennsylvania. Washington Printed By John Colerick, And May Be Had Of The Booksellers In Philadelphia. 1800. 756 p. 8vo.

AzU-L, BLM, CSfU-L, DCU-L, DLC(3), IEN-L, N, MH-L, MWA*, MdBB, MiU-L, MoU-L, NIC-L, NNB, NNC-L, NjP, OU-L, P-L, PBL, PHi, PP, PPL, PU-L, PV-L, TxDaM-L, ViU

Evans 36,763 and 36,764

(a.2) [Second Edition] (Philadelphia 1883).

Note The Law Library Company of the City of Philadelphia had a copy in 1805. Catalogue Number 123. See above 1.07(26)(a).

(37) Rush v. Cobbett, Libel, Supreme Court, 1800

(a) A Report of an Action For A Libel, brought by Dr. Benjamin Rush, against William Cobbett, In the Supreme Court of Pennsylvania, December term, 1799, for certain defamatory publications in a news-paper, entitled Porcupine's Gazette, of which the said William Cobbett Was Editor. [Taken in Shorthand by T. Carpenter] Philadelphia: Printed by W. W. Woodward, No. 17, Chesnut Street. 1800. 70 p.

DLC, MB, MBAt, MH, MH-L, MWA*, N, NIC-L, NN, NNU-L, NcD-L, NjP, PHi(3, 1 imp.), PP, PPL, PU-L, ScC

Evans 37,103, 38,371, and 38,433 Sabin 14,030
Gaines 49a and 49b Parrish 99

Note Brackets in original.

(b) Winthrop and Frances Neilson, Verdict for the Doctor, the Case of Benjamin Rush (New York 1958).

1.08 Delaware

(1) Robinson v. Lessee of Adams, 1788 Case from Court of Errors and Appeals, 1789.

(a) "Law case. In the court of errors and appeals of the state of Delaware. Benjamin Robinson and William Robinson, appellants, against the lessee of John Adams, respondent," 6 American Museum [September 1789] 215-18, above 1.07(9)(a).

Library Locations, above 1.07(9)(a).

Evans 21,650

(b) Law case. . . [November 1789] 394-96, above 1.08(1)(a).

(c) Law case. . . [December 1789] 480-81, above 1.08(1)(a).

(d) Robinson et al. Appellants, v. The Lessee of Adams, Respondent, 4 Dallas xii (Philadelphia 1807).

(2) Sawyer, Negro v. Saunders, Court of Common Pleas, Kent County, 1790.

(a) "Kent county, ss., Court of common pleas: May Term, 1790. Joseph Sawyer, negro, vs. Abraham Saunders. Petition for freedom," 8 American Museum [October 1790] 191-92, above 1.07(23)(a).

(3) Docket Sheet, Court of Common Pleas, New-Castle County, 1792.

(a) Causes for argument and trial, before the Honourable the Court of Common-Pleas, to be held at New-Castle, for the County of New-Castle, at the November term, A.D. one thousand seven hundred and ninety-two . . . [Wilmington] 1792. Broadside 41 x 30 cm.

DeHi

Rink 321

(4) Docket Sheet, Supreme Court, New-Castle County, 1796

(a) Causes for trial and argument, at the April term . . . before the . . . Supreme Court, at New-Castle. First class of trials, commencing Tuesday April 5th, 1796. . . [Wilmington? 1796] Broadside 33 x 2.5 cm.

NjR

Bristol B9,526

1.09 Maryland

(1) Taylor's and Gatchel's Case, Dispute between Lord Baltimore and Maryland, 1723

(a) The Case of Isaac Taylor and Elisha Gatchel, Two Officers of Pennsylvaia, made Prisoners by the Government of Maryland: [Colophon] Printed at Philadelphia [by Andrew Bradford], in the Year 1723. 2 p. fol.

CSmH, DLC, DeWint, NN*, PHi*, PPAmP, PU, RPJCB

Evans 2,482 mp. 39,779 Bristol B642
Sabin 59,957 and 94,466n Hildeburn 196
Huntington 65

Note The heading of Evans 2,482 is "Taylor, Isaac, and Gatchel, Elisha," but the text garbles the title of the imprint, including in the first part, the title of a separate unrelated imprint, "The Honest Man's Interest. . .," which is also correctly entered as Evans 2,749. The microcards reproduce these two Evans entries. Bristol B642 gives the correct text of Evans 2,482 as to both the heading and the title, and this is numbered mp. 39,779. The microcard for mp. 39,779 reproduces the PHi copy. They are the same imprint.

(2) Seven Runaway Servants, Provincial Court, 1734

(a) Maryland ss. Complaint being made to Me, Levin Gale, Esq; Chief Justice of the Provincial Court of Maryland, by Benjamin Tasker, Charles Carrol, and Daniel Dulany, of Annapolis, Esqrs; That Seven Men Servants ran away from them, and others their Partners from their Iron-Works at Potapsco River . . . These are therefore to Require all His Majesty's Subjects within this Province . . . to apprehend the said Runaways . . . Levin Gale [Annapolis? William Parks? 1734] Broadside 15 x 20 cm.

NN*

mp. 40,049 Bristol B930 New York Public 179

Note Bristol uses heading, "Maryland, Provincial Court"; while Short-Title Evans uses heading "Maryland (Colony) Chief Justice, 1734."

(3) Christie's Banishment, 1775

(a) The Case of James Christie, jun. Late of the Province of Maryland, Merchant. . . . [Annapolis: Printed by Frederick Green? 1775] [auction of goods imported against the Act of the American Continental Congress and forfeited under its provisions] 24 p. 8vo.

DLC, RPJCB*

Evans 13,868 Sabin 12,933

(b) Hezekiah Niles, ed., "Annapolis, 1775. In provincial convention, August 7, 1775, the following memorial of James Christie, jun of Baltimoretown, merchant, was read . . . . G. Duvall, clerk," Principles and Acts of the Revolution 222-23 (Baltimore 1822).

(b.2) Centennial Offering Republication of the Principles and Acts of the Revolution in America 262-64 (Samuel Niles Revision 1876).

(4) Sueman's Death Sentence for treason, Court of Oyer and Terminer, 1781

(a) Sentence of Death for High Treason. At a special Court of Oyer and Terminer and Goal Delivery, held at Frederick Town, in the Month of July, 1781. Peter Sueman, Nicolaus

Andrews, Jost Blecher, John George Grases, Adam Graves, Henry Schell, and Caspar Fritchie . . . [English and German. Philadelphia, Melchior Steiner, 1781]
Broadside 18 x 14 cm.

PHi*

mp. 43,990 Bristol B5,302

(5) Baltimore Riot, 1794

(a) To the citizens of Baltimore-Town, After a public enquiry, by witnesses on oath which fully satisfied my judgment that certain persons, in this town, had been guilty of acts of violence that amounted to a riot, I issued a warrant to arrest the persons, and to bring them before me, to be dealt with as the law directs . . . Samuel Chase. Sunday Evening, 7 o'clock, May 4th, 1794. [Baltimore: Printed by James Angell, 1794]
Broadside fol.

MdHi*

Evans 26,762

1.10 Virginia

(1) Hite v. Fairfax, Land Case, High Court of Chancery, 1736-86

(a) See 10.10(2).

(b) Virginia. At a High Court of Chancery held in Richmond, the 8th day of May, 1785. John Hite, Isaac Hite . . . plaintiffs, against the executors. . . of Thomas Lord Fairfax. . . defendants. . . John Brown, C.H.C.C. [Richmond 1785?] Broadside 30.5 x 18 cm.

WHi (not located)

mp. 44,827 Bristol B6,212

(c) Josiah Look Dickinson, "Appendix: The Transcript of the Record of the Hite vs. Fairfax Suit," The Fairfax Proprietary (Front Royal, Virginia 1959).

(2) Kamper v. Hawkins, Constitutional Law, General Court, 1794

(a) Report of a Case, Decided On Saturday, the 16th of November, 1793, in the General Court of Virginia; Wherein Peter Kamper was Plaintiff, against Mary Hawkins, Defendant; on a Question adjourned from the District Court of Dumfries, for Novelty and Difficulty, touching the Constitutionality of an Act of Assembly;

Together with Arguments and Opinions of the respective Judges at Large, and the Order of Court thereon. Published With Their Permission. By a Gentleman of the Bar. [William Tatham] Philadelphia: Printed for A. M'Kenzie, & Co. No. 126, South Front-street, By W. W. Woodward, Franklin's Head, No. 36, Chestnut-street. 1794. 104 p. 8vo.

DLC, MBAt, MH-L, MHi, MWA, MiU-C, PP, PPL*, PU-L, Vi(2), ViHi ViW (Tucker's copy)

Evans 27,777 Sabin 94,411 Sowerby 2,092 Swem 7,790

(3) Wythe's Reports, 1791?-1794 Cases, High Court of Chancery, 1795

(a) Decisions of Cases in Virginia, by The High Court of Chancery, With Remarks upon Decrees By The Court of Appeals, Reversing some of those Decisions. Richmond: Printed by Thomas Nicolson. M,DCC,XCV. 167 p. fol.

DCU-L, DLC, MB, MH-L, MWA, MiU-L, NN, NHi, NNB, NNC, NcD-L, RPJCB, TxDaM-L, Vi* (autograph of P. Lyons), ViHi, ViU (marginal notes by Jefferson), ViW

Evans 29,930 Sabin 100,230 Sowerby 1,759 Swem 7,698

Note A copy was in the library of William Munford on October 10, 1802. See above 1.05(10)(c).

For a discussion of Wythe's motivations in publishing these Reports see Imogene E. Brown, American Aristides: A Biography of George Wythe 252-67 (Rutherford, New Jersey 1981). Of relevance also, see 2 David John Mays, The Letters and Papers of Edmund Pendleton 504-59 (Charlottesville 1967).

This volume of Reports by Wythe was not included among the early Virginia reports numbered in 1933. Citation of Virginia Reports, 159 Va. xxiii (1933).

(b) Decisions of cases in Virginia, by the High Court of Chancery, with remarks upon decrees by the Court of Appeals, reversing some of those decisions. 2d and only complete edition, with a memoir of the author, analysis of the cases, and an index by B. B. Minor. (Richmond 1852).

Note E. Lee Shepard, "George Wythe," in The Virginia Law Reporters Before 1880 90-95 (W. Hamilton Bryson, ed. 1977). This account erroneously says, "After the first edition of his Reports in 1795, Wythe published fourteen additional opinions in pamphlet form." Id. at 94. The correct number is eight, published in seven pamphlets. These seven pamphlets are set forth below as separate entries. The seven cases reported in six of these pamphlets were reprinted by Minor in this 2d edition of Wythe. On case in one pamphlet, Love v. Donelson, below 1.10(14)(a), was not printed in this 2d edition.

(4) Case upon the Statute for Distribution, High Court of Chancery, 1796

(a) Case upon the Statute for Distribution. [By George Wythe] Richmond: Printed by Thomas Nicolson, 1796. 38 p. 8vo.

DLC(2), MH-L (Ms. corrections by Wythe), MWA*, VI(2, one with autograph of Creed Taylor), ViHi, ViU

Evans 31,672 Sabin 105,703 Sowerby 1,760
Swem 823 and 7,858

(a.2) Wythe (2d ed. 1852), above 1.10(3)(b), 302-21.

(5) Aylett v. Aylett, Estate Dispute, High Court of Chancery, 1796

(a) Report of the Case Between Aylett and Aylett, Determined by the High Court of Chancery in which the Decree Was Reversed by the Court of Appeals. [By George Wythe] Richmond: Printed and Sold at T. Nicolson. M,DCC,XCVI.

MH-L, MHi, ViHi, ViU

mp. 47,706 Bristol B9,460

Note Both Bristol and Short-Title Evans list this under the heading "Aylett, Philip, plaintiff." Short-Title Evans says "Not located, 1968."

(a.2) Wythe (2d ed. 1852), above 1.10(3)(b), 219-35.

(6) Field v. Harrison, Liability of Executor, High Court of Chancery, 1796

(a) A Report Of The Case between Field and Harrison, determined by the High Court Of Chancery, in which The decree Was Reversed by the Court of Appeals. [By George Wythe] Richmond: Printed And Sold By Thomas Nicholson. M,DCC,XCVI. 32 p. 8vo.

DLC (Ms. corrections by Wythe), MBAt, MH-L (gift by author to James Iredell), MiU-L(imp.), NcD, Vi*, ViHi, ViU

Evans 31,667 Sowerby 1,761 Swem 4,538 and 7,860

(a.2) Wythe (2d ed. 1852), above 1.10(3)(b), 273-91.

(7) Yates v. Salle, Estate Dispute, High Court of Chancery, 1796?

(a) Between William Yates and Sarah his wife, plaintiffs and Abraham Salle, Bernard Markham, Edward Moseley, Benjamin Harris, and William Wager Harris, defendants. . . . [By George Wythe. Richmond: Printed by Thomas Nicolson. 1796?] 18 p. 8vo.

DLC*, MH-L, ViHi, ViU

Evans 31,671 Sabin 105,702 Sowerby 1,764 Swem 7,856

Note Evans dates this imprint 1796, probably because there are three known imprints from 1796, above 1.10(4), (5), and (6). This date is followed in Short-Title Evans and on the microcard. It should be taken with caution, inasmuch as Evans misdated some other Wythe pamphlets as having been published in 1796. Evans reports this as a 31-page imprint. Mp. 31,671 reproduces DLC copy and says, "No complete copy located." It is probable that the pamphlet only had 18 leaves and is complete. See Sowerby 1,764.

(a.2) Wythe (2d ed. 1852), above 1.10(3)(b), 163-72.

(b) 1 Washington Reports, below 1.10(9), 226-27 (decision in the Court of Appeals, October Term 1793).

(8) Fowler v. Saunders, and Goodall v. Bullock, Statute of Frauds and Sheriff's Liability, High Court of Chancery, 1798

(a) Between, William Fowler and Susanna his wife, plaintiffs, And, Lucy Saunders, an infant, by James Paterson, her guardian, defendant, . . . [at p. 12] Between Parke Goodall and John Clough, plaintiffs, and, John Bullock, the younger, defendant, . . . [By George Wythe. Richmond: Printed by Thomas Nicolson] 28 p. 8vo.

DLC*, MH-L, Vi, ViHi, ViU

Evans 31,668 Sowerby 1,762 Swem 7,855

Note Inasmuch as these cases were decided in 1798, the dating of 1796 given by Evans and followed on the microcard and in Short-Title Evans must be in error.

(a.2) Wythe (2d ed. 1852), above 1.10(3)(b), 322-37.

(b) Fowler v. Saunders, 4 Call 361-63 (1833) (decision in the Court of Appeals, October Term 1798).

(9) Washington's Reports, Volume 1, 1790-1794 Cases, Court of Appeals, 1798

(a) Reports of Cases Argued And Determined in the Court Of Appeals of Virginia. By Bushrod Washington. Vol. I. Richmond: Printed by Thomas Nicolson, M,DCC,XCVIII.
432 p. 8 vo.

CLU-L, CSmH, CSfH, DCU-L, DGW-L, DLC, MB, MH, MH-L, MWA*, MiU-L, MoSW-L, NIC-L, NN, NNB, NcD, OU-L, P-L, PU-L, PV-L, RPJCB, TNJ-L, TU-L(2), TxDaM-L, TxU-L, Vi, ViLxW-L(2), ViRU-L

Evans 34,958 Sabin 100,038 Sowerby 2,090
Swem 7,696 and 7,697

Note The Law Library Company of the City of Philadelphia in 1805 had copies of the two volumes of Washington's Reports. Catalogue Number 124. See above 1.07(26)(a).

The two volumes of Washington's Reports were in the library of William Munford on October 10, 1802.

(a.2) Second edition, very materially corrected, with the addition of references to subsequent determinations of the same court, new marginal abstracts of the cases reported, a new index, and a complete table of cases cited. Vol. I. Philadelphia, Printed and published by Abraham Small, 1823.

Sabin 100,038n Shoemaker 14,787 Swem 7,807

(a.3) 1 Virginia Reports Annotated (Charlottesville 1903) (Volume 1 of Official Virginia Reports).

(b) J. Steven McDorman, "Bushrod Washington," Virginia Reporters, above 1.10(3)(b), 1-6.

(10) Washington's Reports, Volume 2, 1794-1796 Cases, Court of Appeals, 1799

(a) Reports of Cases Argued and Determined in the Court Of Appeals of Virginia. By Bushrod Washington. Vol. II. Richmond: Printed by Thomas Nicolson, M,DCC,XCIX.
332 p. 8vo.

BLM, CLU-L, CSmH, CtY, CSfH, DCU-L, DGW-L, DLC, MB, MH, MH-L, MWA*, MiU-L, MoSW-L, NIC-L, NN, NNB, NNC-L, NcD, P-L, PU-L, PV-L, RPJCB, TNJ-L, TxDaM-L, TxU-L, Vi, ViU, ViLxW-L(2), ViRU-L

Evans 36,670 Sabin 100,038 Sowerby 2,090 Swem 7,806

Note See above 1.05(9)(a).

(a.2) Second Edition. Above 1.10(9)(a.2).

(a.3) 2 Virginia Reports. Above 1.10(9)(a.3).

(11) Wilkins v. Taylor, Construction of Will, High Court of Chancery, 1799

(a) Between, Joseph Wilkins, administrator of his late defunct wife Sarah, one of the grand-daughters and legataries of Thomas Williamson, and widow, when she was married last, of Hartwell Cocke, plaintiff, And, John Taylor, and William Urquhart, executors of the said Thomas Williamson, defendants, . . . [By George Wythe. Richmond: Printed by Thomas Nicolson] 31 p. 8vo.

DLC* (Ms. corrections by Wythe), MH-L, ViHi, ViU

Evans 31,670 Sowerby 1,763 Swem 7,857

(a.2) Wythe (2d ed., 1852), above 1.10(3)(b), 338-54.

(b) 5 Call 150-58 (1833) reports the case in the Court of Appeals, May 1804.

(12) Pleasants v. Logan, Estate Dispute, High Court of Chancery, 1800

(a) Virginia: In the High Court of Chancery, March 16, 1798. Between Robert Pleasants, son and heir of John Pleasants, dec'd. pltf. And Mary Logan, widow and administratrix of Charles Logan, . . . [Dated Mar. 19, 1800, on last page.] 18 p. 8vo.

CSmH (signed Wm. W. Hening C:C), NHi, PPL* (signed Wm. W. Hening clk), ViU

Evans 38,963 Sabin 100,231

(13) Read's Case, 1800

(a) Richard E. Lee's Letter, the Attorney General's Opinion, and the Affidavits accompanying the Governor's Communication to the General Assembly, relative to the conduct of Doctor John K. Read, A Magistrate of the Borough of Norfolk. Richmond: Printed by Meriwether Jones, printer to the Commonwealth. 1800. 32 p. 8vo.

DLC, MWA*

Evans 37,811 Sabin 39,782 and 100,228 Swem 8,003

(b) A Letter from Governor Monroe, Several Documents in the Case of J. K. Reade, and a Statement of the Trials of Certain Negroes. Richmond. Nicholson. Dec. 30, 1800.

[No copy located]

Evans 38,957 Sabin 100,229 Swem 8,004

(14) Love v. Donelson, Land Dispute, High Court of Chancery, 1800?

(a) Love, against Donelson and Hodgson, . . . [By George Wythe. Richmond: Printed by Thomas Nicolson] 34 p. 8vo.

DLC* (Ms. notes by Wythe), ViU

Evans 31,669 Sowerby 1,765 Swem 7,859

Note Evans dates this imprint as having been published in 1796, and this dating is followed in the Short-Title Evans. However, the pamphlet refers to a cause that came on "in the first year of the nineteenth centurie." This would be 1801 if the reference is chronologically accurate, but because of doubts about when it was printed it is included here. Minor apparently did not have a copy when he prepared the second edition of Wythe's Reports, above 1.10(3)(a.2), and so it has never been reprinted but is only available in the original pamphlet.

1.11 North Carolina

(1) Regulators, 1770

(a) An Impartial Relation of the First Rise and Cause of the Recent Differences, in Publick Affairs, In the Province of North-Carolina; and of the past Tumults and Riots that lately happened in that Province. Containing most of the true and genuine Copies of Letters, Messages and Remonstrances, between the Parties contending:--By which any impartial Man may easily gather and see the true Ground and Reasons of the Dissatisfaction that universally reigns all over said Province in a more or less Degree. [By Herman Husbands] Printed for the Compiler. 1770. 104 p. 16vo.

MWA, NcU(imp.), RPJCB*

Evans 11,689 McMurtie: North Carolina 59
Thornton Unofficial 6,607

(a.2) Some Eighteenth Century Tracts Concerning North Carolina 245-333 (William K. Boyd, ed. Raleigh, North Carolina 1927).

(b) A Continuation of the Impartial Relation of the First Rise and Cause of the Recent Differences, in Publick Affairs, in the Province of North-Carolina, &c. Second Part. Printed for the Author, [Newbern?] 1770
39 p. 10.5 x 16 cm.

CSmH*

mp. 42,112 Bristol B3,203 Huntington 299
McMurtrie: North Carolina 60

(c) A Fan for Fanning, and A Touch-Stone to Tryon, containing An Impartial Account of the Rise and Progress of the so much talked of Regulation in North-Carolina, By Regulus. Boston: Printed and Sold at the Printing-Office, opposite the Seat of William Vassel Esq; at the Head of Queen-Street. 1771. 80 p. 8vo.

CtHT-W*, DLC, MWA

Evans 12,081 Thornton Unofficial 6,606

(c.2) Some Eighteenth Century Tracts, above 1.11(1)(a.2), 335-92.

(2) Bayard v. Singleton, 1787 Case from Supreme Court of Law and Equity, 1788

(a) "Law case, tried and determined, at a supreme court of law and equity, for the district of Newbern, North Carolina, on the 30th of November, 1787," 3 Aterican Museum [April 1788] 371-72, above 1.07(9)(a). Library Locations, above 1.07(9)(a).

Evans 20,927

(b) Den on the Dem. of Bayard and wife of Singleton, Martin's Reports 48-51, below 1.11(4)(b).

(3) Sealed Instrument Case, Fayetteville Superior Court, 1796

(a) Report Of A Case, Lately Decided in Fayetteville Superior Court of Law, wherein the following questions are discussed and settled; viz. 1. Whether in the case of a Sealed instrument, Unattested by any Subscribing witness, the Handwriting of the party May be Admitted in evidence? II. Whether an action of Debt lies upon Such an instrument? [By Francis-Xavier Martin] Newbern: Printed by Francois-Xavier Martin. MDCCXCVI 20 p. 12mo.

NcU
Evans 30,743 (Just published, N.C. Gazette, April 6, 1796)
McMurtie: North Carolina 219 Tinker p. 694

(4) Martin's Reports, 1778-1796(1797) Cases, Superior Courts, 1796

(a) A Few Cases, Determined in the Superior Courts of North-Carolina. Newbern: F. X. Martin, 1796.

No Copy Known

Bristol B9,602 McMurtie: North Carolina 220
Tinker p. 694

(b) Notes of a few Decisions in the Superior Courts of the State of North-Carolina, and in the Circuit Court of the U. States, for North-Carolina district. Newbern, Francois-Xavier Martin, 1797.

NcAsS, PU-L, ViW

mp. 48,173 [reproduces MH-L copy of Evans 32,426, which is 1.11(4)(b.2)] Bristol B9,995 McMurtrie: North Carolina 232 Thornton Official 3,254 Tinker p. 694 Weeks 115

(b.2) Notes of a few Decisions in the Superior Courts of the State Of North-Carolina, and in the Circuit Court of the U. States, for North-Carolina District. To which is added a Translation of Latchs's Cases. Newbern: Francois-Xavier Martin. 1797. 420 p. 8vo.

DLC*, MH-L, NN, NNB, NcAsS, NcD, NcU, PU-L, RPJCB

Evans 32,426 Sabin 44,873
McMurtrie: North Carolina 233
Thornton Official 3,254 Tinker p. 694-5

(b.3) 2 Haywood, North Carolina Reports (William H. Battle, ed., 2d ed. 1843).

Thornton Official 3,252

(5) Haywood's Reports, 1789-1798 Cases, Superior Courts of Law and Equity, 1799

(a) Reports of Cases Adjudged in the Superior Courts of Law and Equity of the State of North-Carolina, from the year 1789, to the year 1798. By John Haywood, Esquire, One of the Judges of the Superior Courts of Law and Equity. Halifax: Printed by Abraham Hodge. M,DCC,XCIX. 524 p. 8 vo.

DCU-L, DLC(2), LNT-L, M, MH-L, MWA*, MoU-L, NN, NNB, NNC-L, NcAsS, NcD, NcU, OC-L, PHi, PU-L, RPJCB, TxDaM-L, ViU, ViW-L

Evans 35,607 McMurtie: North Carolina 265
Weeks 123 and 129

(a.2) 1 Haywood, North Carolina Reports (William H. Battle, ed., 2d ed. 1832).

Thornton Official 3,257

(6) Cameron's Reports, 1800 Cases, Superior Courts of Law and Equity, 1800

(a) Reports of Cases determined by the judges of the superior courts of law, and courts of equity of the state of North-Carolina at their meeting on the tenth of June, A.D. 1800, held pursuant to an act of the General Assembly, for settling questions of law or equity arising on the circuit. By Duncan Cameron, Attorney at Law. -- Raleigh -- From the press of Hodge & Boylan, Printers to the State. 1800. 108 p. 8vo.

DCU-L, NcU*, OU-L, TxDaM-L

Evans 37,086 Thornton Official 3,258 Weeks 130

(a.2) Second Edition (William H. Battle, ed. 1844).

1.12 South Carolina

(1) Roupell v. Ann, Vice Admiralty, 1768

(a) Extracts From the Proceedings of the Court Of Vice-Admiralty in Charles-Town, South Carolina; In the Cause, George Roupell, Esq; v. the Ship Ann and Goods: With a few Explanatory Remarks. To which is subjoined, some General Observations on American Custom-House Officers and Courts Of Vice-Admiralty. . . . [By Henry Laurens] America: [Philadelphia] Printed [by W. and T. Bradford] Anno Domini, M,DCC,LXVIII. 24 p. 4to.

MBAt, MWA*, NN, PHi, PPL, PPAmP

Evans 10,945 Sabin 23,532 and 39,925
Adams Independence 57a Turnbull p. 166

(a.2) Boston Gazette, January 9, 1769.

(a.3) 6 Papers of Henry Laurens 184-216 [with commentary] (George C. Rogers, Jr., and David R. Chesnutt, eds. Columbia, South Carolina 1978).

Note Editors state at 185 that the five known copies are identical, but apparently do not state which copy is reproduced.

(b) Extracts From The Proceedings of the High Court of Vice-Admiralty, In Charlestown, South Carolina, upon Six Several Informations, adjudged by The Honourable Egerton Leigh, Esq; Sole Judge of that Court, and His Majesty's Attorney-General in the said Province, In the Years 1767 and 1768. With explanatory Remarks, &c. And Copies of two extraordinary Oaths. To which are subjoined, Recapitulation, Reflections Arising From A Retrospect Of A Late Case, and some General Observations on American Custom-House Officers, And Courts of Vice Admiralty. [By Henry Laurens] Charlestown: Printed by David Bruce. MDCCLXIX. 56 p. 32 cm.

CSmH, MHi, MWA*, NN, PPAmP, RPJCB

mp. 41,950 Bristol B3,015 Sabin 39,926
Adams Independence 57b Huntington 289 Morgan 288
New York Public 411 Turnbull p. 170 [See also 35 Papers of Bibliographical Society of America 294-97 (1941)]

(b.2) The Second Edition, with an Appendix.

ScHi*

Evans 11,307 Sabin 39,926 Adams 57c
Morgan 290 Turnbull p. 170

Note The imprint is described in 6 Papers, above (a.3), at 290-92.

(b.3) 6 Papers of Henry Laurens 287-383 [with commentary] see above (a.3).

Note The editors say at 289 that there are three distinct printing impressions. The NN copy is reproduced.

(c) The Man Unmasked: or, the World Undeceived, in The Author Of A Late Pamphlet, intitled, "Extracts From The proceedings Of The High Court Of Vice-Admiralty In Charlestown, South-Carolina," &c. With Suitable Remarks on that masterly performance. By Egerton Leigh. . . . Charles-Town: Printed by Peter Timothy. M,DCC,LXIX 215 p. 8vo.

DLC, MBAt, MHi, MWA(imp.), NN*, NcD, PPL, RPJCB, ScC

Evans 11,308 Sabin 39,927 Adams Independence 66
Morgan 291 Turnbull p. 171

(c.2) 6 Papers of Henry Laurens 450-567 [with commentary], see above (a.3).

(d) An Appendix to the Extracts from the Proceedings of the High Court of Vice-Admiralty in Charleston, South Carolina &c. Containing Strictures upon, and proper Answers to, A Pamphlet Entitled, The Man Unmask'd, Published by Egerton Leigh. Together With A full Refutation of Mr. Leigh's Attempts to vindicate his Judicial Proceedings. . . . Charlestown: Printed by David Bruce. MDCCLXIX. 66 p. 19.5 x 31 cm.

DLC, NN, PPAmP*, ScHi

mp. 41,949 Bristol B3,014 Morgan 292
Turnbull p. 169

Note This is a separate imprint, but it was also published as the Appendix to the Second Edition of the Charleston printing of Extracts. See 1.12(1)(b.2) above.

(d.2) 7 Papers of Henry Laurens 2-114 [with commentary], see above (a.3), published in 1979.

Note It may be that "A Representation of Facts. . ." published in Charleston in 1767 should be considered the first of this series of imprints. See 7 Papers of Henry Laurens at xv where the editors state, "The paper war had opened with the publication of "A Representation of Facts in November 1767." A Representation, with commentary, is reproduced in 5 Papers of Henry Laurens 391-464, see above (a.3), published in 1976.

(2) Hill v. Slann, 1785 Case from Court of Common Pleas, Charleston, 1787

(a) "Statement of a cause decided in the court of common pleas, Charleston, on the 5th of March 1785," 2 American Museum [November 1787] 466-68, above 1.07(9)(a).

(b) A Review of the Laws of the United States 167, below 3.20(1).

(3) Saunders v. Brisbane, 1785 Case from Court of Common Pleas, Charleston, 1788

(a) "Law Case--Court of common pleas, Charleston, Saunders v. Brisbane," 3 American Museum [January 1788] 83-84, above 1.11(2)(a).

(4) Cart v. Lion, Court of Common Pleas, Charleston 1788

(a) "Statement of a cause decided in the court of common pleas, Charleston, August, 1788, Cart v. Lion," 4 American Museum [September 1788] 275, above 1.07(15)(a).

(5) Parole Gift, 1788 Case from Court of Common Pleas, Charleston, 1789

(a) "Case respecting a parole gift," 6 American museum [November 1789] 393, above 1.08(1)(a).

(6) Parker's Case, 1790

(a) A report of the case against Parker
Morgan 803 (citing City Gazette, October 18, 1790)

(7) Washington's Trial for Counterfeiting, 1791

(a) The whole of the trial of Thomas Washington, alias Walsh, who was lately condemned and executed for gorging [sic], uttering, and counterfeiting the public securities of this state.

Morgan 826 (citing <u>South Carolina State Gazette</u>, April 16, 1791)

(8) Drayton's and Moultrie's Contempt, 1794

(a) An Appeal to the People, On The Conduct Of A Certain Public Body in South-Carolina, Respecting Col. Drayton and Col. Moultrie. By Alexander Moultrie. . . . Charleston: Printed by Markland, M'Iver & Co. MDCCXCIV. 28 p. 8vo.

CLS, MWA*

Evans 27,354 Morgan 939

(9) Court of Wardens Decision, 1795

(a) Being a statement of facts reguarding [sic] a decision in the court of wardens, taken down with great exactness Morgan 988 (citing <u>City Gazette</u>, June 6, 1795)

(10) Bay's Reports, 1783-1795 Cases, Superior Courts of Law, 1798

(a) Reports of Cases Argued and Determined in The Superior Courts of Law, in the State of South-Carolina since the revolution. By Elihu Hall Bay, one of the associate judges of the said state. Vol. I. Charleston, South Carolina: Printed by Elliott & Burd, No. 47 Bay. MDCCXCVIII 529 p. 8vo.

DCU-L, MHi*, MiU-L, NN, NcD-L, TxDaM-L, WvU-L

Evans 33,382 Sabin 87,458 Morgan 1,125
Turnbull p. 346

(a.2) Second edition, with additional notes and references, &c. Volume I. New-York: Printed and Published by I. Riley. For Sale by E. Morford, Willington & co., Charleston; Seymour & Williams, Savannah; Lewis Adams, Richmond; Cole & Thomas, Baltimore; P. Byrne, Philadelphia; R. M'Dermut, and S. Gould, New-York; John West, & co., Boston; Daniel Johnson, Portland. 1809 538 p.

CSmH, DLC, MWA*, NN

Shaw-Shoemaker 18,661 Sabin 87,439
Turnbull p. 448

(b) M. Leigh Harrison, "A Study of the Earliest Reported Decisions of the South Carolina Courts of Law," 16 <u>American Journal of Legal History</u> 51-70 (1972).

(11) Bowman's Trial for Contempt, 1798

(a) A Narrative, &c. The following late transactions, with some remarks upon them, are submitted to the consideration of the citizens of this state, by A Fellow-Citizen. Charleston, 27th March, 1798. [Charleston, South Carolina] [Colophon] Printed by W. P. Young.
16 p. 8 vo.

DLC, NN*

Evans 33,447 Morgan 1,108 Turnbull p. 356

1.13 Georgia

(1) M'Intosh's Case, 1777

(a) The Case of George M'Intosh, Esquire, a Member of the late Council and Convention of the State of Georgia; with The Proceedings thereon in the Hon. the Assembly and Council of that State. . . . Printed in the year MDCCLXXVII. [Savannah?] 29 p. 4to.

DLC, MHi*

Evans 15,383

(a.2) Massachusetts Historical Society, Photostat Americana, Second Series, No. 160 (Boston 1942).

(b) An Addition To The Case Of George M'Intosh, Esquire, Earnestly recommended to the serious Attention of every Reader, particularly those of the State of Georgia. Printed in the year MDCCLXXVII. [Savannah?]
10 p. 4to.

DLC*

Evans 15,384

(c) Strictures On a Pamphlet, entitled, The Case of George M'Intosh, Esq. Published by Order of the Liberty Society. . . . Georgia. Savannah: Printed by Lancaster & Mumford. MDCCLXXVII. 17 p. 4to.

DLC*

Evans 15,605

(d) Remarks on A Pamphlet, entitled, "Strictures on a Pamphlet, entitled the Case of George M'Intosh, Esq. Published by Order of the Liberty Society." to which is

added, a concise Account of the Justice of the Executive and Legislative Bodies of the State of Georgia: together with some Account of the Lives and upright Principles of the Leaders of the Nocturnal Junto. Printed in the year MDCCLXXVII. [Savannah?]
22 p. 4to.

DLC*

Evans 15,385

(2) M'Intoth v. Faming, Superior Court for Chatham, 1789

(a) "Law case respecting payment of interest," 6 American Museum [November 1789] 393-94, above 1.08(1)(a).

1.14 Vermont

(1) Chipman's Reports, Supreme Court, 1793

(a) Reports And Dissertations in two parts. Part I. Reports of Cases determined in the Supreme Court of the State of Vermont, in the years 1789, 1790, and 1791. Part II. Dissertations on the Statute adopting the Common Law of England, the Statute of Conveyances, the Statute of Offsets, and on the Negotiability of Notes. With an Appendix, containing Forms of Special Pleadings in several cases; Forms of Recognizances; of Justices Records; and of Warrants of Commitment. By Nathaniel Chipman, Late Chief Justice. Rutland: Printed by Anthony Haswell, for the author; M,DCC,XCIII.
296 p. 16mo.

BLM, CSmH, CSf-H, DCU-L, DLC, IEN-L, MB, MH-L, MWA*, MWiW, MiU-L, N, NHi, NIC-L, NNB, NcD-L, OU-L, PU-L, RPJCB, TxDaM-L, Vt, VtB, VtBennM, VtHi, VtMiM, VtMiS, VtU

Evans 25,296	Sabin 99,132	Cooley 203
McCorison 256	Parrish 107	

Note A copy of these reports was in the library of Ephrahim Kirby, sold in 1804. See above note to 1.04(5)(a).

(a.2) Second edition (Rutland 1871).

(a.3) Second edition (St. Paul, Minnesota 1888)

(2) Bell's Trial for Extortion, 1797

(a) An Impartial History of the trial of Benjamin Bell, A.M. for the Pretended Crime of Extortion: exemplified in a series of letters. . . . [By Benjamin Bell, Late Pastor of a Church in Windsor and Cornish] Printed at Windsor, by Oliver Farnsworth, at the press of Alden Spooner. M,DCC,XCVII. 155 p. 8vo.

CtY, MB, MBAt, MWA*, NHi, NhHi, VtHi, VtU(imp.)

Evans 31,795 Sabin 4,448 Cooley 361
McCorison 428

1.15 Kentucky

(1) Kenton v. M'Connell, Judges Muter and Sebastian, 1794

(a) Journal Of The House Of Representatives At The First Session Of The Third General Assembly For The Commonwealth Of Kentucky, Begun And Held At The Capitol, In The Town Of Frankfort, On Monday The Third Day Of November, In The Year Of Our Lord, One Thousand, Seven Hundred And Ninety Four; And In The Year Of The Commonwealth. Frankfort: Printed by John Bradford, Printer to the Commonwealth. MDCCXCIV 84 p. 19 x 31.5 cm.

ICU

mp. 47,089 Bristol B8,714 Kentucky Imprints #36

(b) Kentucky Gazette, Numb. XXIV, Vol III, Saturday, February 28, 1795. Lexington: Printed by John Bradford, at his Office on Main Street. . . . p. 2: (Published by particular desire) Kentucky sct. Simon Kenton Compt. against Alex. M'Connell & Francis Keen, Defendants. In Chancery. . . .

MWA

Evans 28,928

(c) Kentucky Gazette, Numb XXV, Vol III, Saturday, March 7, 1795 . . . p. 4: (Concluded from our last.) . . . As I cannot accord with the Court in its decision on this cause, the constitution imposes on me the painful task of delivering my opinion separately to be entered on record. Caleb Wallace.

MWA

Evans 28,928

(d) The Address of George Muter and Benjamin Sebastian, Two of the Judges of the Court of Appeals, To the Free Men of Kentucky. Lexington: Printed by John Bradford.

M,DCC,XCV. [The Kenton v. M'Connell opinions, above (b) and (c), are reprinted at pp. 6-17.]

KyU

Kentucky Imprints #49n

(e) A Reply to the Address, of the Hon. George Muter and Benjamin Sebastian. M,DCC,XCV.

KyU, MBAt, NjP

Evans 29,024 Sabin 44,778 Kentucky Imprints #49

Note Short-Title Evans says "Evans' entry was from Sabin" and does not reproduce on the microcard.

(f) Journal of the House of Representatives, at the first session of the fourth General Assembly, for the Commonwealth of Kentucky; begun and held at the Capitol in the town of Frankfort, on Monday the second of November, in the Year of our Lord, One Thousand, Seven hundred and Ninety-Five and in the fourth year of the Commonwealth. Lexington: Printed by John Bradford, Printer to the Commonwealth. [1795?] 76 p. 18.5 x 30.5 cm.

ICU, Ky

mp. 47,476 Bristol B9,160 Kentucky Imprints #45

Note Short-Title Evans says "Not located, 1968."

2.00

Trial and Law Reports of the United States

2.01 Court Martials and Military Courts of the Revolution

(1) Colonel Henley, 1778

(a) Substance of General Burgoyne's Speeches at a Court-Martial held at Cambridge, for the Trial of Colonel Henley, for stabbing Corporal Rieves, of the 47th Regiment. [John Howe] Newport: Printed by John Howe in Thames-Street, at the Corner of the Parade. 1778. 19 p. 4to.

MH(imp.), RNHI(imp.), RNR(imp.), RP(imp.), RPJCB*

Evans 15,752 Alden 718

(b) The substance of General Burgoyne's speeches, on Mr. Vyner's motion, on the 26th of May; and upon Mr. Hartley's motion, on the 28th of May, 1778. With an appendix, containing General Washington's letter to General Burgoyne, &c. London: Printed for J. Almon, opposite Burlington-House, Piccadilly. MDCCLXXVIII. 42 p. 8vo.

CSmH (1st, 3d, 6th and Dublin), CtHT-W, DLC, MB, MBAt, MH, MWA, MiU-C, NHi, NN (1st--2, 2d, 3d, 6th and Dublin), NjHi, NjP, ViU

Sabin 9,257 and 31,344

Note Six editions were published in London and one in Dublin.

(c) The Proceedings of a General Court-Martial, Held at Cambridge, On Tuesday the Twentieth of January; And continued by several Adjournments to Wednesday the 25th of February, 1778: Upon the Trial of Colonel David Henley. Boston: Printed by J. Gill, in Court-Street. M,DCC,LXXVIII. 88 p. 8vo.

CSmH, DLC, MB, MH-L, MHi, MWA*, NHi, NN, RPJCB

Evans 16,139 Sabin 31,343

Evans Ghost 16,626

(d) Proceedings of a Court Martial, Held at Cambridge, by order of Major General Heath, Commanding the American Troops for the Northern District, for the Trial of Colonel David Henley, Accused by General Burgoyne, of ill treatment of the British Soldiers, &c. Taken in Short Hand by an Officer, who was present. London: Printed by J. Almon, opposite Burlington-House, Piccadilly. MDCCLXXVIII. 148 p.

CLL, CSmH, DLC, MH-L, MWA, MiU-C, NN, NjHi, PHi, Vi, ViU, WHi

Sabin 31,344 Adams Controversy 78-44

Note Adams says, "No copy of a second London edition, as listed by Sabin, has been located."

(e) 2 Travels through the Interior Parts of America; in a Series of Letters. By an Officer. [Thomas Anburey], 102-95. London: Printed for William Lane, Leadenhall Street. M DCC LXXX IX.

CSmH, CtHT-W, DLC, MB, MBAt, MH, MWA, MWiW, MdBE, MdBJ-G, MiU-C, NHi(2), NN(3), NjHi, PBL, PHi, PPAmP, PPL, RPB, Vi, ViU

(e.2) London. 1791.

CtHT-W, DLC, MWA, NjHi, NjP, PPL, NjR, Vi, ViU

(e.3) Voyages Dans Les Parties Intérieures De L'Amérique, Pendant le cours de la derniere guerre. Par un Officer de l'Armée Royale. Traduit de l'Anglois. Tome Premier. A Paris, Chez Briand, Libarie, rue Pavée-Saint-Andre-des Arcs, no. 22, 1790.

PPAmP, ViU

(e.4) Paris. 1792.

ViU

(e.5) Journal D'Un Voyage Fait Dans L'Intérieur De L'Amérique Septentrionale. Ouvrage dans lequel on donne des détails précieux sur l'insurrection des Anglo-Américains, et sur la chute désastreuse de leur papier-monnoie. Traduit de l'Anglois et enrichi de notes par M. Noël ancien Professeur de belles-lettres au College de Louis-le-grand. Avec carte & Figures. Tome Premier. A Paris. Chez La Villette, Librarie, rue du Battoir, No. 8. 1793.

ViU

(e.6) Reisen im Inneren von Nordamerika, welche eine Schilderung der Sitten und Eigenthümlichkeiten des Landes Kanada, Neu-England und Virginien, imgleichen die Geschicte des Feldzuges, der Uebergabe und der ferneren Schicksale der Armee unter dem General Burgoyne enthalten. Aus dem englischen übersetzt von Georg Forster, Berlin, Vossische Buchhandlung, 1792.

(e.7) Thomas Anburey, _Travels through the Interior Parts of America_. (Boston and New York 1923).

(e.8) Whitfield J. Bell, Jr., "Thomas Anburey's 'Travels through America': A Note on Eighteenth-Century Plagiarism," 37 _Papers of the Bibliographical Society of America_ 23-36 (1943).

(f) Peleg W. Chandler, ed., "Trial of Colonel David Henley, before a General Court Martial, for improper conduct as an officer of the American Army, Cambridge Massachusetts, 1778," 2 _American Criminal Trials_ 59-153 (Boston 1844).

(g) John D. Lawson, ed., "The Trial of Colonel David Henley, for improper conduct as an officer of the American Army, Massachusetts, 1778," 3 _American State Trials_ 806-62 (St. Louis 1915).

(2) Major General Lee, 1778

(a) Proceedings of a General Court Martial, Held at Brunswick, In The State of New-Jersey, by order of His Excellency General Washington, Commander In Chief, Of the Army of The United States of America, For the Trial of Major General Lee. July 4, 1778. Major General Lord Stirling, President. Philadelphia: Printed by John Dunlap, in Market-Street. MDCCLXXVIII. 62 p. fol.

[Official and Unofficial Printings]

BLM, CSmH, (2-both printings), DLC, MBAt, MiU-C, NHi, NN* (2-both printings), NjHi, NjR, PHi (Charles Thomson autograph), PPL, RNR, RPJCB, ViU

Evans 16,140 Bristol Additions B4,708a (82 MWA 48)
Sabin 39,711 Church 1,151 Hildeburn 3,784

(a.2) Cooperstown, Printed for the Publisher, by J. H. Prentiss, 1823.

Sabin 39,712 Shoemaker 13,859

(a.3) New York: Privately Reprinted. 1864.

Sabin 39,713

(a.4) 6 Collections of the New-York Historical Society for the Year 1873 1-208 (New York 1874).

(b) John Richard Alden, General Charles Lee (Baton Rouge 1951).

(c) Theodore Thayer, Washington & Lee at Monmouth: The Making of a Scapegoat (Port Washington, New York 1976).

(3) Major General St. Clair, 1778

(a) Proceedings of a General Court Martial, Held at White Plains, in the state of New-York, by Order of his Excellency General Washington, Commander In Chief Of the Army of The United States of America, For the Trial of Major General St. Clair, August 25, 1778. Major General Lincoln, President. Philadelphia: Printed by Hall and Sellers, in Market-Street. MDCCLXXVIII. 52 p. fol.

CSmH, DLC, MDBB, MWA*, MWiW-C, MdBE, MdBE, MiU-C, NHi, NN(2), PHi(2), PPAmP, PPL, RNR, RPJCB

Evans 16,141 Sabin 75,021 Church 1,152
Hildeburn 3,786

(a.2) 13 Collections of the New-York Historical Society for the year 1880 1-172 (New York 1881).

(4) Major General Schuyler, 1778

(a) Proceedings of a General Court Martial, Held at Major General Lincoln's Quarters, near Quaker-Hill, In the State of New-York, By Order of his Excellency General Washington, Commander In Chief Of the Army of The United States of America, For the Trial of Major General Schuyler, October 1, 1778. Major General Lincoln, President. Philadelphia: Printed by Hall and Sellers, in Market-Street. MDCCLXXVIII. 62 p. fol.

CSmH, DLC, MBAt, NHi, NN*(3), PHi, PPL, RNR, RPJCB, ViU

Evans 16,142 Sabin 78,059 Church 1,154
Hildeburn 3,785

(a.2) 12 Collections of the New-York Historical Society for the Year 1879 1-211 (New York 1880).

(5) Colonel Hall and Captain Norwood, 1779.

(a) Proceedings of several General Courts-Martial, Held, By order of Brigadier-general Smallwood, on the Trials of Col. J. Carvil Hall, and Capt. Edward Norwood. Annapolis: Printed by Frederick Green. M,DCC,LXXIX 105 p. 12mo.

MdBP (autograph of Ch. Carroll), MdHi*

Evans 16,334

(6) Major General Arnold, 1779

(a) In Council. Philadelphia, February 3d, 1779. . . . [Resolutions exhibiting the charges of illegal and oppressive conduct against General Benedict Arnold, upon which the attorney-general was directed to prosecute him.] Philadelphia: Printed by Francis Bailey, in Front-Street. [1779] Broadside fol.

MHi*

Evans 16,439 Hildeburn 3,889

(b) Proceedings of the Supreme Executive Council of the State of Pennsylvania, In the Case of Major General Arnold. [Colophon] [Philadelphia] Printed by Hall & Sellers. 1779. 11 p. 4to.

CSmH, DLC*, MHi, MiU-C, PHi, PPAmP, RPJCB

Evans 16,448 Sabin 2,062 Hildeburn 3,935

(c) Proceedings of a General Court Martial of the line, Held by Raritan, in the state of New-Jersey, By Order of his Excellency George Washington, Esq. General and Commander in Chief of the Army Of The United States of America, For the Trial of Major General Arnold, June 1, 1779. Major General Howe, President. Published by Order of Congress. Philadelphia: Printed by Francis Bailey, in Market-Street. M.DCC.LXXX. 55 p. fol.

CSmH, DLC, MBAt, MHi, MWiW-C, MiU-C, NN*, PHi, PPAmP, RPJCB, PPL

Evans 17,047 Sabin 2,060 Church 1,169
Hildeburn 4,049

(d) To The Inhabitants Of America . . . . B. Arnold. New-York, October 7, 1780. Printed by James Rivington, Printer to the King's Most Excellent Majesty. Broadside fol.

NN*

Evans 16,701 Sabin 2,059

(d.2) The Royal Gazette. October 11, 1780. New-York: Published by James Rivington, Printer to the King's most excellent Majesty. 1780. fol.

NN

Evans 16,985 Sabin 2,059

(e) Complot d'Arnold et de Sir Henry Clinton contre les Etats-Unis d'Amerique, et contre le General Washington Septembre 1780 [Barbé-Marbois]. Paris, Didot l'aine, MDCCCXVI.

CSmH, CtHT-W, DLC, MB, MBAt, MWA, MiU-C, NN(2), NjP, P, PHi, PPAmP, PPL, RNR, ViU

Sabin 3,302

(e.2) 2 The American Register; or, Summary Review of History, Politics, and Literature. . . [A Translation by Robert Walsh, Esq.] 3-63 (Philadelphia 1817)

CSmH, DLC, ICN, MB, RP

Shaw-Shoemaker 39,985 Sabin 3,302n

(e.3) Proceedings of a General Court Martial for the Trial of Major General Arnold (New York: Privately Printed, 1865).

Sabin 2,061 and 3,302n

(f) John D. Lawson, ed., "The Trial of Major General Benedict Arnold for Certain Misdemeanors, Raritan, New Jersey, 1779," 6 American State Trials 411-63 (St. Louis 1916).

(7) Major Andre, 1780

(a) Proceedings of a Board of General Officers, Held by Order of His Excellency Gen. Washington, Commander in Chief of the Army of the United States of America. Respecting Major John Andre, Adjutant General of the British Army. September 29, 1780. Philadelphia Printed by Francis Bailey, in Market-Street, M,DCC,LXXX. 21 p. 8vo.

BLM, CSmH, DLC, MB, MBAt, MH, MHi, MWA*(2), MiU-C, NHi, NN, NNC-L, NjHi, NjP, NjR, PHi(3), PPAmP, PPL, RPJCB, ViU

Evans 17,043 Sabin 1,454 Adams Controversy 80-6a
Church 1,165 Hildeburn 4,048

(a.2) Philadelphia Printed -- New-York, Re-printed By James Rivington, opposite the Coffee-House Bridge. [1780] 13 p. 4to.

CSmH*, MiU-C, NHi, NN, NjP, RNR, RPJCB

Evans 17,044 Sabin 1,455

(a.3) Philadelphia, Printed: Hartford: Re-printed by B. Webster, M.DCC.LXXX. 34 p. 8vo.

CSmH, CtHT-W, MHi, MdBJ, NcU, NjP, RPJCB*

Evans 17,045 Sabin 1,454 Church 1,167
Trumbull 1,274

(a.4) Fish-Kill: Printed by Samuel Loudon. M,DCC,LXXX. 23 p.

NHi, NjP*, RPJCB

mp. 43,903 Bristol B5,195
Vail, Patriotic pair p. 412

(a.5) New-London. Reprinted by T. Green, 1780. 16 plus p. 12mo.

No copy located.

mp. 43,904 Bristol B5,196 Trumbull 2d 2,517

(a.6) Philadelphia, Francis Bailey. [1780] 32 p. 8vo.

PHi

Bristol B5,198

(a.7) [Charleston? James Robertson, Donald McDonald, and Alexander Cameron? 1780]

No copy located

Bristol B5,199 Morgan 551 Mosimann 347

(a.8) Norwich: Printed by John Trumbull, near the Court-House. M,DCC,LXXX.

MH-L

mp. 43,905 Bristol B5,197 Trumbull 2d 2,518

Note: Short-Title Evans says "no copy located."

(b) Proceedings of a Board of General Officers, Held by Order of His Excellency Gen. Washington, Commander in Chief of the Army of the United States of America, Respecting Major John Andre, Adjutant General of the British Army. September 29, 1780. To which are appended, The several Letters which passed to and from New-York on the Occasion. Published by Order of Congress. Providence: Printed and Sold by John Carter. [1780] 16 p. 8vo.

CSmH, CtHi, DLC, MB, MH, MWA*, NHi, NjP, PBL, PP, RHi, RNHi, RP, RPAt, RPB, RPJCB

Evans 17,046 Sabin 1,456 Alden 815
Church 1,168 Winship p. 42

(b.2) Proceedings Of A Board of General Officers, Held By Order Of His Excellency Gen. Washington, Commander in Chief of the Army of the United States of America. Respecting Major John Andre, Adjutant General of the British Army. September 29, 1780. To which are appended, All the Letters which passed between Sir Henry Clinton, Generals Washington, Arnold, Robertson, Major Andre, &c. &c. on the Occasion. Printed and published at Philadelphia, by Order of Congress, October 10, 1780. Exeter: Re-printed and Sold by R. Trewman, behind the Guildhall. Price Three-Pence. [1780?] 16 p. 8vo.

CSmH, NN, RPJCB

Adams Controversy 80-6b Church 1,166

(b.3) Printed by Order of Congress, At Philadelphia: --And Dublin Re-printed. By Pat. Byrne, Bookseller, Stationer, &c. No. 35, College-Green, opposite the Statute of King William. M.DCC.LXXXI. 31 p. 8vo.

CSmH, RPJCB

Adams Controversy 80-6c Church 1,178

(c) Major Andre, Written while he was a Prisoner in the American Camp. Ah: Delia, see the fatal hour . . . [Boston? 1780?] Broadside

MB*

mp. 43,820 Bristol B5,111 Ford 2,233 Wegelin 631

(d) The Case of Major John Andre, Adjutant-General to the British Army, Who was put to Death by the Rebels, October 2, 1780. Candidly Represented: With Remarks on the said Case . . . . New-York: Printed by James Rivington. MDCCLXXX. 28 p. 4to.

RPJCB*

Evans 16,731 Sabin 1,453

(e) Brave Paulding and the Spy. [Ballad Sheet of 1783]

No copy located.

(e.2) Death of Major Andre . . . . Printed and Sold at No. 25, High Street, Providence, where may be obtained 100 other kinds. [Henry Trumbull? 1828?]

RPB

Winslow 75 (RPB)

(e.3) Frank Moore, "Brave Paulding and the Spy," Songs and Ballads of the American Revolution 316-21 (New York 1856).

(f) Monody on Major Andre. By Miss Seward (Author of the Elegy on Capt. Cook). To which are added letters addressed to her by Major Andre, in the year 1769. Lichfield, Printed and sold by J. Jackson, for the author; sold also by Robinson, Pater-Noster-Row; Cadell and Evans, in the Strand, London; Prince, Oxford; Merrill, Cambridge; and Pratt and Clinch, Bath. M.DCC.LXXXI. [Price Two-Shillings and Six-Pence.] 52 p. 4to.

NN, ViU

Sabin 79,477 Adams Controversy 81-65a Church 1,185

(f.2) The Second Edition. Lichfield 48 p.

DLC, MB, NjHi, ViU

Sabin 79,478 Adams Controversy 81-65b

(f.3) New-York, Printed by James Rivington. M,DCC,LXXXI. 39 p. 8vo.

Evans 17,368 Sabin 79,479

(f.4) Monody on Major Andre, (Who was executed at Tappan, November--1780.) By Miss Seward, To which are added, Major Andre's Letters, Addressed to Miss Seward, when at his 18th Year. Philadelphia: Printed and Sold by Enoch Story, in Third-Street, Third Door from Chesnut-street. [1782? 1788?] 56 p. 12mo.

MWA*, MdBJ-G, MeHi*, NHi

Evans 17,719 and 21,457 (Book description varies from copy on microcard.)
Sabin 79,480 Hildeburn 4,248

(f.4.a) [The Same] [1782?] 92 p. 12mo.

ViU

(f.4.b) Second American Edition. [n.d.] 48 p. 5 5/8"

MdBJ-G

Sabin 79,481

(f.5) New York: Printed by Harrisson and Purdy, For, and Sold by Thomas Allen, Bookseller and Stationer, No. 16, Queen-Street, Corner of Fly-Market, M.DCC.LXXXVIII. 48 p. 12mo.

DLC*

Evans 21,458 Sabin 79,482

(f.6) The Second New-York Edition. New-York: Printed for T. Allen, Bookseller and Stationer, No. 12, Queen-Street. 1792. 48 p. 12mo.

MBAt, MH, MWA*

Evans 24,782 Sabin 79,483

(f.7) Monody on Major Andre. By Miss Seward. Fourth American Edition. Boston: Printed For And Sold By W. Spotswood, And C. P. Wayne. 1798. 22 p. 12mo.

DLC, MH, MWA*, NN, PPL, RPB, RPJCB

Evans 34,533 Sabin 79,484

(f.8) Amelia; Or, The Faithless Briton. An Original American Novel, founded upon recent facts. To Which Is Added, Amelia, or Malevolence Defeated; And, Miss Seward's Monody On Major Andre. Boston: Printed For And Sold By W. Spotswood, And C. P. Wayne. 1798. 86 p. 8vo.

DLC, MWA*, NN, ViU

Evans 33,290

(f.9) Galatea, A Pastoral Romance; Imitated From Cervantes. By M. De Florian. Translated Into English. To Which Is Added Amelia, Or The Faithless Briton; Amelia, Or Malevolence Defeated; And, Miss Seward's Monody On Major Andre. Embellished With Engravings. Boston: Printed For And Sold By W. Spotswood, And C. P. Wayne. 1798. 207 p. 12mo.

(f.10) Edited by E. C. G. Penzance, Printed by T. Vigurs. 1806.

Sabin 79,485

(f.11) London: Printed for Longman, Hurst, Rees, Orme and Browne. . . . 1817.

Sabin 79,486

(f.12) London: Otridge and Rackham. 1821.

Sabin 79,487

(g) Cow-Chace, In Three Cantos, Published on Occasion of the Rebel General Wayne's Attack Of The Refugees Block-House On Hudson's River, On Friday the 21st of July, 1780. New-York: Printed by James Rivington, MDCCLXXX. 69 p. 8vo.

Evans 16,697 Sabin 1,449 Adams Controversy 80-5a

BLM, CSmH, CtY, MWA, MWiW-C*, MiU-C, NN, PHi, PPL

(g.2) The Cow Chace: An Heroick Poem, in Three Cantos. Written at New York, 1780, by the late Major Andre, With Explanatory Notes, by the Editor . . . London: Printed for John Fielding, No. 23, Pater-Noster-Row, 1781. 32 p. 4to.

BLM, CSmH, CtY, DLC, MB, MH, MWA, PHi, RPJCB

Sabin 1,450 Adams Controversy 80-5b

(g.3) The Cow Chace. In Three Cantos. Written in the year 1780, By Major John Andre, Adjutant-General to the British Army, in North America. A few weeks previous to his capture by the Americans. Litchfield: Re-printed by Thomas Collier [1790] 12 p.

MWA*

mp. 45,811 Bristol B7,299

(h) Reflexions D'Un Gentil'Homme Suisse, Sur La Sentence d'un conseil de guerre Americain, qui a condamne le Major Andre au dernier supplice. Et sur la lettre Ecrite, a cette occasion, par un ami de cet officier au redacteur du Courier du l'Europe, No. XLIII. . . . A Londres Se vend chez M. Bossiere, a la societe Typographique rue St. James. 1781. 37 p. 8vo.

RPJCB

Adams Controversy 81-62

(i) [Edward Burnaby Greene] The Prophecy of Andree. An Ode: Written in the Year 1780 . . . . London: Printed for G. Kearsly, in Fleet-Street; and R. Faulder, in New Bond-Street. M,DCC,LXXXII. 22 p. 4to.

CSmH, RPJCB

Sabin 28,493n Adams Controversy 82-47

(j) [John Newell Puddicombe] The British Hero in Captivity. A Poem. Dedicated To His Royal Highness The Prince of Wales. . . . London: Printed For J. Robson, New Bond-Street; J. Walter, Charing Cross; And J. Sewell, Cornhill. M.DCC.LXXXII. [Price One Shilling and Six Pence.] 23 p. 4to.

BLM, ICN, RPJCB

Adams Controversy 82-75.1

(k) Major Andre's Complaint. . . . Philadelphia Printed at Carr & Co's Musical Repository. [1794] Broadside 4to.

DLC*

Note This is a sheet of music, with words.

(l) Andre: A Tragedy, in Five Acts: [By William Dunlap] As Performed By The Old American Company, New York, March 30, 1798. To which are added Authentic Documents respecting Major Andre; consisting of Letters to Miss Seward, the Cow Chace, Proceedings Of The Court Martial, &c. Copy Right Secured. New York: Printed by T. & J. Swords, No. 99 Pearl-street.--1798--. 112 p. 8vo.

CSmH, DLC, MBAt, MH, MWA*, NN, NjR, PHi(2, 1 imp.), PPL, PU, RPB, RPJCB, ViU

Evans 33,652 Sabin 21,296 Church 1,279
Hill 72

(l.2) Andre: A Tragedy in five acts: As now performing At the Theatre in New York. To which is added The Cow-Chace: A satirical Poem. By Major Andre: With The Proceedings of the Court-Martial; And Authentic Documents concerning him. London: Printed for David Ogilvy and Son, No. 315, Holborn 1799. 110 p.

CSmH, CtY, DLC, ICU, MB, MH, MWA, MiU-C, NN(2), NjP, PU, RPB

Sabin 21,297

(l.3) William Dunlap, Andre. A Tragedy in Five Acts. (The Dunlap Society. New York 1887).

(l.4) Hobson Quinn, Representative American Plays 79-140 (New York 1917).

(l.5) Montrose J. Moses, Representative Plays by American Dramatists, 1765-1819 499-564. (New York 1918).

(m) An Authentic Narrative of the Causes Which led to the Death of Major Andre, Adjutant-General of his Majesty's forces in North-America. By Joshua Hett Smith, Esq. Counsellor at Law, late Member of the Convention of the State of New York. To which is added, A Monody on the Death of Major Andre. By Miss Seward. London, Printed for Mathews and Leigh, 1808. 352 p.

Sabin 40,699

(m.2) New York: Printed for Evert Duyckinck, No. 110, Pearl Street. 1809. 214 p.

DLC, MWA*, NN, NSchU

Shaw-Shoemaker 18,637 and 18,636

(n) The Trial of Major John Andre, Adjutant-General Of The British Army. September 29, 1780. With an Appendix containing sundry interesting Letters interchanged on the occasion. Published by order of Congress. Palmer: [Mass.] Printed By Ezekiel Terry, For Capt. James Warner, Wilbraham. 1810. 24 p.

CSmH, MWA*, NN, NjPT, PPL

Shaw-Shoemaker 21,518

(o) Vindication of The Captors Of Major Andre. [By Egbert Benson, LL.D.] New-York: Published by Kirk & Mercein, At the office of the Edinburgh and Quarterly Reviews, No. 22 Wall-Street. T. & W. Mercein, Printers, No. 93 Gold-street. 1817.

DLC, KyU, MB, MWA*, MeBa, NNPM, NjR, ViU

Shaw-Shoemaker 40,184 Sabin 4,746

(o.2) Vindication of the Captors of Major Andre. By Egbert Benson, L.L.D. With Introduction and Appendix. New York: Privately Printed. [for Francis S. Hoffman] 1865.

Sabin 4,747

(o.3) New York: Reprinted for Joseph Sabin. 1865.

Sabin 4,748

(p) The Glory of Columbia Her Yeomanry! A Play, in five acts. By William Dunlap, Esq. With Songs, Duetts, &c. New-York. Published by David Longworth, At the Dramatic Repository, Shakespeare-Gallery. May--1817. 56 p.

DLC, MWA*(imp.), NIC, NjR, RPB

Shaw-Shoemaker 40,699 Hill 82

(q) Peleg W. Chandler, ed., "Proceedings of a Board of General Officers, Held by Order of General George Washington, respecting Major John Andre, charged with being a spy, New York, 1780," 2 American Criminal Trials 155-81 (Boston 1844).

Sabin 11,868

(r) William Gilmore Simms, "The case of Major Andre," Views and Reviews in American Literature, History and Fiction 101-22 (New York 1845).

(s) Charles J. Biddle, "The Case of Major Andre, with a Review of the Statement of it in Lord Mahon's History of England," Historical Society of Pennsylvania, Contributions to American History 317-416 (Philadelphia 1858).

(t) Andreana. Containing the Trial, Execution, and various matters connected with the History of Major John Andre (Philadelphia 1865).

Sabin 1,458

(u) Minutes of a Court of Inquiry upon the case of Major John Andre, with accompanying documents published in 1780 by order of Congress, with an additional Appendix containing copies of the papers found upon Major Andre when arrested, and other documents relating to the subject. (Albany 1865).

Sabin 1,457

(v) Papers concerning The Capture and Detention of Major John Andre. Collected by Henry B. Dawson. (Yonkers, New York 1866).

(w) Proceedings of a board of general officers respecting Major John Andre (Privately printed by Bradstreet press. New York 1867).

(x) The Fate of Major Andre; A Letter from Alexander Hamilton to John Laurens (Heartman's Historical Series No. 18, New York 1916).

(y) John D. Lawson, ed., "The Trial of Major John Andre for Being a Spy, Tappan, New York, 1780," 6 American State Trials 464-85 (St. Louis 1916).

(8) Colonel Sheldon, 1780

(a) Proceedings of a General Court Martial, Convened at Fish-Kill, on the 25th Day of October, 1780, By Order of His Excellency General Washington, Commander in Chief of the Army of the United States of America. On the Tryal of Colonel Elisha Sheldon, Hartford: Printed by Hudson and Goodwin, M,DCC,LXXX. 16 p. 12mo.

CtHi*, PHi(imp.)

Evans 17,048 Trumbull 2d 2,519

(9) Major General Howe, 1782

(a) Proceedings of a General Court Martial, Held at Philadelphia, In The State Of Pennsylvania, By Order of his Excellency General Washington, Commander In Chief Of the Army of The United States of America, For the Trial of Major General Howe, December 7, 1781. Major General Baron Steuben, President. Philadelphia: Printed by Hall and Sellers, in Market-Street M,DCC,LXXXII. 51 p. fol.

CSmH, DLC, MBAt, MHi, MWA*, MdBB, NHi, NN, PHi

Evans 17,772 Sabin 33,328 Hildeburn 4,237

(a.2) 12 <u>Collections of the New York Historical Society for the year 1879</u> 213-311 (1880).

(10) Admiral Landai, 1784

(a) Memorial, to justify Peter Landai's conduct during the Late War. Boston: Printed by Peter Edes, at his Office, at the American-Exchange, State-Street. M,DCC,LXXXIV. 115 p. 4to.

MBAt, MWA*, NN, NjP, RPJCB(imp.)

Evans 18,549 Sabin 38,827

(b) The Second Part of the Memorial to justify Peter Landai's Conduct, during the Late War. New-York: Printed by Samuel Loudon, at his Office, No. 5, Water-Street. [1785] 52 p. 4to.

MBAt, MWA*, NjP, RPJCB

Evans 19,056 Sabin 38,828

(c) Charges and Proofs Respecting the Conduct of Peter Landais. New-York: Printed by Francis Childs. [1787] 18 p. 4to.

DLC*, MBAt

Evans 20,436 Sabin 38,829

(11) Brigadier General Harmar, 1791

(a) The Proceedings of a Court of Enquiry, Held at the special Request of Brigadier General Josiah Harmar, To Investigate his Conduct, as Commanding Officer of the Expedition against the Miami Indians, 1790: The same having been transmitted by Major General St. Clair, to the Secretary of the United States, for the Department of War. Published by Authority. Philadelphia: Printed by John Fenno. M.DCC.XCI. 35 p. fol.

CSmH, DLC, MBAt, MHi, MiU-C, NHi, NN*, NcD, PHi, RPJCB

Evans 23,905

Note The first paragraph of a letter from Fisher Ames to Thomas Dwight, dated May, 1791, was as follows: "If I can make a rebellious report on Harmer's trial lie peaceably in a sheet of folio paper, I will send it you by this post. Please to communicate it, with my respects, to the worthy old Gentleman, whom God bless. Considering your captainship, there is a propriety in your having it. You will learn to respect the militia, that bulwark of a free country, as the cant is." 2 Works of Fisher Ames (Seth Ames, ed., Boston 1854).

(12) Captain Sever, 1800

(a) Norfolk, 22d April, 1800. Sir, The President of the United States having appointed me to be President of a Court of Inquiry to investigate the causes of the loss of the masts, &c. of the Frigate Congress, . . . [signed: Thomas Truxton, Commander-in-Chief U.S. Navy Norfolk] 14 p.(imp.)

DLC (Photostat in Manuscripts Division) 14 p. (imp.)

2.02 Court of Commissioners of Appeals and Court of Appeals in Cases of Capture, 1775-1787

(1) Active, Admiralty, 1779-1809

(a) The Case of the Sloop Active, &c. . . . [By Richard Peters, Jr.] [Philadelphia: Printed by Hall and Sellers, 1779] 27 p. 4to.

DLC, MiU-C, NHi, NN*, NjP, PHi, PPL

Evans 16,220 Hildeburn 3,858

(b) [No title page. Cadwalader Pamphlet, below 2.02(3), 1-11]

(i) In the Court of Commissioners of Appeals for the United States of America, on the 15th day of December, 1778. Appeal from the Court of Admiralty of the State of Pennsylvania. Thomas Houston, esq. &c--Appellees,

versus Gideon Olmsted, &c. Appellants, and Claimants of the Sloop Active, her Cargo, &c.

(ii) In the Court of Admiralty for the State of Pennsylvania. Thomas Houston, esq. &c. Appellees, versus Gideon Olmsted, Artemas White, Aquila Rumsdale, and David Clark, Appellants, Claimants of the Sloop Active and her Cargo.

PPT-L

(c) Ross v. Rittenhouse, 2 Dallas 160 (Pa. Supreme Ct. 1792), above 1.07(33).

(d) Sundry Documents Relative to the Claim of Gideon Olmsted, against the Commonwealth of Pennsylvania. Respectfully submitted to the Consideration of the Members of the Legislature of said Commonwealth. [Philadelphia: Printed by Robert Cochran, 1808]

DLC, PPB (No copy available for filming 1980)

Shaw-Shoemaker 15,801

(e) The Case of the Sloop Active, including the whole of the evidence adduced on the Trial, The Proceedings In The Court of Admiralty, and before the Committee Of Appeals, and Other Authentic Documents connected with the case. Philadelphia, C. & A. Conrad, 1809 39 p.

ICN*, MB, MH-L, MHi, MiD-B, PP, PU-L

Shaw-Shoemaker 17,163

(f) The Whole Proceedings in the case of Olmsted And Others versus Rittenhouse's Executrices, As contained in documents on record in the courts of the United States and Pennsylvania; together with The Act of the Legislature of the State of Pennsylvania and other matters in relation to this important subject. Collected And Arranged By Richard Peters, Jun. Philadelphia: Published by William P. Farrand and Co. Fry and Kammerer, Printers. 1809. 108 p.

DLC, MH-L, MWA*, MdHi, NIC-L, PPL

Shaw-Shoemaker 18,368 and 19,230 Sabin 57,236

(g) Report of the case of the Commonwealth of Pennsylvania, versus John Smith, Esq. Marshall Of The United States, For The District Of Pennsylvania. Containing The Speeches of the Attorney General and Jared Ingersoll, Esq. on behalf of the Commonwealth, and William Lewis, Esq. on the part of the Defendant. And Also The Opinion Of The Honorable William Tilghman, Esq. Chief Justice of the State of Pennsylvania. By A Member Of The Bar Of Philadelphia. Philadelphia:

Published By David Hogan, No. 51, South Third-Street. April, 1809. T. T. Stiles, Printer. 52 p.

MBAt, MH-L, MHi, MWA*, MdHi, PHi, PPAmP

Shaw-Shoemaker 18,494 and 18,342

(h) A Report of the whole trial of Gen. Michael Bright, and others; before Washington & Peters, in the Circuit Court, Of The United States, in and for The District Of Pennsylvania, In The Third Circuit; on an Indictment for obstructing, resisting and opposing the execution of the Writ Of Arrest, issued out of The District Court Of Pennsylvania; in the case of Gideon Olmstead and others, against the surviving executrices of David Rittenhouse, deceased. By Thomas Lloyd, the arguments of counsel, and charge of the judge, revised by each respectively. Philadelphia; Printed for P. Byrne. 1809. 222 p.

Ct, DLC, MB, MWA*, N-L, NNC-L, PHi, PPAmP, PPB, PPL

Shaw-Shoemaker 18,495 Sabin 7,970

(h.2) Frederick C. Brightly, _Reports of Cases Decided by the Judges of the Supreme Court of Pennsylvania, in the Court of Nisi Prius at Philadelphia, and also in the Supreme Court_, Note at 19-28 (Philadelphia 1851).

(h.2.b) United States v. Bright, _Federal Case_ No. 14,647 (St. Paul 1896).

(i) Report of the Committee to whom were referred that part of the governor's message relative to the case of Gideon Olmstead and the resolutions from the House of Representatives upon the same subject. . . . 7 p.

MWA*

Shaw-Shoemaker 18,341

(j) Sundry Documents (copied from the original) relative to the claim of Gideon Olmsted, against the Commonwealth Of Pennsylvania. Respectfully submitted to the Consideration of the Members Of The Legislature of said Commonwealth. Philadelphia: Printed by Edward Olmsted [1811] 119 p.

MWA*, MiU-C, NHi, PHi, PPB

Shaw-Shoemaker 24,001 Sabin 57,236

(k) United States v. Judge Peters, 5 _Cranch_ 115 (U.S. 1809), (Published New York 1812).

(l) The Case of Gideon Olmsted. [n.p. n.d.] 15 p.

PPAmP

(m) "No. 265: Protest of Pennsylvania against the Decision of the Supreme Court in the Case of Gideon Olmstead, Communicated to the Senate, June 11, 1809," American State Papers, Miscellaneous II 2-7 and "No. 268: Further Proceedings of Pennsylvania in Relation to the Decision of the Supreme Court in the Case of Gideon Olmstead, Communicated to the Senate, December 19, 1809" Id. 11-12 (Walter Lowrie, ed., Washington, D.C. 1834).

Sabin 1,228

(n) Hampton L. Carson, "The Case of the Sloop 'Active'," 16 Pennsylvania Magazine of History 385-98 (Philadelphia 1892).

(o) Louis F. Middlebrook, Captain Gideon Olmsted (Salem 1933).

(p) Kenneth W. Treacy, "The Olmstead Case, 1778-1809," 10 Western Political Science Quarterly 675-91 (Salt Lake City 1957).

(q) Henry J. Bourguignon, "Ch. III: The Case of the Sloop Active--Congress Establishes a Court," The First Federal Court: The Federal Appellate Prize Court of the American Revolution 1775-1787 (Philadelphia 1977).

(r) Edward Dumbauld, "Olmstead's Claim: The Case of the Mutinous Mariner," Yearbook 1976 Supreme Court Historical Society 52-56 (Washington, D.C. 1977).

(2) Chester, Court of Appeals, 1786

(a) [U.S. Continental Congress. . . Resolved, that the Court of Appeals. . . Philadelphia, John Dunlap, 1786]

No copy known.

mp. 44,999 Bristol B6,404 Ford: Bibliographical Notes 545

(3) [No title page. No date. Cadwalader Pamphlet] 1792?

(a) [Six cases, p. 1-25] Below 2.03(2).

(i) Houston v. Olmstead, above 2.02(1)(b).

(ii) Houston v. Olmstead, above 2.02(1)(b).

(iii) Appeal from Boston. Captain Darby and others, Appellants, versus Brig. Ersten and Cargo, Peter Thomson, Appellee.

(iv) Appeal from Pennsylvania. Roger Kean, &c. Libellants and Appellants, versus Brig. Gloucester and Cargo, &c. Mahon and others, Claimants and Appellees.

(v) George Meade, in Behalf of Richard Lake and Others, Petitioner from the Admission of an Appeal from the Decree of the Maritime Court of the State of Connecticut condemning the Brig. Hope, her Apparel, and Cargo, versus John Hurlbutt and Others, Respondents. (Listed as Case. No. 103, The Brigantine Hope, at 131 U.S. xlviii.)

(vi) Alexander Hamilton, esq. in Behalf of Anthony Ameloo and Others, Petitioner for the Admission of an Appeal from the Admiralty Court of the State of South-Carolina condemning the Sloop Chester, her Apparel, and Cargo, versus The Owners, Masters, and Mariners of the Brig Experiment and the Brig Fair American.

(4) Dallas, Volume 2, Federal Court of Appeals, 1798

(a) 2 Dallas, above 1.07(33), contains reports of eight cases under the heading "Federal Court of Appeals," including Darby v. The Brig Erstern, above, 2.02(3)(iii) and Keane v. The Brig Gloucester, above 2.02(3)(iv).

2.03 United States Circuit and District Courts

(1) Brailsford v. Spalding and Douglass v. Executors of Stirk, Revolutionary Confiscations, Circuit Court for the District of Georgia, 1792

(a) The Case of Messrs. Brailsford and Others versus James Spalding, In the Circuit Court for the District of Georgia, Was argued on Friday the 27th Day of April, 1792, and the Court delivered their Opinions, with their Reasons, as within, on Wednesday the 2d of May. Also, Douglass versus The Executors of Stirk, Argued the 28th of April, and decided on the 2d of May. Savannah: Printed by James and Nicholas Johnston. M,DCC,XCII. 36 p. 8vo.

NHi*

Evans 24,353 Sabin 7,328

(b) Cadwalader Pamphlet, below 2.03(2), at 64-88.

(c) For later 1792-94 developments in the Supreme Court, see Georgia v. Brailsford, 2 Dallas 402 and 415, above 1.07(33); 3 Dallas 1, above 1.07(35).

(2) Cadwalader Pamphlet, 1792?

Note: The only known copy was lost in the burning of the Library of the Temple University School of Law. The pamphlet was imperfect, not having a title page, and so not showing either date or place of publication, and it was missing at least one page at the end. It contained 88 pages and reported ten decisions, dating between 1779 and 1792, the last being incomplete. The pamphlet was given to Temple by the Cadwalader estate in the late 1950's.

In addition to the cases separately listed in 2.03 and 2.04 this pamphlet also contains reports of Farquahar's Executors v. State of Georgia, C.C.D. Ga. 1791, p. 43-51. (Proceedings in the Supreme Court reported as Chisholm, Ex'r v. Georgia, see below 2.04(2); and Higginson v. Greenwood, C.C.D.S.C. 1791, p. 51-63.

(3) Ravara's Trial for Sending Threatening Letters, Circuit Court for the District of Pennsylvania, 1793

(a) A Statement Of Facts, concerning Joseph Ravara, written by himself. Philadelphia: Printed by Thomas Dobson, No. 41, South Second-street. 1793. 21 p. 8vo.

MBAt, PPL*, RPJCB

Evans 26,053 Sabin 67,979 Sowerby 3,171

(b) The United States v. Ravara, 2 Dallas 297, above 1.07(33).

(c) Francis Wharton, ed., "Trial of Joseph Ravara, for Sending Threatening Letters to the British Minister. In the Circuit Court of the United States for the Pennsylvania District. Philadelphia, 1793," _State Trials of the United States_ 90-92 (Philadelphia 1849).

(d) United States v. Ravara, _Federal Cases_ No. 16,122 and No. 16,122a (St. Paul 1896).

(4) _Catherine_, Neutrality Case, Admiralty Side, District of New York, 1794

(a) Decree on the Admiralty Side of the District Court of New-York, in which the rights of sovereignty and neutrality concerning captures within neutral bounds; and the treaty of amity and commerce between France and the United States and the jurisdiction of the neutral courts, as far as they are respectively connected with that subject are considered by Judge Duane, in the case of the Catharine on the 28th January, 1794. Published by particular desire. New-York: Printed by Francis Childs and John Swaine. MDCCXCIV 35 p. 8vo.

DLC, MWA (copy not located), NHi*, NN, PPAmP

Evans 26,915 Sabin 20,982

(5) United States v. Hylton, Constitutional Law, Circuit Court for the District of Virginia, 1795

(a) The Substance Of An Argument in the case of the Carriage Duties, delivered before the Circuit Court of the United States, in Virginia, May term, 1795, By John Wickham, counsel for the United States vs. Hylton. Richmond: Printed by Augustine Davis [1795] 15 p. 8vo.

DLC, MHi*, NHi

Evans 29,889 Sabin 103,854

(b) An Argument respecting the Constitutionality of the Carriage Tax; which subject was discussed at Richmond, in Virginia, in May, 1795. By John Taylor. Richmond: Printed by Augustine Davis. [1795] 34 p. 8vo.

DLC, MHi* (autograph of S. G. Tucker), NHi

Evans 29,606 Sabin 94,485

(c) Proceedings in the Supreme Court are reported in Hylton v. United States, 3 Dallas 171, above 1.07(35).

(6) Van Horne's Lessee v. Dorrance, 1795 Ejectment Case, Circuit Court for the District of Pennsylvania, 1796

(a) The Charge of Judge Paterson To the Jury, in the case of Vanhorne's Lessee against Dorrance: Tried at a Circuit Court for the United States, held at Philadelphia, April Term 1795: wherein the controverted title to the Wyoming lands, between the claimants under Pennsylvania and Connecticut, received a decision. Philadelphia: Printed By Samuel H. Smith, No. 118 Chestnut-Street. 1796. 43 p. 8vo.

CSmH, CtY(2), DLC, MH-L, MWA*, MiU-C, PHi(2), PP, PPAmP, PPL, PU-L, RPJCB, ScC

Evans 30,962 Sabin 59,056

(b) Van Horne's Lessee v. Dorrance, 2 Dallas 304, above 1.07(33).

(c) Charge of Judge Patterson, April Term, 1795. Present, Patterson and Peters, Justices. Vanhorne's Lessee versus Dorrance. [Last page sets forth certificate of clerk of the U.S. Supreme Court, dated February 12, 1801, setting forth proceedings in the Supreme Court. This is followed by the colophon] Philadelphia Printed by Z. Poulson, jun. [1801] 24 p. 21.5 cm.

CtSoP, DLC, MHi, MH-L, MWA*, NN, PHi

Shaw-Shoemaker 1,474

(7) Hamilton and Hamilton v. Eaton, British Debts Case, Circuit Court for the District of North Carolina, 1797

(a) Hamiltons versus Eaton: A Case Respecting British debts, Lately Determined in the Circuit Court of the United States, for North-Carolina District, Presided by C. J. Ellsworth. Newbern: Francois-Xavier Martin, 1797. 79 p. 8vo.

CtY, DLC, MH-L, NN(imp.), NNC-L NcAsS

Evans 32,223 (No copy could be filmed) Sabin 30,048
McMurtrie North Carolina 181 and 238 Sowerby 2,167

(a.2) See above 1.11(4).

(b) Hamilton v. Eaton, Martin's Reports [Second Part] 1-77, above 1.11(4)(b).

(8) Morse v. Reid, Circuit Court for the District of New York, 1798

(a) "Law Case At a circuit court for the United States for the district of New-York in the eastern circuit, held at the city of New-York on the 4th day of April, 1798," 5 Collections 123-24, above 1.02(1)(h).

(9) Lyon's Trial for Sedition, Circuit Court for the District of Vermont, 1798

(a) The Scourge of Aristocracy and Repository of Important Political Truths. Published at Fairhaven, M,DCC,XCIII. [Numbers 1-4, Vol. I, October 1 - December 15, 1798.] 194 p. 8vo.

CSmH, CtY, DLC, MWA, NN(imp.), VtHi, VtU-W(No. 3 only)

Evans 34,028 Cooley 442 McCorison 498

(b) Francis Wharton, ed., "Trial of Matthew Lyon for a Seditious Libel. In the Circuit Court of the United States for the Vermont District. Vergennes, October 7, 1798," State Trials of the United States 333-44 (Philadelphia 1849).

(c) Lyon's Case, Federal Case No. 8,646 (St. Paul. 1895).

(d) John D. Lawson, ed., "The Trial of Matthew Lyon for a Seditious Libel, Vergennes, Vermont, 1798," 6 American State Trials 687-94 (St. Louis 1916).

(e) James Morton Smith, "Ch. XI: The Ordeal of the Critical Congressman: Matthew Lyon of Vermont," Freedom's Fetters 221-46 (Ithaca 1956).

(f) Aleine Austin, "9 On Trial for Sedition," and "10 Free Speech Vindicated," Matthew Lyon 108-30 (University Park, Pennsylvania 1981).

(10) United States v. Duane, Sedition Act, Circuit Court for the District of Pennsylvania, 1799

(a) A Letter To George Washington, President Of The United States; containing Strictures On His Address Of The Seventeenth Of September, 1796, Notifying His Relinquishment Of The Presidential Office. By Jasper Dwight, Of Vermont. [Pseudonym of William Duane?] Printed at Philadelphia for the author, and sold by the booksellers. Dec. 1796. 48 p. 8vo.

CSmH, Ct, DLC, MB, MBAt, MH, MWA*, MdBJ-G, MdBP, MiU-C, NHi, NN, NjP, PBL, PHi(4), PPAmP, PPL, PPPrHi, RPB, RPJCB, ScC

Evans 31,315 Sabin 20,989

(a.2) Baltimore: Printed for George Keatinge's Book store. 1799. 44 p. 8vo.

DLC*, MdBP

Evans 32,940

(b) Copy of an Indictment [No. I] In the Circuit Court of the United States in and for the Pennsylvania District of the Middle Circuit. The Grand Inquest . . . . [The second part is a separately-paged "Copy of an Indictment No. II.] [Philadelphia 1799] 7 p. 8vo.

DLC*

Evans 36,513

Note: Brackets in original.

(c) Report, In Part, of the Committee Of Privileges, on the Form Of Proceedings in the case of William Duane [March 22, 1800]. Printed by order of the Senate of the United States. [Philadelphia 1800] 4 p. 8vo.

DLC, MBAt, MWA*, N, NN

Evans 38,814

(d) Further Report, In Part, of the Committee Of Privileges, on the Form Of Proceedings in the case of William Duane. Printed by order of the Senate of the United States. March 25th 1800. [Philadelphia 1800] 4 p. 8vo.

DLC, MBAt, MWA*

Evans 38,733

(e) An Examination of The Question, Who Is The Writer Of Two Forged Letters addressed to The President of the United States? Attributed To John Rutledge, Esq. Member Of Congress From South Carolina [By William Duane. n.p.] 1803 24 p.

MBAt, MWA*, MiU-C, NHi, NN, PPL

Shaw-Shoemaker 4,109 Sabin 20,985 Turnbull p. 400

(e.2) Washington City: Printed By William Duane & Son. 1803 24 p. 22 cm.

DLC*, MWA, NN

Shaw-Shoemaker 4,110

(e.3) Second Edition. Washington City: Printed By William Duane & Son. 1803. 24 p.

DLC, MWA*, NN(2)

Shaw-Shoemaker 4,111

(e.4) Second Edition. Philadelphia 1805.

(f) "United States v. Duane" at p. 5-13, 102-07; "Hollingsworth v. Duane" at p. 46-50, 51-58, 77-101, 141-46; "United States v. Wayne" at 134-38, Reports of Cases adjudged in The Circuit Court of the United States for the Third Circuit. By John B. Wallace. . . . Philadelphia: Published By Asbury Dickens, S.C. Ustick, Printer, 1801. 146 p.

MH-L, MWA*, NjR, PP, PPAmP, PPL

Shaw-Shoemaker 1,600 and 1,558

(g) John B. Wallace, Reports of cases in the circuit court for the Third Circuit in 1801. [A star-paged second edition, containing above materials at the indicated pages] [Philadelphia 1838).

(h) Hollingsworth v. Duane, Federal Cases Nos. 6,614 - 6,618; United States v. Duane, Federal Cases Nos. 14,996 and 14,997; and United States v. Wayne, Federal Case No. 16,454 (St. Paul 1895-96).

(i) James Morton Smith, "Ch. XIII: William Duane, The Aurora, and the Alien and Sedition Laws," Freedom's Fetters 277-306 (Ithaca 1956).

(11) Robbins's Extradition Case, District of South Carolina, 1799

(a) Three Letters, Written, And Originally Published, under the signature of A South Carolina Planter. The first, on the case of Jonathan Robbins; decided under the twenty-sixth article of the treaty with Great-Britain, in the District Court of the United States, for South Carolina. The second, On The Recent Captures of American Vessels By British Cruisers, contrary to the laws of nations, and the treaty between the two countries. The third, On The Right Of Expatriation. By Charles Pinckney, Esquire, Senator in Congress, for South-Carolina. To which is added, An Appendix, containing sundry documents concerning Jonathan Robbins. Philadelphia: Aurora-office, 1799 67 p. 8vo.

BLM, CLL, CLU, CSmH, CtHi, CtHT-W, CtY, DLC(2), ICN, MB, MBAt, MH-L, MHi, MWA*, MdBJ-G, MdBP, MiU-L, N, NHi, NIC-L, NN(2), NcD, NjP, PHi(4), PP, PPAmP, PPL, PPPrHi, RPB, RPJCB, ScC, TxU, ViU(2), ViW(2), WHi

Evans 36,124 Sabin 62,298 and 40,605 Turnbull p. 369

(b) Case of Jonathan Robbins, examined by Charles Pinckney, Esq. Senator in Congress for South Carolina, and late Governor of that State To The Citizens Of The United States. Baltimore: printed by Warner & Hanna No. 3, N. Gay-street. 1799. 36 p. 12mo.

CLU, DLC, MWA*, NN

Evans 36,121 Minick 531 Turnbull p. 368

(c) Three Letters, addressed to the People of the United States, which have lately appeared under the signature of "A South-Carolina Planter." The first, On The Case Of Jonathan Robbins. The second, On The Recent Captures Of The British Cruisers, And The Right Of A Citizen To Expatriate Himself, the third, On The Claims Of The British Creditors, And The Proceedings of the British Commissioners, Under The Sixth Article of Mr. Jay's Treaty. By Charles Pickney, Senator in Congress, for South-Carolina. Charleston: Printed By T. C. Cox, Tradd-Street. Dec. 1799. 71 p. 8vo.

CtMW, DGU, DLC, MWA*, NNC-L, RPJCB

Evans 36,122 Sabin 62,899 Sowerby 3,216 Turnbull p. 369

(d) Speech of the Hon. John Marshall, delivered in the House Of Representatives of the United States, on the resolutions of the Hon. Edward Livingston relative to Thomas Nash, alias Jonathan Robbins. Philadelphia: printed at the office of "The True American." 1800. 45 p. 12mo.

CSmH, CtHT-W, CtY, DLC, MB, MBAt, MH-L, MHi, MWA*, MiU-C, N, NHi, NN(2), NcD, NjP, PHi, PPAmP, PPL, RPJCB, ViU(2)

Evans 37,887

Evans Ghost 36,123 is a composite of Evans 36,122 and 36,124, above 2.03(11)(a) and (c).

(e) Reports of Cases Adjudged in the District Court of South Carolina. By the Hon. Thomas Bee, Judge of that Court. To which is added an Appendix containing Decisions in the Admiralty Court of Pennsylvania. By the Late Francis Hopkinson, Esquire, and Cases determined in other Districts of the United States. Philadelphia: Published by William P. Farrand and Co., Fry and Kammerer, Printers 1810.

Sabin 87,456 Turnbull p. 459

(f) John E. Hall, ed., "District Court, South Carolina, 25th July, 1799. Case of Jonathan Robbins, Present, his honour Judge Bee," 1 Journal of Jurisprudence: A New Series of The American Law Journal 18-32 (Philadelphia 1821).

(g) Francis Wharton, ed., "Proceedings in the Case of Jonathan Robbins, on a Claim for Delivery to the British Government on Charge of Murder. In the District Court of the United States for the South Carolina District. Charleston, 1799," State Trials of the United States 392-457 (Philadelphia 1849).

(h) John D. Lawson, ed., "The Trial of Jonathan Robbins for Extradition Under a Treaty With Great Britain, Charleston, South Carolina, 1799," 7 American State Trials 811-31 (St. Louis 1917).

(i) Larry Cress, "The Jonathan Robbins Incident: Extradition and the Separation of Powers in the Adams Administrations, III Essex Institute Historical Collections 99-121 (1975).

(12) United States v. Fries, Treason, Circuit Court for the District of Pennsylvania, 1799

(a) The Two Trials of John Fries, on an Indictment for Treason; together with a brief report of the trials of several other persons, for Treason and Insurrection, In the Counties of Bucks, Northampton, and Montgomery, in the Circuit Court of the United States, Begun at the City of Philadelphia, April 11, 1799; continued at Norristown, October 11, 1799; -- and concluded at Philadelphia, April 11, 1800; before the Hon. Judges, Iredell, Peters, Washington and Chase. To which is added, A Copious Appendix, containing the evidences and arguments of the counsel on both sides, on the motion for a new trial; the arguments on the motion for removing the case to the county where the crime was committed, and the arguments against holding the jurisdiction at Norristown. Taken in shorthand by Thomas Carpenter. [Copy-Right secured.] Philadelphia: Printed and sold by William W. Woodward, No. 17 Chesnut, near Front street. 1800. 281 p. 8vo.

CLL, CtMW, DLC, M, MB, MBAt, MH-L, MWA*, MdBB, MiU-L(imp.), MoU-L, NIC-L, NN(3), NNB, NNC-L, NNPM, NNU-L, NcD-L, NjP, NjR, PHi, PP, PPAmP, PPL, RPJCB

Evans 37,104 Sabin 25,961 Parrish 100

Evans Ghosts 35,281 and 35,282

Note: Brackets in original.

(a.2) An edition in German was published at Allentown, Pa., in 1839.

(b) Philadelphia: May 20th, 1800. Sir, You are hereby summoned to attend the Philadelphia Gaol, on Thursday next, at five o'clock in the morning, as one of the Posse Comitatus, to attend and assist me, the Marshall of the District of Pennsylvania, from thence to Quaker-Town, in Bucks county, to the end that I may carry into execution the sentence of the last Circuit Court of the United States, held in Pennsylvania, against John Fries, Frederick Heany and John Getman, attainted of treason. Hereof fail not at your peril. John Hall, Marshall. [Philadelphia 1800] [Richard Rush, handwritten addressee] Broadside

PPL*

mp. 49,078 Bristol B11,044

(c) United States v. Fries, 3 Dallas 515, above 1.07(35).

(d) Francis Wharton, ed., "Trial of the Northampton Insurgents. In the Circuit Court of the United States for the Pennsylvania District, Philadelphia, 1799-1800" and "Second Trial of John Fries. In the Circuit Court of the United States for the Pennsylvania District. Philadelphia, April 29, 1800," <u>State Trials of the United States</u> 458-648 (Philadelphia 1849).

(e) United States v. Fries, <u>Federal Cases</u> Nos. 5,126 and 5,127 (St. Paul 1895).

(f) William W. H. Davis, <u>The Fries Rebellion 1798-99</u> (Doylestown, Pa. 1899).

(f.2) Reproduced as part of <u>Mass Violence in America</u> series (New York 1969).

(g) John D. Lawson, ed., "The Trial of John Fries for Treason, Philadelphia, Pennsylvania, 1799," and "The Second Trial of John Fries for Treason, Philadelphia, Pennsylvania, 1800," 11 <u>American State Trials</u> 1-196 (St. Louis 1919).

(h) Dwight F. Henderson, "Treason, Sedition, and Fries' Rebellion," 14 <u>American Journal of Legal History</u> 308-18 (1970).

(13) United States v. Cooper, Libel, Circuit Court for the District of Pennsylvania, 1800

(a) An Account of the Trial of Thomas Cooper, of Northumberland; on a Charge of Libel against the President of the United States; taken in short hand. With a preface, notes and appendix, by Thomas Cooper. Philadelphia: Printed by John Bioren, No. 83, Chesnut Street, for the Author. April 1800. 64 p. 8vo.

CSmH, CtY, DLC, ICN, MB, MBAt, MH, MH-L, MHi, MWA*, MiU-C, NN(3, 2 imp.), NNC-L, NjR, NcD, P-L, PHi(2), PP(2), PPAmP, PPL, RPB, RPJCB, ScC, Vi, WHi

Evans 37,249 Sabin 16,608 Turnbull p. 375

Note This statement is at the bottom of the last page: "Erratum. In the title page this trial is said to be printed for the author: this is a mistake: it is not printed for me. T.C."

(b) William Cobbett, "Trial of Cooper," 12 Porcupine's Works 3-16 (London 1801).

(c) Francis Wharton, ed., "Trial of Thomas Cooper, for a Seditious Libel. In the Circuit Court of the United States for the Pennsylvania District. Philadelphia, 1800," State Trials of the United States 659-81 (Philadelphia 1849).

(d) United States v. Cooper, Federal Case No. 14,865 (St. Paul 1896).

(e) John D. Lawson, ed., "The Trial of Thomas Cooper, For Seditious Libel, Philadelphia, Pennsylvania. 1800," 10 American State Trials 774-812 (St. Louis 1918).

(f) Dumas Malone, "Ch. IV: Republican Politics and Seditious Libel, 1800," The Public Life of Thomas Cooper, 1783-1839, 111-49 (New Haven 1926).

(g) Clark Gavin, Foul, False and Infamous: Famous Libel and Slander Cases of History 69-104 (New York 1950).

(h) James Morton Smith, "Ch. XIV: President Adams, Thomas Cooper, and Sedition," Freedom's Fetters 307-33 (Ithaca 1956), reprinted from 42 Mississippi Valley Historical Review 438-65 (1955).

(14) United States v. Brigstock, Circuit Court for the District of New Jersey, 1800

(a) Circuit Court of the United States, Middle Circuit of the New-Jersey District. The United States (a.) William Brigstock, otherwise called John Johnston. . . . [Trial for Piracy . . . Trenton? March 1st, 1800.] 15 p. 8vo.

CLU, DLC, NN, NjP, MWA*

Evans 38,723 Sabin 96,837 Morsch 461

2.04 United States Supreme Court

(1) West v. Barnes, Procedure, 1791

(a) [Heading] "Supreme Court of the United States. Tuesday, August 2d, 1791. West, Pltf. in error, v. Barnes, et alias Deft." in "The Federal Gazette and Philadelphia Daily Advertise" issues of August 11, 1791 (p. 2, col. 1-3, and p. 3, col. 1) and August 12, 1791 (p. 2, col. 1-2).

MWA, PPL

Evans 23,365

(a.2) [Heading] "The very interesting Case which was determined on the 3d instant, in the Supreme Court of the United States, held in this city, having engaged the public attention, we presume it will be agreeable to our readers to see an accurate statement of the proceedings in that case, which we are authorized to say is authentic. Supreme Court of the United States. Tuesday, August 2, 1791. West, Pltf. in error, v. Barnes, et alias Deft." in "The Gazette of the United States" issues of Saturday, August 13, 1791 (p. 1, col. 1-3) and Wednesday, August 17, 1791 (p. 1, col. 1-2).

DLC, MWA, PPL

Evans 23,404

(a.3) "Supreme Court of the United States. August Term, 1791. West, Plaintiff, versus Barnes et alios, Defendants, in Error," [Cadwalader Pamphlet, above 2.03(2)] p. 26-42.

(b) [Summary only] 2 Dallas 401, above 1.07(33).

(2) Chisholm v. Georgia, Constitutional Law, 1793

(a) Observations upon the Government of the United States Of America. By James Sullivan, Esq. Attorney-General of the Commonwealth of Massachusetts. Boston: Printed and sold by Samuel Hall, No. 53, Cornhill. MDCCXCI. 55 p. 8vo.

BLM, CSmH, DLC, ICN, MB, MBAt, MHi, MWA*, MWiW-C, MiU-L, NHi(2), NN(2), NcD, PPAmP, PPL, RPJCB

Evans 23,812

<u>Note</u> For a book review see "Impartial Review of American Publications," II (or 7) Universal Asylum and Columbian Magazine For September 1791 185-86.

(b) An Enquiry into the Constitutional Authority of the Supreme Federal Court, over the Several States in Their Political Capacity. Being An Answer to Observations upon the Government of the United States of America: By James Sullivan, Esq. Attorney General of the State of Massachusetts. By a

Citizen of South-Carolina. [By Timothy Ford] Charleston: Printed by W. P. Young, Broad-Street M,DCC,XCII 49 p. 8vo.

CSmH, MBAt, MWA*, NHi, NN, NNC-L, NjP, RPJCB

Evans 23, 324 Sabin 22,639 Morgan 851 Turnbull p. 290

Note For a book review see "Impartial Review of American Publications," II (or 9) Universal Asylum and Columbian Magazine for July 1792 41-44.

(c) [Brief news account about the opinions delivered by the judges of the Supreme Court on February 18] in "Dunlap's American Daily Advertiser" issue of February 19, 1793 (p. 3, col. 2-3).

BLM, DLC, MHi, MWA, PHi, PPL, NHi

Evans 25,423

Note Similar news accounts were published in other newspapers.

(d) [Letter signed by S. B. (Samuel Bayard, Clerk of the Supreme Court) giving "accurate" summary of the several opinions in Chisholm v. Georgia] in "Dunlap's American Daily Advertiser," issue of February 21, 1793, (p. 3, col. 3-4).

Note Similar news accounts were published in other newspapers.

(e) [Heading] "Chief Justice Jay's opinion, on the question 'whether a State liable to be sued by a private citizen of another state?'", in "Gazette of the United States," above 2.04(1)(a.2), issues of Saturday August 10, 1793 (p. 1, col. 1-2) and Wednesday, August 14, 1793 (p. 1, col. 1-3).

Evans 25,532

(f) A Case decided in the Supreme Court of the United States, in February, 1793, in which is discussed the question -- "whether a State be liable to be sued by a private citizen of another State?" Philadelphia: Printed by T. Dobson, At The Stone-House, No. 41, South Second-Street. M,DCC,XCIII. 123 p. 8vo.

DLC, GU(2), MH-L, MWA*, MiU-C, NHi, NIC-L, NN(2 variants), NcAsS, NcD, NjP, NjR, PPL, PU-L, RPB, RPJCB, ViU

Evans 25,370

(f.2) [The Same] Published by Authority. Boston: Printed by Adams & Larkin, at the State-Press, Court-Street. M,DCC,XCIII. 80 p. 8vo.

CtY, DLC, GU, MH-L(2), MWA*, PPL, RPJCB, TNJ

Evans 25,371

(f.3) Chisholm Ex'r versus Georgia, 2 Dallas 419, above 1.07(33).

(g) Virginia. In the House of Delegates, Thursday, 28th November, 1793. Resolved, That a State cannot, under the Constitution of the United States, be made a Defendant at the Suit of any Individual or Individuals, and that the decision of the Supreme Federal Court, that a State may be placed in that Situation, is incompatible with, and dangerous to the Sovereignty and Independence of the Individual States, as the same tends to a general Consolidation of these confederated Republicks . . . . (Teste) Charles Hay, C.H.D. 1793 December 3d,. . . [Richmond: Printed by Augustine Davis, 1793] Broadside 4to.

DLC, NN, R, MWA*

Evans 26,391

(h) Chisholm Ex'r v. Georgia, 2 Dallas 419, above 1.07(33).

(3) Penhallow v. Doane's Administrators, Admiralty, 1795

(a) A Report of the Opinions of the Judges in the Important Cause of Penhallow et al. against Doane's Administrators, delivered in the Supreme Court of the United States, at February Term, 1795, On an Appeal from the Circuit Court for the District of New-Hampshire. Taken by Permission, from the notes of the judges. Philadelphia: Printed by and for W. W. Woodward, No. 36, Chesnut-street, south side, (green sign) Franklin's Head. 1795. 73 p. 8vo.

DLC, MBAt, MH, MH-L, MHi, MWA*, NHi, NN, NNU-L, NjP, PHi, PPL, PU-L, RPJCB

Evans 29,284 Sabin 59,653

(b) A Statement of the Cause of the M'Clary Owners, and Doane & Doane's Administrators from its Commencement in 1777, to its Close in the Supreme-Court of the United States, Feb. 1795. . . . [By John Hale] Portsmouth: N.H. Printed by John Meicher. 1795. 67 p.

DLC, MBAt, MH, MHi, MWA*, NHi, NN

Evans 28,788 Sabin 29,638

(c) Penhallow, et al. versus Doane's Administrators, 3 Dallas 54, above 1.07(35).

(d) "[Letter] From John Sullivan, with Petition of John Penhallow; Report on the Case of the Brig Lusanna," 6 Papers of Thomas Jefferson 447-55 (Julian P. Boyd, ed., Princeton 1952).

(e) Kinvin L. Wroth and Hiller B. Zobel, eds., "Case No. 58. Penhallow v. The Lusanna 1777-1795," 2 Legal Papers of John Adams 352-95 (Boston 1965).

(4) Moultrie et al. v. Georgia, Jurisdiction, 1797?

(a) United States, in Equity, To Wit, In the Supreme Court. To the Honourable Oliver Elsworth chief justice and his associate justices of the Supreme Court, of the United States holding jurisdiction in Equity. Humbly complaining, shew unto your Honors your Orators, Alexander Moultrie, Isaac Huger and William Clay Snipes, citizens of the State of South-Carolina complainants . . . [Signed by William Tilghman and Jared Ingersoll, for the complainants, and filed in the Supreme Court on June 24, 1796.] [Philadelphia? 1797?] 18 p. 33 cm.

MiU-C

Bristol B10,008

(b) In thr (sic) Supreme Court of United States. Moultrie, et Al. versus State of Georgia, et Al. In Equity, Complainants Brief. The Bill. [Philadelphia? 1798?]

MiU-C

Bristol B10,402

(b.2) "No. 85. 8th Congress, 1st session. South Carolina Yazoo Company. Communicated to the House of Representatives, December 28, 1803," American State Papers I Public Lands 167-71 (Washington, D.C. 1832).

(5) Grayson v. Virginia, Jurisdiction, 1798 (Date Case Reported by Dallas)

(a) View of the Title to Indiana, A Tract of Country on the River Ohio, Containing Indian Conferences at Johnson-Hall in May, 1765; the deed of the Six Nations to the Proprietors of Indiana; the Minutes of the Congress at Fort Stanwix, in October and November, 1768; the deed of the Indians, settling the boundary line between the English and Indian lands; and the opinion of Counsel on the title of the Proprietors of Indiana. [Samuel Wharton, Philadelphia? 1775] 24 p. 21 cm.

CSmH, DLC, NjP*, RPJCB, WHi

mp. 42,983 Bristol B4,167
Sabin 34,579 and 99,584, and see 96,769
Huntington 394 Vail 649

(a.2) Williamsburg: Printed by J. Dixon & T. Nicholson. M,DCC,LXXIX. [Omits pages 21 to end] 8 p.

RPJCB*

mp. 43,732   Bristol B4,993   Sabin 99,584

(a.3) Philadelphia: Printed by Styner and Cist in Second-street, near Arch-street. M DCC LXXVI. 46 p. 8vo.

DLC, MBAt, MWA*, PHi, PPL

Evans 15,219 Sabin 25,595, 34,780, and 99,584
Hildeburn 3,490 Huntington 394 Vail 652

(b) William Trent, Robert Callender, David Franks, Joseph Simons, Levy Andrew Levy . . . Proprietors of a certain tract . . . called . . . Indiana. To all unto whom these presents shall come, Greeting . . . [Philadelphia 1776] Broadside fol.

No copy located

mp. 43,049   Bristol B4237   Rosenbach 68

(c) Indiana business. Richmond, November 8, 1791. The following anonymous letter has been industriously circulated among . . . the delegates of the General Assembly . . . in order to prejudice them against the Indiana memorialists claim . . . George Morgan. Agent for the Indiana Company. [Richmond 1791] Broadside 34.5 x 22 cm.

WHi (not located)

mp. 46,225   Bristol B7,762

(d) [Bill in Equity] In the Supreme Court of the United States. To the Honorable John Jay, Esquire, Chief Justice, and his Associates, Judges of the Supreme Court of the United States, sitting in Chancery: Humbly complaining shew unto your honors, your orators, William Grayson . . . William Lewis, William Rawle . . . [colophon] Printed by D. Humphreys, Philadelphia [1792] 28 p. 35 cm.

PPL*, Vi

mp. 45,777 and 46,198   Bristol B7,251 and B7,735

(d.2) 6 _Calendar of Virginia State Papers_ 1-36 (Richmond 1886).

Note There are duplicate entries in _Bristol_ and _Short-Title Evans_, both erroneously dated. Bristol B7,251 and mp. 45,777 date the imprint "179?", list it under the heading "Lewis, William", and locate a single copy at PHi, but the microcard reproduces the PPL copy. Bristol B7735 and mp. 46,198 date the imprint as "1791", list it under the heading "Indiana Company" and locate copies in PPL and Vi, the PPL copy being reproduced on the microcard. The 1886 reprinting of the Vi copy also prints the notice dated August 11, 1792, served by Benjamin R. Morgan, Solicitor for Complainants, on James Innes, Attorney-General of the Commonwealth of Virginia.

(e) Grayson v. Virginia, 3 Dallas 320, above 1.07(35).

(f) Hollingsworth, et al. v. Virginia, 3 Dallas 378, above 1.07(35).

(6) Cutting, Adm'r v. South Carolina, Jurisdiction, 1798 (Date Case Reported by Dallas)

(a) Facts and Observations, justifying the Claims of the Prince of Luxembourg, against the State of South Carolina, and against Alexander Gillon, Esq. Late Commodore of the Navy of the said State. [Charleston, 1784] 52 p. 8vo.

PPL*

mp. 44,528 Bristol B5,891 Sabin 87,825
Morgan 614 Turnbull p. 246

(b) Huger v. South Carolina, 3 Dallas 339, above 1.07(35).

(c) D. E. Huger Smith, "Commodore Alexander Gillon and the Frigate South Carolina," 9 _South Carolina Historical and Genealogical Magazine_ 189-219 (1908).

(d) D. E. Huger Smith, "The Luxembourg Claims," 10 _South Carolina Historical and Genealogical Magazine_ 92-115 (1909).

(7) Dallas's Reports, Volume 2, 1798

(a) Reports of Cases . . . By A. J. Dallas. Vol. II. Philadelphia . . . 1798. Above 1.07 (33).

(8) Clarke v. Russel, Diversity of Citizenship, 1798 (Date Case Reported by Dallas)

(a) Declaration. Rhode-Island District sc. Circuit Court of the United States, June Term 1798. Nathaniel Russel of Charleston in the district of South Carolina, . . . complains of John Innis Clark of Providence . . . surviving partner of the company of Joseph Nightingale, now deceased, and the said John Innis Clark, . . . [Providence 1798]. 8 p. 8vo.

RHi*, RNHi, RPJCB

Evans 34,908 Alden 1,598 Winship p. 69

Note This is probably a copy of the record in the Supreme Court

(b) Clark v. Russel, 3 Dallas 415, above 1.07(35).

(9) Dallas's Reports, Volume 3, 1799

(a) Reports of Cases . . . By A. J. Dallas. Volume III. Philadelphia . . . 1799. Above 1.07(35).

(10) Bingham v. Cabot, Diversity of Citizenship, 1795 and 1798 (Case Reported by Dallas in 1799)

(a) February Term, 1795. Bingham, Plaintiff in Err. versus Cabbot, et al, 3 Dallas 19, above 1.07(35).

(b) February Term, 1798. Bingham, Plaintiff in Error, versus Cabot, et al., 3 Dallas 382, above 1.07(35).

(c) Proceedings Relative to the Danish Brig Hope, and cargo. [by William Bingham. Philadelphia? 1800?] 46 p.

CSmH, MWA*, PHi, PPAmP

Evans 38,328 Sabin 96,935

(d) Statement of a case, Mess. Cabots, &c. versus the United States: The case of the Danish Brig the Hope, and Cargo, with the proceedings thereon. [1802?]

Sabin 96,930A

2.05 Federal Claims Commissions

(1) William Cunningham & Company's Claim, 1798

(a) The Claim and Answer, in the case of William Cunningham & Co. against The United States; under the sixth article of the Treaty of Amity, Commerce and Navigation, between his Brittanic Majesty and the United States of America. Philadelphia: Printed By John Fenno. M,DCC,XCVIII. 183 p. 4to.

BLM, DLC, MBAt, MHi, MWA*, MiU-C, NN, PHi, PPL, PU-L, Vi

Evans 34,906

(b) The reply of William Cunningham & Co. to the answer of the United States to their Claim and Memorial. Philadelphia: Printed by James Humphreys, 1798. 36 p. 8vo.

DLC, MBAt, MWA*, NN, NNC-L, PHi, PPL, PU-L, RPJCB, Vi

Evans 34,906

(2) Inglis's Claim, 1798

(a) Commissioners' Office, Philadelphia, May 21, 1798. In the Case of the Right Reverend Charles Inglis. . . . [Philadelphia 1798] Broadside 23 x 19 cm.

NN*

mp. 48,648 Bristol B10,268 New York Public 1,228

(b) Commissioners' Office, 19th February, 1799. Present. Mr. MacDonald, Mr. Rich, Mr. Fitzsimons, Mr. Sitgreaves, Mr. Guillemard. In the Case of the Right Reverend Charles Inglis . . . . ["In the case of Samuel Brailsford," p. 60; "In the case of Joseph Anderson," p. 62 "In the case of Daniel Dulaney," p. 63.] 63 p. 8vo.

PHi, RPJCB*

mp. 48,222 Bristol B10,744

(c) Commissioners' Office, Philadelphia, July 31st, 1799. Present. Mr. MacDonald, Mr. Rich, Mr. Fitzsimons, Mr. Sitgreaves, Mr. Guillemard. In the Case of the Right Reverend Charles Inglis . . . . [Philadelphia: Printed by Humphreys? 1799] 40 p. 8vo.

DLC, MBAt, NN, PHi

Part of (d) below?

(d) The Claim and Answer with the Subsequent Proceedings, in the case of the Right Reverend Charles Inglis, against The United States; under the sixth article of the Treaty of Amity, Commerce and Navigation, between his Britannic Majesty and the United States of America. Philadelphia: Printed by R. Aitken, No. 22, Market-Street. MDCCXCIX. 151 p. 8vo.

CSmH, DLC, MBAt, MHi, MWA*, MiU-C, NHi, NN, NjHi, PHi, PPAmP, RPJCB

Evans 36,504 (Book has apparent error as to printer)

(3) Allen's Claim, 1799

(a) The Claim and Answer with the Subsequent Proceedings in the case of Andrew Allen, Esquire, against The United States. Under the sixth article of the Treaty of Amity, Commerce and Navigation, between his Britannic Majesty and the United States of America. Philadelphia: Printed by James Humphreys, opposite the Bank of the United States. 1799. 50 p. 8vo.

CaOOA, DLC, MBAt, MHi, MWA*, MiU-C, NN(2), PHi, PPAmP

Evans 36,503

(4) Commissioners under Jay Treaty, 1799

(a) [Pages 19-26 of a pamphlet with no other pages contains the following reports: Claim of W. R. Lidderdale for Thomas Mann Randolph; Clark, Administrator of Russel, for the Debt of J. Dorsey; In the Case of John Bowman, and others, surviving partners of Spiers, Bowman and Co.; In the Case of George Anderson, surviving Partner of Anderson & Horseburgh]

DLC (Manuscripts Division)

(5) Commissioners Opinions, 1800

(a) A Brief Statement of Opinions, given in the Board of Commissioners, under the Sixth Article of the Treaty of Amity, Commerce, and Navigation, with Great Britain: With An Appendix, containing certain articles of the Treaties with Great-Britain; the Commissions under the said Sixth Article of the Treaty of Amity:--And References to Opinions Delivered by Judges of the Supreme and circuit Courts of the United States; By one of the Commissioners under the said Sixth Article. Philadelphia: Printed by James Humphries, No. 106, South Side of Market-Street. 1800. 71 p.

DLC

3.00

American Trials and Cases Principally Published in England

3.02 Massachusetts

(1) Hutchinson's 1637, Antinomian Trial, 1644

(a) Antinomians and Familists Condemned By the Synod of Elders in New England; With the Proceedings of the Magistrates against them, And their Apology for the same. Together with A Memorable example of God's Judgement upon some of those Persons magistrated against. London. Printed for Ralph Smith at the signe of the Bible in Corn hill near the Royall Exchange. 1644. 66 p. 4to.

BLM, BDT, CSmH, CtHT-W, CtY, MB, MH, NN, P, RPB, RPJCB

Church 465 Wing W-3,094

(a.2) A Short Story of the Rise, reign, and ruin of the Antinomians, Familists & Libertines, that infected the Churches of New England: And how they were confuted by the Assembly of Ministers there: As also of the Magistrates proceedings in Court against them. Together with Gods strange and remarkable judgements from Heaven upon some of the chief fomenters of these Opinions; And the lamentable death of Ms. Hutchison, Very fit for these times; being here the same errours amongst us, and acted by the same spirit. Published at the instant request of sundry, by one that was an eye and earewitnesse of the carriage of matters there . . . London, Printed for Ralph Smith at the signe of the Bible in Cornhill neare the Royall Exchange. [John Winthrop or Thomas Welde] 1644. 66 p. 4to.

BDT, BEN, BLM, BMR, BOB, CSmH, CtY, DLC. ICN, MBAt, MH, MHi, MSaE, MWA, MiU-C, N, NHi, NN, RHi, RPJCB

Sabin 104,848   Church 466   Wing W-1,269

(a.3) London, Printed for Tho. Parkhurst, at the Bible and Three Crowns at the lower end of Cheapside, near Mercer's Chappel, 1692.

BCU, BLC, BLM, BOB, CtY, DLC, ICN, MH, MWiW-C, MiU-C, PHi, RPJCB

Sabin 104,849   Wing W-1,270

Note: David D. Hall, The Antinomian Controversy (1968), at page 200 says, "A third edition, reset, was published in 1644, and a fourth in 1692." It is this third edition, according to Hall, that was reprinted by Adams, below (f), and is also reprinted by Hall. Inasmuch as Hall does not report any distinguishing features in the title pages of the second and third editions, only one edition is listed above as (a.2).

(b) Mercurius Americanus, Mr. Welds his Antitype, Or, Massachusetts great Apologie examined, Being Observations upon a Paper styled, A short story of the Rise, Reign, and Ruine of the Familists, Libertines, &c. which infected the Churches of New-England, &c. Wherein some parties therein concerned are vindicated, and the truth generally cleared. By John Wheelwright junior London: Printed, and are to be sold at the Bull near the Castle-Tavern in Cornhill. 1645.

BEN, BLM, BOB, CSmH, MH, RPJCB

Wing W-1,605

(b.2) Charles Bell, ed., John Wheelwright, His Writings 179-228 (Publications of the Prince Society. Boston 1876).

(c) The History of the Colony of Massachusetts-Bay, from the First Settlement thereof in 1628. Until its incorporation with the Colony of Plimouth, Province of Main, &c., by the Charter of King William and Queen Mary in 1691 . . . . [Volume one.] By Mr. Hutchinson, Lieutenant-Governor of the Massachusetts Province. Boston, New-England: Printed by Thomas & John Fleet, at the Heart and Crown in Cornhill. MDCCLXIV. 574 p. 8vo.

CSmH, MB, MBAt, MWA*, MiU-C, NN(2), NjR, RPJCB, ViW

Evans 9,705   Sabin 34,075

(c.2) The Second Edition. London: Printed for M. Richardson, in Paternoster Row. M DCCLXV. [Some copies erroneously dated MDCCLX] 566 p.

CSmH, KWi, MSaE, MWiW, MiU-C, NN, NNPM, NjP, NjR (both variants), P, PBL, PHi, PPL, RPB, ViU(2), ViW

Sabin 34,076 Church 1,032

(c.3) The Third Edition. With additional notes and corrections. Printed at Salem, by Thomas C. Cushing, for Thomas and Andrews, No. 45, Newbury-Street, Boston. 1795. 488 p. 8vo.

CSmH, DLC, KWi, MBAt, MBU, MH, MHi, MSaE, MWA*, MWiW-C, MiU-C, NHi, NN, NjP, PHi, PPPRHi, RPB, RPJCB, ViU

Evans 28,878 Sabin 34,077 Tapley p. 359

(c.4) The History of New England from 1630 to 1649. By John Winthrop, Esq. . . . By James Savage, . . . A New Edition. Vol I. . . . Boston M DCCC LIII

(c.5) Lawrence Shaw Mayo, ed., 1 <u>History of the Colony and Province of Massachusetts-Bay. By Thomas Hutchinson. Edited from the author's own copies of volumes I and II and his Mss. of volume III, with a memoir and additional notes</u> 49-67 (Cambridge 1936).

(c.6) <u>Anne Hutchinson in Massachusetts. From Governor Hutchinson's History of Massachusetts Bay.</u> (Old South Leaflets, General Series, Vol. 8, No. 178. Boston 1907).

(d) "Appendix II: The Examination of Mrs. Hutchinson at the court at Newtown," The History of the Province of Massachusetts-Bay from the Charter of King William and Queen Mary, in 1691, until the year 1750. By Mr. Hutchinson, Lieutenant-Governor of the Province. [Volume Two] Boston, New England: Printed by Thomas & John Fleet, in Cornhill, and sold in Union-Street, opposite to the Cornfield. MDCCLXVII. 547 p. 8vo.

KWi, MB, MSaE, MWA*, NN(2), PPL, RPJCB, ViW

Evans 10,658 Sabin 34,078

(d.2) The Second Edition. [482-520] London: Printed by J. Smith near Wellclose-Square; for G. Kearsly, at No. 1 in Ludgate-Street; and W. Davenhill, at No. 8 in Cornhill. MDCCLXVIII. 540 p.

MSaE, MWiW, MdBJ-G, NN, NjP, RPB, PHi, ViU(3), ViW

Sabin 34,079

(d.3) "Appendix II," History of Massachusetts, from the First Settlement Thereof in 1628, until the year 1750. By Thomas Hutchinson, Esq. Late Governor of Massachusetts . . . . In Two Volumes. Vol. II. The Third Edition. With additional Notes and Corrections. [423-47] Printed at Boston. By Manning and Loring. For Thomas and Andrews, No. 45, Newbury-Street, Boston, 1795. 452 p.

DLC, DGU, KWi, MB, MBAt, MBU, MH, MHi, MSaE, MWA*, MWiW-C, NHi, NN, RPJCB, ViU

Evans 28,879 Sabin 34,080

(d.4) The History of New England from 1630 to 1649. By John Winthrop, Esq. . . . By James Savage, . . . A New Edition. Vol II . . . . Boston M DCCC LIII

(d.5) Lawrence Shaw Mayo, ed., 1 History of the Colony and Province of Massachusetts-Bay. By Thomas Hutchinson. Edited from the author's own copies of volumes I and II of his Mss. of volume III, with a memoir and additional notes 366-91 (Cambridge 1936).

(e) Peleg W. Chandler, ed., "Trial of Anne Hutchinson before the General Court of Massachusetts for sedition and heresy," 1 American Criminal Trials. 1-29 (Boston 1841).

Sabin 11,868

(f) "A Report of the Trial of Ann Hutchinson before the Church in Boston, March, 1638" Massachusetts Historical Society, 4 Proceedings, Second Series 1887-89 159-91 (Boston 1889).

(g) Charles Francis Adams, Three Episodes of Massachusetts History (Boston 1892).

(h) Charles Francis Adams, ed., "Antinomianism in the Colony of Massachusetts Bay," 21 Prince Society Publications (Boston 1894).

(i) Winnifred K. Rugg, Unafraid, A Life of Anne Hutchinson (Boston 1930).

(j) Perry Miller, Orthodoxy in Massachusetts, 1630-1650 (Cambridge 1933).

(k) Edward S. Morgan, "The Case Against Anne Hutchinson," 10 New England Quarterly 675-97 (1937).

(l) Emery Battis, <u>Saints and Sectaries: Anne Hutchinson and the Antinomian Controversy in the Massachusetts Bay Colony</u> (Chapel Hill 1962).

(m) David E. Hall, <u>The Antinomian Controversy, 1636-38</u> (Middletown 1968).

(n) William K. Stoever, <u>A Faire & Easie Way to Heaven: Covenant Theology & Antinomianism in Early Massachusetts</u> (New York 1978).

(2) Quakers, General Court, 1659

(a) A Declaration of the General Court of the Massachusetts Holden at Boston in New-England, October 18, 1659. Concerning the Execution of two Quakers . . . Cambridge. Printed by Samuel Green. 1659. Broadside

No copy located

Evans 51 (Erroneously listed under 1658)

(a.2) Printed by their order in New-England. Edward Rawson, Secretary. Reprinted in London, 1659.

BLM, BOB, MH

Wing M-1,001

(a.2.a) Massachusetts Historical Society, Americana Series No. 194 (1927).

(a.3) A true Relation of the Proceedings against certain Quakers, at the generall Court of the Massachusetts holden at Boston in New-England October. 18. 1659. . . . Edward Rawson Secret. London Printed by A.W. 1660. Broadside

BLM, CSmH

Wing T-3,019

(a.3.a) Massachusetts Historical Society, Americana Series No. 194 (1927).

(b) The Heart of New-England Rent at the Blasphemies of the present Generation; or a brief Tractate, concerning the Doctrine of the Quakers, Demonstrating the destructive nature thereof, to Religion, the Churches, and the State; with consideration of the Remedy against it, p. 2 by John Norton Teacher of the Church of Christ at Boston. Printed by J.H. for John Allen at the Rising Sunne in St. Pauls Church-yard. London 1660.

<u>Note</u>: The source of this entry is <u>Powers</u>, below 3.02(2)(n), 323 at note 9.

(c) The Humble Petition and Address Of the General Court sitting at Boston in New-England, unto the High and Mighty Prince Charles The Second. And presented unto his Most-Gracious Majesty Feb. 11, 1660. Printed in the Year 1660. [London] 8 p. 4to.

BLM, BOB, CSmH, CtY, MB, MBAt, MH, MHi, NN, RPJCB

Sabin 33,696 Church 566 Wing H-3,426

Evans Ghost 61

(d) A Declaration of the Sad and Great Persecution and Martyrdom Of the People of God, called Quakers, in New-England, for the Worshipping of God. Whereof 22 have been Banished upon pain of Death. 03 have been Martyred. 03 have had their Right-Ears out. 01 hath been burned in the Hand with the letter H. 31 Persons have received 650 Stripes. 01 was beat while his Body was like a jelly. Several were beat with Pitched Ropes. Five Appeals made to England, were denied by the Rulers of Boston. One thousand forty-four pounds worth of Goods hath been taken from them (being poor men) for meeting together in the fear of the Lord, and for keeping the Command of Christ. One now lyeth in Ironfetters, condemned to dye. Also, Some Considerations, presented to the King, which is in Answer to a Petition and Address, which was presented unto Him by the General Court at Boston: Subscribed by J. Endicot, the Chief Persecutor there; thinking thereby to cover themselves from the Blood of the Innocent. [By Edmund Burroughs] . . . London, Printed for Robert Wilson, in Martins Le Grand. [1660] 32 p.4to.

BBB, BLF, BLM, CSmH, CtSo-P, DLC, MB, MWi-C, N, NN, PHC, PHi, RPJCB

Sabin 9,455 Church 563 Wing B-5,994

(e) An Examination of the grounds of causes which are said to induce the Court of Boston in New England to make that order or law of banishment upon pain of death against the Quakers . . . As also of some further grounds for justifying of the same, in an appendix to John Norton's book . . . and likewise of the arguments briefly hinted in that which is called, a true relation of the proceedings against the Quakers, etc. Isaac Penington, the Younger. Printed for L. Lloyd next to the Sign of the Castle in Cornhill. London 1660 4to.

BBB, BCU, BEU, BLF, BLM, CSmH, CtY, MH, MWiW-C, MiU-C, PHC, RPJCB

Wing P-1,166

(f) New England Judged, Not by Man's but the Spirit of the Lord: And the Summe sealed up of New Englands Persecutions. Being a Brief Relation of the Sufferings of the People called Quakers in those parts of America, from the beginning of the

Fifth Moneth 1656 (the time of their first Arrival at Boston from England) to the later end of the Tenth Moneth, 1660. Wherein the Cruel Whippings and Scourgings, Bonds and Imprisonments, Beatings and Chainings, Starvings and Hunting, Fines and Confiscation of Estates, Burning in the Hand and Cutting of Ears, Orders of Sale for Bond-men, and Bond-women, Banishment upon pain of Death, and Putting to Death of those People, are Shortly touched; With a Relation of the Manner, and Some of the Other most Material Proceedings; and a Judgement thereupon. In Answer to a Certain Printed Paper, Intituled, A Declaration of the General Court of the Massachusetts holden at Boston, the 19. October, 1658. Apoligizing for the same. By George Bishope . . . . London. Printed for Robert Wilson, in Martins Le Grand, 1661.
198 p. 4to.

BBB-N, BCT, BLF, BLM, BOB, CSmH, CtSoP(2), CtY, DLC, MB, MH, MSaE, MdBJ-G, NN, NNUT, PBL, PHi, PSC-Hi, RPJCB

Sabin 5,628, 5,629, and 5,630 Baer 53 Church 571
Garrett 35 Wing B-3,003

(g) New England Judged. The Second Part. Being a Relation of the Cruel and bloody Sufferings of the People called Quakers, in the Jurisdiction chiefly of the Massachusetts; Beginning with the Sufferings of William Ledra, whom they murthered, and hung upon a Tree at Boston, the 14th of the first month, 1660/1. barely for being such a one as is called a Quaker, and coming within their Jurisdiction; And ending with the Sufferings of Edward Wharton, the 3d month, 1665. And the remarkable Judgements of God in the Death of John Endicot, Governour, John Norton, High Priest, and Humphrey Adderton, Major General. By George Bishope . . . . London, Printed in the Year, 1667. 148 p. 4to.

BBB-N, BLF, BLM, BOB, CSmH, CtSoP, CtY, IU, MH, MdBJ-G, NN, NNUT, PBL, PHC, PSC-Hi, RPJCB

Sabin 5,630 Baer 62 Church 598 Wing B-3004

(h) Several Epistles Given forth by Two of the Lords Faithful Servants, Whom he sent to New-England, to Bear Witness to his Everlasting Truth. And were there (by the Priests, Rulers, and Professors) after cruel and long Imprisonment, and inhumane Whippings and Banishment, put to death; for no other Cause, but for keeping the Commandments of God, and Testimony of Jesus. William Robinson. William Leddra. Here is also perfixed (sic) W.R. his Testimony of his Call to that Service, for obedience unto which, he underwent the wrath of Men, but hath obtained Everlasting Peace and Rest with God . . . . London, Printed in the Year, 1669 12 p. 4to.

BBB, BLF, BLM, BOB, CSmH, CtY, MB, MH, N, NN, RPJCB

Sabin 72,199 Church 607 Wing R-1,722

(i) Ellis Hookes, An Addition to the Book, Entitled, The Spirit of the Martyrs Revived. London 1682.

Note For source see above 3.02(2)(b), note at p. 345 and note 68.

(j) [Daniel Gould] A Brief narration of the sufferings of the People Called Quakers; who were put to Death at Boston in New-England. Also An account from their own hands, of their Coming to Boston, and of their staying in their jurisdiction after Banishment. With A Precious Epistle of William Robinson, to us his fellow-Prisoners, and other Epistles hereunto Annexed. . . . [Philadelphia 1700] 35 p. 4to.

BLF, MHi*, RPJCB (imp.)

Evans 911 Sabin 28,099 RPJCB 4th p. 413
Wing G-1,415

(j.2) Massachusetts Historical Society, Americana Series No. 55 (Boston 1921).

(k) New England Judged. . . Printed and sold by T. Sowle, in White-Hart Court in Gracious-Street. London 1703.

MSaE, MdBJ-G, MiU-C

(l) Peleg W. Chandler, ed., "Trials of the Quakers before the General Court and Court of Assistants, Massachusetts, 1656-1661," 1 American Criminal Trials 31-64 (Boston 1841).

Sabin 11,868

(m) John D. Lawson, "The Trials of the Quakers William Robinson, Marmaduke Stevenson Dyer, and others, Massachusetts, 1659 1 American State Trials 813-24 (St. Louis 1914).

(n) Edwin Powers, "Ch. 10 Quakers and Their 'Damnable Heresies'," Crime and Punishment in Early Massachusetts 1620-1692: A Documentary History 321-66 (Boston 1966).

(3) Checkley's 1724 Deist Trial, 1730

(a) The Short and Easy Method with the Deists: To which is added, A Discourse concerning Episcopacy; In Defence of Christianity, and the Church of England, against the Deists and Dissenters. . .

Note See (b) below. No American edition dating 1730 or earlier is known. The first English edition was published in 1698, with the title, "A Short and Easie Method with the Deists. Wherein the truth of the Christian religion is demonstrated. . ." This was followed by other English editions with variant titles following the basic, "A Short and Easy Method with the Deists." The first known American edition, and having such a variant title, is "The Fifth Edition. Printed and Sold by William Parks, at his Printing-Offices, in Williamsburg, and Annapolis, 1733. This is Evans 3,675, the DLC copy being reproduced on the microcard. Later 18th century American editions are Evans 17,999 (1783); mp. 47,822, Bristol B9,594 (1796); Evans 32,373 (1797); mp. 48,166, Bristol B9,990 (1797), with Evans 5,619 and 33,993 probably being ghosts.

James Grindlay, South Carolina lawyer who died in 1765, owned a copy of "A Short and Easy Method with the Deists & Jews" which was valued at 5 shillings in the inventory of his estate. Herbert Johnson, Imported Eighteenth Century Law Treatises in American Libraries 1700-1799 75 (Knoxville, Tennessee 1798).

(b) The Speech of Mr. John Checkley upon his Tryal, At Boston in New-England, For Publishing The Short and Easy Method with the Deists: To which is added, A Discourse concerning Episcopacy; In Defence of Christianity, and the Church of England, against the Deists and Dissenters . . . To which is added: The Jury's Verdict, His Plea in Arrest of Judgment; and the sentence of Court. London: J. Welford. 1730.

MB, MBAt, MH, MWA, NN, PPPrHi, RPJCB

Sabin 12,365

(b.2) The second edition. London: Printed by J. Applebee, in Bolt-Court, Fleet Street. M.DCC.XXXVIII.

CtHT-W, DLC, ICN, MB, MSaE, MWA, MiU-C, NN, PPL, RHi, RNR, ViW

(b.3) The Speech of Mr. John Checkley, upon his trial at Boston, in 1724. (Morrisania, New York 1868).

(c) Edmund Farwell Slafter, John Checkley: or the Evolution of Religious Tolerance in Massachusetts bay. 2 vols. (The Prince Society. Boston 1897).

3.04 Connecticut

(1) Moheagan Indians 1743 Proceedings, 1769

(a) Governor and Company of Connecticut, and Moheagan Indians, by their Guardians. Certified Copy of Book of Proceedings before Commissioners of Review, MDCCXLIII. London: Printed by W. and J. Richardson. MDCCLXIX 283 p. 27.5 cm.

CtHi

(b) 4 Acts of Privy Council of England, Colonial Series 723-24 (1911); 5 Id. 218 (1912).

3.05 New York

(1) Atwood's Case, 1703

(a) The case of William Atwood, Esq; By the late King William of Glorious Memory, constituted Chief Justice of the Province of New York in America, and Judge of the Admiralty there, and in neighbouring colonies. With a true account of the government and people of that Province; particularly of Bayard's Faction, and the treason for which he and Hutchins stand attainted; but reprieved before the Lord Cornbury's arrival, upon acknowledging their offences, and begging pardon. London: Printed in the Year MDCCIII. 8vo.

DLC, MdBB, MiU-C, NN

Sabin 2,346

(a.2) 13 Collections of the New-York Historical Society for the Year 1880 237-319 (1881).

Note See also 1.05(2).

(2) Revolutionary Conspiracy of 1776, 1786

(a) Minutes of the Trial and Examination of certain persons, in the Province of New York, Charged with being engaged in a Conspiracy against the Authority of the Congress, and the Liberties of America. London: Printed for J. Bew, No. 28, Pater-Noster Row, MDCCLXXXVI [Price One Shilling] 46 p. 8vo.

BLM, CSmH, DLC, MiU-C, NN, PHi, RPJCB, ViU

Sabin 49,386 Adams Controversy 76-97 Church 1,134

(b) Minutes of A Conspiracy Against the Liberties of America. Philadelphia: John Campbell. MDCCCLXV.

Sabin 49,387

(3) Gordon's English Court Martial, 1781

(a) The Trial of Lieut. Col. Thomas, Of The First Regiment Of Foot-Guards, On A Charge Exhibited By Lieut. Col. Cosmo Gordon, For aspersing his Character, By accusing him of Neglect of Duty before the Enemy, as Commanding Officer of the First Battalion of Guards, on the 23d of June, 1780, near Springfield, in the Jerseys: Containing The Whole Proceedings Of A General Court-Martial, Held at New-York on the 16th of September last, and continued by several

Adjournments to the 26th of the same Month. London: Printed for J. Ridley, in St. James's Street. MDCCLXXXI 119 p. 8vo.

BLM, CSmH, CtY, DLC, ICN, InU, LNT, MiU-C, NN, PHi, RPJCB

Sabin 95,390 Adams Controversy 81-70

(b) The Trial Of The Hon. Col. Cosmo Gordon, Of The United Regiment Of Foot-Guards, For Neglect of Duty before the Enemy, On the 23rd of June, 1780, Near Springfield, in the Jerseys: Containing The Whole Proceedings Of A General Court-Martial, Held at the City of New-York on the 22nd of August, and continued by several Adjournments to the 4th of September, 1782. London: Printed for Geo. Harlow (late Mr. Ridley's) St. James's Street. MDCCLXXXVIII. 146 p. 8vo.

BLM, CSmH, CtY, DLC, ICN, InU, MB, MH, MiU-C, NN, RPJCB

Sabin 27,972 Adams Controversy 83-36

3.06 New Jersey

(1) Fenwick v. Edridge & Warner, 1675

(a) Friends, These are to satisfie you, . . . that we shall no doubt find, but that New Cesarea or New Jersey, which is the place which I did purchase: together with the Government thereof, is a healthy, pleasant, and plentiful Country: . . . and the character given thereof, by John Ogliby in his America, which I herewith send . . . dated this 8th of the 1st month, 1675. [By John Fenwick] 1 p. fol.

NcAsS, PHi

Sabin 24,081 Vail 164

(b) A Testimony against John Fenwick, concerning his Proceedings about New-Cesaria, or New-Jersey, in the Province of America: Also John Fenwick's Letter of Condemnation sent to Friends; upon their Testifying against his Proceedings. [London 1675] 1 p. fol.

BLF

Sabin 24,082 Vail 165 Wing T-804

(c) The True State of the Case between John Fenwick, Esq., and John Edridge & Edmund Warner, concerning Mr. Fenwick's Ten Parts of his Land in West-New-Jersey, in America. London: Printed in the Year 1677. [Signed Edm. Saunders] 11 p.

PHi

See Evans 9,970 cf. Sabin 24,083 Vail 183

(d) [The Same] And, Philadelphia, Re-printed by Andrew Steuart for John Hart, MDCCLXV. 8 p. 8vo.

PHi*

Evans 9,970 Sabin 24,083 Hildeburn 2,176 Vail 560

3.07 Pennsylvania

(1) Keith's Case, 1726

(a) The Case of the Heir at Law and Executrix of the late Proprietor of Pennsylvania, &c. in Relation to the Removal of Sir William Keith, and the Appointing Major Patrick Gordon to succeed him as Deputy-Governor there. [Philadelphia: Printed by Andrew Bradford 1726] 16 p.

DLC, MWA*, PHi

Evans 2,735 Sabin 59,959 Hildeburn 270

Note The attribution to Andrew Bradford and a Philadelphia printing is seemingly inconsistent with the "there" in the title of the pamphlet.

(a.2) Massachusetts Historical Society, Americana Series No. 101 (1923).

(b) A Just and Plain Vindication of Sir William Keith, Bart. Late Governour of Pennsilvania, From the Untruths and Aspersions contained in a Paper, Printed at London, and now Reprinting at Philadelphia, under the Title of The Case of the Heir at Law and Executrix of the late Proprietor of Pennsylvania, &c. . . . [by Sir William Keith? Philadelphia: Printed by Samuel Keimer? 1726.] 10 p. fol.

DLC, NN*, PHi, PPAmP, PPL, RPJCB

Evans 2,753 Hildeburn 279

(b.2) A Just and Plain Vindication of Sir William Kieth (sic), Bart. Late Governour of Pensilvania, From the Untruths and Aspersions contain'd in a Paper printed at London, under the Title of The Case of the Heir at Law and Executrix of the late Proprietor of Pensilvania, &c. Printed in the Year 1726. 31 p.

PPL*

Evans 2,754 Hildeburn 278

(c) A more Just Vindication Of the Honourable Sir William Keith, Bart. Against the unparalleled Abuses put upon him, in a Scandalous Libel call'd, A Just and plain Vindication of Sir William Keith, &c. . . . [Philadelphia: Printed by Andrew Bradford. 1726] 4 p. fol.

DLC, NN*, PHi, PPAmP, RPJCB

Evans 2,759 Hildeburn 283

(d) Remarks on Sir William Keiths Vindication. . . . [By James Logan. Philadelphia: Printed by Andrew Bradford. 1726] 24 + p. 8vo.

PHi*(imp.)

Evans 2,808 Hildeburn 288

3.09 Maryland

(1) Lord Baltimore's Case, 1653

(a) The Lord Baltemore's Case, Concerning the Province of Maryland, adjoyning to Virginia in America. With full and clear Answers to all material Objections, touching his Rights, Jurisdiction, and Proceedings there. And certain Reasons of state, why the Parliament should not impeach the same. Unto which is also annexed a true copy of a Commission from the late King's Eldest Son, to Mr. William Davenant, to dispossess the Lord Baltemore of the said Province, because of his adherence to this Common-Wealth. London, Printed in the Yeare, 1653. 20 p. 4to.

BLM, MHi, MdHi, NN

Baer 38 Clayton-Torrence 70 Garrett 22
Wing L-3,040

(a.2) Clayton Colman Hall, Narratives of Early Maryland, 1633-1684 161-80 (New York 1910).

(a.2.a) Reprinted in 1925.

(b) Virginia and Maryland. or, The Lord Baltamore's Printed Case, uncased and answered Shewing, the illegality of his Patent and usurpation of Royal Jurisdiction and Dominion there. With, the Injustice and Tyranny practiced in the Government, against the Laws and Liberties of the English Nation, And the just Right and Interest of the Adventurers and Planters . . . . London, printed, and are to be sold at the Crown in Popes-head-Alley, and in Westminister Hall, 1655. 52 p. 4to.

BLM, CSmH, MH(imp.), MdBJ-G, PHi

Sabin 100,546 Baer 45 Church 541A
Clayton-Torrence 73 Garrett 23 Wing F-1,457

(b.2) Clayton Colman Hall, Narratives of Early Maryland, 1633-1684 181-230 (New York 1910).

(b.2.a) Reprinted 1925.

(b.3) 2 Peter Force, Tracts, No. 9 (Washington, D.C. 1838).

(b.4) Massachusetts Historical Society, Americana Series No. 137 (1925).

3.10 Virginia

(1) Lord Baltimore's Case, 1653

See above 3.09(1).

(2) Hellier's 1678 Execution for Murder, 1680.

(a) The Vain Prodigal Life, and Tragical Penitent Death of Thomas Hellier Born at Whitchurch near Lyme in Dorset-shire: Who for Murdering his Master, Mistress, and a Maid was Executed according to Law at Westover in Charles City, in the Country of Virginia, neer the Plantation called Hard Labour, where he perpetrated the said Murders. He suffer'd on Munday the 5th of August, 1678. And was after Hanged up in Chains at Windmill-Point on James River. London: Printed for Sam. Crouch, at the Princes Arms, a corner-shop of Popes-head-alley in Cornhil, 1680. 43 p. 21.5 cm.

CSmH, DLC, NN(2), RPJCB, Vi, ViHi, ViU

Sabin 31,252 Clayton-Torrence 86 McDade 467
RPJCB 4th p. 76-77 Swem 5,861 Wing V-19

(a.2) 1 Plantation and Frontier Documents: 1649-1863 357-65 (Ulrich B. Phillips, ed., Cleveland 1909) (Extract only.)

(b) T. H. Breen, James H. Lewis, and Keith Schlesinger, "Motive for Murder: A Servant's Life in Virginia, 1678," 40 William and Mary Quarterly (3d Series) 106-20 (1983).

3.12 South Carolina

(1) Bonnet's 1718 Trial for Piracy, 1719

(a) The Tryals of Major Stede Bonnet, and other Pirates, Viz Robert Tucker, Edward Robinson, Neal Paterson, William Scot, Job Bayley, John William Smith, Thomas Carman, John Thomas, William Morrison, William Livers alias Evis, Samuel Booth, William Hewet, John Levit, William Eddy alias Nedy, Alexander Annand, George Ross, George Dunkin, John Ridge, Matthew King, Daniel Perry, Henry Virgin, James Robbins, James Mullet alias Mullet, Thomas Price, John Lopez, Zachariah Long, James Wilson, John Brierly, and Robert Boyd. Who were all condemn'd for Piracy. As also The Tryals of Thomas Nichols, Rowland Sharp, Jonathan Clarke, and Thomas Gerrat, for Piracy, who were Acquitted, at the Admiralty Sessions held at Charles-Town, in the Province of South Carolina, on Tuesday the 28th of October, 1718. and by several adjournments continued to Wednesday the 12th of November, following. To which is Prefix'd, an Account of the Taking of the said Major Bonnet, and the rest of the Pirates. London: Printed for Benj. Cowse at the Rose and Crown in St. Paul's Church-Yard. M.DCC.XIX.

CSmH, DLC, MH, MH-L, NN, NjP

Sabin 6,326 Turnbull p. 57

(b) "Chap. IV. Of Major Stede Bonnet, And his Crew," A General History of the Robberies and Murders Of the most notorious Pyrates, and also Their Policies, Discipline and Government, From their first Rise and Settlement in the Island of Providence, in 1717, to the present Year 1724 . . . . By Captain Charles Johnson. [60-86] London, Printed for Ch. Rivington at the Bible and Crown in St. Paul's Church-Yard, J. Lacy at the Ship near the Temple-Gate, and J. Stone near the Crown Coffee-house in the back of the Greys-Inn, 1724.

Note See above 1.02(4)(c) Note.

(c) "Appendix to the First Volume, Of Major Bonnet," A General History of the Robberies and Murders of the most notorious Pyrates. . . Vol. II. By Capt. Charles Johnson. . . 320-23, above 1.02(4)(c).

(d) "CLXXXVI. The Trials of Major Stede Bonnet and Thirty Three others, at the Court of Vice-Admiralty at Charles-Town in South-Carolina, for Piracy, Octob. 30, &c. 1718. 5 Geo. I., A Complete Collection of State-Trials, and Proceedings upon High-Treason, and other Crimes and Misdemeanours; from The Reign of King Richard II. To The End of the Reign of King George I. The Sixth Volume. With an Alphabetical Table to the two Supplemental Volumes. [156-88] London: Printed in the Year M.DCC.XXX.

DLC, NcAsS, ViU

Sowerby 1,951

Note The report of Bonnet's Trial in State Trials was one of the authorities relied on by John Adams in his representation of the defendant in Rex v. Corbet. L. Kinvin Wroth and Hiller B. Zobel, eds., 2 Legal Papers of John Adams 276 at 284 and 287 (Cambridge 1965)

(d.2) "CLXXXIX," The Fourth Edition. Volume the Sixth. cols. 155-88 (London 1777).

(d.3) Thomas B. Howell, "Case No. 457," 15 A Complete Collection of State Trials. cols. 1231-1302 (London 1816).

(e) John D. Lawson, ed., "The Trials of Major Stede Bonnet and Thirty-Three others for Piracy. Charleston, South Carolina, 1718," 4 American State Trials 652-722 (St. Louis 1915).

3.20 United States

(1) American Cases, 1790

(a) "Ch. X: Late judicial determinations in the courts of the United States, and in the Courts of Westminster Hall, relating to the United States, &c. &c.," A Review of the Laws of the United States of North America, the British Provinces, and West India Islands: with Select Precedents and Observations upon Divers Acts of Parliament and Acts of Assembly and a comparison of the Courts of Law and Practice there with that of Westminster Hall. [162-88] London: Printed for William Otridge, No. 134, and John Otridge, No. 158, in the Strand. M,DCC,XC.

CSmH, MBAt, MiU-L, NN, PU-L, RPB

4.00

Grand Jury Charges and Petitions

4.05 New York

(1) Chief Justice's Charge, New York City, 1727

(a) The Charge Given by The Chief Justice Of The Province of New-York, To The Grand Jury Of The City of New-York, In March Term, 1726-7. Printed at the Request of the said Grand Jury. New York, Printed and sold by John Peter Zenger, 1727. (pr. 6d.) 19 p. 4to.

PHi*

Evans 2,933 Rutherfurd p. 139, No. 2

(2) De Lancey's Charge, City and County of New York, 1734

(a) The Charge of The Honourable James De Lancey, Esq; Chief Justice of the Province of New-York, to the Gentlemen of the Grand-Jury for the City and County of New-York, on Tuesday the 15th Day of January, Annoq; Domini 1733. Printed at the Request of the Grand-Jury. . . . [Colophon] New-York, Printed and Sold by William Bradford 1733. 6 p. fol.

DLC, NN*, PHi, PPL

Evans 3,696 Sabin 19,340

(b) Some Observations on the Charge given by the Honourable James De Lancey, Esq; Chief Justice of the Province of New-York, to the Grand Jury, the 15th day of January, 1733. . . . [Colophon] New-York, Printed and sold by J. Peter Zenger, Price Is. 1733-4. 18 p. fol.

CSmH, DLC, NHi, NN*

Evans 3,835 Sabin 84,557 and 19,341
Rutherfurd p. 149, No. 2

Note Authorship attributed by Prof. Osgood to William Smith and James Alexander and by Livingston Rutherfurd to Lewis Morris.

(3) De Lancey's Charge, 1734

(a) The Charge of the Honourable James DeLancey, Esq. Chief Justice of the Province of New-York, to the gentlemen of the grand jury, July 1734. [New-York: Printed by William Bradford. 1734]

N (Lost in Fire)

Evans 3,811 Sabin 19,342

(4) De Lancey's Charge, City and County of New York, 1734

(a) The Charge of The Honourable James De Lancey, Esqr. Chief Justice of the Province of New-York, to The Gentlemen of the Grand-Jury for the City and County of New-York, on Tuesday the 15th of October, 1734. . . . Printed at the Request of the said Grand-Jurors. . . . [Colophon] Printed and Sold by William Bradford in New-York, 1734. 8 p. fol.

NN*

Evans 3,812

(5) Jay's Charge, Ulster County, 1777

(a) The Charge delivered by The Honourable John Jay, Esq; Chief Justice, of the State of New-York, to the Grand Jury, at the Supreme Court, Held in Kingston, in Ulster County, September 9, 1777. Kingston: Printed by John Holt, Printer to the State of New-York. 12 p.

MH, MHi*

Evans 15,376 Sabin 35,831 Vail
Patriotic Pair p. 403

(a.2) Hezekiah Niles, ed., Principles and Acts of the Revolution in America 62-64. (Baltimore 1822).

(a.3) Hezekiah Niles, ed., Centennial Offering Re-publication of the Principles and Acts of the Revolution in America 180-82 (Samuel V. Niles Revision. New York, Chicago, New Orleans, 1876).

(6) Mayor's Charge, City and County of New York, 1788

(a) Charge of his honour the mayor of New York, delivered to the grand jury at the opening of the general sessions of the peace, for the city and county of New York, May 6, 1788, 3 American Museum [June 1788] 530-34, above 1.11(2)(a).

4.06 New Jersey

(1) Grand Jury's Petition, 1736

(a) A Copy Of The Petition of the President, Council, the Speaker and some of the Members of the House of Assembly of New-Jersey, To His Majesty, For a Separate Governor, on the Death of Col. Cosby. Given to His Grace the Duke of New-Castle, Secretary of State, and a Duplicate thereof lodged in the Council Office, the 11th of May, 1736, by Richard Patridge, Agent for the said Province. . . . A Copy Of The Grand Jury's Petition, from New-Jersey, To the King, On the Death of Col. Cosby, for a Separate Governor, March 19. 1735,6, and Received May 11. 1736. And that Day lodg'd in the Council Office by Richard Patridge, Agent for said Province. [New York 1736] 4 p. fol.

NN*

Evans 4,046

(2) Burlington, 1787

(a) Singular Charge of a judge to a grand jury, 2 American Museum [October 1787] 402, above 1.07(9)(a).

(3) Smith's Charge, Gloucester County, 1800

(a) A Charge, Delivered by the Honourable Isaac Smith Esq. Second Justice of the Supreme Court, to the Grand-Jury, Circuit Court holden, at Woodbury, in and for the County of Gloucester, on Tuesday, the seventh day of October, 1800: -- and the Answer of the Grand-Jury to the same. . . . Broadside 46.5 x 40 cm.

NjHi*

Evans 38,517 Morsch 472

4.07 Pennsylvania

(1) Logan's Charge, Philadelphia, 1723

(a) The Charge Delivered from the Bench to the Grand-Jury, At the Court of Quarter Sessions, held for the County of Philadelphia, the second day of September 1723. Published at the Desire of the said Grand-Jury. [By James Logan] Together with Their Address. Philadelphia, Printed and Sold by Andrew Bradford, at the Sign of the Bible, in the Second Street, MDCCXXIII. 16 p. 4to.

CSmH, DLC, MH-L, NHi, NN, NjR, P, PHi*, PP, PPAmP, PPL, RPJCB

Evans 2,441 Sabin 41,793 Hildeburn 206

(2) Norris's Charge, Philadelphia, 1727

(a) The Speech Delivered from the Bench in the Court of Common Pleas held for the City and County of Philadelphia, the 11 day of September, 1727. [By Isaac Norris] [Philadelphia: Printed by Andrew Bradford. 1727] 4 p. fol.

RPJCB*

Evans 2,937 Hildeburn 311

(b) A modest Reply to the Speech of Isaac Norris, Esq; delivered from the Bench, in the Court of Common-Pleas, Held for the City and County of Philadelphia, the 11th Day of September, 1727, and afterwards Printed. [By Sir William Keith] [Philadelphia: Printed by Andrew Bradford. 1727] 4 p. fol.

PPAmP*

Evans 2,890 Hildeburn 309

(c) A Confutation of the Reply to the Speech, &c. . . . [By Isaac Norris] [Philadelphia: Printed by Andrew Bradford. 1727] 4 p. fol.

CSmH*

Evans 2,938 Hildeburn 310

(3) Logan's Charge, Philadelphia, 1733

(a) The latter part of The Charge Delivered from the Bench to the Grand Inquest, at a Court of Oyer and Terminer and Gaol Delivery, held for the City and County of Philadelphia, at Philadelphia the 24th Day of September

1733. Published at the request of said Inquest. With their Address. . . . [Philadelphia: Printed by B. Franklin. 1733] 3 p. fol.

PHi, PU*, NNU-L

Evans 3,711 Hildeburn 463

(4) Logan's Charge, Philadelphia, 1736

(a) The Charge Delivered from the Bench to the Grand Inquest, At a Court of Oyer and Terminer and General Goal-Delivery, held for the City and County of Philadelphia, April 13th, 1736. [By James Logan] Philadelphia; Printed and Sold by B. Franklin. M,DCC,XXXVI. 24 p. sm. 4to.

NN, PHi*, PPL, RPJCB

Evans 4,061 Sabin 41,794 Hildeburn 540

(a.2) Printed at Philadelphia: Re-printed at London, and Sold by J. Roberts, near the Oxford-Arms in Warwick Lane, 1737. [Price Sixpence.] 36 p. 20 cm.

MH-L, MdBJ-G, NN, RPJCB

Sabin 41,795

(a.3) Charge [of the Honourable James Logan, esq.:] delivered from the bench to the grand inquest at a Court of Oyer and Terminer and General Goal-Delivery held for the City and County of Philadelphia, April 13, 1736, [Being a scheme of morals from their first principles in nature.] Printed at Philadelphia, Reprinted at London, and sold by J. Roberts . . . 1737. 35 p. 20 cm.

Sabin 41,795

(5) M'Kean's Charge, York, 1778

(a) A Charge delivered to the Grand-Jury, By the Honourable Thoms M'Kean, Esquire, Chief Justice of Pennsylvania, At a Court of Oyer and Terminer, and General Goal Delivery, held at York, for the County of York, on the 21st Day of April 1778; and published at the special Request of the said Grand-Jury. Lancaster: Printed by Francis Bailey, in King's Street. M,DCC,LXXVIII. 18 p. 8vo.

DLC*

Evans 15,876 Hildeburn 3,738

(6) Philadelphia, 1788

(a) Charge to grand Jury Feb. 13, 1788, 2 Columbian Magazine [February 1788] 101-02, above 1.07(16)(a).

(7) Edwards's Charge, Philadelphia, 1791

(a) Introduction to a Charge Delivered to a Grand Jury for the county of Philadelphia, March 7th. By Enoch Edwards Esq. President of the Court of Common Sessions, [6] The Universal Asylum, and Columbian Magazine, For March 1791. [158-61] Philadelphia: Printed for the Proprietors, by William Young, Bookseller, No. 52, Second-Street, the corner of Chesnut Street.

DLC, MBAt, MdBJ-G, NN, NjP, P, PBL, PHi, PPAmP, PPL, RPB, RPJCB, TxU, ViU

Evans 23,930

(8) Addison's Charge, Fifth Circuit, 1797

(a) Causes And Error of Complaints And Jealousy of The Administration of the Government: being, a Charge to the Grand Juries of the Counties Of The Fifth Circuit, of the State of Pennsylvania, At March Sessions, 1797. By Alexander Addison, President of the Courts of Common Pleas of that Circuit. Philadelphia; Printed by T. Dobson, at the Stone-House, No. 41, South Second-Street. 1797. 24 p. 8vo.

DLC, MH-L, NN*, PHi, PPAmP

Evans 31,694

(a.2) "No. XX. Causes and Error of Complaints and Jealousy of the Administration of the Government," Reports of Cases. . . By Alexander Addision. . ., above 1.07(36)(a), at 207-21.

(9) Addison's Charge, Fifth Circuit, 1798

(a) Liberty Of Speech, and Of The Press. A Charge to the Grand Juries of the County Courts of the Fifth Circuit of the State Of Pennsylvania. By Alexander Addison, President of those Courts. Washington [Pennsylvania]: Printed by John Colerick, for the Author. 1798. 24 p. 8vo.

DLC, MBAt, MWA*, MiU-C, NHi, NNC-L, P-L, PPL, RPJCB, ScC

Evans 33,267 Sabin 377

(a.2) Albany: Printed by Loring Andrews. [1798? 1800?] 16 p. 12mo.

CSmH, DLC*, MB

Evans 33,266 and 36,762 Sabin 377

(a.3) [Another Edition 1798] 16 p.

PPL*

mp. 48,328 Bristol B10,192

Note Short-Title Evans dates as 1797.

(a.4) [Another Edition. Boston. Printed by Benjamin Russell, January 1799. Presented to the readers of the Columbian Sentinel as a New-Year's Gift.] 2 p. fol.

DLC, MH, MHi, MSaE, MWA*, NHi, NN, PPL

Evans 35,323 Ford 2,903

(a.5) Albany: Printed by C.R. and G. Webster, At their Bookstore, in the White-House, Corner of State and Pearl-streets. 27 p.

MWA*

mp. 48,766 Bristol B10,683

(a.6) "No. XXV. Liberty of Speech and of the Press," Reports of Cases. . . By Alexander Addison. . ., above 1.07(36)(a), at 270-89.

(10) Rush's Charge, Luzerne County, 1798

(a) A charge delivered by the Hon. Judge [Jacob] Rush to the Grand Jury of Luzerne County, Pennsylvania, 30th June, 1798. Philadelphia: Printed by Andrew Brown? 1798. 12mo.

No Copy located.

Evans 34,498 Sabin 74,249

(a.2) Reprinted in Glasgow, 1798.

MH

Evans 34,398n.

(a.3) Reprinted in Dublin, 1799.

MH, NN

(11) Addison's Charge, Fifth Circuit, 1799

(a) On the Alien Act. A Charge to the Grand Juries of the County Courts of the Fifth Circuit of the State of Pennsylvania, At

December Sessions, 1798; by Alex. Addison, President of those courts. Published at the request of the Grand Juries of the Counties of Allegheny, Westmoreland, Somerset, and Greene. Washington: Printed by John Colerick. 1799. 23 p. 12mo.

DLC(2), MBAt, MH-L, MWA*, NN, P-L, PPL, RHi, RPJCB

Evans 35,077 Sabin 376

(a.2) "No. XXVI. A Defence of the Alien Act," Reports of Cases. . . By Alexander Addison. . ., above 1.07(36)(a), at 289-310.

(b) A Charge to the Grand Juries of the County Court Of The Fifth Circuit, of the State Of Pennsylvania. By Alexander Addison, President of those courts. Vergennes [Vermont]: Printed for Samuel Chipman. 1799. 32 p. 12mo.

BLM, MH-L, MWA*

Evans 35,078 Cooley 470 McCorison 512

(12) Preston's Charge, Wayne County, 1800

(a) A Charge Delivered to the Grand Jury of Wayne County. By Samuel Preston, Esq., first associate judge of said county. Easton, printed by Sam. Longcope. MDCCC. 22 p. 12mo.

NN, PHi*

Evans 38,321

(13) Addison's, Grand Jury Charges, 1800

(a) Reports of Cases. . . By Alexander Addison. . ., above 1.07(36)(a).

4.08 <u>Delaware</u>

(1) Chew's Charge, Newcastle, 1741

(a) The Speech of Samuel Chew, Esq; Chief Justice of the Government of New-Castle, Kent and Sussex upon Delaware; Delivered from the Bench to the Grand-Jury of the County of New-Castle, Nov. 21. 1741; and now published at their Request. Philadelphia: Printed and sold by B. Franklin. M,DCC,XLI. 16 p. 4to.

NN*, PHi

Evans 4,708 Hildeburn 695

<u>Evans Ghost</u> 4,709 (2d edition).

Note Brackets in original.

(a.2) The Speech of Samuel Chew, Esq. Chief Judge of the Counties of Newcastle, Kent, and Sussex, on Delaware. On the Lawfulness of Defence against an Armed Enemy. Delivered from the Bench to the Grand Jury of the County of Newcastle, Nov. 21 1741. First Published at the request of said Grand Jury; and now re-published by desire of several Gentlemen. Philadelphia: Printed and Sold by R. Aitken, Front-Street. M.DCC.LXXV. [Price Two Coppers.] 8 p. 8vo.

PPL*

Evans 13,867 Hildeburn 3,182

(2) Chew's Charge, Newcastle, 1742

(a) The Speech of Samuel Chew, Esq; Chief Justice of the Government of New-Castle, Kent and Sussex upon Delaware: Delivered from the Bench to the Grand-Jury of the County of New-Castle, Aug. 20, 1742. and now published at their Request. Philadelphia: Printed and Sold by B. Franklin, M,DCC,XLII. 16 p. 8vo.

PU*

Evans 4,930 Hildeburn 756

4.10 Virginia

(1) Gooch's Charge, Williamsburg, 1730

(a) A Charge to the Grand Jury. At a General Court, held at the Capitol of the City of Williamsburg, in Virginia, on Monday the 19th day of October, 1730. By the Honourable William Gooch, Esq; Governour of Virginia. Publish'd at the Request of several Gentlemen. Williamsburg: Printed and Sold by William Parks. M,DCC,XXX. 4 p.

Fulham Palace Library, NN(photostat)*, ViU (film)

Evans 3,370 Sabin 99,977

(a.2) Lawrence C. Wroth, _William Parks. Printer and Journalist of England and Colonial America_ (William Parks Club, Richmond 1926).

4.11 North Carolina

(1) Newbern (?), 1771

(a) Presentment of the Grand Jury, approving the proposal by Governor Tryon to go in person to suppress the insurgents together with the Association. Newbern, James Davis, 1771.

No copy known.

mp. 42,260 Bristol B3,369

McMurtrie: North Carolina 64

(2) Ashe's Charge, Wilmington, North Carolina, 1782

(a) A Charge Given to the Grand-Jury at Wilmington, Nov. 30, 1782, by the Hon. Samuel Ashe, Esq; one of the Judges of the Superior courts. Broadside 29.5 x 38 cm.

NcU (No copy located)

mp. 44,095 Bristol B5,411

McMurtrie: North Carolina 111

(3) Edenton, 1788

(a) Address of the grand jury of Edenton, North Carolina November 12, 1787, 3 American Museum [January 1788] 72-74, above 1.11(2)(a).

4.12 South Carolina

(1) Whitaker's Charge, Charleston, 1741

(a) At a Court of General Sessions of the Peace, Oyer and Terminer, Assize and General Goal Delivery, Holden at Charles-Town, in the Province of South-Carolina, on the First Day of October, 1741. The Chief Justice's Charge to the Grand Jury for the body of this Province. . . . South-Carolina, [By Daniel Whitaker] Charles-Town, Printed by Peter Timothy, M,DCC,XLI. 40 p. 4to.

RPJCB*

Evans 4,812 Sabin 82,356 Morgan 80
Turnbull p. 97

(2) Drayton's Charge, Charleston, 1776

(a) A Charge, on the Rise of the American Empire, delivered by the Hon. William-Henry Drayton, Esq; Chief-Justice of South-Carolina: to The Grand Jury for the District of Charlestown. Charlestown: Printed by David Bruce in Church-Street, M DCC LXXVI. 27 p. 8vo.

CSmH, MBAt, MWA*, PPAmP, PPL, PU

Evans 14,741 Sabin 20,918 Morgan 435
Turnbull p. 202

(a.2) The New-England Chronicle: or, the Essex Gazette. July 25, 1776. Cambridge: Printed by Samuel and Ebenezer Hall. 1776 fol.

MHi

Evans 14,741 note, and 14,898

Note Morgan, 1,251 lists a grand jury charge by Drayton in October 1776. The source is Douglas C. McMurtrie, "The Correspondence of Peter Timothy, Printer of Charlestown, with Benjamin Franklin, 35 South Carolina Historical and Genealogical Magazine 123, 128 (1934). McMurtrie prints a letter from Peter Timothy to Benjamin Franklin, in which he says that he is sending "6 copies also of Chief Justice Drayton's Charge to a Grand Jury in October last and a set of Gazettes." Although Bristol used Morgan as a source, he apparently did not consider this sufficient evidence of an imprint so as to include it in his Supplement.

(a.3) John Drayton, "The Charge to the Grand Jury," 2 Memoirs of the American Revolution 259-74 (Charleston, S.C. 1821).

Sabin 20,914 Shoemaker 5,206

(a.4) Hezekiah Niles, ed., "Judge Drayton's Charge," Principles and Acts of the Revolution in America 72-80 (Baltimore 1822).

Sabin 55,312 Shoemaker 9,718

(a.5) Timothy Pitkin, "Appendix No. 21: Extract from the charge of the Hon. William Henry Drayton, Chief Justice of South Carolina, to the grand jury, in April, 1776. . . .," A Political and Civil History of the United States of America from the year 1763 to the Close of the Administration of President Washington, in March, 1797 488-95 (New Haven 1828).

Sabin 63,045

(a.6) Peter Force, ed., 5 American Archives: Fourth Series 1026-34 (Washington, D.C. 1844).

Sabin 25,053

(a.7) Hezekiah Niles, ed., Centennial Offering Republication of the Principles and Acts of the Revolution in America 327-35 (Samuel V. Niles Revision. New York, Chicago, New Orleans 1876).

(a.8) William M. Dabney and Marion Dargan, "Appendix," William Henry Drayton & the American Revolution 177-92 (Albuquerque, New Mexico 1962).

(3) Grimke's Charge, Cheraws and Camden Districts, 1783

(a) State of South-Carolina. At the Courts of General Sessions of the Peace held for the districts of Cheraws and Camden, the 15th and 26th of November, 1783, before the Hon. Judge Grimke, the Grand Juries of the above districts having requested that the Charge delivered by the Court be published, together with their Presentments. Ordered that they be printed accordingly. . . . [Charleston? 1783] 4 p. 27.5 cm.

MHi*

mp 44,457 Bristol B5,806 Morgan 603

(4) Pendleton's Charge, Gagetown, Cheraws, and Camden Districts, 1787

(a) Part of Judge Pendleton's Charge to the Grand Jurors of Gagetown, Cheraws, and Camden Districts, in the State of Carolina, 1 American Museum [June 1787] 483-87. Philadelphia: Printed by Mathew Carey. M DCC LXXXVII. Library Locations, above 1.07(9)(a).

Evans 20,193

(b) Niles, above 4.12(2)(a.4), 404-06.

(b.2) Niles, above 4.12(2)(a.7), 327-35.

(5) Grimke's Charge, Charleston, 1789

(a) Charge of the hon. John Faucheraud Grimke, to the grand jury in Charleston, October 1789, 8 American Museum [August 1790] Appendix II, 31-35, above 1.07(23)(a).

(6) Grimke's Charge, Beaufort and Orangeburgh Districts, 1798

(a) Charge delivered to the grand juries of Beaufort And Orangeburgh Districts, by the honorable J: F. Grimke, one of the associate Judges of the state of South-

Carolina, November Term, 1798. Charleston: Printed by Benjamin F. Timothy 1798. MDCCXVIII. 23 p. 8 vo.

DLC*, PHi

Evans 33,824 Sabin 87,450 Morgan 1,124
Turnbull p. 349

4.20 United States

(1) Jay's Charge, U.S. Circuit Court for Eastern Circuit, 1790

(a) The Charge of Chief Justice Jay to the Grand Juries on the Eastern Circuit: At the Circuit Courts held in the Districts of New-York, on the 4th, of Connecticut on the 22d day of April; of Massachusetts on the 4th, and of New-Hampshire on the 20th days of May, 1790. Portsmouth, (N.H.) Printed and to be sold by George Jerry Osbourne, jr., at his office. Guttenberg's Head, Congress-Street. 15 p. 8vo.

DLC, MWA*, NHi, NNC, NhHi

Evans 22,587 Whittemore 513

(b) Independent Chronicle: and the Universal Advertiser. May 27, 1790. Printed and published by Thomas Adams, Printer to the honourable the General Court of the Commonwealth of Massachusetts, at his Printing-Office, opposite the new Court-House, Court Street. 1790. fol.

DLC, MBAt, MHi, MWA

Evans 22,583

(c) Charge of chief justice Jay, to the grand juries, on the eastern circuit, 8 American Museum [October 1790] Appendix II 57-60, above 1.07(23)(a).

(2) Wilson's Charge, U.S. Circuit Court for Pennsylvania District, 1790

(a) Charge of the hon. James Wilson, esq. judge of the federal circuit court for district of Pennsylvania, to the grand jury of said court, delivered April 12, 1790, 7 American Museum [May 1790] Appendix II 35-42, above 1.07(22)(a).

(3) Wilson's Charge, U.S. Circuit Court of Pennsylvania District, 1791

(a) A Charge Delivered to the Grand Jury at a special Circuit Court held at Philadelphia on the twenty-first day of February, 1791, for the District of Pennsylvania, in the

Middle Circuit. [By James Wilson] Philadelphia: Printed by James & Johnson, No. 147, High-Street. M,DCC,XCI. 23 p. 8vo.

PHi

Bristol B7,850

(4) Wilson's Charge, U.S. Circuit Court for Virginia District, 1791

(a) A Charge delivered by The Hon. James Wilson, Esq. One of the Associate Justices of the Supreme Court of the United States, to the Grand Jury, impannelled for the Circuit Court of the United States, Holden for the Middle Circuit at the Capitol, in the City of Richmond, and District of Virginia, On Monday, the 23rd Day of May, 1791. Richmond: Printed by Augustine Davis. M,DCC,XCI. 29 p. 8vo.

DLC*, MiU-C, PPAmP, ViU

Evans 24,006 Sabin 104,626 Sowerby 3,193

(5) Wilson's Charge, U.S. Circuit Court for Pennsylvania District, 1791

(a) An Inquiry into the Reasons and Principles on which Exclusive Property is established and protected* [Footnote: From the Hon. Judge Wilson's charge to the Grand Jury, at a special court of the united states, in and for the district of Pennsylvania, held on the 15th of August, 1791, for the trial of Eleanor Mc. Donald, charged with having committed a larceny on the high seas], II (or 7) The Universal Asylum, and Columbian Magazine, For September 1791 [151-52] Philadelphia: Printed, for the Proprietors, by William Young, Bookseller, No. 52, Second-Street, the corner of Chesnut Street.

DLC, MdBJ-G, NN, NjP, P, PBL, PHi, PPAmP, PPL, RPB, RPJCB

Evans 23,931

(6) Wilson's Charge, U.S. Circuit Court for Maryland District, 1791

(a) Observations on Criminal Jurisprudence, and the means of rendering Punishments fit preventatives of crimes* [Footnote: From the hon. Judge Wilson's charge to the grand-jury, at a circuit court of the united states, for the state of Maryland, held at Easton, Nov. 7th, 1791, II (or 7) The Universal Asylum, and Columbian Magazine, For December 1791, 400-03, above 4.20(5)(a).

(7) Iredell's Charge, U.S. Circuit Court for South Carolina District, 1792

(a) A Charge delivered to the grand jury for South Carolina district, in the circuit court of the United States for the said district, held in Columbia, the 14th day of May last, by James Iredell, one of the associate judges of the supreme court of the United States, 12 American Museum [October 1792] 34-41. Philadelphia: From the Press of M. Carey, No. 118, Market-Street. M.DCC.XCII.

CtHT-W, DLC, MWiW, MdBE, MdBP, NHi, NN, NjP, NjR, P, PBL, PHi, PPL, RPB, RPJCB, TxU, ViU

Evans 24,046

(8) Jay's Charge, U.S. Circuit Court for Virginia District, 1793

(a) A Charge, delivered by the Hon. John Jay, Esq., Chief Justice of the United States Court, Virginia. Richmond: Printed by Samuel Pleasants and Co. 1793. 12 p. 4to.

No copy known

Evan 25,657 Sabin 35,832

Note In a letter to Alexander Hamilton dated June 24, 1793, Jay wrote, "The G. Jury at Richmd. requested a Copy of the Charge, the Burden of which was neutrality, and directed it to be printed. I requested Mr. Marshall the Clerk of the Court to send you two copies of it. I hope he will not forget it. I wish I had thought of making the like Request of mr Carrington." 15 Papers of Alexander Hamilton 20 (Harold C. Syrett, ed. 1969). Wharton, below (b), 49 note says the charge was printed by the government for the purpose of explaining abroad the position of the United States.

(b) Francis Wharton, "Trial of Gideon Henfield, for Illegally Enlisting in a French Privateer in the Circuit Court of the United States for the Pennsylvaia District, Philadelphia, 1793," State Trials of the United States 49-89 (Philadelphia 1849).

(b.2) Henfield's Case, Federal Case No. 6,360 (1895).

(c) John D. Lawson, ed., "The Case of Breach of Neutrality By Citizens of the United States, Richmond, Virginia, 1793" and "The Trial of Gideon Henfield for Enlisting in a French Privateer, Philadelphia, 1793," 4 American State Trials 600-36 (St. Louis 1915).

5.00

Confessions, Narratives, and Dying Speeches of Criminals

5.01 New Hampshire

(1) Ruth Blay, Concealing Birth, 1768

(a) The declaration and confession of Ruth Blay who was tried . . . in Portsmouth, New-Hampshire, September 21st, 1768 for concealing the birth of her infant, which was found dead; and is to be executed the 30th day of December 1768. [Portsmouth, 1768] Broadside 36.5 x 14 cm.

MSaE

Bristol B2,849

(2) Elisha Thomas, Murder, 1788

(a) The Last Words, and Dying Speech of Elisha Thomas, Who was Executed at Dover, on the 3d June, 1788 -- for the Murder of Captain Peter Drowne. . . . [n.p. 1788] Broadside 44 x 34 cm.

MWA*

mp. 45,373 Bristol B6,817 Ford 2,523

(b) Life and Dying Speech Of Elisha Thomas, who Suffered at Dover, June 3, 1788, -- for the Murder of Capt. Peter Drowne. . . . [1788] Broadside 34 x 21.5 cm.

NhHi*

mp. 45,374 Bristol B6,818 Whittemore 466

(c) A brief account of the Execution of Elisha Thomas. . . . Printed and Sold at the Printing-Office in Market Street, Portsmouth. [1788?] Broadside 34.5 x 22.5 cm.

PHi

Bristol B6,676 Winslow 52 (PHi)

(d) Verses addressed to Mr. Elisha Thomas, together with a brief account of his execution &c. Portsmouth: Printed by George Jerry Osborne, 1788.

No copy located

Evans 21,545 Wegelin 818

(3) Thomas Powers, Rape, 1796

(a) The Narrative and Confession of Thomas Powers, A Negro, formerly of Norwich in Connecticut, who was in the 20th year of his age. He was Executed at Haverhill, in the State of New-Hampshire, on the 28th July, 1796, for committing a rape. Price Single, 4½. Norwich, Printed [by John Trumbull] August 19th, 1796. 12 p. 12mo.

DLC*

Evans 31,037 Trumbull 2d 2,510

Evans Ghosts 31,034, 31,035 (Cooley 329 and McCorison 396), and 31,036

(b) A Sermon delivered at Haverhill, New Hampshire, July 28, 1796, at the Execution of Thomas Powers, Who was Executed for a Rape, Committed at Lebanon, on the 7th of December, 1795. By Noah Worcester, A.M. Pastor of a Church in Thornton. Haverhill, New-Hampshire: Printed and Sold by N. Coverly. MDCCXCVI. 33 p. 8vo.

MWA*, RPJCB

Evans 31,657

5.02 Massachusetts

(1) James Morgan, Murder, 1686

(a) A Sermon Occasioned by the Execution of a Man found Guilty of Murder: Preached at Boston in New-England, March 11th 1685/6. (Together with the confession, Last Expressions and Solemn Warning of that Murderer, to all Persons; especially to Young Men; to beware of those Sins which brought him to his Miserable End.) By Increase Mather. Teacher of a

Church of Christ. . . . . Boston, Printed for John Dunton Book-Seller, lately Arrived from London; and are to be Sold by him, both at his Shop over against the Town-House and his Shop in Salem. 1686. 48 p.

CtY(imp.), NHi*, RPJCB(imp.), ViU

mp. 39,232 Bristol B75 2 Increase Mather 115-A[1] RPJCB 4th p. 167 Wing M-1,246

(a.2) Boston: Printed for Joseph Brunning Book-Seller, & are to be Sold at his Shop, at the Corner of the Prison Lane next the Town-House. Anno 1686 48 p. 8vo.

CtY, MWA*, RPJCB

Evans 417 Sabin 46,735
2 Increase Mather 115-A[2]
RPJCB 4th p. 167-68 Wing M-1,247

(a.3) Boston, Printed for John Dunton and Reprinted at London, in the Year 1691.

BLM, BOB, MB, MWA

2 Increase Mather 115-C Wing M-1,249

(b) Call of the Gospel Applyed, unto All men in general, and unto a Condemned Malefactor in particular. In A Sermon Preached on the 7th d. of the 1st m. 1686. At the Request, and in the Hearing of a man under a just Sentence of Death for the horrid Sin of Murder. By Cotton Mather, Pastor to a Church at Boston in N.E. . . . Printed at Boston, by R. P. [ierce] Anno supradict; [1686] [Second Title] An Exhortation to a condemned malefactor Delivered March 7 1685/6. By Joshua Moodey, Preacher of the Gospel at Boston in N. England. . . . Printed at Boston in N. England. Anno praedict. [1686] 96 p. 16 mo.

MB, MH, MWA*(imp.), NHi, RPJCB(2)

Evans 413 Sabin 46,244 Cotton Mather 43-A

Increase Mather 115-A RPJCB 4th p. 167
Wing M-1,087

(c) A Sermon Occasioned by the Execution of a man found Guilty of Murder Preached at Boston in N.E. March 11th 1685/6. (Together with the Confession, Last Expressions, & solemn Warning of that Murderer to all persons; especially to Young Men, to beware of those Sins which brought him to his miserable End.) By Increase Mather, Teacher of Church of Christ. The Second Edition. . . . Boston: Printed by R. P.[ierce] Sold by J. Brunning Book-seller, at his Shop at the Corner of the Prison-Lane next the Exchange. Anno 1687. [Second

Title] The Call of the Gospel, Applyed Unto All men in general, and Unto a Condemned Malefactor in particular. In a Sermon, Preached on the 7th Day of March. 1686. At the Request, and in the Hearing of a man under a just Sentence of Death for the horrid Sin of Murder. By Cotton Mather. Pastor to a Church at Boston in N.E. The Second Edition. . . . Printed at Boston, by Richard Pierce. 1687. [Third Title] An Exhortation To A Condemned Malefactor Delivered March the 7th 1686. By Joshua Moody, Preacher of the Gospel at Boston in New England. . . . Printed at Boston by R. P.[ierce] Anno 1687. 128 p. 16 mo.

BLM, CtHi, CtY(imp.), MB, MH, MWA*, NN, RPJCB

Evans 432 2 Increase Mather 115-B
RPJCB 4th p. 168 Wing M-1,248

Note John Dunton, London bookseller visiting in Boston, described this execution in a March 25, 1686, letter to George Larkin in London. Perry Miller and Thomas H. Johnson, ed., The Puritans (New York 1938), reprinting from John Dunton's Letters from New-England 118-36 (W.H. Whitmore, ed., Prince Society, Boston 1867).

(2) Esther Rodgers, Murder, 1701

(a) Death The certain Wages of Sin to the Impenitent: Life The sure Reward of Grace to the Penitent: Together with the only Way for Youth To avoid the former, and attain the latter. Deliver'd in three Lecture Sermons; Occasioned by the Imprisonment, Condemnation and Execution, of a Young Woman, who was guilty of Murdering her infant Begotten in Whoredom. To which is added, An Account of her manner of Life & Death, in which the glory of free grace is displayed. By Mr. John Rogers, Pastor of the Church of Ipswich. . . . Boston: Printed by B. Green, and J. Allen, for Samuel Phillips at the Brick Shop. 1701. 166 p. 12 mo.

MB*

Evans 1,020

(3) David Wallis, Murder, 1713

(a) The Sad Effects of Sin. A True Relation of the Murder Committed by David Wallis, On his Companion Benjamin Stolwood: On Saturday Night, the first of August, 1713. With his Carriage after Condemnation; His Confession and Dying Speech at the Place of Execution, &c. To which are added, The Sermons Preached at the Lecture in Boston, in his Hearing, after his Condemnation; And on the Day of his Execution, being Sept. 24. 1713. [Cotton Mather] Boston, N.E.: Printed by John Allen, for Nicholas Boone, at the Sign of the Bible in Cornhil. 1713. 118 p.

CSmH, MB, MH, MHi, MWA*, RPJCB, ViU(2)

Evans 1,626 and 1,619 3 Cotton Mather 339 McDade 1,034

(b) Hainous [sic] Nature of the Sin of Murder. And The Great Happiness of Deliverance from it. As it was Represented in a Sermon at the Lecture in Boston, Sept. 24. 1713. Before the Execution of one David Wallis. By Benjamin Colman, Pastor of a Church in Boston. Boston, N.E. Printed by John Allen, for Nicholas Boone, at the Sign of the Bible in Cornhill. 1713. 34 p. 24mo.

CSmH, MB, MH, MHi, MWA*, NN, RPJCB, ViU(2)

Evans 1,601

(4) Joseph Quasson, Murder, 1726

(a) Summary Account of the Life and Death Of Joseph Quasson, Indian; Who on the 28. Day of August 1725. at Arundel in the County of York, & Province of Main, in New-England, Shot his Fellow-Soldier and Kinsman, John Peter: So that he died of the Wound in a few Days. For which Murder being Apprehended, Tried, and after Conviction, condemned at York in the Province aforesaid, on the 12th of May following; he was there Executed on the 29th of June, 1726. By Samuel Moodey, M.A. Pastor of the Church in York Boston, Printed for S. Gerrish, the lower End of Cornhill. 1726. 46 p. 15.5 cm.

DLC, MWA*

Evans 2,782 Sabin 50,303 McDade 780

(5) Richard Wilson, Robbery, 1732

(a) The Wages of Sin; or, Robbery justly Rewarded: A Poem Occasioned by the untimely Death of Richard Wilson, Who was Executed on Boston Neck, for Burglary, On Thursday the 19th of October, 1732. . . . Boston: Printed and Sold at the Heart and Crown in Cornhill. Broadside 31.5 x 19 cm.

NHi*

mp. 40,012 Bristol B893 Ford 619
New York Public 172 Wegelin 826 Winslow 38 (DLC)

(6) Julian, Murder, 1733

(a) Poor Julleyoun's Warnings to Children and Servants to shun the ways of Sin, and those particularly which hath brought him to his doleful End. . . . Published at his Desire, in Presence of two Witnesses. Boston: Printed for B. Gray and A. Butler. [1733] Broadside 33.5 x 20 cm.

MB*

mp. 40,022 Bristol B903 Ford 629 Wegelin 746

(b) Advice from the Dead to the Living; or, a Solemn Warning to the World, Occasioned by the untimely Death of poor Julian, Who was Executed on Boston Neck, on Thursday the 22d. of March, 1733. for the Murder of Mr. John Rogers of Pembroke the 12th of September, 1732. . . . Boston: Printed and Sold [by Thomas Fleet] at the Heart and Crown in Cornhill. . . .
Broadside 8 1/8" x 13¼"

MB*

Evans 13,791 (erroneously dates as "1775"?) Ford 630
Wegelin 478 Winslow 39 (MB)

Note The following is at the bottom: "Note. There being a foolish Paper printed, called Julian's Advice to Children and Servants, said to be published at his Desires this may certify, that the said paper is false and spurious, and disowned by the said Julian in the Presence of three Persons."

(c) The last Speech and dying Advice of poor Julian, Who was Executed the 22d of March, 1733. for the Murder of Mr. John Rogers of Pembroke. Written with his own Hand, and delivered to the Publisher the Day before his Execution. . . . Printed and Sold by T. Fleet, at the Heart and Crown in Cornhill, Boston. [1733]
Broadside 33 x 21 cm.

MB*

mp. 40,021 Bristol B902 Ford 628

(7) Rebekah Chamblit, Concealing Birth, 1733

(a) The Declaration, Dying Warning and Advice of Rebekah Chamblit A Young Woman Aged near Twenty-seven Years, Executed at Boston, September 27. 1733. according to the Sentence pass'd upon her at the Superiour Court holden there for the County of Suffolk, in August last, being then found Guilty of Felony, in concealing the Birth of her spurious Male Infant, of which she was Deliver'd when alone the Eighth Day of May last, and was afterwards found Dead, as will more fully appear by the following Declaration, which was carefully taken from her Mouth. . . . Boston: Printed and Sold by S. Kneeland and T. Green, in Queen-street. [1733]
Broadside 39 x 30 cm.

MBAt, MWA*, NHi

Evans 3,639 Sabin 11,808 McDade 167

(b) Lessons of Caution to Young Sinners. A Sermon Preach'd on Lord's-Day Sept. 23, 1733. Upon the affecting Occasion of An unhappy Young Woman present in the Assembly under Sentence of Death. By Thomas Foxcroft, M.A. Pastor to the Old Church in Boston. With a Preface by Mr. Cooper. And Mr. Byles's Conference with the Prisoner as she walk'd to the Place of

Execution . . . . Boston: N.E. Printed and Sold by S. Kneeland and T. Green, in Queen-street. MDCCXXXIII. 80 p. 8vo.

MBAt, MH*, MHi, MWA(imp.)

Evans 3,655 Sabin 25,397 McDade 168

(8) Matthew Cushing, Burglary, 1734

(a) The Declaration & Confession of Matthew Cushing, A Young Man aged about Twenty two Years, who was try'd for Burglary at the Superior Court held at Boston in August last; and had Sentence of Death passed upon him for the same; which he deliver'd to us on Tuesday Sept. 24 and confirm'd the same before credible Witnesses the Day of his Execution, to be published for the benefit of Mankind. [Boston 1734?] Broadside

MB*

mp. 40,042 Bristol B925 Ford 642

(b) The Greatness of Sin improv'd by the Penitent as an argument with God for a Pardon. A Sermon At the Thursday Lecture in Boston, October 17th. 1734. Preach'd in the Hearing of John Ormesby, and Matthew Cushing, Two Condemned Malefactors On the Day of their Execution, The One for Murder, and the other for Burglary. By John Webb, A.M. Pastor of a Church in Boston. With an Appendix, Giving a faithful Account of the Behaviour of Matthew Cushing, after his Condemnation, and at the Time of his Execution. By the Reverend Mr. Cooper. Boston: Printed and Sold by S. Kneeland & T. Green, in Queen-street over against the Prison. 1734. 42 p. 16mo.

MBAt, MWA*

Evans 3,851

(c) A few Lines Upon the awful Execution of John Ormsby & Matth. Cushing, October 17th. 1734. One for Murder, the other for Burglary. . . . Printed and Sold at the Printing House in Queen-Street, over against the Prison. Broadside

MB*

mp. 40,044 Bristol B927 Ford 652 Wegelin 489

(d) A Mournful Poem on the Death of John Ormsby and Matthew Cushing, who were appointed to be executed on Boston Neck, the 17th of October, 1734. . . . Sold at the Heart and Crown in Boston. [Thomas Fleet] Broadside 8 3/4" x 13 3/4"

MB*

mp. 40,054 Bristol 935 Ford 653 Wegelin 648
Winslow 40 (MB)

(9) John Ormsby, Burglary, 1734

(a) The Last Speech and Dying Words of John Ormsby. Who was appointed to be Executed on Boston Neck, the 17th of October, 1734. Written with his own Hand, the Day before he was to suffer; And Recommended to all People, for their serious Perusal. . . . Boston, Printed and sold by Thomas Fleet, at the Heart and Crown in Cornhill. 1734. Broadside

MB*

mp. 40,058 Bristol B939 Ford 651

(b) See above 5.02(8)(b).

(c) See above 5.02(8)(c).

(d) See above 5.02(8)(d).

(10) Patience Boston, Murder, 1735

(a) The Confession, Declaration, Dying Warning and Advice of Patience Sampson, alias Patience Boston, who was executed at York, July 24th, 1735, for the murder of Benjamin Trot of Falmouth in Casco Bay, a child of about eight years of age, which she drowned in a well, July 9th, 1734, and went immediately and accused herself before one of his Majesty's justices of the peace, continuing her self-accusation from first to last; even on her trial; standing to it also from her condemnation, to the very time of her execution. [Boston: Printed and sold by S. Kneeland and T. Green 1735] 8 p. 8vo.

DLC, MB (Copy not found)

Evans 3,890

(b) A Faithful Narrative of the Wicked Life and Remarkable Conversion of Patience Boston alias Samson; Who was Executed at York [Maine], in the County of York, July 24th. 1735, for the Murder of Benjamin Trot of Falmouth in Casco Bay, a Child of about Eight Years of Age, whom she Drowned in a Well. With a Preface by the Reverend Messi. Samuel & Joseph Moody, Pastors of the churches in said Town. . . . Boston: Printed and Sold by S. Kneeland and T. Green in Queen-Street over against the Prison, 1738. 39 p. 16mo.

MHi, MWA*

Evans 4,245 McDade 123

(11) Hugh Henderson, House-Breaking, 1737

(a) The Confession and Dying Warning of Hugh Henderson, Who was Executed at Worcester for House-Breaking Nov. 24. 1737. . . . Boston: Printed and Sold at the Printing House in Queen Street over against the Prison. 2 p. fol.

MWA*

Evans 4,144 Ford 679 Wegelin 201

<u>Note</u> The microcard reproduction reverses the order.

(b) After Souls by Death are separated from their Bodies they come to Judgment. asserted in a Sermon Deliver'd at Worcester, November 24th, 1737. Being the Day of the Execution of John Hamilton, alias Hugh Henderson. [With his Confession and Dying Warning.] By John Campbell, M.A. And Pastor of the Church in Oxford, N.E. . . . Boston: Printed & Sold by S. Kneeland & T. Green, in Queen-Street over against the Prison, 1738. 42 p. 8vo.

MWA*

Evans 4,230

<u>Note</u> Brackets in original.

(12) Philip Kennison, Burglary, 1738

(a) Short and Plain, but Faithful Narrative of the Wicked Life of Philip Kennison, who was executed at Cambridge on the 25th of September, 1738. Written by Himself. Boston: Printed & Sold by Thomas Fleet. 1738.

No copy located.

Evans 4,258

(b) The Dying Lamentation and Advice of Philip Kennison, Who was Executed at Cambridge in New-England (for Burglary) on Friday the 15th Day of September, 1738. in the 28th Year of his Age. All written with his own Hand, a few Days before his Death: And published at his earnest Desire, for the good of Survivors. . . . Boston, Printed and sold at the Heart and Crown in Cornhill: where may be had a Narrative of his Life, written with his own Hand. [1738]
Broadside 32 x 19 cm.

NN*

mp. 40,143 Bristol B1,026 New York Public 186

(c) A Sermon Preach'd at Cambridge, September 15. 1738. On Occasion of the Execution of Philip Kennison, For the Crime of Burglary. By William Williams, M.A. Pastor of the Church in Weston. . . . With the Confession of his Faith. Boston: Printed and sold by Thomas Fleet, at the Heart and Crown in

Cornhill; where may be had the Narrative of Kennison's Life, written by himself. 1738. 23 p. 8vo.

MBAt, MSaE, MWA*

Evans 4,326

(13) Edward Fitz-Partrick, Murder, 1744

(a) The Examination & Confession Of Edward Fitz-Partrick, After his committing Murder on the Body of Daniel Campbell at Rutland, on the 8th Day of March 1743,4 . . . Sold by Benjamin Gray, near the Market. 1744. Broadside 31 x 19 cm.

MH*

mp. 40,330 Bristol B1,240 McDade 307

(14) Jeffrey, Murder, 1745

(a) Declaration and confession of Jeffrey, a Negro, who was executed at Worcester, Oct. 17, 1745, for the murder of Mrs. Tabitha Sandford, at Mendon, the 12th of September preceding. Boston: Printed & Sold by T. Fleet. 1745.

No copy located

Evans 5,571

(15) William Welch, Murder, 1754

(a) The last Speech & Dying Words of William Welch, 23 Years of Age, who was Executed at Boston in New-England, on the 11th Day of April, 1754. for the Murder of Darby O'Brian, on the Evening of the 19th Day of November, 1753. . . . Broadside

MHi*

Evans 7,333 Ford 1,004

(16) William Wieer, Murder, 1754

(a) The horrid nature, and enormous Guilt of Murder. A Sermon Preached at the Thursday-Lecture in Boston, November 19. 1754. The Day of the Execution of William Wieer, For the Murder of William Chism. By Charles Chauncy, D.D. One of the Pastors of the first Church in Boston. . . . Boston: Printed by Thomas Fleet. 1754. 24 p. 8vo.

BLM, MBAt, MWA*, RPJCB

Evans 7,168

(b) A Warning to Young & Old: In the Execution of William Wieer, at Boston, the 21st of November, 1754, for the

Murder of William Chism, on the 6th of April last. [Boston 1754] Broadside 31 x 24 cm.

MWA(facsimile)*, NN, RPJCB

mp. 40,730 Bristol B1,694 Ford 1,003
New York Public 249

(17) Mark and Phyllis, Murder, 1755

(a) The last & dying words of Mark, aged about 30 years, a negro man who belonged to the late Captain John Codman, of Charlestown: who was executed at Cambridge, the 18th of September, 1755, for poysoning his abovesaid master . . . [Boston] Sold next to the prison in Queen-Street. [1755]
Broadside 42.5 x 31 cm.

MHi (Copy not located)

mp. 40,760 Bristol B1,726

(a.2) Reprinted Cambridge, Massachusetts 1883.

(b) A few Lines On Occasion of the untimely End of Mark and Phillis, Who were Executed at Cambridge, September 18th for Poysoning their Master, Capt. John Codman of Charleston. . . .
Broadside 8½ x 12½

NHi*

Evans 7,415 Ford 1,008 Wegelin 588
Winslow 42 (NHi)

(b.2) Abner C. Goodell, "The Murder of Captain Codman," 20 Massachusetts Historical Society Proceedings 122-57 (Boston 1884).

(c) John Lawson, ed., "The Trial of Mark and Phillis (negro slaves) for Petit Treason, in the Murder of Captain John Codman, their Master, Cambridge, Massachusetts, 1755," 11 American State Trials 511-27 (St. Louis 1919).

(18) John Harrington, Murder, 1757

(a) The Agonies of a Soul departing out of Time into Eternity. A few Lines occasioned by the untimely End of John Harrington, Who is to be Executed at Cambridge this Day, being the 17th of March, 1757, for the Murder of Paul Learnard, the 1st of September last. . . . [Boston 1757]
Broadside 8¼" x 12 3/4"

MHI*

mp. 40,872 Bristol B1,849 Ford 1,078
Wegelin 481 Winslow 42 (MHi)

(b) The Last Words and Dying Speech of John Harrington, Aged 43 Years. Who was executed at Cambridge, March 17, 1757, for the Murder of Paul Learned. . . . Sold next to the Prison, in Queen-Street, 1757. . . . [Boston]
Broadside 38 x 21.5 cm.

MHi*

mp. 40,889   Bristol B1,871   Ford 1,077

Note   The following is at the bottom of the imprint: "Since I delivered the above to be Printed, one Thing more has come into my Mind, and that is relating to the false Reports which have been spread in the World, of my destroying my Brother's Son; which, as a dying Man, and as my last Words, I do now solemnly declare to be an innocent of, as if I never had a Being. J.H."

(19) Seth Hudson, Counterfeiting, 1762

(a) The Humble Confession of that Notorious Cheat, Doctor Seth Hudson. 1762. . . . [Boston, 1762]
Broadside 9" x 6½"

PHi*

mp. 41,274   Bristol B2,287   Ford 1,269

(b) A Serious-Comical Dialogue Between the Famous Dr. Seth Hudson, And the Noted Joshua How, Who were lately tried, in Boston, and convicted of Counterfeiting and passing Counterfeit Treasurer's Notes. . . . Boston: Printed and Sold by Benjamin Mecom, at the New Printing-Office, opposite to the Old Brick Meeting, near the Town-House. 1762.
28+ p. 21.5 cm.

MWA*(imp.)

mp. 41,309   Bristol B2,325

(c) H-ds-n's Speech from the Pillory. . . . Sold by N. Hurd, near the Exchange, and at the Heart and Crown in Cornhill, Boston. [1726]   Broadside fol.

MB*

Evans 9,144   Ford 1,268

(20) Joseph Lightly, Murder, 1765

(a) The Last Words and Dying Speech Of Joseph Lightly, Who was Executed at Cambridge, November 21, 1765. For the Murder of Elizabeth Post, at a Place called Ware. . . . [Boston 1765]
Broadside

MHi*

mp. 41,556 Bristol B2,590 Ford 1,349

(21) Magnus Mode, Richard Hodges and J. Newington Clark, Passing Counterfeit Dollars, 1767

(a) A few Lines on Magnus Mode, Richard Hodges & J. Newington Clark. Who are Sentenc'd to stand one Hour in the Pillory at Charlestown; To have one of their Ears cut off, and to be Whipped 20 Stripes at the public Whipping-Post, for making and passing Counterfeit Dollars, &c. . . . [Boston: Printed by Zachariah Fowle. 1767] Broadside 26 x 20 cm.

NN, PHi*

mp. 41,706 Bristol B2,752 New York Public 385
Ford 1,407 Wegelin 587 Winslow 44 (PHi)

(22) Arthur, Rape, 1768

(a) The Life, and dying Speech of Arthur, a Negro Man; who was Executed at Worcester, October 20th 1768. For a Rape committed on the Body of one Deborah Metcalfe. . . . Boston: Printed and Sold in Milk-Street. 1768 Broadside

MWA*, NHi

Evans 10,822 Ford 1,426

(b) The Power and Grace of Christ display'd to a dying Malefactor. A Sermon Preached at Worcester, October the Twentieth, 1768. Being the Day of the Execution of Arthur, a Negro of a [sic] about 21 years old, for a Rape. By Thaddeus Maccarty, A.M. Pastor of the Church in Worcester. . . . Boston: Printed and Sold by Kneeland and Adams, next to the Treasurer's Office, in Milk-Street. MDCCLXVIII. 28 p. 16mo.

BLM, CSmH, CtHi, DLC, MB, MBAt, MWA*, NHi, NN, RPJCB

Evans 10,952 Sabin 42,995

(23) Cooke, Counterfeiting?, 1770

(a) Cooke's Speech from the Pillory. . . . Sold at the Printing-Office in Back-Street. [Printed by Zachariah Fowle Boston 1770] Broadside

PHi*

mp. 42,077 Bristol B3,167 Ford 1,514

(24) Cot-er, Counterfeiting, 1770

(a) Cot-er's Speech from the Pillory. [Who was sentenced by the Superior Court held at Boston, to set in the

Pillory one Hour, be whip'd 20 Stripes, and pay Costs of prosecution, for counterfeiting Quarters of Dollars.] [Printed by Zachariah Fowle. 1770?] Broadside 12" x 7"

PHi*

mp. 42,078 Bristol B3,168 Ford 1,515

Note First set of brackets in original.

(25) William Linsey, Burglary, 1770

(a) The dying Speech and Confession of William Linsey, to be Executed at Worcester, October 25th 1770. For the Crime of Burglary. . . . [Dated] Worcester Goal, Oct. 18, 1770. Boston, Printed and Sold in Milk-Street 1770.
Broadside 35 x 42 cm.

MHi(imp.), MWA*, NHi

mp. 42,114 Bristol B3,205 Ford 1,525

(b) The most heinous Sinners capable of the saving Blessings of the Gospel. A Sermon Preached at Worcester, October 25th. 1770. On Occasion of the Execution of William Linsey, for Burglary. By Thaddeus Maccarty, A.M Pastor of the Church in Worcester. . . . Boston: Printed and Sold by Kneeland and Adams, next to the Treasurer's Office, in Milk-Street. MDCCLXX. 28 p. 16 mo.

DLC, MHi, MWA*, NN(2, 1 imp.)

Evans 11,707 Sabin 42,995

(26) William Shaw, Murder, 1770

(a) A Poem, On the Execution of William Shaw, at Springfield, December 17 1770, for the Murder of Edward East, in Springfield Goal. . . . [By William Carpenter] [Hartford 1771]
Broadside 11" x 15"

PHi*

Evans 12,200 Ford 1,511 New York Public 459

(a.2) [Another issue.] [Salem? Samuel Hall? 1771]

MWA* (photostat)

mp. 42,223 Bristol B3,332 Ford 1,512

(a.2.a) Heartman's Historical Series, No. 21 (1916).

(b) The Ungodly Condemned in Judgment. A Sermon Preached at Springfield, December 13th 1770. On Occasion of the

Execution of William Shaw, For Murder. By Moses Baldwin, A.M. Pastor of the Church in Palmer. . . . Boston: Printed and Sold by Kneeland and Adams, next to the Treasurer's Office in Milk-Street. MDCCLXXI. 24 p. 8vo.

MHi, MSaE, MWA*, N, RPJCB

Evans 11,973

(b.2) The Second Edition. . . . Boston: Printed and Sold by Kneeland and Adams, next to the Treasurer's Office in Milk-Street. MDCCLXXI. 24 p. 8vo.

MSaE(imp), MWiW*

Evans 11,974

(b.3) The Third Edition. . . . Boston: Printed and Sold by Kneeland and Adams, next to the Treasurer's Office in Milk-Street. MDCCLXXI. 24 p. 8vo.

BLM, DLC, MBAt, MWA*, RPJCB

Evans 11,975

(b.4) New-London: Printed and sold by T. Green, 1771. 14 p. 19.5 cm.

Ct(imp.), CtHi, CtNlC, CtY, MB, MH, MHi, MWA*, N, NBuG, NHi, NN, PPL, RPJCB

mp. 42,212 Bristol B3,318
New London 915 Trumbull 2d 1,887

(27) Bryan Sheehen, Rape, 1772

(a) Salem, January 16. 1772. An Account of the Life of Bryan Sheehen, this Day executed in Salem, for committing a Rape on the Body of Abial Hollowell, Wife of Benjamin Hollowell, of Marblehead; . . . To be sold at the Printing Office Portsmouth also, Verses on said Occasion. Broadside 14¼" x 9"

PHi*

Evans 12,559 Ford 1,633 Tapley p. 311

(b) S . . . An Account of the . . . this Day executed in Salem, for com . . . Hollowell, Wife of Benjamin Hollow . . . he was convicted before the Superior C . . . in November last, and received Sentence . . . ordered to be executed on the 19th De . . . prieved to the 2d, and then to this 16th Day of . . . [Salem 1772] Broadside 34.5 x 21.5 cm.

MSaE(imp.) (No copy available for reproduction)

mp. 42,309 Bristol B3,419 Ford 1,634
Tapley p. 310

(c) A Sermon, Preached at Salem, January 16, 1772. Being this Day on which Bryan Sheehen was executed for commiting a Rape, On the Body of Abial Hollowell, the Wife of Benjamin Hollowell, Of Marblehead. By James Dimon, A.M. Pastor of the Second Church in Salem. . . . Salem: Printed by Samuel and Ebenezer Hall, near the Exchange. MDCCLXXII. 24 p. 8vo.

MSaE, MWA*, RPJCB

Evans 12,375 Tapley p. 310

(28) Solomon Goodwin, Murder, 1772

(a) The last Words and Dying Speech of Solomon Goodwin, lately executed at Falmouth, Casco-Bay, for the Murder of David Wilson, may be had at the Printing-Office in Salem. Broadside?

No copy located.

mp. 42,343 Bristol B3,453 Ford 1,613
Tapley p. 310

(b) Sovereign Grace displayed in the Conversion and Salvation of a Penitent Sinner, Set forth in a Sermon Preached before the Execution of Solomon Goodwin, Who was Executed at Falmouth, November 12, 1772, for the murder of David Wilson, on the 25th of May last. Published at the Desire of many who heard it. By Ephraim Clark Of Cape-Elizabeth, and Pastor of the Church there. . . . Boston: Printed by John Boyles in Marlborough-Street, MDCCLXXIII. 24 p. 12mo.

DLC, NHi, NN*

Evans 12,725 McDade 361

(29) Ansell Nickerson, Piracy, 1773

(a) The following Circumstances Relating to the Famous Ansell Nickerson, And concerning the Boy, (mentioned in Trial to be carried away by the Pirates) who, they say, is arrived at Martha's Vineyard: Also, the Testimony of Two Men, belonging to Seaguin, who were robbed by a Top-Sail Schooner with four Boats, on the Fourteenth of November: To which is added, the Declaration of a Justice of the Peace, respecting Mr. Nickerson's Innocence of the Murder and Robbery in Nov. All which particulars have transpired since his Trial and Acquittal. [Boston? 1773?] Broadside 35.5 x 15.5 cm.

PHi (microcard not yet issued 4-1-82)

mp. 42,475 Bristol B3,562 Ford 1,678

(b) L. Kinvin Wroth and Hiller B. Zobel, eds., "Case No. 57. Rex v. Nickerson 1772-1773," 2 Legal Papers of John Adams 335-51 (Cambridge 1965).

(30) John Richardson, Intended Murder, 1773

(a) Inhuman Cruelty: Or Villany Detected. Being a true Relation of the most unheard-of, cruel and barberous Intended Murder of a Bastard Child belonging to John and Ann Richardson, of Boston, who confined it in a small Room, with scarce any Victuals, or Cloathing to cover it from the cold or rain, which beat into it, for which Crime they were both of them Sentenc'd to set on the Gallows, with a rope around their Necks, &c. . . . [Boston, Draper? 1773?]
Broadside 12½" x 7"

PHi*

mp. 42,454 Bristol B3,578 (see also B2,478)
Ford 1,686 Winslow 43 (PHi)

(31) Elizabeth Smith and John Sennet, Thievery and Beastiality, 1773

(a) A Dialogue between Elizabeth Smith, and John Sennet, Who were convicted before his Majesty's Superior Court, Elizabeth Smith For Thievery, and John Sennet for Beastiality: and each sentenced to Set upon the Gallows for the space of one Hour, with a Rope round their Necks. Elizabeth Smith to receive Twenty Stripes upon her naked Back, And John Sennet, Thirty-nine. . . . [Boston, Draper 1773]
Broadside 15" x 6"

PHi*

mp. 42,502 Bristol B3,553 Ford 1,692

(32) Levi Ames, Burglary, 1773

(a) A Prospective View Of Death: Being, A solemn Warning to inconsiderate Youth, occasioned by the Trial and Condemnation of Levi Ames, Aged Twenty-two Years, who was convicted of Burglary, and received Sentence of Death, Sept. 10, 1773. Who is soon finally to leave the World, and launch into an awful Eternity. To which is added, his Trial and Life. His Death-Warrant has been read to him by the High-Sheriff, by which it appears he is to be executed on Thursday the Fourteenth Day of October next: Who desires the Prayers of all the Churches. . . . Boston: Printed and Sold by E. Russell, next the Cornfield, Union-street, near the Market.
Broadside 42 x 36 cm.

mp. 42,485 Bristol B3,622

(b) The Dying Groans of Levi Ames, Who was Executed at Boston, the 21st of October, 1773, for Burglary. . . . [Boston 1773]
Broadside 36 x 21.5 cm.

PHi*, RPB

mp. 42,400 Bristol B3,518 New York Public 490
Ford 1,641 Winslow 48 (PHi)

(c) An Exhortation to young and old to be cautious of small Crimes, lest they become habitual, and lead them before they are aware into those of the most heinous Nature. Occasioned by the unhappy Case of Levi Ames, Executed on Boston-Neck, October 21st, 1773, for the Crime of Burglary. . . . [Boston 1773] Broadside 29 x 16 cm.

PHi*

mp. 42,436 Bristol B3,558 Ford 1,642
Winslow 49 (PHi)

(d) A few Lines wrote upon the intended Execution of Levi Ames, For Burglary, and being sent to him for his Improvement, are now published at his Desire. . . . [Boston 1773]
Broadside 8½" x 11½"

PHi*

mp. 42,438 Bristol B3,560 Ford 1,643
Wegelin 590

(e) The last Words and Dying Speech of Levi Ames, Who was Executed at Boston, on Thursday the 21st Day of October, 1773, for Burglary. Taken from his own Mouth, and Published at his desire, as a solemn Warning to all, more particularly Young People. . . . Boston: Printed and Sold at the Shop opposite the Court-House in Queen-Street. [1773]
Broadside 49.5 x 37.5 cm.

DLC, MB, MHi, MWA*, MiU-C, NHi, RPB

mp. 42,401 Bristol B3,519 See Evans 12,642
Ford 1,644

(e.2) The last Words and dying Speech of Levi Ames, Executed at Boston, Octo. 21, 1773, for Burglary. Taken from his own Mouth, and published at his Desire, as a solemn Warning to all, particularly young People. . . . Printed and Sold at the Printing-Office in Salem.

DLC*

Evans 12,641 Ford 1,645 Tapley p. 312

<u>Evans Ghost</u> 12,642

(f) A Solemn Farewell to Levi Ames, Being a Poem written a few Days before his Execution, for Burglary, Oct. 21, 1773. . . .

Boston: Printed and Sold at Draper's Printing-Office, in N[ewbury-Street.] Broadside 32 x 20 cm.

PHi*

mp. 42,506 Bristol B3,645 Ford 1,646
Wegelin 771

(g) The Speech of Death to Levi Ames. Who was Executed on Boston-Neck, October 21, 1773, for the Crime of Burglary. . . . [Boston 1773] Broadside 31 x 19 cm.

CSmH, MHi*, PHi, RPB

mp. 42,508 Bristol B3,647 Huntington 340
Ford 1,647 Wegelin 787 Winslow 50 (PHi)

(h) Theft and Murder: A Poem on the Execution of Levi Ames, Which is to be on Thursday, the 21st of October inst. for robbing the House of Mr. Martin Bicker, and was convicted of Burglary. Sold near the Mill-Bridge: and at the Printing Office near the Market. [Boston 1773] Broadside

MH*, RPB

mp. 42,518 Bristol B3,657 Ford 1,648 Wegelin 792

Note The colophon text is taken from Bristol. It is not on the microcard, probably because of faulty reproduction.

(i) An Address to the Inhabitants of Boston, (Particularly to the thoughtless Youth:) Occasioned by the Execution of Levi Ames, Who so early in Life, as not 22 Years of Age, must quit the Stage of action in this awful Manner. He was tried for Burglary on the 7th of September, and after a fair and impartial examination of Facts, the Jury went out but soon returned, who upon their Oaths pronounced him Guilty. . . . [Boston 1773] Broadside 36 x 21.5 cm.

PHi, RPJCB*

mp. 42,396 Bristol B3,513 Ford 1,640
New York Public 479 Wegelin 477B

(j) Boston, October 21, 1773. The dying Penitent; or, the affecting Speech of Levi Ames, Taken from his own Mouth, as Delivered by him at the Goal in Boston the Morning of his Execution. . . . [Boston] Sold opposite the Court House in Queen Street. [1773] Broadside 34.5 x 21.5 cm.

MHi*

mp. 42,399 Bristol B3,517

(k) Two Sermons: The First from Psalm CII. 19, 20. Delivered the Lord's-Day before the Execution of Levi

Ames. Who was executed at Boston, Thursday October 21, for Burglary, AEt. 22. This Discourse was preached at the Desire of the Criminal, who also attended on the Occasion. The Second from Proverbs XVII. 25. Preached the Lord's-Day after his Execution; and designed as an Improvement of that awful Event, by Way of Caution to others. To Which Is Added, At the Request of many, An Account of the Exercise of his Mind, from the Time of his Condemnation, till he left the World; together with the Conversation the Author had with him as he walked with him from the Prison to the Gallows. By all which, compared with his latter Conduct, he may be thought in a Judgment of Charity, to have died, A Penitent Thief. By Samuel Stillman, A.M. Pastor of the First Baptist Church in Boston. . . . Boston: Printed by John Kneeland, in Milk-Street, for Philip Freeman, in Union-Street. MDCCLXXIII. 67 p. 8vo.

MH*, MSaE

Evans 13,030

(k.2) The Second Edition. Boston: Printed and Sold by J. Kneeland, in Milk-Street;--Sold also by Philip Freeman, in Union-Street. MDCCLXXIII. 67 p. 8vo.

MWA*, RPJCB, ScC

Evans 13,031

(k.3) The Second Edition. Boston: N.E. Printed and Sold by E. Russell, next to Cornfield, Union-Street. Sold also by A. Ellison in Marlborough street. M,DCC,LXXIII. 31 p. 20 cm.

MWA*

mp. 42,513 Bristol B3,652

(k.4) The Fourth Edition. Boston: N.E. Printed and Sold by E. Russell next the Cornfield, Union-street. Sold also by A. Ellison in Marlborough-street. M,DCC,LXXIII 32 p. 20 cm.

CSmH, MHi, MWA*

mp. 42,514 Bristol B3,653

(l) Christ's Promise to the penitent Thief. A Sermon Preached the Lord's-Day before the Execution of Levi Ames, Who suffered Death for Burglary, October 21, 1773. Aet. 22. By Andrew Eliot, D.D. Pastor of a Church in Boston. . . . M.B. This discourse was preached at the desire of the prisoner, who was present when it was delivered. Boston: Printed and Sold by John Boyle, next Door to the Three Doves in Marlborough-Street. 1773. [Second Title] The Life, last words, and dying speech of Levi Ames, who was executed at Boston, on

Thursday afternoon, the twenty-first of October, 1773, for Burglary, Taken from his own mouth, and published at his desire, as a solemn warning to all, more particularly young people. . . . Boston: Printed by John Boyles, 1773.
39 p. 8vo.

BLM, DLC, MBAt* (lacks second title), RPJCB (lacks second title)

Evans 12,759

(m) Christ sent to heal the Broken Hearted. A Sermon, Preached at the Thursday Lecture in Boston, on October 21st. 1773. When Levi Ames, A young Man, under a sentence of Death for Burglary, to be Executed on that Day, Was present to hear the Discourse; by Samuel Mather, D.D. Pastor of a Church in Boston, New-England. . . . To which is added, his Life written by himself Boston: Printed and Sold at William M'Alphine's Printing-Office in Marlborough-Street. M,DCC,LXXIII
36 p. 12mo.

RPJCB*

Evans 12,862

(m.2) Boston: Printed and Sold by E. Russell, near the Corn Fields in Union Street. M,DCC,LXXIII.
36 p. 12mo.

MBAt, MH*, RPJCB

Evans 12,863

(33) Valentine Duckett, Desertion, 1774

(a) The Life, Last Words, And Dying Speech of Valentine Duckett; who was shot for Desertion, on Boston Common, Friday Morning, Sept. 9, 1774, agreeable to the Sentence of a General Court-Martial held in Boston Camp, the 30th Day of August, 1774 . . . [Dated] Boston Camp (at mid-night) 9th Sept. 1774. Sold at the Printing-Office in School-street. Price Six Coppers. [Boston 1774] Broadside 49 x 35 cm.

MWA*

mp. 42,589 Bristol B3,728 Ford 1,722

(34) William Brooks, James Buchanan, Ezra Ross, and Bathsheba Spooner, Murder, 1778

(a) The Cruel Murder Or a Mournful Poem Occasioned by Sentence of Death being pass'd upon William Brooks, James Buhannon, Ezra Ross and Bethsheba Spooner, who were tried and found guilty of Murdering Mr. Joshua Spooner, of Brookfield, and who are all ordered to be executed at Worcester on thursday the 2d Day of July next, which awful sight grant, may be a

warning to all. . . . Boston: Printed and Sold by the Gross or Dozen, at N. Coverly's Printing-Office.
Broadside 34 x 20 cm.

NHi (No copy located)

mp. 45,460 Bristol B6,928 (Dated 1789?)

(b) The dying Declaration of James Buchanan, Ezra Ross and William Brooks, who were executed at Worcester, on Thursday July the 2d. 1778, for the Murder of Mr. Jashua Spooner. . . . [Worcester, Isaiah Thomas, 1788]
Broadside 42.5 x 33 cm.

MWHi, NHi*

mp. 43,422 Bristol B4,651 New York Public 664
Sabin 105,350 McDade 898

(a.2) The Dying Declaration of James Buchanan, Ezra Ross, And William Brooks, Who were executed at Worcester, July 2, 1778, for the Murder of Mr. Joshua Spooner. . . . [Worcester, 1778?]
8 p. 23cm.

MWA*

mp. 43,423 Bristol B4,652 McDade 897

(c) The last Words and dying Speech Of James Buchanan, Ezra Ross, and William Brooks, who are executed this day at Worcester, for the Murder of Mr. Joshua Spooner. . . . Boston: Printed and Sold by Draper and Folsom, at the Corner of Winter-Street. [1778] Broadside 41 x 31 cm.

NjP*

mp. 43,427 Bristol B4,653

(c.2) [Boston? 1778?] Broadside 41.5 x 86 cm.

NN*

mp. 43,426 Bristol B4,654 Ford 2,129
New York Public 665

(d) The last Words and dying Speech Of Ezra Ross, James Buchanan and William Brooks, Who were executed at Worcester on Thursday the 2d Day of July 1778, For the Murder of Mr. Joshua Spooner, of Brookfield. Bathsheba Spooner, who was convicted of being accessary to the Murder of her Husband, was also executed at the same time. . . . [n.p. 1778]
Broadside 43 x 33 cm.

MWA*

mp. 43,424 Bristol B4,792

(d.2) Massachusetts Broadsides, above 1.02(15)(e.6), 95.

(e) The Lives, Last Words, and Dying Speech of Ezra Ross, James Buchanan, and William Brooks, who were executed at Worcester, on Thursday, the 2d day of July, 1778, for the Murder of Mr. Joshua Spooner, of Brookfield. Bathsheba Spooner, who was convicted of being accessory to the Murder was also executed at the same Time. [Worcester? 1778?] 8 p.18.5 cm.

MWA*

mp. 43,425 Bristol B4,793 McDade 901

(f) A mournful Poem: Occasioned by Sentence of Death being pass'd upon William Brooks, James Buhannon, Ezra Ross and Bathsheba Spooner, who were tried and found guilty of Murdering Mr. Joshua Spooner, of Brookfield, and who were all executed at Worcester on Thursday the 2d day of July 1778. . . . [Boston 1778] Broadside 33.5 x 21.5 cm.

MWA*(imp.), RPB

mp. 43,501 Bristol B4,730

Note Bristol describes imprint as mutilated and reproduction on microcard seems to confirm this description.

(g) The guilt of innocent blood put away. A Sermon, Preached at Worcester, July 2, 1778. On Occasion of the Execution of James Buchanan, William Brooks, Ezra Ross, and Bathshua Spooner, for the Murder Of Mr. Joshua Spooner, at Brookfield, On the Evening of the first of March preceeding. Together with An Appendix, giving Some Account of those Prisoners in Their Last Stage. By Thaddeus Maccarty, A.M. Pastor of the Church in said Worcester. Worcester: Massachusetts-Bay, Printed and sold by Isaiah Thomas, & Co. MDCCLXXVIII. 40 p. 8vo.

MB, MHi, MWA*, NHi, PMA, RPJCB

Evans 15,872 Sabin 42,995 McDade 900

(g.2) Norwich, Printed and sold by John Trumbull, near the Meeting-House. M,DCC,LXXVIII. 28 p. 8vo.

MWA*, NHi, NN(imp.), RPJCB

Evans 15,873 Trumbull 1,035 McDade 899

(h) The Rev. Mr. Maccarthy's Account of the Behaviour of Mrs. Spooner after her Commitment and Condemnation for being Accessary in the Murder of her Husband at Brookfield, March 1, 1778. . . . [n.p. 1778?] 4 p. 17.5 cm.

DLC, MWA*

mp. 43,485 Bristol B4,714 McDade 902

(i) A Sermon preached at Brookfield March 6, 1778. on the Day of the Interment of Mr. Joshua Spooner, Who was most barbarously murdered at his own Gate, on the Lord's-Day Evening preceeding, by three Ruffians, who were hired for the purpose by his Wife. By Nathan Fiske, A.M. Pastor of the third Church in Brookfield . . . . Boston, New-England: Printed by Thomas & John Fleet, 1778. 20 p. 8vo.

MBAt, MWA*, NHi, NcD, PHi, RPJCB

Evans 15,793

(i.2) The third edition. Danvers, near Boston: Printed By E. Russell, next the Bell-Tavern. M,DCC,LXXVIII 16 p. 17.5 cm.

DLC, MSaE, MiU-C, NN

mp. 43,454 (No such edition located)
Bristol B4,683 New York Public 669
Tapley p. 332

(i.3) Norwich: Printed by Green & Spooner. M,DCC,LXXVIII. 16 p. 18 cm.

DLC, MWA*, RPJCB

mp. 43,453 Bristol B4,682 Trumbull 2d 2,148

(j) Peleg W. Chandler, ed., "Trial of Bathsheba Spooner and others before the Superior Court of Judicature, for the murder of Joshua Spooner, of Brookfield, Massachusetts, 1778," 2 American Criminal Trials 1-58 (Boston 1844).

(k) Samuel Swett Green, "The Case of Bathsheba Spooner," 5 American Antiquarian Society Proceedings (New Series) 430-36 (Worcester 1889).

(l) John D. Lawson, ed., "The Trial of Bathsheba Spooner, William Brooks, James Buchanan and Ezra Ross for the Murder of Joshua Spooner, Massachusetts, 1778," 2 American State Trials 175-201 (St. Louis 1914).

(35) Robert Young, Rape, 1779

(a) The Last Words and Dying Speech of Robert Young, Who is to be Executed at Worcester this Day, November 11th, 1779, for a Rape committed on the Body of Jane Green, a Child, eleven years of age, at Brookfield, in the County of Worcester, on the third Day of September Last. . . . Printed and sold at the Printing Office, in Worcester. [1779] Broadside fol.

MWA*

Evans 19,448 Sabin 106,092 Ford 2,212

(a.2) The Last Words, and Dying Speech of Robert Young, Who was Executed at Worcester on Thursday last, November 11th, . . . Sold at the Printing-Office: New-London. [1779] Broadside 9½" x 14½"

CSmH*, NjR(imp.)

Evans 16,688 Sabin 106,093 Huntington 444
New London 1,094

(a.3) <u>Massachusetts Broadsides</u>, above 1.02(15)(e.6), 97.

(b) The Dying Criminal: Poem, By Robert Young, on his own Execution, which is to be on this Day, November 11th, 1779, for Rape committed on the Body of Jane Green, a Child eleven years of age, at Brookfield, in the County of Worcester, on the third Day of September last. Corrected from his own Manuscript . . . . Printed and sold at the [Printing Office, in Worcester 1779] Broadside 37 x 20.5 cm.

MWA*

mp. 43,738 Bristol B4,999 Sabin 106,090
Ford 2,211 New York Public 713 Wegelin 470

(b.2) The Dying Criminal: A Poem. By Robert Young, on his own Execution, which was on Thursday last, November 11th 1779, for a Rape committed on the Body of Jane Green, a Child eleven Years of Age, at Brookfield, in the County of Worcester, on the 3d Day of September last. Corrected from his own Manuscript. . . . Sold at the Printing-Office, New-London [1779?] Broadside 24 x 37 cm.

CSmH*, RPB

mp. 43,739 Bristol B5,000
Sabin 106,091 Huntington 443
New London 1,093 Wegelin 469

(36) William Huggins and John Mansfield, Murder, 1783

(a) The Last Words of William Huggins and John Mansfield, Who are to be Executed this Day, June 19th, 1783, at Worcester, in the Commonwealth of Massachusetts, for Burglary, committed in October last. . . . Printed and sold at the Printing-Office in Worcester [Printed by Isaiah Thomas] Broadside

MWA*, NjP

Evans 17,994 Ford 2,360 Wegelin 621

(37) Cassumo Garcelli, Murder, 1784

(a) The Life, Last Words, and Dying Speech of Cassumo Garcelli, Who was this day (Thursday, January 15, 1784,) executed for the willful, cruel and inhuman murder of Mr. John Johnson on the Evening of the Sixth November, 1783 translated by an . . . Boston, January 15, 1784. . . . [Boston] Printed and sold at the Printing-Office in Marlborough-Street [1784]
Broadside 43.5 x 35 cm.

MWA*(imp.)

mp. 44,534 Bristol B5,898

(38) Dirick Grout and Francis Coven, Burglary, 1784

(a) The Life, Last Words and Dying Speech Of Dirick Grout, a Dutchman, of New-York State, aged 36; and Francis Coven, a Frenchman, belonging to Marseilles, aged 22; who were Executed this Day, pursuant to their Sentence, for the Crime of Burglary. Thursday, October 28, 1784. . . . [n.p. 1784]
Broadside 50 x 35 cm.

NHi*

mp. 44,543 Bristol B5,907 Ford 2,385

(39) Richard Barrick and John Sullivan, Highway Robbery, 1784

(a) The American Bloody Register: containing a true and complete History of the Lives, Last Words, and Dying Confessions of three of the most noted Criminals, that have ever made their Exit from a Stage in America, viz. Richard Barrick and John Sullivan, Highway Robbers. Together with the Dying Confession of Alexander White, a Murderer and Pirate, Who were executed at Cambridge, (New England) on Thursday, November 18, 1784. . . . Boston, Printed and Sold by E. Russell at his Office next Door below Liberty-Pole; where Allowance is made to Purchasers by the Quantity. MDCCLXXI 32 p. 16mo.

MBAt, MH-L, MWA*, MiU-C

Evans 18,324 Sabin 103,349A (Revised 1,066)
McDade 1,082

(b) The Lives and Dying Confessions of Richard Barrick, and John Sullivan, Highway Robbers. Together with the Last Words of Alexander White, Murderer and Pirate, Who were Executed at Cambridge, on Thursday, November 18, 1784. Printed and Sold at Worcester. Sold also by Edward Houghton, Post-Rider. [1784] 12 p. 12mo.

MWA*

Evans 18,559 Sabin 3,625 McDade 1,084

(40) Alexander White, Murder, 1784

(a) A Narrative of the Life and Conversion of Alexander White, AET. 23, Who was Executed at Cambridge, November 18, 1784, for the Murder of a Captain White, At Sea. Containing extracts from his manuscripts, and some letters written by him a short time before his execution. Printed and published, by Powars and Willis, in Boston. [1784] 23 p. 8vo.

DLC, MB, MH-L, MWA*, NHi

Evans 18,886 Sabin 103,350 McDade 1,083

(b) The life, last words and dying speeches of Alexander White, and John Sullivan, who were . . . executed this day. . . . [Boston] E. Russell [1784] Broadside 44.5 x 35.5 cm.

PPRF (Not located)

mp. 44,633 Bristol B6,006

(c) Paradise promised by a dying Saviour to the penitent Thief on the Cross. A Sermon Delivered at Cambridge, On Thursday the Eighteenth of November, immediately preceeding the Execution of Alexander White, Richard Barrick and John Sullivan. With an Appendix, Exhibiting some Account of their Conversation and Behaviour in Prison, &c. By Timothy Hilliard, A.M. Pastor of the First Church in Cambridge. Boston: Printed and Sold by E. Russell, in Essex-Street, next Door to Liberty-Pole. M,DCC,LXXXV. 32 p. 8vo.

MBAt, MWA*, RPJCB

Evans 19,037

(d) See above 5.02(39).

(41) American Bloody Register, 1784

(a) The American bloody register. . . . [No. II] Boston, E. Russell, 1784.

MBAt, MH

Bristol B5,857

(42) Johnson Green, Burglary, 1786

(a) The Life and Confession of Johnson Green, Who is to be Executed this Day, August 17th, 1786, for the Atrocious Crime of Burglary; Together with his Last and Dying Words. . . . Worcester Gaol, August 16, 1786. . . . Printed and Sold at the Printing-Office at Worcester. Broadside fol.

DLC, MWA*

Evans 19,693 Ford 2,437 Porter 89

(43) Isaac Coombs, Murder, 1787

(a) The Last words and dying speech of Isaac Coombs, who was executed at Salem, the 21st of December last, for the murder of his wife. Portsmouth: Printed and sold by George Jerry Osborne. 1787 Broadside

No copy located

Evans 20,299 Whittemore 415

(b) A Sketch of the life and confession of Isaac Coombs, who was executed at Salem, on December 21, 1786, for the murder of his wife; containing an account of his assistance in roasting an Indian prisoner to death by a slow fire. . . . The Murder of his wife, and her appearing to him afterwards, attended by two great devils. Middletown: Printed and sold by Woodward and Green. 1787.

No copy located

Evans 20,300 Trumbull 2d 2,612

(c) The Prayer of a true Penitent for Mercy; or, the Publican's Prayer, Illustrated. A Sermon, Delivered at Salem, Dec. 21, 1786, Previous to the Execution of Isaac Coombs, an Indian, whose crime was Murder of his Wife. By Joshua Spalding, A.M. Pastor of the Tabernacle Church, in Salem. [Published by Desire.] Salem: Printed by Dabney and Cushing, MDCCLXXXVII. 24 p. 8vo.

MH*

Evans 20,721

Note Brackets in original.

(44) John Sheehan, Burglary, 1787

(a) Life, Last Words and Dying Speech of John Sheehan, Who was Executed at Boston, on Thursday, November Twenty-second, 1787, for Burglary. . . . Boston: Printed and sold by E. Russell, at his Office, next Lib. Pole. . . . Broadside 53 x 33 cm.

MWA*

Evans 20,702 Ford 2,500

Evans Ghost 20,701

(45) John Bly and Charles Rose, Burglary, 1787

(a) A Narrative of the Life, together with the last words and dying confession of John Bly and Charles Rose, two insurgents, who were executed at Lenox, in the County of Berkshire, and Commonwealth of Massachusetts, on Thursday the 16th day of December 1787. This narrative contains some secrets proper to be known:--and much good advice to their brethren in iniquity. Boston: Printed and sold by E. Russell, next Liberty-Pole. 1788.

No copy located

Evans 20,974

(b) A Sermon; Preached in Lenox, in the County of Berkshire, and Commonwealth of Massachusetts; December, 6th, 1787: At The Execution Of John Bly, and Charles Rose, for Crimes of Burglary. By Stephen West, A.M. Pastor of the Church in Stockbridge. Published at the Desire of a great Number of the Hearers. [Commonwealth of Massachusetts.] Pittsfield: Printed by Elijah Russell, M,DCC,LXXXVII. 12 p. 12mo.

CtHi*

Evans 21,598 (microcard varies from Evans entry)

<u>Note</u> Brackets in original.

(b.2) Hudson: Printed by Ashbel Stoddard, M,DCC,LXXXVIII. 22 p.

NHi*

Evans 21,599

(46) Joseph Taylor, Robbery, 1788

(a) [Cover Title] The Wonderful Monitor: Or, Memorable Repository. Containing, A curious and most astonishing account of the Revivication of young Jo. Taylor. [Title p. 3] God's tender Mercy and infinite Compassion surmounting Man's Severity; in a remarkable and surprising Manner exemplified, in the following Curious and very Extraordinary Narrative of the Revivication of young Joseph Taylor, Who was supposed to have been Hanged to Death, (in Company with that notorious Highwayman, Pickpocket and Housebreaker, Archibald Taylor) on Boston-Neck, on Thursday, the Eight of May, 1788, for a violent Assault and Robbery on the Highway, committed on the Person and Property of Mr. Nathaniel Cunningham, Butcher, in October, 1787. In a Letter from said Joseph Taylor, to his kind Friend and Countryman, Mr. Phelim Donance, in Boston. With attestation Of the Truth of the Facts, by said Donance, &c. and Many other interesting Particulars, relating to this very extraordinary and memorable Transaction. . . . Boston: Printed and sold by E. Russell, next Liberty-Pole. M,DCC,LXXXVIII. 16 p. 16mo.

MWA*

Evans 21,487 and 21,488 Sabin 94,518

(a.2) [Same Cover Title. Variations in Title] Sixth Edition. America: Printed for, and Sold by A. Nelson, Travelling Trader, Pownalboro': (Pr. gd.) Who has for, sale, Trial of Sir Richard Rum, the Min. Funeral Sermon, Prod. Daughter, Bloody Register, No. IV, Oracle, or a Pack of Cards turned into a complete Fortune-Teller. [Boston. E. Russell. 1788?] 16 p. 18 cm.

MWA*

mp. 45,371 Bristol B6,815
Sabin 94,521

(b) Narrative of the Revivication of Joseph Taylor, Who was supposed to have been hanged to death, on Boston-Neck, on Thursday the Eighth day of May, 1788, for Robbery. Printed in the year 1790. [Price four Coppers.] 12 p. 17 cm.

MWA*, NN

mp. 45,998 Bristol B7,501 New York Public 973
Sabin 94,519

Note Brackets in original.

(c) A Remarkable and Extraordinary Narrative of the Revivification of Joseph Taylor, Who was supposed to have been hanged to Death, on Boston Neck, on Thursday the 8th of May, 1788, for a violent Assault and Robbery on the Highway, committed on the Person and Property of Mr. Nathaniel Cunningham; and who was, by Means of several Persons, recovered to Life and Health, notwithstanding it was Two Hours and Forty-three Minutes after he was cut down, before they could render him any Assistance. Published by himself in a Letter to his Friend, Mr. Phelim Donance, in Boston, dated Capes of Delaware, May 12, 1788--then on his way home to Sweden. A certain person, well known in Boston, has spread a false Report, contradicting the Truth of this Narrative; but without the least Effect; as the Public in that State have received satisfactory and undeniable Attestations from uncontrovertible Witnesses. Boston: Printed--Baltimore: Re-printed and sold by S. & J. Adams, for Isaiah Isaacs, 1790. 8 p. 17 cm.

MWA*

mp. 45,999 Bristol B7,502

(c.2) Carlisle: Printed by Kline & Reynolds. 1790.

Sabin 94,520

(47) Rachel Wall, High-way Robbery, 1789

(a) Life, Last Words and Dying Confession, of Rachel Wall, Who with William Smith and William Dunogan, were executed at Boston, on Thursday, October 8, 1789, for High-Way Robbery. . . . Broadside

MB, MBAt, MWA*

Evans 22,235 Ford 2,555

(b) The Prisoner's Magazine. Or malefactor's bloody register. No. IV. Containing the life and confession of Rachel Wall, William Durogan and William Smith. Boston: Printed and sold by E. Russell, near Liberty Stump. 1789.

No copy located

Evans 22,083

(c) The Lives and confessions of Rachel Wall, William Smith, William Denosse [sic], executed in Boston. Neither of the above had arrived to the age of thirty years, but have been old offendors [sic]--The woman in particular. Keene, N.H. Printed and sold by James D. Griffith. 1789.

No copy located

Evans 22,236 Whittemore 499

(48) John Bailey, Burglary, 1791

(a) Life, last Words, and Dying Confession of John Bailey. A Black Man, who was Executed at Boston this Day, being Thursday, October 14, 1790, for Burglary. . . . Boston: Printed by E. Russell, next Liberty-Pole; cheap to Travelling-Traders, Town-Flys &c.--where also may be had, cheap by the thousand, hundred gross, dozen, or single, Bickerstaff's Boston Almanack, or Federal Calendar, for 1791. Broadside 45.5 x 31 cm.

MHi*

mp. 45,816 Bristol B7,305 Ford 2,560a

(49) Samuel Frost, Murder, 1793

(a) The Confession and Dying Words of Samuel Frost, Who is to be Executed this day, October 31, 1793, for the Horrid Crime of Murder. . . . Printed and sold at Mr. Thomas's printing office in Worcester. Price 6d. Also, A Poem on the Occasion. Price 3d. Broadside 51 x 46 cm.

MWA*

Evans 25,521   McDade 326

Evans Ghost 25,522 (Trumbull 2d 2,173)

(b) A Poem. On the Execution of Samuel Frost, Who is to be Executed this Day, October 31, 1793, for the Murder of Capt. Elisha Allen, of Princeton, Massachusetts. . . .

MWA*

Evans 26,013   Ford 2,681   Wegelin 728

(c) The Confession and Dying Words of Samuel Frost, Who was executed at Worcester, the 31st day of October, 1793, for Horrid Crime of Murder. . . . Printed and sold by Henry Blake & Co.--Keene, State of New-Hampshire. [1793] Broadside 44.5 x 27.5 cm.

MWA*

mp. 46,757   B8,345

(d) The Importance of a Religious Education Illustrated and Enforced. A Sermon: delivered at Worcester, October 31, 1793, occasioned by the Execution of Samuel Frost, on that day, for the Murder of Captain Elisha Allen, of Princeton, on the 16th Day of July, 1793. By Aaron Bancroft, A.M. Pastor of the Second Church in Worcester. Printed at Worcester, Massachusetts, By Isaiah Thomas. Sold at the Worcester bookstore. MDCCXCIII.

CSmH, MBAt, MHi, MWA*, NHi, NN, NNUT, PHi, RPJCB

Evans 25,137

(50) Matthew Womble, Murders of 1784, 1793

(a) A true account, how Matthew Womble murdered his wife, (who was pregnant) and his four sons on June 19th, 1784 . . . by John Leland, V.D.M. Stockbridge, Printed for Richard Lee, 1793. 8 p. 17 cm.

MH-L (not located), MWA* (T. p. wanting), NBuG

mp. 46,808   Bristol B8,396

(a.2) Norwich: Printed for Richard Lee. 1797. 8 p.

N.D. Scotti, Providence, R.I. (1970)
Bristol B9,989a   Stoddard 142

(51) Edmund Fortis, Rape and Murder, 1795

(a) The Last Words and Dying Speech of Edmund Fortis, a Negro Man, Who appeared to be between thirty and forty years of age, but very ignorant. He was executed at Dresden, on

Kennebeck River, on Thursday the twenty-fifth day of September, 1794, for a Rape and Murder, committed on the body of Pamela Tilton, a young Girl, of about fourteen years of age, daughter of Mr. Tilton of Vassalborough, in the County of Lincoln. Printed and Sold at Exeter--1795.
12 p. 16 cm.

MWA*

mp. 47,425 Bristol B9,101 McDade 312

(a.2) Exeter. MDCCXCVI 8 p. 17.5 cm.

Present location unknown

mp. 47,782 Bristol B9,545 Porter 85

Note Edmund Fortis is listed under Massachusetts because Vassalborough, where the murder occurred, was in Maine.

(52) Pomp, Murder, 1795

(a) Dying Confession of Pomp, A Negro Man, who was executed at Ipswich, on the 6th of August, 1795, For Murdering Capt. Charles Furbush, of Andover, taken from the mouth of the Prisoner, and penned by Jonathan Plummer, Jun. . . . [Newburyport, printed by Blunt & March, 1795.] Broadside

MSaE*, RPB

Evans 29,329 Ford 2,759 McDade 760

(53) John Stewart, Burglary, 1797

(a) The Confession, last Words, and Dying Speech of John Stewart, A Native of Ireland. Taken from himself, at his own particular Request. . . . [Boston 1797] Broadside fol.

MWa*, NHi

Evans 32,879 Ford 2,843

Evans Ghost 32,880

(54) Stephen Smith, Burglary, 1797

(a) Life, Last Words and Dying Speech of Stephen Smith. A Black Man, who was executed at Boston this Day being Thursday, October 12, 1797 for Burglary. . . . [Boston 1797]
Broadside fol.

MB*

Evans 32,852

(55) Samuel Smith, Burglary, 1799

(a) Last Words and Dying Speech of Samuel Smith, Who was Executed at Concord, in the County of Middlesex, and Commonwealth of Massachusetts, the 26th of December, A.D. 1799, for the Crime of Burglary. . . . To be sold at Mr. Reuben Bryant's Book-Store, Concord. -- Also at the Printing-Office, in Kilby-Street, Boston. Broadside

MWA* (two variants reproduced), NHi

Evans 36,321 Ford 2,939

(b) Love To Our Neighbour Explained and Urged in a Sermon, delivered at Concord, Massachusetts, December 26, 1799, Being the Day on which Samuel Smith was executed for Burglary. By Ezra Ripley, A.M. Minister of Concord. Published for the Benefit of Criminals. Printed by Samuel Hall, No. 53, Cornhill, Boston. 1800. 31 p.

CtY, DLC, MBAt*, MHi, MWA, NHi, NN, RPJCB

Evans 38,410

5.03 Rhode Island

(1) Jeremiah Meacham, Murder, 1715

(a) The Lord's Voice, Crying to His People: in some Extraordinary Dispensations Considered In a Sermon. . . . preached 27d. I m. [Mar. 27] 1715. Occasioned By the Terrible Tragedies of a Man Barbarously Murdering his Wife and her Sister, and then Burning his House, March 22. 1715. Together With some Account about the Poor Man. Written for the Benefit of the Living. By Nathaniel Clap, M.A., Preacher of the Gospel at Newport, R. Island. Boston: Printed by B. Green, Sold at the Booksellers Shops 1715. 140 p. 12mo.

DLC, MB*, MHi, MWA(imp.), NHi, RHi(imp.), RPJCB

Evans 1,729 Sabin 13,204 McDade 675

(b) Sinners Directed to Hear & Fear, and do no more so Wickedly. Being an Impartial Account of the Inhumane and Barbarous Murder, Committed by Jeremiah Meacham, On his Wife and her Sister, at Newport on Rhode-Island, March 22d. 1715. With some Account of his Life, Tryal, Carriage before and after Condemnation; his Confession, Prayers, and Last Dying Words at the Place of Execution, which was April the 12th. 1715. Also a Sermon Preached in his Hearing. . . . . By Nathaniel Clap, Minister of the Gospel in Newport, Rhode-Island. Boston. Printed by J. Allen, for N. Boone, at the Sign of the Bible in Cornhill, 1715. 80 p. 13.3 cm.

DLC, MHi, MWA*, RHi(imp.)

mp. 39,607 Bristol B464 McDade 676

(c) A Broken Heart Acceptable with God through Christ. A Sermon preached at Newport, March 27, 1715. [By Nathaniel Clap]. . . . on a murder committed by Jeremiah Meacham (the prisoner being present at the meeting, and addressed by the preacher), with the dying words of the criminal at the execution, at Newport, on Rhode Island, April 21. 1715. [Printed for, and Sold by Nicholas Boone, at the Sign of the Bible in Cornhill, Boston.] 56 p. 16mo.

RHi(2, 1 imp.)

Evans 1,728 Sabin 13,202

Note Microcard for Evans 1,728 says this is a ghost of Evans 1,728, above 5.04(1)(a). Considering the major discrepancies between the two entries, doubts must be expressed.

(2) Fortune, Arson, 1762

(a) The Dying Confession and Declaration of Fortune, a Negro Man, Who was executed in Newport, (Rhode-Island) on Friday the 14th of May, 1762, for setting Fire to the Stores on Long Wharf. Boston: Printed by Fowle & Draper at their Office opposite [illegible], Marlborough [illegible] MDCCLXII.

Unidentified photocopy*

Evans 9,116

(3) John Shearman, Burglary, 1764

(a) The last Words and Dying Speech of John Shearman, Executed at Newport, Rhode-Island, on Friday the Sixteenth Day of November, 1764, for Burgulary [sic]. . . . Boston: Printed and Sold by R. and S. Draper's Printing-office in Newbury-street, and at Green and Russell's in Queen-street. 1764. Broadside 33 x 23 cm.

PHi

Bristol B2,515 Ford 1,335

(b) [Bottom of col. 1] . . . And as I am now about resigning this transitory Life, by Way of Expiation to offended Justice, I ardently . . . May all . . . take Warning by the awful Spectacle which this Body of mine will exhibit when suspended in the Place destined for its suffering. . . John Shearman. Boston, Printed, and Sold by Z. Fowle, at his Printing-Office in Back-Street. 1764. Broadside 30.5 cm.

MWA*(imp.)

mp. 41,487 Bristol B2,516

(4) Daniel Wilson, Rape, 1774

(a) The Life and Confession of Daniel Wilson, Who was executed at Providence (Rhode-Island) on Friday the 29th of April, 1774, for committing a Rape,. . . [Providence or Boston? 1774] Broadside 30.5 x 21 cm.

MWA*

Evans 13,774 Alden 573 Ford 1,780

(5) Thomas Hickey, Sedition and Mutiny, 1776

(a) The Last Speech, and Dying Words of Thomas Hickey, (A Soldier in the Continental Army) Who was executed in a Field near the City of New-York, on Friday June 28, 1776, for joining in Sedition and Mutiny, and of treacherously corresponding with, inlisting, and receiving pay from the Enemies of the United American Colonies. . . . I die in the twenty-eighth year of my age. And may the Lord have mercy upon my soul. Thomas Hickey. By a vessel arrived yesterday. . . Newport, July 4, 1776. [Newport, Printed by Solomon Southwick, 1776] Broadside 35 x 23 cm.

NHi*, RNHi

mp. 43,046 Bristol B4,232 Alden 634

(b) Revolutionary Conspiracy, <u>above</u>, 3.05(2).

(6) Thomas Mount, Burglary, 1791

(a) The Confession, &c. of Thomas Mount, Who was executed at Little-Rest, in the State of Rhode-Island, on Friday the 27th of May, 1791, for Burglary. [Colophon] Printed and sold by Peter Edes, in Newport. 21 p. 8vo.

MH, MWA, NHi, RHi*, RNHi(imp.), RP(imp.), RPJCB

Evans 23,773 Sabin 41,144 Alden 1,259 Winship p. 57

(a.2) Newport Printed: New-Haven Re-Printed, 1791. [T. & B. Green] Sold at the Printing-office. 22 p. 8vo.

CtHi*

Evans 23,774 Trumbull 1,131

(a.3) Middletown [Conn.]: Printed by Moses H. Woodward For Isaac Riley, & Co. [1791] 23 p. 8vo.

RPJCB*

Evans 23,775 Trumbull 2d 2,622 Winship p. 57

(a.4) Portsmouth: Printed and Sold by J. Melcher, at his Office in Market-Street [1791?] 24 p. 17.5 cm.

MWA*

mp. 46,227 Bristol B7,764

(7) Zilpha Smith, 1798

(a) A narrative of the life of Zilpha Smith, alias Sylva Wood . . . She hung herself in Herkemer Gaol . . . Providence, Bennett Wheeler, 1798.

No copy known

mp. 48,519 Bristol B10,404 Alden 1,567

5.04 Connecticut

(1) Isaac Frazier (or Frasier), Burglary, 1768

(a) Account of the life and abominable thefts of Isaac Frazier, under the sentence of death for burglary. New Haven: Printed by Samuel Green. 1768. 16 p. 16mo.

CtY*

Evans 10,808 Trumbull 2d 2,169

(a.2) A Brife [sic] Account Of the Life, and abominable Thefts, of the Notorious Isaac Frasier, (Under Sentance [sic] of Death, for Burglary) penned from his own Mouth, signed by him, a few Days, before his Execution. With his dying Speech. [New Haven: Printed by T. & S. Green. 1768] 15 p. 17 cm.

NN*(imp.)

mp. 41,823 Bristol B2,880
New York Public 391 Trumbull 732

(b) A Brief Account Of the Life, and abominable Thefts, of the notorious Isaac Frasier, who was Executed at Fairfield, Sept. 7th, 1768, penned from his own Mouth, and signed by him, a few Days before his Execution. New-London: Printed and Sold by Timothy Green. [1768] 16 p. 12 mo.

MWA* New London 850

Evans 10,808 (microcard) Trumbull 3d 2,839

(b.2) Printed & sold by T. & S. Green, in New Haven. [1768?] 16 p. 20 cm.

CtHi, CtY, MWA*, RPJCB

mp. 41,822 Bristol B2,879
Trumbull 2d 2,170

(c) Excessive Wickedness, the Way to an untimely Death. A Sermon Preached at Fairfield, in Connecticut, September 7th, 1768. At The Execution Of Isaac Frasier. By Noah Hobart, A.M. Pastor of the First church in Fairfield. . . . New-Haven: Printed and Sold by Thomas and Samuel Green. [1768] 24 p. 8vo.

CtHi, NHi*

Evans 10,926 Trumbull 839

Note The execution of Isaac Frazier is confirmed by a news account in the Connecticut Courant, September 12, 1768, p. 3. Frazier's petition to the General Assembly for commutation of his sentence was denied. Apparently his disappointment at this led him to burn the Fairfield jail where he was confined. Richard Gaskins, "Changes in the Criminal Law in Eighteenth Century Connecticut," 25 American Journal of Legal History 309, 329 note 84 (1981).

(2) Burglar, 1769

(a) A Poem, wrote upon the Execution of a Man, who [was] Whipt, Cropt, and Branded at Fairfield, for Burglary, the first Day of March, in the Year 1769. . . . [n.p. 1769]
Broadside 23.5 x 17 cm.

CtHi*(imp.?)

mp. 41,994 Bristol B3,066

(3) Moses Paul, Murder, 1772

(a) New-Haven, September 2, 1772. A short Account of the Life of Moses Paul, (an Indian) who is this Day to be executed in New-Haven, for the Murder of Mr. Moses Cook, of Waterbury; of which Crime he was convicted before the Honorable Superior Court, held in this Place, in December last, and received Sentence of Death accordingly; and was to have been executed on the 17th of June last, but was reprieved to this Day.
Broadside 42.5 x 19 cm.

NHi*

mp. 42,358 Bristol B3,468

(b) A Sermon, Preached at the Execution of Moses Paul, An Indian, Who was executed at New-Haven, on the second of September, 1772; for the Murder of Mr. Moses Cook, Late of Waterbury, on the 7th of December, 1771. 24 p. 8vo.

CSmH, CtHi, CtHT-W, CtNlC(imp.), CtY, DLC, MDeeP, MH, MWA*, NN, NSm, PPPrHi, RPJCB(imp.)

Evans 12,493 Sabin 56,635 New London 950
Trumbull 2d 2,478 McDade 730

(b.2) New-Haven; Printed and Sold T. & S. Green. [1772] 32 p. 8vo.

CSmH, CtHT-W, MBAt, MWA*, MWiW-C, NN, PPPrHi, ViU

Evans 12,494 Sabin 56,635 McDade 731

(b.3) The Third Edition. New-London: Printed and sold by T. Green. 1772. 24 p. 8vo.

CtHi, DLC, ICN, MH, MWA*, NAuT, NjR

Evans 12,495 Sabin 56,635 New London 951
Trumbull 2d 2,479 McDade 732

(b.4) The Fourth Edition. New-London: Printed and sold by T. Green. 1772 24 p. 4to.

CSmH, CtHT-W, DLC, ICN, MWA*, NHi, NN

Evans 12,496 Sabin 56,635 McDade 733
New London 952 Trumbull 2d 2,480

(b.5) Boston: Printed and Sold by Richard Draper in Newbury-Street. And John Boyles in Marlborough-Street. 1773. 32 p. 4to.

CSmH, DLC, ICN, MB, MWA*

Evans 12,907 Sabin 56,635 McDade 733n.

(b.6) Boston, Printed and Sold by John Boyles, next Door to the Three Doves in Marlborough Street. 1773. 32 p. 19 cm.

CSmH, CtHT-W, MB, MHi(imp.) MSaE, MWA*

mp. 42,478 Bristol B3,610

Note Microcard says that MWA "has a variant with the imprint reading 'Boyles, in Marlborough-Street.'"

(b.7) Boston, Printed and sold by Richard Draper in Newbury-Street. 1773. 32 p. 19.5 cm.

CSmH*, ViU

mp. 42,479 Bristol B3,611 Huntington 334

(b.8) Boston: Printed and Sold by John Boyles, next Door to the Three Doves in Marlborough-Street. 1773. 24 p. 8vo.

DLC, ICN, MWA*, NN, RPJCB

Evans 12,908 Sabin 56,635 McDade 733n.

(b.9) Hartford: Re-printed and sold by Ebenezer Watson. [1772 or 1773] 24 p. 4to.

MWA*, NN

Evans 12,909 Sabin 56,635 McDade 733n.
Trumbull 2d 2,481

(b.10) Salem: Printed and sold by S. and E. Hall, near the Town-House. 1773. 31 p. 8vo.

MWA*

Evans 12,910 Sabin 56,635 McDade 733n.
Tapley p. 313

(b.11) The Ninth Edition. Boston: Printed for and Sold by Eldad Hunter. MDCCLXXIV. 24 p. 8vo.

MB, MWA*, RPJCB

Evans 13,508 Sabin 56,635 McDade 733n.

(b.12) London Edition, 1789.

MBAt, P

Sabin 56,635 McDade 733n.

(b.13) Northampton. 1801

Sabin 56,635

(b.14) Exeter: Printed for Josiah Richardson, the Lord's Messenger to the People. 1819.

Sabin 56,635 McDade 733n.

(b.15) Bennington: William Watson. [After 1820]

Sabin 56,635

(b.16) Springfield: Henry Brewer, Printer. [n.d.]

DLC

Sabin 56,635

(c) Letter form J---h J-----n, one of the Mohegan Tribe of Indians, to his countryman, Moses Paul, under Sentence of Death, in New-Haven Goal. Mohegan, in New-London County, A.D. 1772, March 29. . . . [New Haven? 1772] 8 p.

CSmH, CtHi, DLC*

Evans 12,634 Huntington 321 New London 947
Trumbull 2d 2,296

(d) Mr. Occom's Address to his Indian Brethren. On the Day that Moses Paul, an Indian, was executed at New-Haven, on the 2d of September, 1772, for the Murder of Moses Cook . . . . [n.p. 1772?] Broadside 34 x 21 cm.

MWA*

mp. 42,362a Bristol B3,473 Wegelin 291

(d.2) Mr. Occom's Address to his Indian Brethren, On the Day that Moses Paul, an Indian, was executed at New-Haven, on the 2d of September, 1772, for the Murder of Moses Cook. Put in Metre . . . . Sold [by T. and J. Fleet] at the Heart and Crown in Boston, and by Bulkeley Emerson at Newburyport. [1773] Broadside 8¼" x 12"

CSmH, NN (photostat)*

Evans 12,911 Ford 1,629 Huntington 322
McDade 733n. Winslow 47 (NN photostat)

(e) A Sermon at the Execution of Moses Paul, an Indian; who had been guilty of Murder, Preached at New Haven in America. By Samson Occom, A native Indian, and Missionary to the Indians, who was in England in 1776 [1766] and 1777, [1767] collecting for the Indian Charity Schools. To which is added A Short Account of the Late Spread of the Gospel; among the Indians. Also Observation on the Language of the Muhhekaneew Indians; Communicated to the Connecticut Society of Arts and Sciences, By Jonathan Edwards, D.D. New Haven, Connecticut; Printed 1788.

CtHT-W, NN

mp. 45,316 Bristol B6,763 Sabin 56,636

Note Bristol lists the imprint described, saying that there are two copies at NhD. Short-Title Evans and mp. 45,316 say the description of an American imprint is "a ghost of the London printing", and reproduces the London imprint from a Dartmouth

College copy.

(e.2) [The Same] London: Reprinted, 1788, and Sold by Buckland, Paternoster-row; Dilly, Poultry; Otridge, Strand; J. Lepard, No. 92, Newgate-street; T. Pilcher, No. 44, Barbican; Brown, on the Tolsey, Bristol; Binns, at Leeds; and Woolmer, at Exeter.

DLC, MB, NN, NNUT, NhD*, NjP, PHi, PPL

mp. 45,316 Bristol B6,763 Sabin 56,636

Note See Note to (e).

(e.3) London: Reprinted, 1789, and sold by Buckland (2 issues, one with and one without appendix)

CtHT-W, DLC, MB, NN

Sabin 56,636

(4) Elizabeth Shaw's 1744 Execution for Murder, 1772

(a) A brief Relation of a Murder committed by Elizabeth Shaw, Who was executed at Windham, on the 18th of Nov. 1744, for the Murder of her Child . . . . New-London: Printed in the Year 1772. Broadside 27.5 x 16.5 cm.

CtHi*, ICN

mp. 42,321 Bristol B3,431 New London 936

(5) Moses Dunbar, High Treason, 1777

(a) The Last Speech and Dying Words of Moses Dunbar Who was executed at Hartford on Wednesday the 19th day of March 1777 for high treason against the State of Connecticut. (Printed at the request of his son.). No copy known (NNPM has contemporary manuscript.)

mp. 43,245 Bristol B4,460 (Cf. Evans 15,607)
Trumbull 2d 2,090

(a.2) The Calendar. August 22, 1846 [Superseded by The Churchman (Hartford, Conn.)]

(a.3) Joseph Anderson, ed., 1 The Town and City of Waterbury, Connecticut 434-36 (New Haven 1896).

(b) The Reasons and Design of public Punishments; a Sermon, Delivered before the People who were collected to the Execution of Moses Dunbar, Who was condemned for High Treason against the State of Connecticut, and executed March 19th A.D. 1777. By Nathan Strong, Pastor of the first Church in Hartford . . . . Hartford: Printed and Sold by Eben. Watson, M,DCC, LXXVII. 18 p. 4to.

MWA*, NHi

Evans 15,607 Trumbull 1,460

(6) Thomas Goss, Murder, 1778

(a) The Last Words and dying Speech of Thomas Goss, In a private Conference, previous to his Execution. . . . [n.p. 1778]
Broadside 48 x 27 cm.

NN*

mp. 43,459 Bristol B4,688 McDade 368
New York Public 672

(7) Barnett Davenport, Murder, 1780

(a) A Brief Narrative of the Life and Confession of Barnett Davenport, Under Sentence of Death, for a Series of the most horrid Murders, ever perpetrated in this country, or perhaps any other, on the Evening following the 3rd of February, 1780. Is to be executed at Litchfield, on the 8th of May. [Hartford?] Printed in the Year M,DCC,LXXX. 15 p. 16 mo.

CSmH, DLC, MWA*, NHi

Evans 16,756 McDade 242

(b) A Brief Narrative of the Life and Confession. . . . Barnett Davenport. Litchfield Goal, April 29th, 1780. [Hartford? 1780?] 14 p. 20 cm.

MWA(imp.) (microcard not yet issued 3-31-82)

mp. 43,792 Bristol B5,073

(c) The Continental Journal, and Weekly Advertiser. June 1, 1780. A Narrative of the Life and Confession of Barnett Davenport, who was executed at Litchfield, on the 8th of May instant, for a series of the most horrid murders, ever perpetrated in this country, or perhaps any other, on the evening following the 3d of February 1780. Boston: Printed by John Gill, in Court-Street. 1780. fol.

MHi

Evans 16,752

(8) William Beadle, 1782

(a) A Poem, Occasioned by the most shocking and Cruel Murder That ever was represented on the Stage; or the most deliberate Murder that ever was perpetrated in Human Life. . . . Sold near Liberty-Stump and next the Swan-Tavern, South End. (Price 6 Coppers single.) --The Sermon refer'd to above will be immediately printed as soon as, it comes to Hand.

[Hartford, B. Webster. 1782] Broadside 42 x 33.5 cm.

MiU-C*

mp. 44,246 Bristol B5,571 Winslow 51 (MiU-C)

(b) Providence. January 1, 1783. The following is the most particular Account we have been able to obtain of the late cruel Murders committed at Weathersfield, in Connecticut;--it is extracted from a Hartford Paper of the 17th Ultima, and published by Desire of a Number of Gentlemen who expected to have seen it in last Saturday's Paper--but were disappointed. . . . Providence: Printed and Sold by B. Wheeler. [1783] Broadside fol.

MWA*

Evans 19,431

(c) A Narrative of the Life of William Beadle, Of Wethersfield, in the State of Connecticut. Containing I. The Particulars of the "horrid Massacre" of himself and Family. II. Extracts from the Rev. Mr. Marsh's Sermon at the Funeral of his Wife and Children. Hartford: Printed and sold by Bavil Webster, 1783. 24 p. 8vo.

CtHT-W(imp.), MWA*, NN, RPJCB

Evans 17,828 Sabin 4,102 McDade 74
Trumbull 2d 2,423

(c.2) A narrative of the life of William Beadle, of Wethersfield, Connecticut. Containing I. The particulars of the horrid massacre of himself and family. II. Extracts from the Rev. Mr. Marsh's sermon at the funeral of his wife and family. III. A true account of the situation of the house on the morning after the dredful catastrophe. [By Stephen Mix Mitchell] Bennington [Vt.]: Printed by Anthony Haswell, 1794. 47 p. 8vo.

NHi*(imp.)

Evans 26,629 Cooley 240 McCorison 304
McDade 77

<u>Note</u> Microcard reproduces pages 3 through 40. Title page missing.

(c.3) Windsor: Re printed by Alden Spooner, M,DCC,XCV. 24 p. 12mo.

MWA*

Evans 28,246 Sabin 4,102 McCorison 351
Cooley 274 McDade 77n.

(d) The great Sin and Danger of striving with God. A Sermon preached at Wethersfield, December 13, 1782. At the funeral of Mrs. Lydia Beadle, wife of the late William Beadle, And their Four Children, Who were all murdered by his own Hands, on the Morning of the 11th Instant. By John Marsh, A.M. Pastor of the First Church of Wethersfield. To which is annexed A Letter, from a Gentleman in Wethersfield to his Friend, containing a Narrative of the Life of William Beadle, (so far as it is known) and the Particulars of the Massacre of himself and Family. Hartford: Printed by Hudson and Goodwin. [1783] 39 p. 8vo.

CSmH, CtHT-W, DLC, MB, MBAt, MH, MHi, MWA*, NHi, NN, RPJCB

Evans 18,009 Sabin 44,743 McDade 75
Trumbull 1,072

(d.2) Middleborough, (County of Plymouth) Printed and sold by N. Coverly M,DCC,LXXXVIII. 39 p. 8vo.

CSmH, DLC, MB(imp.), MWA*, NN, RPB

Evans 21,216 Sabin 44,743 McDade 76

(e) Men's sins not chargeable on God, but on themselves. A Discourse Delivered at Wallingford, December 22, 1782, occasioned by the tragical exit of William Beadle, His Wife and four Children, at Wethersfield, on the morning of the 11th instant, by his own hands. By James Dana, D.D. Pastor of the first Church in Wallingford. . . . New-Haven: Printed by T. & S. Green. [1783] 28 p. 4to.

MBAt, MHi, MWA*

Evans 17,903

(f) A Poem Occasioned by the horrid Crime of William Beadle, Late of Wethersfield, in Connecticut, who on the 11th of December 1782, . . . murdered his wife and four promising children. . . . Broadside 37.5 x 25 cm.

[n.p. 1783?]

MAJ

Bristol B5,787

(g) William Beadles Lebens-Beschreibung, Nebst der Ermordung seiner Familie und sich selbst Wie auch die Ursachen und Beweisgruende, die er hinterliess sich zu rechtfertigen. Ephrata: Nach-gedrucht . . . Benjamin Mayer, 1796. 16 p. 8vo.

PHi*

Evans 30,042

(9) Joseph Mountain, Rape, 1790

(a) Sketches of the Life of Joseph Mountain, A Negro, Who was executed at New-Haven, on the 20th Day of October, 1790, For a Rape, Committed on the 26th Day of May last. [The writer of this history has directed that the money arising from the sales thereof, after deducting the expense of printing, &c. be given to the unhappy girl, whose life is rendered wretched by the crime of the malefactor.] New-Haven: Printed and Sold by T. & S. Green. 20 p.8vo.

CtHi*, CtY, NHi

Evans 22,441 Porter 203 Trumbull 1,132

Note Brackets in original.

(a.2) Sketches of the Life of Joseph Mountain, A Negro, Who was executed at New-Haven, on the 20th Day of October, 1790. For a Rape, Committed on the 26th Day of May last. The writer of this narrative assures the public, that the facts related were taken from the mouth of the culprit. In no instance has any fact been substantially altered, or in the least exaggerated. On the 28th of September the writer applied to Joseph, to learn if he persisted in affirming the truth of the foregoing story. By the direction of the criminal his name was then set to this history, and he declared, in presence of the subscribing witnesses, that it contained nothing but the truth, Joseph Peck Samuel Punderson. Norwich: Printed by John Trumbull. [1790?] 16 p. 20 cm.

NHi*

mp. 45,856 Bristol B7,350

(a.3) Sketches of the Life of Joseph Mountain, A Negro, Who was executed at New-Haven, on the 20th Day of October, 1790, For a Rape, Committed on the 26th Day of May last. [The writer of this history has directed that the money arising from the sales thereof, after deducting the expence of printing, &c. be given to the unhappy girl, whose life is rendered wretched by the crime of the malefactor.] Hartford: Printed and Sold by Nathaniel Patten. [1790] 15 p. 20 cm.

MWA*

mp. 45,855 Bristol B7,349 Trumbull 2d 2,613

Note Brackets in original.

(a.4) Independent Chronicle: and the Universal Advertiser. November 18, 1790, above 4.20 (1)(b).

(b) The Intent of Capital Punishment. A Discourse Delivered in the City of New-Haven, October 20, 1790. Being the day of the Execution of Joseph Mountain, for a Rape. By Dana, D.D. Pastor of the first church in said city. New-Haven; Printed by T. and S. Green. [1790] 28 p. 8vo.

MWA*, NIC-L, NN, RPJCB

Evans 22,446 Trumbull 549

(c) [The singular adventures, &c. n. p. 179?] 32 p. 18.5 cm.

Cty* (title page lacking)

mp. 45,763 Bristol B7,237 Porter 204

(d) The Life and Adventures of Joseph Mountain, a Negro Highwayman. Who practised robbing in England, France, Spain and Holland, about ten years, without detection, and was finally executed at New-haven, in Connecticut, on the 20th of October, 1790, for committing a Rape, on the body of a respectable young girl of that town. Taken from his own mouth in the presence of respectable witnesses. . . . [By David Daggett] Bennington, [Vermont] Printed by Anthony Haswell, M,DCC,XCI. 28 p. 19 cm.

VtBennM*

mp. 46,146 Bristol B7,675 Cooley 150 McCorison 198

<u>Evans Ghosts</u> 22,442 and 22,443

(e) Die Wunderbare Lebens-Beschreibung von Joseph Mountain, eines Negers, Welcher den 20sten October 1790, in Neu-Haven, im Staat Connecticut wegen einer Nothzüchtigung gehencket worden ist. Worinnen dessen viele verübte Räubereyen in England, Franckreich, Holland, &c. Sehr wunderbar zu lesen, und Anzeigt wie tief die menschliche Natur fallen kan. Lancaster, Gedruckt und zu haben in der Neuen Buchdruckerey. [n.d.] 24 p. 22 cm.

PHi

(f) Das Leben und die Begebenheiten von Joseph Mountain, einem Neger, welcher zu Neu-Haven, an 20sten October, 1790 . . . hingerichtet worden . . . [Philadelphia, C. Cist, 1791] 16 p. 8vo.

PPL

Bristol B7,674a

5.05 New York

(1) Peter Vine, Rape and Murder, 1744

(a) A Warning piece to all clergymen; being an impartial account of the life, character, behaviour and last dying words of Peter Vine, who was executed. . . . 1743, for a rape and murder. New-York. Re-printed by H. De Foreest 1744.

No copy located

Evans 5,507

(2) Owen Syllivan, Counterfeiting, 1756

(a) A Short Account Of the Life, of John **** Alias Owen Syllavan, Alias John Livingston, alias John Brown, by which Names he stood indicted by the Grand Jury, and was found Guilty by the Supreme Sessions for the City and County of New-York, for Counterfeiting and passing the current Bills of that colony emitted in the Year 1737: And was Executed on Monday the 10th Day of May 1756. Shewing what Manner of Life he led from his Infancy. Taken from his own Mouth. To which is added, His Dying Speech At the Place of Execution. New-York Printed. Boston: Re-printed and Sold by Green & Russell at their Printing-Office near the Custom-House, and next to the Writing School in Queen-Street. 1756. 12 p.

MWA*

Evans 7,796

(3) Joseph Andrews, Piracy and Murder, 1769

(a) An Account of the Trial of Joseph Andrews for Piracy and Murder, Together with his Confession to the Gentlemen of the Clergy who visited him during his Confinement, and to the Keepers of the Goal the Day before his Execution; the Account he gave them of his Parentage and Manner of Life; also his Character and Dying Speech. America. [New-York] Printed for every Purchaser. M,DCC,LXIX. 8 p. 4to.

PPL*

Evans 11,149 McDade 8

(b) An Account of The Trial of Joseph Andrews, for Piracy and Murder, Together with his Confession to the Gentlemen of the Clergy who visited him during his Confinement, and on the Day of his Execution; the Account he gave them of his Parentage and Manner of Life, also his Character and Execution. . . . [New-York 1769] 2 p. fol.

PPL*

Evans 11,150 McDade 9

(c) A Narrative Of Part of the Life and Adventurers [sic] of Joseph Andrews, Particularly of his Piracy and the Murder of Capt. Duryee and his Company, for which he was tried on the 17th Instant, and condemn'd to be hang'd this day, the 23d of May, 1769, on the Shore between the Air Furnace and the Town, and his Body afterwards hung in Chains on Bedlow's Island. . . . [New York 1769] 2 p. fol.

PPL*

Evans 11,151 McDade 11

(d) The Last dying Speech and Confession, of Joseph Andrews. Who was Executed at New-York, on Tuesday the 23d of May, 1769. For Piracy and Murder. . . . [Signed] Joseph Andrews. A true Copy. [New York] Printed for and published by L. Swiney and J. Stewart. [1769] Broadside fol.

PPL*

Evans 11,152 McDade 10

(4) John Jubeart, Counterfeiting, 1769

(a) The Confession and Dying Words of John Jubeart, Who was Executed at New-York, upon Wednesday the Sixth of September, 1769; For Coining and Passing Counterfeit Dollars. . . . [New York] Printed for the Sober John Stewart, Esq; and Co. and sold from their Fists in every Quarter of this City. [1769] Broadside fol.

PPL*

Evans 11,303

(5) John Campbell, Robbery, 1769

(a) A Short Account of the Life and Character of John Campbell, Now under Sentence of Death, for Robbery, and to be executed this 29th of December, 1769. . . . [New-York 1769] Broadside fol.

PPL*

Evans 11,463

(6) John Clarkewight, Horse Stealing, 1770

(a) The last Speech and dying Words of John Clarkewight, who was executed at Poughkeepsie, on Friday the 20th of July Instant, for horse stealing. . . . [New York 1770] Broadside fol.

PPL*

Evans 11,602

(7) John Smith, Counterfeiting, 1773

(a) The Last Speech, Confession and Dying words of John Smith, Who was executed at Albany on the fifth Day of February 1773, for counterfeiting the currency of the Province of New-York, &c. Contained in Two Letters, written by Himself, and addressed to the Printers. Albany: Printed by Alexander and James Robertson, 1773.

No copy located.

Evans 13,019

(a.2) Albany Printed. Hartford: Reprinted [by Ebenezer Watson] in the Year 1773. 8 p. 8vo.

NN*

Evans 13,020 Trumbull 1,386

(a.3) Re-printed and Sold at the Printing-Office in New-Haven. [1773] 8 p. 8vo.

CtY*

Evans 13,021 Trumbull 2d 2,615

(8) John Wall Lovey, Counterfeiting, 1773

(a) The Last Speech, Confession and Dying Words, of John Wall Lovey. Who was executed at Albany Friday the 2d of April, 1773 for counterfeiting the Currency of the Province of New-York . . . . [New York? 1773]
Broadside 35 x 21 cm.

CtHi*

mp. 42,531 Bristol B3,584

(9) Francis Burdett Personel, Murder, 1773

(a) An Authentic and Particular Account of the Life of Francis Burdett Personel, Written by Himself. Who was executed at New-York, September 10th, 1773; in the Twenty-sixth year of his Age, for the Murder of Robert White. New-York: printed in the year M.DCC.LXXIII. 23 p. 12mo.

MWiW-C, NHi*

Evans 12,936 Sabin 61,069 McDade 740

(a.2) Sold at the Printing Office in New Haven. [1773?] 23 p. 16.5 cm.

CtHi*, NN

mp. 42,483 Bristol B3,620 McDade 741
New York Public 508 Trumbull 2d 2,498

(a.3) Another printing. [n.p. 1773?]

NjR(imp.)

Bristol B3,619

(10) Joseph Bill Packer, Counterfeiting, 1773

(a) A Journal of the Life and Travels of Joseph-Bill Packer, now under sentence of death in the City-Hall of Albany, for counterfeiting the currency. Written by himself and published at his request. Albany: Printed by Alexander and James Robertson, 1773. 12 mo.

No copy located

Evans 12,914 (microcard duplicates reproduction of 5.05(10)-(b) below)

(b) A Journal, of the Life and Travels of Joseph-Bill Packer. To the Printers. Gentlemen, Whereas I am now under sentence of death in the City-Hall of Albany, for having as it is supposed, counterfeited. . . . 15 p.

MH*(imp.)

Evans 12,915 Trumbull 926

(11) William Tryon, Treason, 1776

(a) The Speech of William Try--n, Esq; Who was executed on Thursday the 18th of March, 1776. . . . [New-York 1776] Broadside 4to.

DLC, NHi, NN*

Evans 15,095

(11a) Thomas Hickey, 1776

(a) See 5.03(a) above.

(12) Francis Uss, Burglary and Robbery, 1789

(a) The Narrative of the life of Francis Uss, who was executed at Poughkeepsie, in the County of Dutchess, on Friday the 31st of July, 1789. [Poughkeepsie?] Printed in August 1789. 8 p. 21.5 cm.

NN*(imp.)

mp. 45,728 Bristol B7,204 Sabin 98,185

New York Public 947

(13) Whiting Sweeting, Murder, 1791

(a) The Narrative of Whiting Sweeting, Who was executed at Albany, the 26th August, 1791. . . . [Albany? 1791?] 54 p. 12mo.

MWA*, N

mp. 46,293 Bristol B7,835 McDade 960(a)

(a.2) [Albany? 1791] 47 p.

NHi, RPJCB

McDade 960(b)

(a.3) Printed for Silvester Tiffany, Lansingburgh. [1791] 72 p.

MWA*, MiU-C

Evans 23,814 Sabin 94,043 McDade 960

(a.4) Hartford: Re-Printed by Hudson and Goodwin. [1791] 36 p. 12mo.

CtHi, MH, MH-L, MWA*, NN

Evans 23,815 Sabin 94,044 McDade 960(c) Trumbull 1,479

(a.5) Philadelphia: Re-Printed by Daniel Lawrence, and sold by most of the booksellers in the city. M.DCC.XCII 72 p. 12mo.

NHi, PPPrHi*

Evans 24,836 McDade 960(d)

(a.6) Printed at Albany: Reprinted at Providence, and sold by Bennett Wheeler [1792] 64 p.

MWA*, NHi, RPB

Evans 24,838 Alden 1,297 McDade 960(e)

(a.7) Printed at Concord by Elijah Russell. MDCCXCIII. 40 p. 8vo.

DLC, MWA*, NN

Evans 26,237 McDade 960(g)

(a.8) Printed at Albany:--Re-printed at Providence, by Bennett Wheeler, and sold at his Office in the Market-House Chamber--1794. 59 p. 8vo.

DLC, MH-L, RPB*

Evans 27,767 Sabin 94,052 Alden 1,391
McDade 960(k)

(a.9) Windham: Printed for Mr. James Huntington. 1797. 47 p. 8vo.

BLM, CSmH, CtHi, CtY, DLC, MWA*, NHi, NIC-L, NN

Evans 32,899 McDade 960(m) Trumbull 1,480

(b) A Remarkable Narrative of Whiting Sweeting; who was executed at Albany, in the State of New-York, for Murder. . . . Exeter: Printed and sold by H. Ranlet, at his office in Main-Street, 1793. 40 p. 8vo.

MH-L, MWA*, NIC-L, NN, RPJCB

Evans 26,238 Sabin 94,049 McDade 960(h)

(b.2) Printed at Exeter, by Henry Ranlet, and sold at his book-store, in Main-Street 1794. 52 p.

BLM, DLC, MH-L, MWA*

Evans 27,768 (microcard) McDade 960(i)

(b.3) Second Exeter Edition. Printed at Exeter, by Henry Ranlet, and sold at his book-store, in Main-street. 1794. 51 p. 12mo.

DLC, MWA, NIC-L

Evans 27,768 (book) McDade 960(j)

(b.4) The Fourth Edition. Printed at Dover: By Samuel Bragg, Jr. 1796. 70 p. 16.5 cm.

PHi*

mp. 47,926 Bristol B9,715

Evans Ghosts 24,837 [McDade 960(f) and Rink 325] and 29,598 [McDade 960(l)]

(14) William Cunningham, Forgery, 1791

(a) William Cunningham's Life, confession and last dying words. Formerly British Provost Marshal of the City of New York: Executed in London for Forgery, August 10, 1791. [New York 1791] Broadside fol.

No copy located

Evans 23,303

(a.2) "The Life, confession, and last dying words of captain William Cunningham, formerly British provost marshal, in the city of New York, who was executed in London, the 10th of August, 1791," The American Apollo, containing the publications of the Historical Society, Essays, Moral, Political, and Poetical, and the Daily Occurrences in the Natural, Civil, and Commercial World. No. 7, February 17, 1792, Vol. I, Printed at Boston, by Belknap and Young, State Street. 1792.

BLM, DLC, MBAt, MH, MWA, RPJCB

Evans 24,035

(a.3) Hezekiah Niles, ed., <u>Principles and Acts of the Revolution in America</u> 274-75 (Baltimore 1822).

(a.4) Niles, above 4.12(2)(a.7), at 510-11.

(15) John Ryer, Murder, 1792

(a) Proclamation By His Excellency George Clinton, Esquire, Governor of the State of New-York, General and Commander in Chief of all the Military, and Admiral of the Navy of the same . . . John Ryer . . . twenty-fourth day of May in the year 1792. . . . Broadside fol.

DLC*

Evans 25,906

(b) Narrative of the Life and Dying Speech of John Ryer, Who was executed at White-Plains, in the County of Westchester, State of New-York, October 2d, 1793, for the murder of Dr. Isaac Smith, Deputy-Sheriff of that county. [Poughkeepsie?] Printed for, and sold by, the Flying-stationers. [1793] 24 p. 12mo.

NHi, RPJCB*

Evans 26,118 Sabin 74,542 McDade 847 Vail 954

(b.2) Printed in Danbury, by Nathan Douglas. For the Publisher--1793. Copy-Right secured according to Law. 15 p. 21.5 cm.

MWA*, NHi, NN

mp. 46,873 Bristol B8,473 McDade 846 Vail 953

5.06 New Jersey

(1) Samuel Stoddard, Murder, 1762

(a) A Narrative of the Unhappy Life and Miserable End of Samuel Stoddard, late of the County of Burlington, and Province of New-Jersey; who was tried at a Supreme Court, held at Burlington, aforesaid, on Saturday, the Six of November 1762, for the barbarous, cruel and inhuman Murder of Jacob Cole; of which crime he was found guilty, and according to sentence, was executed at Burlington, on Tuesday, the 23d of the same Month. Philadelphia: Printed by Andrew Steuart, 1762.

No copy located

Evans 9,197 Sabin 91,939 Hildeburn 1,832

(2) John Grimes, John Fagan, and John Johnson, Burglary, 1765

(a) The Last Speech, confession, birth, parentage and education of John Grimes, John Fagan, and John Johnson, alias Johnson Cochran, who were executed at Gallows-Hill., in the city of Burlington, on Wednesday the 28th of August 1765, for burglary and felony, committed in the county of Burlington . . . . [Woodbridge: Printed by James Parker? 1765] Broadside fol.

PPL (mislaid)

Evans 10,036 Humphrey 82

(3) William Jones, Murder, 1791

(a) The Wonderful and surprising Resurrection of William Jones, Who was executed the 6th of May, at Newark, for the Murder of Samuel Shotwell. In a letter from him to E--- W---, in New-York, dated M--- T----, May 13, 1791 . . . . [Newark: Printed by John Woods, 1791] Broadside fol.

NHi*

Evans 23,475 Morsch 142

(4) Abraham Johnstone, Murder, 1797

(a) The Address of Abraham Johnstone, A Black Man, who Was hanged at Woodbury, in the County of Glocester [sic], and State of New Jersey, on Saturday the the [sic] 8th day of July last; To The People Of Colour. To which is added his dying confession or declaration. Also, a copy of a letter to his wife, written the day previous to his execution. Philadelphia: Printed [By Robert Bell] for the Purchasers. 1797. 47 p. 12mo.

BLM, DLC, MH, MBAt, MWA*, NN(2), NjR

Evans 32,320 Sabin 36,390 McDade 535 Porter 170

5.07 Pennsylvania

(1) John Morrison, Robbery, 1751

(a) An Account of the Robberies Committed by John Morrison, And his Accomplices, in and near Philadelphia, 1750. Together with The Manner of their being discover'd, their Behaviour on their Tryals, in the Prison after Sentence, and at the Place of Execution. Philadelphia, Printed [By Anthony Armbruster] in the Year 1750-1. 16 p. 4to.

PHi, PPRF*

Evans 6,624

(2) Hugh Davis and George Chambers, 1755

(a) The Last speech and dying words of Hugh Davis and George Chambers, who were executed at Lancaster, Saturday, the 14th of June, 1755, which was spoken to a numerous crowd of spectators a few moments before they were turned off, and is now printed at their desire, to deter others from evil practices. Printed at Lancaster by W. Dunlap. 1755. 8 p.

No copy located

Evans 7,404 Metzger 176

(3) John Myrick, Murder, 1755

(a) The Life and confession of John Myrick, who was executed for the murder of his wife and children. Philadelphia: Printed by James Chattin. [1755] 4to.

No copy located

Evans 7,494 Hildeburn 1,417

(4) John Lewis, Murder, 1760

(a) A Narrative of the Life, together with the last speech, confession and solemn declaration of John Lewis; who was executed, at Chester, on Saturday the 21st of September, 1760, for the most inhuman, barbarous and bloody murder of his wife; which unnatural deed he committed on Friday the 27th of June, preceding. With his letter to Mr. Raine, the sub-sheriff of Chester, concerning the publication of the said Narrative: and a penitential prayer, which he composed just before his execution. Philadelphia: Printed by Andrew Steuart. 1760.

No copy located.

Evans 8,638 Hildeburn 1,687 McDade 605n

(b) A Narrative Of the Life, Together with The last Speech, Confession and solemn Declaration, of John Lewis, Who was executed at Chester, on Saturday the 21st of September, 1760, for the most inhuman, barbarous and bloody Murder of his Wife; which unnatural Deed he committed on Friday the 27th of June, preceding. With His Letter to Mr. Raine, the Sub-Sheriff of Chester, concerning the Publication of the following Narrative: and a penitential Prayer which he composed just before his execution. . . . New-Haven: Re-Printed by James Parker and Company, at the Post-Office, 1762. [Dated, 'From my cell, in Chester-Jail September 30, 1760.] [New-Haven 1762] 10 p. 8vo.

CtHi, DLC, MWA*, NHi, NjP

Evans 9,157 and 9,120 Sabin 40,815 McDade 605
Trumbull 1,135

Note See 6.12(1)(a) below for an extract from a sermon issued in the same imprint. The imprint also included a full sermon of 220 pages.

(5) Henry Halbert, Murder, 1765

(a) Last Speech and Confession, of Henry Halbert, Who was executed at Philadelphia, October 19, 1765, for the inhuman Murder of the Son of Jacob Woolman. To which is added, A Letter from the Criminal to the Father of the murdered Son . . . Philadelphia: Printed by Anthony Armbruster, in Race-Street [n.d.] 8 p. 8vo.

PPL*

Evans 9,996 Sabin 29,602 Hildeburn 2,130 McDade 425

(6) Herman Rosencrantz, Counterfeiting, 1770

(a) The Life and Confession of Herman Rosencrantz; Executed in the City of Philadelphia, on the 5th Day of May, 1770, for Counterfeiting and Uttering the Bills of Credit of the Province of Pennsylvania. In which is an Account who were his Confederates. Taken from him own Mouth, in one of the Cells of the Gaol, a short Time before he was Executed; and, by his Request, Published, as a Warning to all others . . . Philadelphia: Printed [By Joseph Crukshank] for James Chattin, and Sold by him at Mr. Graham's, in Second-street, the second Door from Market-street Corner, and next door to Mr. Milnes, Jeweller. [1770] 11 p. 8vo.

NHi*

Evans 11,839 Hildeburn 2,554

(7) Samuel Brand, Murder, 1774

(a) Erzehlung derer durch Samuel Brand verübten gantz unmenschlichen Thaten, und seiner darauf erfolgren Hinrichtung . . . Andere Auflage. Welcher ein erbaulicher und denen meisten unbekanter gesang beygefügt worden Lancaster: Gedruckt und zu finden ben Francis Bailey. 1774. 34+ p. 8vo.

PPL*(imp.)

Evans 13,269 Hildeburn 3,012 McDade 130n.

(b) A Melancholy Narrative of the unhappy Samuel Brand, Who was executed at Lancaster, in the Province of Pennsylvania, on the 18th Day of December, 1773. For the Barbarous and Inhuman Murder of his Only Brother containing a succinct account of his Person, Parentage, Principles and Temper:- Interspersed with some interesting Reflections, moral and religious. . . . Translated from the German. Lancaster: Printed by Francis Bailey. 1774. 15 p. 19.5 cm.

MWA, RPJCB

Evans 13,436 Hildeburn 3,059 McDade 130

Note: Short-Title Evans locates a copy of Evans 13,436 at MWA, but corrected microcard does not reproduce; instead says, "Adv. Pa. Gazette, Feb. 16, 1774."

(8) John Hurrin and Alexander Buchan, Burglary, 1774

(a) The Last solemn Confession and Declaration of John Hurrin, and Alexander Buchan, who were executed at Easton, Northampton County, in the Province of Philadelphia, on the first of January, 1774. The first for Murder committed in the year 1768, and the last for a late Burglary committed at Easton. Containing a Particular Account of the many Thefts, &c. they have been guilty of from their Childhood, and by which they have been unhappily led, as it were step by step, to this ignominious and untimely End. Philadelphia: Printed and sold by James Humphreys, junior. 1774.

No copy located

Evans 13,369 Sabin 34,012 Hildeburn 3,039

(9) Elizabeth Wilson, Murder, 1786

(a) A Faithful Narrative of Elizabeth Wilson; Who was executed at Chester, January 3d, 1786. Charged with the Murder of her Twin Infants. Containing some account of her Dying Sayings, With some serious reflections. Drawn up at the request of a friend unconnected with the deceased. Philadelphia: Printed in the year 1786 8 p. 19 cm.

MH-L, MWA*, NHi, PHi, PP

Evans 19,636 Sabin 104,617 McDade 1,106

(a.2) Carlisle: Printed and sold by Kline & Reynolds, 1786.

MH-L

Evans 19,635 (origin of entry unknown)
McDade 1,106n

(a.3) Printed in Hudson, by Ashbel Stoddard, M,DCC,XXXVI 16 p. 16 cm.

NHi*

mp. 44,881 Bristol B6,278

(a.4) New-Haven: Re-printed in the year 1786. 12 p.

CtY*

mp. 44,882 Bristol B6,279 Trumbull 2d 2,122

(a.5) Philadelphia: Printed for the Purchaser. 1807.

DLC

Sabin 104,617

Evans Ghosts 19,637, 19,638 (Trumbull 2d, 2,123), and 19,639 (Trumbull 2d 2,124)

(10) John Burns, John Logan, John Ferguson, John Bennet, and Daniel Cronan, Murder and Robbery, 1789

(a) Some account of John Burns, John Logan, John Ferguson, John Bennet, and Daniel Cronan, who were executed upon the commons in the city of Philadelphia, on Monday the 12th of October, 1789, for the murder and robbery of John M'Farland. . . . [Philadelphia? 1789?] Broadside 37.5 x 18.5 cm.

PHi*

mp. 45,594 Bristol B7,067

(11) Benjamin Bailey, Murder, 1798

(a) The confession of Benjn. Bailey, who was executed at Reading, Pennsylvania, the sixth day of January, 1798; for the murder of a certain Jost Follhaber, on the eleventh day of August, 1797. Made the morning of his execution; Judge Rush's charge, together with the letters which passed between him and his wife, the week previous to his exectiion [sic], concluding with his favorite prayer. Reading: J. Schneider & Comp. M,DCC,XCVIII. 20 p. 16.5 cm.

NCooHi (Not located 1968)

mp. 48,344 Bristol B10,214 McDade 59

5.10 Virginia

(1) Charles O'Donnel, Murder, Morgantown 1797

(a) The Extraordinary life and confession of Charles O'Donnell, who was executed on the 19th day of June, 1797, at Morgan-Town, Monongahela-County, Virg. for the willful murder of his son. This account was taken days before his execution, in which are recounted some of the most extraordinary acts of villany and cruelty ever recorded. [By Simon Cochrun] Washington, (Pennsylvania): Printed by John Colerick. 1797.

No copy located

Evans 31,951

(b) The life and confession of Charles O'Donnel . . . executed at Morgantown, June 19, 1797, for the wilful murder of his son; though he had murdered a woman about 27 years before . . . not discovered . . . As related by himself, to the Rev. Simon Cochrun . . . Lancaster, Printed and sold by W. & R. Dickson, 1798. 14 p. 21 cm.

NHi (microcard not yet issued 4-6-82)

mp. 48,554 Bristol B10,448

5.12 South Carolina

(1) George Burns, Robbery, 1768

(a) The Confession and Declaration of George Burns, Now a Prisoner in Charles-Town Goal, Convicted of the Robbery of Mr. John Scott, Which he voluntarily makes concerning the said Robbery and his Accomplices, this 9th day of February, 1768 . . . George Burns. [Colophon] Charles-Town: Printed by John-Hugar Van Huerin, at his Printing-Office in King-Street [1768] 2 p. 31.5 x 19.5 cm.

MWA*

mp. 41,806 Bristol B2,862 Morgan 1,241

5.14 Vermont

(1) Elizabeth Wood's Son, Murder, 1793?

(a) A Most Bloody and Cruel Murder, committed on the body of Mrs. Elizabeth Wood, by her own son. Made public with a view of warning the youth from the snares and temptations of the wicked; and to embrace virtue and [to find] the sure road to happiness. To which is added Two Appropriate Hymns. Bennington: Printed by Anthony Haswell [1793?] 8 p. 17.5 cm.

RPJCB*

mp. 45,782 and 46,827 Bristol B7,260 and B8,418
Cooley 489 McCorison 272

5.20 United States

(1) Three Pirates, Boston 1794

(a) Dying Confession of three Pirates, viz. Collins, Furtado and Palacha, who were executed at Boston, this Day, being the thirtieth of July, 1794, for the Murder of Mr. Enoch Wood . . . [Boston] Sold at the Office, No. 2, near Liberty-Pole, and by the Flying-Traders. [Price Four Pence]
Broadside 46 x 30 cm.

MWA*(imp.)

Evans 27,819 McDade 204

Note Second brackets in original.

Evans Ghost 26,926

(2) Joseph Baker, Murder and Piracy, Philadelphia 1800

(a) The Confession of Joseph Baker, a Canadian by birth, who, for Murder & Piracy committed on the high seas, on board the Schooner Eliza, Captain Wm. Wheland, in a voyage from Philadelphia bound to St. Thomas was tried on the 25th of April, 1800, before the Hon. Samuel Chase and Richard Peters, judges of the District Court of the United States, for the District of Pennsylvania, and now under sentence of Death in the solitary cells of the Penitentiary House of the City and County of Philadelphia. Printed by Richard Folwell, No. 63, North Front-Street. (Copy-Right secured according to Law.)
8 p. 19.5 cm.

DLC, MWA*, MiU-C, MoU-L

Evans 36,873 McDade 62

(b) The Last Words and Dying Confession of Three Pirates, who were executed this day (May 9th, 1800.) From Folwell's Press, No. 63, North Front-street. Philadelphia. (Copyright secured according to law.) [1800] 16 p. 21 cm.

CtY, DLC, KWi, MBAt, MWA*, MiU-C, P, PHi, RPJCB

Evans 39,087 McDade 64

5.?? Location Unknown

(1) John Rice, Malefactor, 1763

(a) A Genuine Account of the . . . life . . . of J. Rice, broker, for forgery; P. Lewis, a highwayman; and Hannah Dagoe, for stealing . . . confession. 1763 8vo.

BLM

(a.2) [The same] 4to.

BOL

Note The source is Bibliography of Eighteenth Century Legal Literature (Bell Project 1982). There are duplicate entries. The entry at page 875 is classified as 923: individual American law case; the entry at page 495 is classified as 345: an English case concerning tithes.

6.00

Sermons on Judicial Proceedings (Particularly Executions)

6.01 New Hampshire

(1) Penelope Kenny and Sarah Simpson, Murder, 1739

(a) Religious Education of Children Recommended. In a Sermon Preach'd in the Church of Portsmouth December 27th. 1739 Being the Day appointed for the Execution of Penelope Kenny. By Arthur Browne, A.M. And Missionary from the Society for the Propagation of the Gospel in Foreign Parts. Published at the Desire of the Church Wardens and Vestry. Boston: Printed and Sold by S. Kneeland and T. Green, in Queenstreet over against the Prison. 1739. 21 p. 8vo.

MB, MHi*

Evans 4,478

(b) The Faith and Prayer of a dying Malefactor. A Sermon Preach'd December 27. 1739. On Occasion of the Execution of two Criminals, Namely, Sarah Simpson and Penelope Kenny, and in the Hearing of the Former. By William Shurtleff, A.M. Pastor of a church in Portsmouth, New-Hampshire. To which is annex'd a brief Narrative concerning the said Criminals: And a preface by the Reverend Mr. Fitch. Boston: Printed by J. Draper, for D. Henchman, in Cornhill. 1740. 38 p. 8vo.

MB, MBAt, MWA*, NHi

Evans 4,599 Sabin 86,794 McDade 874

(2) Thomas Powers, 1796

(a) See above 5.01(3)(b).

6.02 Massachusetts

(1) Benjamin Goad, Immoral Acts and Lusts, 1674

(a) The Cry of Sodom Enquired into; Upon Occasion of The Arraignment and Condemnation of Benjamin Goad, For his Prodigious Villany [sic]. Together with A Solemn Exhortation to Tremble at Gods Judgements, and to Abandon Youthful Lusts. By S. D. [Samuel Danforth]. . . . Cambridge: Printed by Marmaduke Johnson: 1674. 29 p. 4to.

MB, MWA*

Evans 186 Wing D-176

(2) Wicked Man's Portion, Murder, 1675

(a) The Wicked mans Portion Or, A Sermon (Preached at the Lecture in Boston in New-England the 18th day of the 1 Moneth 1674. when two men were executed, who had murthered their Master.) Wherein is shewed That excesse in wickedness doth bring untimely Death. By Increase Mather, Teacher of a Church of Christ. . . . Boston, Printed by John Foster. 1675. 29 p.

BOB, CSmH, DLC, MB, MH, MWA*, NN, RPJCB, ViU

Evans 210 Sabin 46,758 Church 635 Huntington 6
2 Increase Mather 174A RPJCB 4th p. 9 Wing M-1,260

(a.2) A Sermon (Preached at the Lecture in Boston in New-England the 18th of the 1. Moneth 1674. When two men were Executed, who had Murthered their Master) Wherein Is Shewed That Excess in wickedness doth bring Untimely Death. The Second Impression. By Increase Mather, Teacher of a Church of Christ. . . . Printed by R.P. for J. Brunning in Boston 1685. 40 p.

Ct, DLC, MB, MBAt, MH, MHi, MWA*, RPJCB, ViU

Evans 394 Sabin 46,736
2 Increase Mather 174-B RPJCB 4th p. 155
Wing M-1,250

(3) James Morgan, 1686

(a) Morgan, above 5.02(1).

(4) Hugh Stone, Murder, 1690

(a) Speedy Repentance urged. A Sermon Preached at Boston, Decemb. 29. 1689. In the Hearing, and at the Request of One Hugh Stone: A Miserable Man Under a just Sentence of Death, for a Tragical and Horrible Murder. Together with some Account concerning the Character, Carriage, and Execution of that Unhappy Malefactor. To which are Added, certain Memorable Providences Relating to some other Murders; & some great Instances of Repentance which have been seen among us. By Cotton Mather Pastor of a Church in Boston. Boston, Printed by Samuel Green, and Sold by Joseph Browning at the corner of the Prison Lane, and Benj. Harris at the London Coffee house. 1690. 110 p.

CtY, DLC, MB, MBAt, MH, MH-AH, MWA*, MHi, RPJCB

Evans 539 Sabin 46,528 Cotton Mather 373
McDade 926 Wing M-1,156

(5) Witchcraft Trials, 1692

(a) Salem Witchcraft Trials, above 1.02(1)(b).

(6) Two Malefactors, Murder?, 1693

(a) Warnings from the Dead. Or Solemn Admonitions Unto All People; but Especially unto Young Persons to Beware of Such Evils as would bring them to the Dead. By Cotton Mather. In Two Discourses, Occasioned by a Sentence of Death, Executed on some Unhappy Malefactors. Together with the Last Confession, made by a Young Woman, who Dyed on June 8. 1693. One of these Malefactors. Boston in New-England; Printed by Bartholomew Green, for Samuel Phillips, at the West End of the Exchange. 1693. 69 p.

MHi, MWA*, ViU

Evans 655 3 Cotton Mather 440 Wing M-1,166

(7) Infanticide, 1698

(a) Impenitent Sinners Warned of their Misery And Summoned to Judgment. Delivered in Two Sermons: the former on the Sabbath, Nov. 6. the other on the Lecture following, Nov. 10, 1698. Occasioned by the Amazing instance of a Miserable Creature, who stood Condemned for murdering her Infant begotten in Whoredom. To which are subjoyned the Solemn Words spoken to her, on those Opportunities. Published for the Warning of others. By Samuel Willard, Minister of the Gospel, and Teacher of a Church in Boston, N.E. . . . Boston, Printed by B. Green, & J. Allen. Sold by Michael Perry, at his Shop over against the Town-House. 1698. 60 p.

DLC*(imp.), MH

Evans 856 Wing W-2,281

(8) Criminal, ?, 1699

(a) The Folly of Sinning, Opened & Applyed, In Two Sermons, Occasioned by the Condemnation of one that was Executed at Boston in New-England, on November 17th. 1698. By Increase Mather, Praesident of Harvard Colledge in Cambridge, and Preacher of the Gospel at Boston in N.E. . . . Boston, Printed by B. Green, & J. Allen, for Michael Perry over against the Town House and Nicholas Buttolph at the corner of Gutteridges Coffee-House, 1699. 96 p. 12mo.

DLC*, MB, MBC, MH, MWA

Evans 879 1 Increase Mather 56 Wing M-1,212

(9) Pillars of Salt, ?, 1699

(a) Pillars of Salt. An History Of Some Criminals Executed in this Land, For Capital Crimes. With some of their Dying Speeches; Collected and Published, For the Warning of such as Live in Destructive Courses of Ungodliness. Whereto is added For the better Improvement of this History, A Brief Discourse about the Dreadful Justice of God, in Punishing of Sin, with Sin. . . . [By Cotton Mather] Boston in New-England. Printed by B. Green, and J. Allen, for Samuel Phillips at the Brick Shop near the Old-Meeting-House. 1699. 112 p. 12mo.

CSmH, CtY, MB, MH, MWA*

Evans 877 Cotton Mather 284-A Wing M-1,140

(a.2) "An Appendix, Containing an History of Some Criminals Executed in New England for Capital Crimes; with some of their Dying Speeches, Book VI," Magnalia Christi Americana: Or, the Ecclesiastical History of New-England, from its First Planting in the Year 1620 unto the Year of our Lord, 1698. in Seven Books. . . . By the Reverend and Learned Cotton Mather, M.A. And Pastor of the North Church in Boston, New-England. [37-49] London: Printed for Thoms Parkhurst, at the Bible and Three Crowns in Cheapside. MDCCII 578 p.

BENew, BEU(2), BLM(3), BLU, BOB, CSmH, CSt, Ct, CtHT-W, CtHi, CtY, DLC, ICN, MB, MBAt, MBC, MH(6), MH-AH, MHi(2), MLy, MSaE, MWA(2), MWiW-C, MeB, MiU-C, N, NHi, NIC, NN, PPL, PPRF, RPJCB(3), ViU

Sabin 46,392 Cotton Mather 213A Vail 294

(a.2.a) First American Edition, from the London Edition of 1702 (Hartford 1820).

Sabin 46,393 Shoemaker 2,183

(10) Sarah Smith's 1698 Execution, Murder, 1699

(a) Warnings to the Unclean: In a Discourse From Rev. XXI. 8. Preacht at Springfield Lecture, August 25th, 1698. At the Execution of Sarah Smith. By Mr. John Williams, Pastor of the Church at Deerfield. Boston, Printed by B. Green, and J. Allen, for Michael Perry, at his Shop over against the Town-House. 1699 64 p. 8vo.

Evans 902

MWA, NHi*

(11) Esther Rodgers, 1701

(a) See above 5.02(2)(a).

(12) John Quelch and Other Pirates, 1704

(a) See above 1.03(3)(a).

(13) Josias and Joseph, Murder, 1710.

(a) The Woful [sic] Effects of Drunkenness A Sermon Preached at Bristol Octob. 12, 1709. When Two Indians, Josias and Joseph, Were Executed for Murther, Occasioned By the Drunkenness both of the Murthering & Murthered Parties. By Samuel Danforth, Pastor of the Church of Taunton. . . . Boston in New-England. Printed by B. Green: Sold by Samuel Gerrish at his Shop near the Old Meeting-House, in Corn Hill. 1710 54 p. 16mo.

MWA*

Evans 1,452

(14) David Wallis, 1713

(a) See above 5.02(3)(a) and (b).

(15) Infanticide, 1715

(a) [First Title] A Sorrowful Spectacle. In Two Sermons, Occasioned by a Just Sentence of Death, on a Miserable Woman, for the Murder of a Spurious Offspring. The One Declaring, The Evil of an Heart Hardened, under and against all Means of Good. The Other Describing, The Fearful Case of such as in a Suffering Time, and much more such as in a Dying Hour, are found without the Fear of God. With some Remarkable Things, relating to the criminal, proper for All to be Informed of. By Cotton Mather, D.D. and F.R.S. . . . Boston: Printed by T. Fleet & T. Crump, for Samuel Gerrish, on the North Side of the Town-House, in King-street. 1715 [Second Title] The Divine Compassions Declar'd and Magnified: To Engage and Encourage the greatest Sinners unto a Speedy and Earnest Repentance. A Sermon, Preach'd at the Lecture in Boston, June 2. 1715. Upon the Sorrowful occasion of a Miserable Woman present, under Sentence of Death for the Murder of her Spurious Infant. By Benjamin Colman, A.M. Boston: Printed by T. Fleet & T. Crump, for Samuel Gerrish, on the North Side of the Town House, in King Street. 1715. 150 p.

BOB, DLC, MB, MHi, MWA*, NNPM, RPJCB

Evans 1,764 3 Cotton Mather 367

(16) Murderer, 1717

(a) The Valley of Hinnom. The Terrours of Hell demonstrated. And the Methods of Escaping the Terrible Miseries of the Punishments on the Wicked there, declared. In a Sermon Preached in the Hearing, and at the Request, of a Man under a Sentence of Death for a Murder; Just before the Execution of the Sentence; and upon a Text by himself assigned for the Sermon to insist upon. At Boston, 13 d. IV. m 1717, . . . [By Cotton Mather] Boston, Printed by J. Allen, for Robert Starke, at his Shop near the New North Meeting-House 1717. 58 p. 12mo.

CtY, MHi*

Evans 1,910 3 Cotton Mather 421

(17) Joseph Hanno, Murder, 1721

(a) Tremenda. The Dreadful Sound with which The Wicked are to be Thunderstruck. In a Sermon Delivered unto a Great Assembly, in which was present, a Miserable African just going to be Executed, for a most Inhumane and Uncommon Murder. At Boston, May 25th. 1721. By Cotton Mather. To which is added, a Conference between a Minister and the Prisoner, on the Day before his Execution. . . . Boston: Printed by B. Green for B. Gray & J. Edwards & Sold at their Shops. 1721. 43 p. 8vo.

MB, MWA*, ViU

Evans 2,251 3 Cotton Mather 407

Evans Ghost 2,252 (2d ed.) (See 3 Cotton Mather 1119)

(18) John Phillips and Other Pirates 1724

(a) The Converted Sinner. The Nature of a Conversion to Real and Vital Piety: And the Manner in which it is to be Pray'd & Striv'n for. A Sermon Preached in Boston, May 31. 1724. In the Hearing and at the Desire of certain Pirates, a little before their Execution. To which there is added, A more Private Conference of a Minister with them. [By Cotton Mather]. . . . Boston: Printed for Nathaniel Belknap, and

Sold at his Shop the Corner of Scarletts-Wharff. 1724.
55 p. 8vo.

KWi, MWA*

Evans 2,551

(a.2) George Francis Dow and John Henry Edmonds, "Ch. XVII: John Phillips Whose Head was Cut off and Pickled," The Pirates of the New England Coast 1630-1730. (Marine Research Society, Salem 1923).

(19) Pirates, 1726

(a) See above 1.02(7)(b) and (c).

(20) Murderer, 1733

(a) [First Title] Murder a great and crying Sin. A Sermon Preach'd on the Lord's-Day March 4th. 1732-3. To a poor Prisoner Under Sentence of Death for that Crime. By Samuel Checkley, A.M. Pastor of a Church of Christ in Boston. . . . Boston: Printed by T. Fleet, at the Heart and Crown in Cornhill. 1733. [Second Title] Mercy with God for the chief of Sinners. A Sermon Preach'd on the Lord's Day March 4th To a Prisoner Under Sentence of Death for Murder. By Samuel Checkley, A.M. Pastor of a Church of Christ in Boston. . . . Printed in the year 1733. [Third Title] Sinners minded of a future Judgment. A Sermon preached to, and at the Desire of, A condemned Prisoner, March 18th 1732--3. Being the Lord's Day before his Execution. By Samuel Checkley, A.M. Pastor of a Church of Christ in Boston. . . . Boston: Printed in the year 1733. 90 p. 8vo.

MB*, MBAt, MHi

Evans 3,642, 3,641, and 3,643

(21) Rebekah Chamblit, 1733

(a) See above 5.02(7)(b).

(22) Matthew Cushing, 1734

(a) See above 5.02(8)(b).

(23) Hugh Henderson, 1737

(a) See above 5.02(11)(b).

(24) Philip Kennison, 1738

(a) See above 5.02(12)(c).

(25) Murderer, 1751

(a) The Prayer and Plea of David, To be delivered from Blood-Guiltiness, Improved in a Sermon At the ancient Thursday-Lecture in Boston, May 16th 1751. Before the Execution of a Young Negro Servant for Poisoning an Infant. By Mr. Byles. . . . Boston: Printed and Sold by Samuel Kneeland, opposite the Prison in Green-Street. 1751 20 p. 8vo.

BLM, MBAt, MWA*, RPJCB

Evans 6,647

(26) William Wieer, 1754

(a) See above 5.02(16)(a).

(27) Bristol, Murder, 1764

(a) The Blood of Abel, and the Blood of Jesus considered and improved, in A Sermon Delivered at Taunton, December the First, 1763. Upon the Day of the Execution of Bristol, A Negro Boy of about Sixteen Years old, for The Murder of Miss Elizabeth McKinstry. By Sylvanus Conant, A.M. Pastor of the First Church in Middleborough. . . . Boston: Printed and Sold by Edes and Gill, in Queen-Street, M,DCC,LXIV. 36 p.

MBAt, MH, MWA*, NHi

Evans 9,616 Sabin 15,092 McDade 131

Evans Ghost 9,355

(28) Arthur, 1768

(a) See above 5.02(22)(b).

(29) Boston Massacre, 1770

(a) See above 1.02(15)(m) and (x).

(30) William Linsey, 1770

(a) See above 5.02(25)(b).

(31) William Shaw, 1770

(a) See above 5.02(26)(b).

(32) Bryan Sheehen, 1772

(a) See above 5.02(27)(c).

(33) Solomon Goodwin, 1772

(a) See above 5.02(28)(b).

(34) Levi Ames, 1773

(a) See above 5.02(32)(k), (l), and (m).

(35) William Brooks, et. al, 1778

(a) See above 5.02(35)(g) and (i).

(36) Alexander White, 1784

(a) See above 5.02(40)(c).

(37) John Dixson, Burglary, 1784

(a) The Paradise of God opened to a penitent Thief, in Answer to his dying Prayer to a dying Saviour, considered and improved in A Sermon; The Substance of which was delivered at Taunton, November 11, 1784. Upon the Day of the Execution of John Dixson, for Burglary, AEtat 24. With an Appendix, On the Nature and Enormity of Burglary. And A Sketch of Dixson's Life. By Peres Fobes, A.M. A.A.S. Pastor of the Church in Raynham. . . . Providence: Printed by Bennett Wheeler. [1784] 48 p. 8vo.

CSt, DLC, MB, MBC, MBev, MWA*, RHi, RPJCB

Evans 19,407 Sabin 24,932n. Alden 1,008 Winship p. 48

Evans Ghost 18,470

(38) Isaac Coombs, 1786

(a) See above 5.02(43)(c).

(39) John Bly and Charles Rose, 1787

(a) See above 5.02(45)(b).

(40) Abiel Converse, Murder, 1788

(a) A Sermon, preached at the Execution of Abiel Converse, Who was executed at Northampton for the Murder of her Infant Bastard Child, July 6th, 1788. By Aaron Bascom, A.M. Pastor of the Church in Chester. Northampton: Printed by William Butler. M,DCC,LXXXVIII. 25 p.

MWA*

Evans 20,955

(41) Joshua Abbott, Murder, 1792

(a) Sermons preached to Joshua Abbot; at York, September 3, 1792; preparatory to the sixth; the day appointed for his execution: when his pardon was publicly read by the minister, at the desire of the sheriff, in the meeting-house to a numerous assembly of people. By Mathew Merriam of Berwick, and Joseph Buckminster of Portsmouth. Printed and sold by John Mycall. [Newburyport 1792] 83 p. 8vo.

DLC, MB, MBAt, MWA*, NHi, RPJCB

Evans 24,540

(42) Samuel Frost, 1793

(a) See above 5.02(49)(d).

(43) Henry Blackburn, Murder, 1796

(a) A Sermon: Delivered at Salem, January 14, 1796, occasioned by the Execution of Henry Blackburn, on that day, For the Murder of George Wilkinson. By Nathaniel Fisher, A.M. Rector of Saint Peter's Church, Salem. Published at the desire of the wardens and vestry. Printed by S. Hall, in Boston, for J. Dabney, in Salem. 1796. 21 p. 8vo.

BLM, DLC, MBAt, MH, MSaE, MWA*, NHi, RPJCB

Evans 30,424 Tapley p. 361

(44) Samuel Smith, 1799

(a) See above 5.02(55)(b).

6.03 Rhode Island

(1) Jeremiah Meacham, 1715

(a) See above 5.03(1)(b).

(2) Thirty-Six Pirates, 1723

(a) See above 1.03(1)(b).

6.04 Connecticut

(1) Katherine Garret, Murder, 1738

(a) A Sermon Preached on the Occasion Of the Execution Of Katherine Garret, an Indian-Servant, (Who was Condemned for the Murder of her Spurious Child.) On May 3d. 1738. To which is Added some short Account of her Behaviour after her Condemnation. Together with her Dying Warning and Exhortation, Left under her own Hand. By Eliphalet Adams, A.M. and Pastor of the Church of Christ in N. London. N. London: Printed and sold by T. Green, 1738. 48 p. 16mo.

CtHi, CtNlC, CtY, ICN, MBAt, MBC, MWA*

Evans 4,215 New London 352

(2) Isaac Frazier, 1768

(a) See above 5.04(1)(c).

(3) John Jacobs, Murder, 1768

(a) A Sermon, Delivered at Litchfield, on the 2d Day of November, A.D. 1768. On the Day of the Execution of John Jacobs, An Indian Native, Pursuant to Sentence of Death passed upon him by the Hon. Superior Court, For the Murder of James Chockrer. Preached upon the Desire of the Criminal and published at the request of some of the Hearers. By Timothy Pitkin, A.M. Pastor of the first Church in Farmington. . . . Hartford: Printed by Green & Watson, near the Great Bridge.
18 p. 12mo.

Ct*(imp.)

Evans 11,045 Trumbull 1,349

(4) Moses Paul, 1772

(a) See above 5.04(3)(b) and (e).

(5) Moses Dunbar, 1777

(a) See above 5.04(5)(b).

(6) William Beadle, 1783

(a) See above 5.04(8)(d) and (e).

(7) Hannah Ocuish, Murder, 1786

(a) God admonishing his People of their Duty, as Parents and Masters. A Sermon, preached at New-London, December 20th, 1786. Occasioned By the Execution of Hannah Ocuish, a Mulatto Girl, Aged 12 Years and 9 Months. For the Murder of Eunice Bolles, Aged 6 Years and 6 months. By Henry Channing, M.A. . . . . New-London: Printed by T. Green, M,DCC,LXXXVI
31 p. 20 cm.

CSmH, CtHi, CtY-L, DLC, MB, MBAt, MWA*, NHi

Evans 19,547 Sabin 11,898 McDade 720

(a.2) The second Edition. New-London: Printed by T. Green. M,DCC,LXXXVII. [sometimes dated 1786]
31 p.

DLC, MB, MWA*, NHi

Evans 20,264 McDade 720n.

(8) Joseph Mountain, 1790

(a) See above 5.04(9)(b).

(9) Richard Doane, 1797

(a) A Sermon, Preached in Hartford, June 10th, 1797, at the Execution of Richard Doane. By Nathan Strong, minister of the North Presbyterian Church in Hartford. To which is added, A Short Account Of His Life, as given by himself: also of the state of his mind during the time of his confinement, and at his death. Hartford: Printed by Elisha Babcock. 1797. 21 p. 20.5 cm.

BLM, CSmH, CtHi, CtY, DLC, MWA*, NHi, NN

Evans 32,888 Sabin 92,970 McDade 254 Trumbull 1,466

(a.2) Second Edition. Hartford: Printed by Elisha Babcock. 1797. 21 p.

No copy located

Evans 32,889 Sabin 92,970

(10) Thomas Starr, Murder, 1797

(a) A Sermon Preached at Haddam, June 14, 1797. On the day of the Execution Of Thomas Starr, condemned for the Murder of his Kinsman, Samuel Cornwell, by seven wounds given him, by a penknife, in the trunk of his body, July 26th, 1796, of which he languished a few days and died: with a sketch of the life and character of said Starr. By Enoch Huntington, A.M., pastor of the first Church in Middletown. . . . Middletown: Printed by Moses H. Woodward. 24 p. 12mo.

CtHi, MBAt, MH, MWA*, NHi, NNUT, PBL, RPJCB

Evans 32,292 McDade 906

(b) Life and character of Thomas Starr, who was executed on the 14th inst. for murder. Middletown: Printed by Moses H. Woodward. 1797.

No copy located

Evans 32,293 McDade 906n.

Note: mp. 32,293 reports that entry is based on an item, "For sale at this office, Middletown Gazette, June 16, 1797." At the end of Evans 32,292 there is a two-page "Life and Character of Thomas Starr," which suggests that this entry may be a ghost.

(11) Anthony, Rape, 1798

(a) A Sermon, Preached at Danbury, November 8th, A.D. 1798, being the Day of the Execution of Anthony, A Free Negro, pursuant to sentence of Death passed upon him by the Hon. Superior Court, for the crime of a Rape. By Timothy Langdon, A.M. Pastor of the First Church in Danbury. . . . [Danbury: Douglas & Nichols, 1798] 23 p. 8vo.

CtHi, MWA*

Evans 33,979

6.05 New York

(1) Hugh Gillapsie, Robbery, 1759

(a) God will trouble the Troublers of his People. A Sermon Preached at Poughkeepsie, in Dutchess-County, In the Province of New-York, July 14th, 1758. Being the Day of the Execution of Hugh Gillapsie, for Felony. By the Rev. Chauncy Graham, M.A. Minister of the Gospel in Rumbout. Published at the Request of the Hearers. . . . New York: Printed and Sold by H. Gaine, of the Bible and Crown, in Hanover-Square, 1759. 23 p. 12mo.

CtY, MHi, NNUT, PPRF*

Evans 8,356

6.06 New Jersey

(1) Matthias Gotleib, Murder, 1796

(a) A Sermon, Preached at the Execution of Matthias Gotleib, for Murder; at Newton, October 28, 1796. By Holloway Whitfield Hunt, A.B. & V.D.M. Printed in Newton, New-Jersey: Nov. 11, 1796 8 p. 20.5 cm.

MWA*

Evans 30,607 McDade 369 Morsch 311

6.12 South Carolina

(1) The Deluded Dutartres, Adultery, Resisting Arrest, and Murder, 1762

(a) Brief Account Of the Deluded Dutartres; Extracted From a Sermom [sic], Preached by the Rev. Mr. Alexander Garden, A.M. At Charlestown, in South Carolina. New Haven: Printed and Sold by James Parker and Company, at the Post-office, 1762. 8 p.

MWA*

Evans 9,120

Note See above 5.07(4)(b) for John Lewis's last speech and confession issued in the same imprint.

7.00

Impeachments

7.07 Pennsylvania

(1) John Nicholson, 1790

(a) Address to the People of Pennsylvania; containing a Narrative of the Proceedings against John Nicholson, Comptroller-General of the said Commonwealth. Philadelphia: Printed by Francis Bailey, at Yorick's Head, in Market-Street. M,DCC,XC.
68 p. 8vo.

DLC*, NHi, PPAmP, PPL

Evans 22,735 Sabin 55,226

Note Evans gives pagination as being 56. Last numbered page on microcard is 68.

(b) The Pennsylvania State Trials: Containing the Impeachment, Trial, and Acquittal of Francis Hopkinson, and John Nicholson, Esquires. The former being Judge of the Court of Admiralty, and the latter, the Comptroller-General of the Commonwealth of Pennsylvania. Vol. I. . . . [66-776] Philadelphia: Printed by Francis Bailey, at Yorick's Head, No. 116, High-Street, for Edmund Hogan. M,DCC,XCIV. 788 p. 8vo.

BLM, CLL, CtHT-W, DLC(2), ICU-L, M, MB, MBAt, MH, MH-L, MWA*, MdBB, MdBP, MiU-C, NHi, NIC-L, NN, NNC-L, NNU-L, NjP, NjR, P-L, PHi, PPAmP, PPL, PU-L, PV-L, RNR, RPJCB, TxDaM-L, ViU(2), ViW

Evans 27,132 Sabin 32,418 and 55,226 Parrish 240

(2) Francis Hopkinson, 1794

(a) An Account of the Impeachment and Trial of the late Francis Hopkinson, Esquire, judge of the court of admiralty for the commonwealth of Pennsylvania. Philadelphia: Printed by Francis Bailey, at Yorick's head, No. 116, High-street. M,DCC,XCIV. 65 p. 23 cm.

CLU-L (Missing February 13, 1981).

Sabin 32,976

(b) The Pennsylvania State Trials, above 7.07(1)(b), 1-65.

(3) Francis Johnston, 1799

(a) Proceedings in the case of Francis Johnston, Esq. Late Receiver-General of the Land-Office, Prosecuted for Delinquencies in the Said Office. [By Samuel Bryan] Lancaster, Printed by Francis & Robert Bailey. 1799. 27 p.

MBAt, MHi, MiU-C, NHi, PHi, PPL*, PPAmP, RPJCB

Evans 36,065 Sabin 36,360

7.11 North Carolina

(1) William Smith, 1740

(a) A True and Faithful Narrative Of the Proceedings of the House of Burgesses of North-Carolina, Met in Assembly for the said Province of Newbern, February 5th 1739. On the Articles of Complaint exhibited before them against the Honourable William Smith, Esq. Chief Justice of the said Province, for high Crimes and Misdemeanors done and committed by the said William Smith in the execution of his Office. Published for the Justification of the Gentlemen Members of that House, who voted the said Articles sufficiently proved for the said Chief Justice to be charged therewith. Addressed to the Freeholders of North-Carolina. . . . [Williamsburg or Boston 1740?] 54 p. 8vo.

MHi*,

Evans 4,582 Thornton Unofficial 12,801

(a.2) Massachusetts Historical Society, Photostat Americana, Second Series, No. 22 (Boston 1936.

7.20 United States

(1) Robert Randall and Charles Whitney, 1796

(a) Proceedings of the House of Representatives of the United States in the Case of Robert Randall and Charles Whitney. [December 28, 1795, to January 13, 1796.] Published by order of the House of Representatives. [Philadelphia: Printed by Francis Childs] 32 p. 8vo.

CSmH, CtY, MB, MBAt, MWA*, NN, RPJCB

Evans 31,364

(b) "Report on the Case of Robert Randall. Rep. A. Baldwin. December 29, 1795," Journal of the House of Representatives of the United States, at the First Session of the Fourth Congress. Anno M.DCC.XCV. and of the Independence of the United States the Twentieth [62-64, 72-78] Philadelphia: Printed by Francis Childs, M.DCC.XCV. 572 p. 8vo.

CSmH, MB, MBAt, MH, MWA*, NN, PPAmP

Evans 31,354

(c) Annals of Congress, 4th Cong., 1st Sess. 166-70, 171-95, 200-29 (1849).

(2) William Blount, 1797

(a) In Senate of the United States, July 6th, 1797. The Committee to whom was referred that part on the President's message which relates to a letter purporting to have been written by William Blount, Esq. one of the Senators from the State of Tennessee, together with the papers accompanying the same, having had the same under their consideration beg leave to make a farther report. That Mr. Blount having declined an acknowledgment or denial of the letter imputed to him; and having failed to appear or give any satisfactory explanation respecting it, your committee sent for the original letter which accompanies this report and is in the following words . . . [Philadelphia, 1797] 5 p. 20.5 cm.

DLC*, MBAt, MiU-C

mp. 48,290 Bristol B10,143

(b) Report of the committee of the House of Representatives of the United States, appointed to prepare and report Articles of Impeachment against William Blount, a Senator of the United States, impeached of high crimes and misdemeanors, made in pursuance of a resolution of the House of Representatives, authorizing the said committee to sit during the recess of Congress, and instructing them "to enquire, and, by all lawful means, to discover the whole nature and extent of the offence whereof the said William Blount stands impeached, and who are the parties and associates therein." Printed by order of the House of Representatives. [Philadelphia:] Printed by John Fenno. [1798] [Dec. 16, 1797] 184 p. 8vo.

CLU, CSmH, DLC, GU, MB, MBAt, MH-L, MWA*, MdBE, MdBP, MiU-C, NHi, NN, NNC-L, NNPM, NcD, P, PBL, PHi, PPAmP, PPL, RPB, RPJCB, ScC, TU, ViU

Evans 34,785 Sabin 6,003 Huntington 728

(c) As the question whether the House of Representatives have a right to impeach . . . Constitutionalist. December 10, 1797 [n.p. 1797] Broadside 24 x 19.5 cm.

DLC, MBAt (Only known copy cannot be reproduced)

mp. 48,042 Bristol B9,843

(d) Further Report from the committee appointed on the eighth of July last, to prepare and report Articles of Impeachment against William Blount, A Senator of the United States, impeached by the House of Representatives, of high crimes and misdemeanors. [Philadelphia 1798] 4 p. 20.5 cm.

DLC, MB, MWA(imp.), NN, PPL*, ViU

Evans 34,793 (no copy located has Evans pagination)

(e) [No Title Page] (1) Letter from the Chevalier d'Yrujo, Minister Plenipotentiary to the United States, from Spain, to the Chairman of the Committee appointed to prepare and report Articles of Impeachment against William Blount, dated January 19, 1798. . . . [At page 2] (2) Letter from John Phillips Ripley. . . . 4 p. 8vo.

DLC, MB, MBAt, MWA*, MiU-C, NN, PHi, PPL, ViU

Evans 34,788

(f) Further Report of the committee, appointed on the eighth July last, to prepare and report Articles of Impeachment against William Blount, a Senator of the United States, impeached by the House of Representatives, of High Crimes and Misdemeanors. 25th January, 1798. [Committed to a Committee of the whole House, on Monday next.] [Philadelphia:] Printed by John Fenno. [Philadelphia 1798] 26 p. 20 cm.

MdBJ-B, ViU

(g) The Testimony given before A Committee of the Whole of the House of Representatives of the United States, in relation to A Report of Their Committee of Privileges On the 5th, 6th and 8th of February, 1798. [Philadelphia 1798] 26 p. 20 cm.

MdBJ-G, ViU

(h) Deposition of Gen. Elijah Clark, of the State of Georgia, respecting a Letter from him to Don Diego Morphy, Consul of

His Catholic Majesty, At Charleston, South-Carolina, containing the answers of the said Deponent, to certain interrogatories framed by the Committee Appointed on the 2d of February last, "To take all such steps as may be necessary for obtaining the testimony of the said Elijah Clark, or any other person or persons, on the subject matter of said Letter." Taken before certain Commissioners empowered by the said committee, for the purpose of taking the said depositon. 27th April, 1798, Ordered to lie on the table. [Philadelphia: Printed by William Ross, 1798] 8 p. 8vo.

DLC, MBAt, MHi, MWA*, NN, PPL, ViU

Evans 34,786

(i) Report, In Part, of the Committee, Appointed on the 18th instant, To consider what Rules are necessary to be adopted by the Senate, in the trial of William Blount. 20th December, 1798. Printed by order of the Senate of the United States. Philadelphia: Printed by Way & Groff, No. 48, North Third-Street. [1798] 4 p. 8vo.

DLC, MBAt, MWA*

Evans 34,789

(j) Further Report of the Managers appointed to conduct the Impeachment against William Blount 20th December, 1798, Ordered to lie on the table. [Published by order of the House of Representatives.] [Philadelphia: Printed by William Ross, 1798] 4 p. 8vo.

DLC, MWA*, NN, PPL, RPB

Evans 34,790

Note First brackets in original.

(k) Message from the Senate, communicating A Copy Of The Plea, filed by the counsel in behalf of William Blount. 26th December, 1798. Referred to the Managers appointed to conduct the impeachment against William Blount, with instructions to proceed thereon, as they shall deem adviseable. [Published by order of the House of Representatives.] [Philadelphia: Printed by William Ross, 1798] 4 p. 8vo.

DLC, MBAt, MWA*, MiU-C, PHi, PPL

Evans 34,791 and 36,558

Note First brackets in original.

(l) Report of the Committee appointed to report the proper measures to be adopted relative to the Articles Of Impeachment againt William Blount. Published by order of the

Senate of the United States. [Philadelphia] Printed by W. Ross. [1798] 6 p. 22 cm.

MBAt, NN*

mp. 48,714 Bristol B10,585 New York Public 1,260

(m) Proceedings of the Impeachment of William Blount, a Senator of the United States from the State of Tennessee, for High Crimes And Misdemeanors. Philadelphia: Printed by Joesph Gales. 1799. 102 p. 23 cm.

BLM, CSmH, DLC, M, MB, MH, MH-L, MHi, MWA*, MdBJ-G, NHi, NIC-L, NNPM, P-L, PHi, PP, PPAmP, PPL, RPB, RPJCB, ScC, TxU, ViU

Evans 36,561 Sabin 6,002

(n) Correspondence qui dévoile la trahison du senateur americain W. Blount; les intrigues du ministre anglais Liston; et l'étrange neutralité observée par le secrétaire d'État des Etats-Unis, Timothy Pickering, Ecuyer. Philadelphie: Imprimé par C. Parent, Cinquième rue Sud, no. 32. 85 p. 22 cm.

DLC

Evans Ghosts 34,787 and 34,798

(o) William Cobbett, "Impeachment of William Blount," 9 Porcupine's Works 135-80 (London 1801).

(p) "Record Of The Proceedings of the High Court Of Impeachment, on the trial of William Blount; consisting of the Senate Of The United States, as is provided By The Constitution, And In Pursuance Of A Resolution Of Senate," Journal of the Senate Of The United States, in cases of Impeachments. 20th February, 1805. Printed conformably to a resolution of the Senate. [3-31] Washington City: Printed By William Duane & Son. 1805. [Bound with Journal of the Senate, 8th Congress, Second Session, 1804) 140 p.

DLC*

Shaw-Shoemaker 9,532

(q) Report of the Secretary of War on the Petition of David Henley. June 9, 1812. Read and referred to a committee of the whole house on Thursday next. Washington: A. and G. Way, Printers. 1812

(r) 2 American State Papers, Foreign Relations 20-27 (1832).

(s) Francis Wharton, ed., "Impeachment of William Blount A Senator of the United States, for Misdemeanour," American State Trials 200-321 (Philadelphia 1849).

(t) "Impeachment of William Blount, Senator of the United States, for Misdemeanor, 5th Congress, 1798-99," 7 _Annals of Congress_ 34-46, 448-66, 499-502, 672-79, 947-52, 953-55; 8 _Id_. 2245-2415 (Washington, D.C. 1851).

(u) Marcus J. Wright, _Some Account of the Life and Service of William Blount_ (Washington, D.C. 1884).

(v) "Record of the Proceedings. . .," _Extracts from Journal of the Senate of the United States of America in Cases of Impeachments_ 5-15 (Washington, D.C. 1904).

(v.2) Senate Document 876, 62d Congress, Second Session. (Washington, D.C. 1912).

(w) F. J. Turner, "Documents on the Blount Conspiracy, 1795-1797," 10 _American Historical Review_ 574-606 (New York 1905).

(x) William H. Masterson, _William Blount_ (Baton Rouge 1954).

8.00

American Printings and Reprintings of Foreign Trials and Law Reports

8.02 Massachusetts

(1) Quakers' Bermuda Trial, 1682

(a) A Publick Tryal of the Quakers in Barmudas Upon the first Day of May, 1678. . . .Thirdly, Being found Guilty . . . Sentenced, . . . brought forth unto the deserved Execution of the Presse. By Samson Bond late Preacher of the Gospel in Barmudas . . . Boston in New-England: Printed by Samuel Green, upon Assignment of Samuel Sewall: 1682. 104 p. 12mo.

CSmH, DLC, MH, MHi, MWA*, RPJCB

Evans 313 Wing B-3,585

(2) English Unjust Judges, 1732

(a) The Triumphs of Justice over Unjust Judges: Exhibiting, I. The Names and Crimes of Four and Forty Judges Hang'd in one year in England, as Murderers for their corrupt Judgments. II. The Case of the Lord Chief Justice Tresilian, Hang'd at Tyburn, and all the rest of the Judges of England (save one) banisht in K. Richard the 2d's Time. III. The Crimes of Empson and Dudley, Executed in K. Henry the 8th's Days. IV. The Proceedings of the Ship-money Judges in the Reign of King Charles the First. V. Diverse other Presidents both Antient and Modern. To which is added, VI. The Judges Oath, and some Observations thereupon. Humbly Dedicated to the Lord Chief Justice Scroggs. . . . Re-printed in the Year 1732. [Boston, S. Kneeland and T. Green] 31 p. 21 cm.

MHi, MWA*

mp. 40,005 Bristol B886

(3) Goodere's Trial for Murder, 1741

(a) Some Account of the Trial of Samuel Goodere, Esq; Late Commander of the Ruby Man of War, Matthew Mahoney, and Charles White, Who were tried on March 26, before the Right Worshipful Henry Combe, Esq; Mayor of Bristol, and the Worshipful Michael Foster, Esq; Serjeant at Law, Recorder of the said City, &c. For the Murder of Sir John Dinely Goodere, Bart. On board the Ruby, in King-Road, Bristol. Boston: Printed and Sold at the Printing-House in Queen-street, over against the Prison. 1741. 24 p. 8vo.

MHi, MWA*

Evans 4,809 Sabin 86,587

Evans Ghost 4,681

(4) Methodists' Trial, 1744

(a) A Brief Account of the Occasion, Process, and Issue of a Late Trial At the Assize Held at Gloucester, March 3. 1743,4. between some of the People call'd Methodists, Plaintiffs, and certain Persons of the Town of Minchin-Hampton, in the said County, Defendants. By George Whitefield, A.B. late of Pembroke College, Oxford . . . . London, Printed 1744. Boston: Re-printed and Sold by Rogers & Fowle in Queen-street, near the Prison. 1744 15 p. 12mo.

DLC, MHi, MWA*, NN

Evans 5,518

(5) Stirn's Behaviour, Murder, 1761

(a) A Curious and Authentic Account of the Remarkable Behaviour of Francis David Stirn (A Foreign Gentleman and Scholar) Who was convicted of the Murder of Mr. Matthews, a Surgeon, in London. Boston: Re-printed and Sold by B. Mecom, at the New Printing-Office, near the Town-House. 1761. 24 p.

MWA*

Evans 8,829

(6) Calvert's Trial for Rape, 1768

(a) The Trial of Frederick Calvert, Esq; Baron of Baltimore, in the Kingdom of Ireland, for A Rape on the Body of Sarah Woodcock; and of El. Griffinburg, & A. Harvey, otherwise Darby, as Accessories before the Fact. For procuring, aiding, and abetting him in committing the said Rape. At the Assizes held at Kingston for the Couuty [sic] of Surry, on Saturday, the 26th of March, 1768. Before the Hon. Sir

Sydney Stafford Smythe, Knt. One of the Barons of his Majesty's Court of Exchequer. Published by Permission of the Judge. Taken in Short-Hand by Joseph Gurney. London: Printed in the Year M DCC LXVIII. [Boston, Mein & Fleeming] 142 p.

MBAt, MWA*, MdBE

Evans 10,919 (No Philadelphia edition) Hildeburn 2,406

(7) Allen's Trial for Forgery and Counterfeiting, 1773

(a) The Trial of the Reverend John Allen, taken exact from the Proceedings on the King's Commission of the Peace, Oyer and Terminer, and Goal-Delivery for the City of London. Held at Justice-Hall in the Old-Bailey On Thursday the 12th, Friday the 13th, Saturday the 14th, Monday the 16th, and Tuesday the 17th of January 1769. Published at the Request of Many. Boston: Printed and Sold by Kneeland and Davis, in Queen-Street. M,DCC,-LXXIII. 20 p. 8vo.

MBAt, MWA*

Evans 13,047

(8) Somersett's Case, Slavery, 1774

(a) An Argument in the case of James Sommersett A Negro, lately determined by the Court of King's Bench: Wherein it is attempted to demonstrate The Present Unlawfulness of Domestic Slavery In England. To which is prefixed A State Of The Case. By Mr. Hargrave, One of the Counsel for the Negro. London Printed: Boston: Re-printed and sold by E. Russell next the Corner of Union-street. M,DCC,LXXIV. 56 p. 8vo.

MHi, MWA*, NHi, NN

Evans 13,318

(9) Parker's Trial for Mutiny, 1797

(a) The Trial of Richard Parker, Complete; President of the Delegates, for Mutiny, &c. On board the <u>Sandwich</u>, and others of his Majesty's Ships, at the Nore, in May, 1797. Before a Court Martial, Held on Board the <u>Neptune</u>, of 98 Guns, Laying off Greenhithe, near Gravesend, on Thursday, June 22, 1797, and following Days. Taken in short hand on board the <u>Neptune</u>, By Job Sibly. Boston: Printed by Samuel Etheridge, for William T. Clap, Fish-street, Corner Proctor's Lane. 1797. 60 p. 12mo.

MWA*, NN(imp.), RPJCB

Evans 32,837

(b) The Tryal, Last Dying Words, Speech and Confession of Richard Parker, (alias Admiral Parker) Late President of the Mutinous Fleet, at the Nore (England) Who was executed on Friday the 30th of June, 1797, on Board the Sandwich Man of War, at Blackflakes near Sheerness, for Mutiny & High Treason. . . . [New York? 1797?] Broadside 44 x 27 cm.

NHi*

mp. 48,214 Bristol B10,049

(10) Pirates' Trial for Little's Murder, 1797

(a) The Interesting Trials of the Pirates, for the Murder of William Little, Captain of the Ship American Eagle. Newburyport: Re-printed at the Herald Press, From a late London Publication. [1797] 59 p. 12mo.

KWi, MBAt, MH-L, MSaE*

Evans 32,308 Sabin 41,527

(11) Cuckold's Chronicle, 1798

(a) The Cuckhold's Chronicle. Being Select Trials for Adultery, Incest, Imbecility, Ravishment, & etc. Volume I. Boston: Printed for those who wish to purchase. 1798. 196 p. 8vo.

MB*

Evans 33,585

Evans Ghost 33,584 (Mineck 425)

8.04 Connecticut

(1) Peake's Nisi Prius Reports, 1790-1794 Cases, 1795

(a) Cases determined at Nisi Prius: in the Court Of King's Bench. From the Sittings after Easter Term, 30 George III. 1790, To the Sittings after Michaelmas Term, 35 George III. 1794; both inclusive. By Thomas Peake, of Lincoln's-Inn. . . . A new edition, with improvements. By Thomas Day, Counsellor at Law. Hartford: Printed by Hudson and Goodwin [1795?] 281 p.

DCU-L, MdB, MiU-L, NjP, P-L, RPJCB*

mp. 47,528 Bristol B9,218

(2) M'Lean's Trial for High Treason, 1797

(a) The Trial, Condemnation and Horrid Execution of David M'Lean, Formerly of Pennsylvania, for High Treason, Against the British Government, at the City of Quebec, on the 21st of July last. Who was hanged, drawn, quartered and beheaded on the above day, with all the attendant circumstances of cruelty and barbarity. Windham: Printed [By John Byrne] 1797. 12 p. 16mo.

CtHi*

mp. 48,170 Bristol B10,133 Trumbull 2d 2,683

(3) Captain Kidd's Dying Words, 1800

(a) The dying Words of Captain Kidd, A noted Pirate, who was hanged at Execution Dock, . . . Printed & Sold in New London. [1800?] Broadside 37 x 18.5 cm.

NHi*

mp. 49,100 Bristol B11,070

8.05 New York

(1) Disney's Montreal Trial for Burglary and Mayhem, 1768

(a) The Trial of Daniel Disney, Esq; Captain of a Company in His Majesty's 44th Regiment of Foot, and Town-Major of the Garrison of Montreal, at the Session of the Supreme-Court of Judicature, holden at Montreal, on Saturday the 28th day of February, and thence continued by Adjournments to Wednesday the 11th Day of March, 1767, before the Honourable William Hey, Esq; Chief-Justice of the Province of Quebec, upon an Indictment containing two Charges, the one for a Burglary and Felony, in breaking and entering Mr. Thomas Walker's House, at Montreal, on the Night of the 6th Day of December, in the Year 1764, with an Intention to murder the said Thomas Walker, the other for feloniously and of Malice aforethought, cutting of the Right Ear of the said Thomas Walker, with Intention thereby to disfigure him, against the Form of the Statute of 22 and 23 Car. II. Cap. i. in that Case made and provided. Supposed to be written by Francis Maseres, Esq; Attorney General of Quebec. Qubec [sic], Printed: New-York, reprinted and Sold by John Holt; at the Exchange. M,DCC,LXVIII. 68 p. 8vo.

MBAt*, PHi

Evans 10,958

(2) Buller's Nisi Prius, 1788

(a) An Introduction to the Law relative to Trials at Nisi Prius. The Fifth Edition. With Additions and Corrections. By Francis Buller, Esq; Of the Middle Temple. London, Printed: New-York: Re-printed by Hugh Gaine, at his Book-Store and Printing-Office, at the Bible, in Hanover-Square. M,DCC,LXXXVIII. 372 p. 8vo.

BLM, CLU-L, CSmH, DCU-L, MH-L, MWA*, NN, PP, RPJCB, ViU, ViW

Evans 20,987

(3) Williams's Trial for Assault and Wounding, 1791

(a) The trial of Renwick Williams, commonly called the monster, for assaulting and wounding Miss Ann Porter. Taken in shorthand by Edward Hodgson. Ornamented with a striking likeness of the prisoner. New York: Printed by Thomas Greenleaf. Sold by Andrew Marschalk. 1791.

No copy located

Evans 23,445

(b) The Trial of Renwick Williams, commonly called the Monster, for assaulting and wounding Miss Ann Porter. Taken in short-hand, by L. Williams, esq. London, Printed; New York: Re-printed and sold by A. Marschalk, No. 3, Queen-street, and at No. 2, John-street. M,DCC,XCI. 55 p. 17 cm.

PHi (Only known copy cannot be reproduced)

mp. 46,359 Bristol B7,903

(4) Muir's Scottish Trial for Sedition, 1794

(a) An Account of the Trial of Thomas Muir, Esq. Younger, of Huntershill, before the High Court Of Justiciary At Edinburgh, on the 30th and 31st days of August, 1793, for Sedition. . . . -- New-York--printed and sold by Samuel Campbell; No. 37, Hanover Square, 1794. 148 p. 8vo.

CtHi, CtHT-W, DLC, MB, MH-L, MHi, MWA*, MdBB, MdBP, NN, NNC-L, NjR, PP, PPL, RNR, RPJCB

Evans 27,633

(a.2) [With second American edition appendix]

PHi, ViU

(a.3) The second American edition. . . . -- New-York -- printed and sold by Samuel Campbell; No. 37, Hanover Square. 1794. 119 p. 8vo.

CLU-L, DLC, MB, MWA*, NHi, NN, ViU

Evans 27,634

(a.4) The third American edition. . . . -- New-York -- Printed and Sold by Samuel Campbell, No. 124 Pearl-Street. M,DCC,XCIV 112 p. 8vo.

CSmH, DLC(2), MWA*, PP

Evans 27,635

(a.5) New-York: Printed by W. Durell, No. 208, Pearl-Street, 1794. 142 p. 19 cm.

CtHi, MWA, NHi

Bristol B8,854

Note Ezra Stiles made the following entry in his diary under date of April 23, 1794: "Revising MS. Copy Hist. Judges. Readg Trial of Mr Muir who with a presb. Minister is banished for 14 y. to Botany Bay for malicious Imputation of Sedition in Scotland." 3 Literary Diary of Ezra Stiles 521 (Franklin Bowditch Dexter, ed. New York 1901).

(5) Rowan's Trial for Libel, 1794

(a) Report of the Trial of Archibald Hamilton Rowan, Esq. on An Information, filed, ex officio, by The Attorney General, for the Distribution Of A Libel; with the Subsequent Proceedings Thereon. Containing The Arguments of Counsel, the Opinion of the Court, and Mr. Rowan's Address to the Court, At Full. Dublin: Printed, March 12, 1794. New-York: Re-printed by Tiebout & O'Brien, No. 358, Queen-Street, near the Friends Meeting-House. 1794. 155 p. 8vo.

CSmH, DLC, MBAt, MHi, MWA*, MdBP, MiU-C, NN, P-L, PHi, PPAmP, PPL, ViU

Evans 27,643

(6) Gerrald's Scottish Trial for Sedition, 1794

(a) The Trial of Joseph Gerrald, delegate from the London Corresponding Society, to the British Convention. Before the High Court Of Justiciary At Edinburgh, on the 3d, 10th, 13th and 14th of March, 1794. For Sedition. Taken in short-hand by Mr. Ramsey. New-York: Printed and Sold by Samuel Campbell, No. 124, Pearl-Street. 1794. 207 p. 8vo.

CSmH, DLC, MBAt, MWA*, MdBB, MdBP, MiU-C, NHi, NN, NjR, NcD-L, NjP, PP, PPL, ViU

Evans 27,591

(7) Eaton's Trial for Libel, 1794

(a) The Trial of Daniel Isaac Eaton, For Publishing a Supposed Libel, Comparing the King of England to a Game Cock In a Pamphlet Intituled Politics for the People; or Hog's Wash At Justice Hall in the Old Bailey, February Twenty-Fourth, 1794. London, Published New York Reprinted for L. Wayland. 1794. 50 p. 8vo.

CtHi, CtHT-W, DLC, MWA*, MiU-C, NN, NjHi, PHi, PPL, RPJCB

Evans 26,931

(a.2) [Half-title and title pages reversed] 50 p. 8vo.

MBAt, MHi*, ViU(imp.)

Evans 26,930

(8) Faulder's Trial for Libel, 1800

(a) Epistle to Peter Pindar. By the Author of the Baviad and Maeviad. . . . To which is added, The Trial Of Mr. Faulder, Bookseller, for publishing a libel on Anthony Pasquin [John Williams], set forth to be contained in the Baviad; Additional Notes To The Maeviad and a Preface To The Sixth London Edition of the work. New-York, Printed by G. and R. Waite, for J. W. Fenno, 1800. 159 p.

CtY, DLC, MBAt*, MH, N, TxU

Evans 37,514 (141 p.) and 37,376 (159 p.)

8.07 Pennsylvania

(1) Mooney's Life, 1752

(a) The Life of Nicholas Mooney. Wherein is contained, His Parentage and Education; an Account of his joining the Rebel Army at Carlisle, and the Part he acted therein, 'till the Defeat thereof at Culloden Moore: the Adventuers [sic] he met with before and after this, 'till he took to the Highway, with a brief Account of his vicious Life, 'till he committed the Robbery at Bristol, for which he was executed on Friday, April 24th, 1752. Together with his moral religious and [sic] Reflections upon the most remarkable Passages of his whole Life; and an Account of his Conversation the Sunday before his Trial. Taken from his own Mouth, by a Friend; and publish'd at his Request. . . . The Fourth Edition. London. Philadelphia Reprinted and Sold by William Bradford, at the Sign of the Bible, in Second Street. M,DCC,LII. 48 p.

PHC*

Evans 6,886 Hildeburn 1,265

(a.2) The sixth edition. London, Printed: Philadelphia, reprinted and sold by William Bradford, at the sign of the Bible in Second-street, M,DCC,LIII. 46 p. 20 cm.

PHi, PPL

Evans 7,063 Metzger 160

Note Microcard says "From an adv."

(2) Duke of Cumberland's Trial for Criminal Conversation, 1770

(a) The Trial of His R.H. the D[uke] of C[umberland] for Criminal Conversation with Lady Harriet G[rosveno]r. To which is prefixed, An Introductory Discourse from the Ancient and Modern Punishments of Adultery, and the uncommon Progress of that Crime. Including All The Letters Which have passed between His Royal Highness and her Ladyship, and were read in Court. Philadelphia: Re-printed by John Dunla, at the Newest Printing-Office, the South Side of the Jersey Market, and three Doors below Second-Street, N DCC LXX. 58 p. 12mo.

MWA*

Evans 11,898 Hildeburn 2,610

(3) Elwall's 1726 Trial for Heresy, 1784

(a) An Appeal to the Serious and Candid Professors of Christianity. . . . By Joseph Priestly, L.L.D. F.R.S. and a Lover of the Gospel. To which are added, A concise History of the Rise of those Doctrines: and the Triumph of Truth; Being An Account of the Trial of Mr. E. Elwall, for Heresy and Blasphemy, at Stafford Assizes. . . . Philadelphia: Printed and Sold by Robert Bell, in Third-Street, M,DCC,LXXIV. 59 p. 12mo.

MHi, MWA*, MiU-C, NHi, PHi, PPL, PPPrHI

Evans, 18,741 Hildeburn 4,543

(a.2) Philadelphia: Printed by Thomas Dobson, at the Stone House No. 41, South Second-Street M,DCC,XCIV 60 p.

BLM, DLC, MBAt, MHi, MWA*, PPL, RPJCB

Evans 27,552

(4) Lee's 1752 Execution, 1793

(a) Some Account of the Life and Death of Matthew Lee, Executed at Tyburn, October 11, 1752, in the 20th Year of his Age. Philadelphia: Printed by Johnston & Justice at Franklin's Head, No. 41 Chestnut-street, Third House from Second-Street;

for William Glendinning, Preacher of the Gospel. 1793. 23 p.

DLC*, P

mp. 46,877 Bristol B8,477

(b) Philadelphia; Printed in the year 1795. 23 p. 16mo.

DLC, MBAt, MWA*, PHi, PPL

Evans 28,960

(5) Walker's Trial for Treason, 1794

(a) The Whole Proceedings on the Trial of Indictment against Thomas Walker of Manchester, merchant, Samuel Jackson, James Cheetham, Oliver Pearsal, Benjamin Booth, and Joseph Collier; for A Conspiracy To Overthrow The Constitution And Government, and To Aid And Assist The French, (being the King's Enemies) in case they should invade this kingdom, tried At the Assizes of Lancaster, April 2, 1794, Before The Hon. Mr. Justice Heath, one of the judges of his Majesty's court of common pleas. Taken in short-hand By Joseph Gurney. Philadelphia: printed for Samuel Harrison Smith, by W. Woodward. 1794. 123 p. 8vo.

DLC, MBAt, MH-L, MHi, MSaE, MWA*, MoU-L, NHi, NN, NNU-L, PHi, PPAmP, PPL, RPB

Evans 27,076

(6) Lacombe's French Trial for Treason, 1795

(a) A Specimen of the Patriotism of the Jacobins in France, or, the Trial of Jean Baptiste Lacombe, late president of the military commission at Bordeaux; condemned to death as an exacter, an extortioner, a prevaricator, a corrupter of morality and of the public mind, and, as such, A Traitor to his Country, on the 27th Thermidor, second year of the French Republic, one and indivisible. Translated from the French. Philadelphia: printed for the translator by Ormrod & Conrad, at the Old Franklin's Head, No. 41, Chesnut-Street. 1795. 32 p.

BLM, MWA*, PHi(2), PPAmP, PPL

Evans 28,941

(7) <u>Two Friends</u> Libel in Bermuda Vice Admiralty, 1795

(a) Proceedings of the Trial of the Ship <u>Two Friends</u>, in the Court of Vice Admiralty in Bermuda. Copy. Philadelphia: Printed by Ormrod and Conrad at Franklin's Head, No. 41, Chestnut-Street. M,DCCXCV. 151 p. 8vo.

DLC, MWA*, MdBB, MiU-C, NHi, NN, PP, PPL, PU-L, ScC

Evans 29,667

(8) Orr's Irish Trial for Being a United Irishman, 1798

(a) The Trial of William Orr, at Carrickfergus Assizes, for being An United Irishman; with his Dying Declaration, &c. &c. &c. Philadelphia: Printed By J. Carey, No. 19, Carter's Alley, for G. Douglas, No. 2, South Third-Street. 1798. 20 p. 8vo.

MWA, NHi, PPB, PPAmP

Evans 34,281

(9) Robinson's Admiralty Reports, 1798-1799 Cases, 1800

(a) Reports of Cases argued and determined in the High Court of Admiralty; (Great Britain) commencing with the Judgments of The Right Honorable Sir William Scott, Michalmas Term 1798. By Chr. Robinson, LL.D. Advocate. Volume The First. Philadelphia, Re-Printed: (From the London Copy of A. Strachan, Law Printer to His Majesty) And Sold By James Humphreys, No. 106, South side of Market-street. 1800. 348 p. 8vo.

DCU-L, DLC, MBAt, MH-L, MWA*, MdBB, MiU-C, NcD-L, NjP, RPJCB, ViU

Evans 38,414

8.08 Delaware

(1) Irish Highwaymen, 1799

(a) A Genuine History of the Lives and Actions of the most notorious Irish Highwaymen, Tories and Rapparees, from Redmond O'Hanlon, the famous Gentleman-Robber, to Cahier na Gappul, the great Horse-Catcher, who was executed at Maryborough, in August, 1735. To which is added, the Gold-Finder: Or, the History of Manus Mac Oneil, who under the Appearance of a stupid, ignorant Country Fellow, (on the Bog of Allen, by the help of his Man Andrew) played the most notorious Cheats, and remarkable Tricks on the People of Ireland, that ever was known. Also, the Remarkable Life of Gilder Roy, a Murderer, Ravisher, Incendiary and Highwayman, With several others, not in any former Edition. The Edition, with Additions. By J. Cosgrave. Wilmington: Printed and Sold by Bonsal & Niles. 1799. 140 p. 24mo.

MWA*

Evans 35,355 Rink 499

8.09 Maryland

(1) Father Moor's Murderers, 1785

(a) The Horror of Murder, Blasphemy, and Sacrilege, Containing A true account, of a most shocking Murder, Committed on the Body of the Rev. Father Moor, at Tralee, in Ireland. Frederick-Town. Printed by M. Bargis. M,DCC,LXXXV. 8 p. 15 cm.

MdHi*

mp. 44,700 Bristol B6,084 Wheeler 371

(2) 'Espinasse's Nisi Prius Reports, 1793-1794 Cases, 1795

(a) Cases Argued And Ruled at Nisi Prius, in the Courts of King's Bench, and Common Pleas, from Easter term 33 George III. -- to Hilary term 34 George III with Some Additional Cases, of an earlier period. By Isaac 'Espinasse, of Gray's Inn. Esq. Barrister at Law. . . . First American edition with additional references. London, printed: Baltimore: Re-printed by Clayland, Dobbin, & Co. for Keatinge's Book-Store. 1795. 148 p. 8vo.

CLU-L, CSt-L, DCU-L, MB, MBAt, MH-L, MHi, MWA*, MdBB, MdBE, MdBP, MdHi, MoU-L, PU-L, RPJCB

Evans 28,636 Minick 233

8.11 North Carolina

(1) Cagliostro's Defence Before Parliament of Paris, 1789

(a) The Defence of Count Cagliostro, before the Parliament of Paris, in presence of Cardinal Prince of Rohan, the Countess de La Motte, and Miss Le Gay D'Oliva, co-accused; against the Attorney General, accused. Newbern?: Printed and sold by Hodge & Willis. 1789.

No copy located

Evans 21,724 McMurtrie North Carolina D-7

(2) Latch's King's Bench Reports, 1624-1627 Cases, 1793

(a) Cases determined in the Court of King's Bench; during the I, II and III years of Charles I. Collected by John Latch, of the Middle Temple, Esquire, First published, in Norman-French, [1661,] by Edward Walpoole, of Gray's Inn, Esquire. Translated into the English Language, by Francois-Xavier Martin. Newbern: From the Translator's Press. 1793. 243 p. 8vo.

CLU-L, CSmH, DCU-L, DLC, MH-L, MWA, MdBB, NN*(2), NNB, NNC-L, NcAsS, NcD, NcD-L, NcU, NjP, PPB, PU-L, RPJCB

Evans 25,451 and 25,702 McMurtrie: North Carolina 182 Thornton Unofficial 5,124

Note Brackets in original.

(b) See above 1.11(4)(a.3).

8.12 South Carolina

(1) Gordon's Trial for Treason, 1781

(a) The Trial of Lord George Gordon

Morgan 570

Note Morgan cites Royal Gazette, April 21, 1781. Bristol deleted the entry for B5,376, which is where this imprint would be listed. A report of George Gordon's trial for high treason was published in Edinburgh and London in 1781.

(2) Worsley v. Bisset, 1782

(a) The Trial, with the Whole of the Evidence, between the Right Honourable Sir Richard Worsley, Bart. Plaintiff, and George Maurice Bisset.

Morgan 584

Note Morgan cites Royal South Carolina Gazette, July 9, 1782. There was a trial for criminal conversation between Worsley and Bisset published in London in 1782.

8.20 Trials and Reports Reprinted in More than One State

(1) Admiral Captain Byng's Court-Martial, 1757

(a) The Proceedings of the Court-Martial on the Trial of Admiral Byng, Held on Board his Majesty's Ship St. George, in Portsmouth Harbour; begun December 27, 1756, and continued till January 27, 1757. Containing a Summary of the Evidence as delivered each Day in Court, methodically digested, and the Proofs and Arguments as well for as against him, fairly and impartially stated. To which is added, The Admiral's Defence, as presented by him, and read in the Court January 18, 1757. Together with an account of his Behavior in his last Moments . . . London: Printed. Boston; New England, Re-printed and Sold by Green & Russell, at their office in Queen-street, and by R. Draper, in Newbury-street. M.DCC.LVII. 76 p. 4to.

CLU, MBAt, MHi, MWA*

Evans 7,892 and 7,865 (second part) Parrish 91

(b) The trial of the Honourable Admiral John Byng, at a court-martial . . . London. Printed. And New-York. Re-printed, and sold by H. Gaine, at the printing-office at the Bible and Crown . . . 1757. 8vo.

CSmH

Evans 7,891 Huntington 205

Note The microcard for Evans 7,891, as well as the Short-Title Evans entry under "Charles Ferne" says this Evans entry is "Apparently a ghost of 7890", but the Short-Title Evans entry under "John Byng" refers to a CSmH copy.

(c) The Trial Of the Honourable John Byng, at a Court-Martial, As taken by Mr. Charles Ferne, Judge-Advocate of his Majesty's Fleet. Published by Order of The Right Honourable the Lords Commissioners of the Admiralty, At the Desire of the Court-Martial. To which is Added, An Account of Admiral Byng's Behavior in his last Moments. Also, a Copy of a Paper delivered by Him to William Brough, Esq; Marshall of the High Court of Admiralty, immediately before his Death. London: Printed. And, New-York, Re-printed, by J. Parker and W. Weyman, at the New-Printing-Office, in Beaver-Street. 1757. 46 p. 8vo.

CLU, DLC, MWA*(imp.)

Evans 7,890 Parrish 91

(d) The Chronicle of B---g, [Byng], the Son of the Great B---G [Byng] That Lived in the Reign of Queen Felicia [Queen Anne]. Containing An Account of his Mighty Transactions against Gallisoniere, His Flight and happy arrival at G-------R [Gibralter] and from thence to sp---th---d [Spithead]. By Israel Ben Ader Of the Tribe of Levi . . . Written in the Eastern Style. London, Printed: 1756. Boston: Re printed and sold at the Heart and Crown in Cornhill, 1757. 8 p. 8vo.

MWA*

Evans 7,927

(2) Wilkes's Trial and Habeas Corpus, 1763

(a) An Authentick Account of the Proceedings Against John Wilkes, Esq; Member of Parliament for Aylesbury, and late Colonel of the Buckinghamshire Militia. Containing All the Papers relative to this interesting Affair, from that Gentleman's being taken into Custody by his Majesty's Messengers, to his Discharge at the Court of Common Pleas. With An Abstract of that precious Jewel of an Englishman, The Habeas Corpus Act. Also, The North Briton, No. 45. Being the Paper for which Mr. Wilkes was sent to the Tower. Addressed to all Lovers of Liberty. London, Printed. Philadelphia, Re-Printed: And to be Sold by W. Dunlap in Market-Street, M,DCC,LXIII.
48 p. 8vo.

CSmH, MH, MWA*, PHi, PPAmP, PPL

Evans 9,542 Hildeburn 1,872

(a.2) London, Printed. Boston, Re-Printed, And Sold by Richard and Samuel Draper, in Newbury-Street, Thomas and John Fleet, at the Heart & Crown in Cornhill; and Edes and Gill, next the Prison in Queen-Street, 1763. 36 p. 8vo.

BLM, DLC, MB, MBAt, MH, MHi, MSaE, MWA*, NHi, NN, RPJCB

Evans 9,543

<u>Evans</u> <u>Ghost</u> 9,544

(3) LaFayette's Impeachment, 1793

(a) Impeachment of Mr. LaFayette: containing His Accusation, (Stated in the Report of the Extraordinary Commission to the National Assembly, on the 8th of August, 1792,) supported by Mr. Brissot of Warville; and His Defence by Mr. Vaublanc: with a Supplement, Containing the Letters, and other authentic Pieces relative thereto. Translated from the French, by William Cobbett. . . . Philadelphia: Printed by John Parker, No. 259, North Second-street. M,DCC,XCIII. 104 p. 8vo.

CSmH, DLC, MBAt, MWA*, NN, NjR, NcD, PBL, PHi, PPL

Evans 25,497

(b) Impeachment of Mr. LaFayette: containing His Accusation, (Stated in the Report of the Extraordinary Commission to the National Assembly, on the 8th of August, 1792,) Supported by Mr. Brissot, And his Defence by Mr. Vaublanc: with A Supplement, Containing the Letters and other authentic Pieces relative thereto. Translated from the French, by William Cobbett. . . . Hagerstown, Printed by Stewart Herbert. M,DCC,XCIV. 81 p. 8vo.

CSmH, MWA*, PHi

Evans 26,996

(4) Paine's Trial for Libel, 1793

(a) The Celebrated Speech of the Hon. T. Erskine, in support of the Liberty Of The Press. Delivered At Guildhall, December 18, 1792. To which is prefixed a Preface by a Scotch Member of Parliament. Taken in short hand by Guerney, the principal short hand writer in London. Edinburgh Printed. New-York: Re-printed by John Buel, No. 28, Wall-Street: sold by C. Cleland, J. Fellows, and the Printer. M,DCC,XCIII. 68 p. 8vo.

NN*

Evans 25,456

(b) The Trial of Thomas Paine, for a Libel, contained in the Second Part of Rights of Man. Before Lord Kenyon, and a Special Jury, At Guildhall, December 18, 1792. With the Speeches of the Attorney General and Mr. Erskine, at large. Printed at Boston, by I. Thomas and E. T. Andrews, Faust's Statue, No. 45, Newbury Street. Sold at their Bookstore, by D. West, No. 36, Marlborough Street, and E. Larkin, jun. No. 50, Cornhill. MDCCXCIII. 43 p. 8vo.

CSmH, CtHi, CtY, DLC, MBAt, MH, MHi, MWA*, MWiW-C, MiU-C, MiU-L, NIC-L, NN, PPL

Evans 26,280 Sabin 96,914

(c) The Trial of Thomas Paine, for certain False, Wicked, Scandalous and Seditious Libels inserted in the Second Part of the Rights of Man, before The right hon. Lord Kenyon and a Special Jury, at Guildhall, on Tuesday the 18th December, 1792. Copied from the minutes taken in court. Philadelphia: From the Press of John Parker, No. 259, North Second-street. M DCC XCIII. 28 p. 8vo.

NN, PHi, PPAmP, PPL*

Evans 26,281 Sabin 96,915

(d) Christianity Vindicated, in the Admirable Speech of the Hon. Tho. Erskine, in the Trial of J. [sic] Williams, for publishing Paine's "Age of Reason." 25th June, 1797. From The Twelfth London Edition. Philadelphia: Printed by J. Carey, No. 83, N. Second-Street, for G. Douglas, No. 2, South Third-Street, 1797. 15 p. 8vo.

DLC, MHi, NIC, NN, MSaE, PPL*

Evans 32,092

(e) The Speeches of the Hon. Thomas Erskine, in the Court Of King's Bench, June 28, 1797, Before the right hon. Lloyd

Lord Kenyon, And A Special Jury, on the Trial The King versus Thomas Williams, for publishing the Age of Reason, written by Thoms Paine: Together with Mr. Stewart Kyd's Reply, and Lord Kenyon's Charge To The Jury. Philadelphia: Printed for, and sold by William Cobbett, opposite Christ Church. Nov. 1797. 23 p. 8vo.

MBAt, MWA*, RPJCB

Evans 32,093

(f) Speeches of Messrs. Erskine and Kydd, On a trial for publishing Paine's Age of Reason. With Lord Kenyon's Charge to the Special Jury. Published at the particular request of several clergymen. Washington, Ky.: Hunter & Beaumont. 1798.

No copy located

Evans 33,698 Kentucky Imprints 70

<u>Evans</u> <u>Ghosts</u> 25,457 (Trumbull 2d 2,117) and 25,458

(5) Louis XVI's Trial, 1793

(a) A Discourse upon the question Whether the King shall be tried? Delivered before the Society of the Friends of the Constitution at Paris, at a Meeting July 10, 1791. By J. P. Brissot de Warville, Member of that Society. Translated by P. J. G. De Nancrede, Preceptor of the French Language, in the University of Cambridge. The First American Edition. Printed at Boston, by J. Belknap and A. Young. Sold at their printing-office, No. 34, Newbury Street, and by the Booksellers in town and country. MDCCXCI 36 p. 12mo.

BLM, DLC, MBAt, MH, MHi, MSaE, MWA*, NHi

Evans 23,222

(b) Trial of Louis XVI, Late king of France; by the National Convention, at several adjourned sittings. Translated from the French. Philadelphia: from the press of John Parker, No. 259, North Second-street, M,DCC,XCII. 30 p. 8vo.

DLC, MWA*, MiU-C, PU-L, RPJCB

Evans 25,499

(c) The Trial, &c. of Louis XVI. Late King Of France, And Marie Antoinette, His Queen. Embellished with copperplate engravings. Lansingburgh, Printed by Silvester Tiffany, for, and sold by, Thomas Spencer, at his Book-Store, in Market-street, Albany, 1794. 38 p. 18 cm.

MWA*

mp. 47,100 Bristol B8,724

(d) The Tragedy of Louis Capet: Being a True and Authentic Narrative of the horrid and barbarous Execution of the late unfortunate Monarch, Louis XVIth of France. . . . [Colophon] Printed next the venerable Stump of Liberty-Tree. for J. Plumer, jun. Trader, of Newbury-Port. [Price 2s. and 8d. per Dozen and Four Pence single.] [Printed by E. Russell] 2 p.

DLC*, MHi

Evans 22,943 Ford 2,700

Note Price brackets in original.

(d.2) [Boston: Printed by Ezekiel Russell for J. Plumer 1793] Broadside fol.

DLC, MHi*

Evans 26,271

(d.3) Sold next the venerable Stump of Liberty-Tree. [Price Two Shillings and Eight Pence per Dozen, and Four Pence single.] Broadside fol.

MSaE*

Evans 26,272 Ford 2,701

Note Brackets in original

(d.4) Springfield. Printed and Sold by Edward Gray. 1793. Broadside fol.

MWA*

Evans 26,273 Ford 2,702 Wegelin 802

(e) The Trial of Louis the XVIth, King of France, Before the National Convention, For High Treason against the State, Containing the whole Proceedings, the King's Defence, the Names of the Members who voted for and against his Death, His final Sentence pronounced on the 17th of January, and lastly the Manner of his Execution, which took place on the Twenty first of January 1793. Translated from the Original French. New-York: Printed in the Year 1793. 12 p. 17 cm.

MHi*

mp. 46,811 B8,400

(f) Columbian USA centinel. No. 33 of Vol. XVIII. Whole No. 917. Wednesday, January 2, (No. 32 of Vol. XX. Whole No. 1020. Saturday, December 28, 1793.) Printed and published, on Wednesdays and Saturdays, by Benjamin Russell, in State-Street, Boston, 1793. fol.

DLC, MB, MBAt, MH, MHi, MSaE, MWA, NHi, NN, PHi

Evans 25,317

Evans Ghosts 25,500 and 26,274

(6) Margarot's Scottish Trial for Sedition, 1794

(a) The Trial of Maurice Margarot, Before the High Court Of Justiciary, At Edinburgh, On the 13th and 14th of January, 1794, on an Indictment for Seditious Practices. Taken in shorthand By Mr. Ramsey. London: Printed.-- New-York: RePrinted, by James Carey, No. 91, Broad-Street. [1794] 166 p. 8vo.

DLC, MB, MH-L, MHi, MWA*, MdBJ-G, MdBP, NN(2), NjR, PHi, PP, PPL, RPB, RPJCB, ViU

Evans 27,594

(b) The Trial of Maurice Margarot, Delegate From London, to the British Convention, before the High Court of Justiciary, at Edinburgh, on the 13th and 14th of January, 1794. For Sedition. Taken in short-hand by Mr. Ramsey. Carefully corrected, and many sentences added, which owing to the low tone of voice used by some of the Witnesses, are omitted in the London Copy. The Public may therefore be assured that this is the Genuine Edition. Philadelphia: Printed by Wrigley and Berriman; for Alexander M'Kenzie & Co. No. 126, South Front Street. M.DCC.XCIV 163 p. 8vo.

DLC, InNd-L, MWA*, MDBB, MdBJ-G, MoU-L, NN, NNU-L, PHi, PPL, ViU, RPJCB

Evans 27,596

(c) "6. Trial of Maurice Margarot before the High Court of Justiciary, at Edinburgh, for Seditious Practices," Select Pamphlets. . . . Philadelphia: Published by Mathew Carey, No. 118, Market-Street. 1796. (Price two Dollars.) 166 p.

MWA*, PPL

Evans 31,173

(c.2) "No. 5 Trial of Maurice Margarot . . .," Select Pamphlets. . . . Philadelphia: Sold by the Booksellers. 1802.

Not in Shaw-Shoemaker

Evans Ghosts 27,592, 27,593, and 27,595

(7) Captain Corran's Trial for Murder, 1794

(a) Account of a Horrid Murder committed by Captain William Corran, of the Brig Falmouth, on the body of Mr. Joseph Porter, his passenger. With particulars of his Trial and Execution, at Halifax, July 16-21, 1794. Philadelphia: Printed Aug. 27, 1794. [Price six cents.] 12 p. 12 mo.

MWA*

Evans 26,534

Note Brackets in original.

(b) Murder. Narrative of the Trial, Conviction and Execution of Captain William Corran. Master of the Brig Falmouth, who was executed at Halifax, Nova Scotia, July 21, 1794, for the most barbarous, inhuman and bloody Murder of Mr. Joseph Porter, a Passenger on board said Brig, by hewing him in in [sic] Pieces with a remarkable large and heavy Cutlass. Halifax, Printed, July 27, Newport, Reprinted, September 12, 1794. 8 p.

RHi*

Evans 26,820

(c) Account of a Horrid Murder, committed by Captain William Corran, of the Brig Falmouth, on the body of Mr. Joseph Porter, his passenger. With the particulars of his Trial and Execution at Halifax, July 17-21, 1794. New-York: Printed by Citizens Loudon and Cook. [Price Six-Pence.] [1794?] 12 p. 19 cm.

CtHi

Bristol B8,564

Note First Brackets in original.

(d) Shocking Narrative of the Murder of Mr. Joseph Porter, by Captain William Corran; on board of the Brig Falmouth, the 27th Day of May, 1794. Being on a voyage from Port Royal, in Jamaica, to Belfast, in Ireland. Containing, An account of the conduct of the Captain, previous to the Murder; also, the securing of him by the people afterwards; who then put into a port near Halifax, where the Captain was sent, tried and sentenced to be hanged, which sentence was put in execution on Monday, the 21st of July, 1794. Printed at Walpole, Newhampshire, by I. Thomas and D. Carlisle, jun. MDCCXCV. 10 p. 19 cm.

MWA*(imp.)

mp. 47,599 Bristol B9,293a

Evans Ghost 31,995 (Cooley 367 amd McCorison 452)

(8) Watt's Scottish Trial for Treason, 1794

(a) The Trials At Large of Robert Watt, and David Downie, for High Treason, at the Session of Oyer and Terminer, At Edinburgh, August 27, September 3d, and September 5th, 1794. At which they were Both Found Guilty, and sentenced to be Hanged, Drawn, and Quartered, on the 15th October. Taken in short hand By an English Barrister. New-York: Printed by Tiebout & O'Brien, 358 Pearl-street, M.DCC.XCIV. 88 p. 8vo.

DLC, MB, MWA*, NHi, NIC-L

Evans 27,815

(a.2) Philadelphia: Printed for Alexander M'Kenzie & Co. No. 126, South Front Street, and Wrigley & Berriman, No. 149, Chestnut Street, December 4, 1794. [Price a Quarter of a Dollar.] 41 p. 8vo.

BLM, DLC, MH-L, MHi*, MdBJ-G, NNU-L, NjR, RPJCB

Evans 27,816

Note Brackets in original.

(9) James, Captain, Hanged for Murder, 1799

(a) Captain James, Who was hung and gibbeted in England, for starving to death his Cabbin-Boy [sic]. . . . Nathaniel Coverly, Jun. Printer, Milk-Street, Boston. [1799?] Broadside

MH*

mp. 48,896 Bristol B10,731 Ford 2,920 and 2,922

(a.2) Boston, Wholesale and retail on Cross Street, near Mercantile Wharf [1799?] Broadside

MSaE

Bristol 10,732

(a.3) [n.p. 1799?] Broadside

MHi*(imp.)

mp. 48,895 Bristol B10,733 Ford 2,922a

(a.4) Deming [Boston 1799?] Broadside

CtHi

mp. 48,897 Bristol B10,734

Note Bristol does not show an mp. number for B10,734, but Short-Title Evans lists this imprint as mp. 48,897, and says "Not located, 1968."

(a.5) Second Newburyport Edition. Printed for, and Sold by, the Travelling Stationers in Town and County. Sold also at N.4, Middle-street. [Newburyport 1800] Broadside

MSaE*

Evans 37,094 Ford 2,919

Ford Ghost 2,921

9.00

English Trials Relating to America

(1) Quo Warranto, 1682

(a) A Letter from New-England Concerning their Customs, Manners, and Religion. Written upon occasion of a Report about a Quo Warranto Brought against that Government. [By W. J.] London, Printed for Randolph Taylor near Stationers Hall, 1682. 9 p.

BEN, BGH, BOB, CSmH, ICN, MWA, NN, RPJCB

Sabin 52,641 Church 674 Wing W-J59

(a.2) Club for Colonial Reprints (George Parker Winship, ed., Providence, Rhode Island 1905).

(b) At the Court at Whitehall, the 20th of July, 1683. . . . [Colophon] London, Printed by the Assigns of John Bill deceas'd; And by Henry Hills, and Thomas Newcomb, Printers to the Kings most Excellent Majesty, 1683. 4 p. 29 cm.

BLM, CSmH, NN, RPJCB

Sabin 45,929 Church 681

(2) Penn v. Baltimore, 1709-1750

(a) The Case of William Penn, Proprietary and Governor in Chief of the Province of Pennsilvania, and Territories, against the Lord Baltimore's Pretensions to a Tract of Land in America. [London 1709]

PPL

(b) Articles of Agreement made and concluded upon between the Right Honourable the Lord Proprietary of Maryland,

and the Honourable the Proprietary of Pensilvania, &c. Touching the Limits and Boundaries of the Two Provinces. With the Commission, Constituting certain Persons to execute the same. Philadelphia: Printed by B. Franklin, at the New Printing-Office, near the Market. M,DCC,XXXIII. 19 p. fol.

MdBJ-G, NN*, PHi

Evans 3,710 Hildeburn 455

(c) Articles of Agreement, &c. [Endorsement] True Copies of I. The Agreement between Lord Baltimore and Messieurs Penn, dated 10 May 1732. II. The Commissions given to the Commissioners to mark out the Lines between Maryland, and Pensilvania and the Three Lower Counties on Delaware. III. The Return or Report of the Commissioners on both Sides, made 24 Nov. 1733. Shewing for what Reasons the Lines were not mark'd out within the Time appointed for that Purpose. [London 1733-34] 8 p. fol.

MdBJ-G, RPJCB

(d) Articles of Agreement, &c. [Philadelphia 1734?]

PPL*

Evans 4,182 Hildeburn 549

Note   Page 8 of entry (d) has same text as Endorsement in entry (c).

(e) The Case of Messieurs Penn, and the People of Pennsilvania, and the three lower Counties of Newcastle, Kent, and Sussex, on Delaware, in relation to a Series of Injuries and Hostilities made upon them, for several Years past, by Thomas Cressap, and others, by the Director of Authority of the Deputy-Governor of Maryland [London 1737] 8 p. fol.

MdBJ-G, PHi

Sabin 59,685 and 59,962

(a.2) Massachusetts Historical Society, Photostat Americana, Second Series, No. 66 (Boston 1938).

(f) The Case of the Province of Maryland, touching the outrageous Riots which have been committed in the Borders of the Province by the Inhabitants of Pennsylvania [signed by J. Strange. London 1737]

DLC, MdBJ-G

Sabin 45,099

(g) In Canc' John Penn, Thomas Penn, and Richard Penn, Esqrs. Plaintiffs. Charles Calvert Esq; Lord Baltimore in the

Kingdom of Ireland, Defendant The Plaintiffs Case. [London 1740] 13 p.

MdBJ-G (unbound and printed on one side only)

Sabin 34,416

(h) In Chancery--Breviate. John Penn, Thomas Penn, and Richard Penn, Esqrs; Plaintiffs. Charles Calvert Esq.; Lord Baltimore in the Kingdom of Ireland, Defendant. For the Plaintiffs. Upon a Bill to compell a Specifick Execution of Articles of Agreement entered into between the Partys for setling the Boundarys of the Province of Pensilvania, the Three Lower Countys, and the Province of Maryland, and for perpetuating Testimony, &c. Mr. Attorney General Sir Dudley Ryder. Mr. Solicitor General Murray. Mr. King's Council Noell. Paris and Weston, Sollicitors [London 1742] 116 p. fol.

DLC, MH, MdBJ-G, NN, NjP, P-L, PHi, PPL

Sabin 34,416

(h.2) 16 <u>Pennsylvania Archives, Second Series</u> 639 (Wm. H. Egle, ed. Harrisburg, Pennsylvania 1890).

(i) Upon the 24th and 25th of May, 1743, the Cause depending in Chancery between Messrs. Penns, Proprietors of Pensilvania, Complainaints [sic], and Lord Baltimore, Proprietor of Maryland, Defendants . . . [Philadelphia? 1743? or England?] Broadside 14 x 11.5 cm.

PHi*

mp. 40,320 Bristol B1,226

(j) Penn against Ld. Baltimore In Chancery. Copy of Minutes on Hearing. Lord Chancellor. Tuesday, May 15. 1750. . . . [Philadelphia, Franklin and Hall, 1750] 15 p. 42.5 cm.

DLC, PHi, PPL*

mp. 40,534 Bristol B1,476 Metzger 140

(k) Pen against Lord Baltimore, 1745, Ridgeway Reports temp. Hardwicke 332-38 (1794), 27 English Reports 847-48 (1903).

(l) Penn v. Lord Baltimore, 1750, 1 Vesey Senior (1771) (444-56, 4th ed. 1818), 27 English Reports 1132-40 (1903). [The first edition of Vesey Senior was published in 1771.]

(m) Penn v. Lord Baltimore, 1750, Vesey Senior Supplement (1817) (194-98, 2d ed. 1825), 28 English Reports 498-500 (1903). [The first edition of Vesey Senior Supplement was published in 1817.]

(n) Penn v. Lord Baltimore, 1755, Dickens 273 (1803), 21 English Reports 273 (1903).

(o) Nicholas B. Wainwright, "The Missing Evidence: Penn v. Baltimore," 80 _Pennsylvania Magazine of History and Biography_ 227-35 (1956).

(3) Lawson v. Tait, 1779

(a) Private case before the House of Lords, between James Lawson and Jno. Tait, relative to Estates in the Province of Maryland, and to tracts of Land on the Ptomack and Occoquan in Virginia, held by John Sempill, with full descriptions of the Estates which were purchased of Col. Ewell. London: Privately Printed. 1779. 40 p. fol.

Sabin 39,450 (Title from J. Camden Hotten's Catalogue)

10.00

American Appeals to the Privy Council

10.01 New Hampshire

(1) Dering (or Deering) v. Packer, 1760

(a) New England. Thomas Dering, Executor of Henry Dering, late of Boston, in the Province of the Massachusetts Bay, Esquire, deceased, Appellant. Thomas Packer, of Portsmouth, in New Hampshire, Gentleman, Respondent. The Appellant's Case. 3 p.

BLM (Add. Ms. 36,218, f. 44)

(b) New Hampshire. Thomas Deering, Executor of Henry Deering, of the said Province of New Hampshire, Appellant. Thomas Packer, of the said Province, Esq; Respondent. The Respondent's Case. 5 p.

BLM (Add. Ms. 36,218, f. 46)

(c) Deering, Appellant, versus Parker, Respondent, 4 Dallas xxiii (1807).

(2) Sherburne v. Sherburne, 1762

(a) New Hampshire. John Sherburne, Gentleman, youngest Son of Henry Sherburne, late of New Hampshire, Esquire, deceased, Appellant. Samuel Sherburne, eldest Son of the said Henry Sherburne the Father, deceased, Peter Gilman, Esquire, and Dorothy his Wife, and Joseph Langdon, and Ann his Wife, which said Dorothy and Ann are the Two Daughters of the said Henry Sherburne, deceased, Respondents. The Appellant's Case. 3 p.

BLM (Add. Ms. 36,218 f. 147)

(b) New Hampshire. John Sherburne, of Portsmouth, in New Hampshire. Gentleman, younger Son of Henry Sherburne, of the said Province, Esq; deceased, Appellant. Samuel Sherburne, of Portsmouth aforesaid, eldest Son and Heir of the said Henry Sherburne, and Peter Gilman and Joseph Langdon, Esqrs. who married two of the said Henry Sherburne's Daughters, Respondents. The Respondents Case. 3 p.

BLM (Add. Ms. 36,218, f. 149)

(3) Trecothick v. Wentworth, 1762

(a) New Hampshire. Barlow Trecothick, of London, Merchant, Plaintiff below and now Appellant. Samuel Wentworth, of New Hampshire, Merchant, Defendant below, and now Respondent. The Appellant's Case. 5 p.

BLM (Add. Ms. 36,218, f. 151)

(4) Rolfe v. Proprietors, 1762

(a) New Hampshire. Benjamin Rolfe, Esquire, Daniel Carter, Timothy Simons, John Evans, John Chandler, Abraham Colby, and Abraham Kimball, Appellants. The Proprietors of the Common and Undivided Lands lying within the Township of Bow, in the Province of New Hampshire, Respondents. The Appellants Case. 7 p.

BLM (Add. Ms. 36,218, f. 181)

(b) New Hampshire. Benjamin Rolfe, Esq. Daniel Carter, Timothy Simons, John Evans, John Chandler, Abraham Colby, and Abraham Kimball, Appellants. The Incorporated Proprietors of the Township of Bow, in his Majesty's Province of New Hampshire, Respondents. The Respondents Case. 6 p.

BLM (Add. Ms. 36,218, f. 185)

(c) Rolfe against Bow. Appendix containing Depositions for the Respondents. 3 p. and map

BLM (Add. Ms. 36,218, f. 189)

(d) [Plans and Explanations of plans of Massachusetts and New Hampshire touching the boundary question and the bounds of certain towns as Rumbord, Cuncook, Bow.] 6 p. Ms. and 5 maps

BLM (Add. Ms. 15,487, ff. 96-103)

10.02 Massachusetts

(1) Vassall v. Fletcher, 1754

(a) See above 1.02(10).

10.03 Rhode Island

(1) South Kingstown, 1748

(a) In the Matter of the Capture of the Ship South Kingstown, and her Cargo. Benjamin Hassard, Robert Carr, and John Easton, Merchants and Jonathan Hassard, Yeoman, all of Rhode-Island in New England, Owners of the Sloop called the South Kingstown, with her Cargo, unduly and illegally taken as Prize by the Bilander Privateer the Young Eagle, John Rous Commander, Appellants. John Rous, of Boston, in the Province of the Massachusetts Bay, late Commander of the Bilander Privateer of the same Province named the Young Eagle, Respondent. The said John Rous, Appellant. The said Benjamin Hassard, Robert Carr, John Easton, and Jonathan Hassard, Respondents. The Case of the Appellants in the Original, and Respondents in the Cross-Appeal. 4 p. fol.

NN

Ford Briefs p. 90

(2) McSparran v. Hassard, 1752

(a) Rhode Island. James McSparran D.D. as the present Incumbent of the Church of England, called St. Paul's, within the Petequamscut Purchase, in the Narroganset Country, in Rhode-Island, and in the Right of the said Church, Plaintiff below, and now Appellant. Robert Hassard Gent., Defendant below, and now Respondent. On a Suit for 280 (the remaining Part of 300) Acres of Land in South Kingston in the Narroganset Country, Parcel of the said Petequamscut Purchase; which 300 Acres were originally given by the Proprietor's Deed in 1668, for an Orthodox Person, to preach God's Word to the Inhabitants. The Appellant's Case. 4 p.

BLM (Add. Ms. 36,217, f. 1)

(b) Rhode Island. The Reverend James M'Sparran, of North Kingston, in the County of King's County, in the Colony of Rhode-Island, Plaintiff and Appellant. Robert Hassard, of South-Kingston, in the said County of King's County, in Rhode-Island, Defendant and Respondent. The Respondent's Case. 7 p.

BLM (Add. Ms. 36,217, f. 3)

(c) See also 1.04(2).

(3) Catherina, 1752

(a) Lord Commissioners of Prizes. The Catharina, a Dutch Ship, condemned in Rhode-Island. John Paasch, a Subject of the States-General of the United Provinces, Master of the said Ship Catharina, on behalf of Jan Ambrosius Duan, an Inhabitant of Curacoa, and a Subject of the said States General, Owner of the said Ship, and the greatest Part of her Cargo; and also on behalf of himself, and the other Officers of the said Ship, Subjects of the said States General, Owners of the rest of the Cargo on board the said ship at the time of the capture; John Sweet, Commander of a Rhode-Island Private Ship of War, called the Defiance, Respondent. The Appellant's Case. 4 p. fol.

NN(2)

Ford Briefs p. 98-99

(b) Rhode Island. In the Matter of the Sloop Catharina. John Paas, Commander of the Sloop Catharina, on behalf of Jan Ambrosius Duan, the pretended Owner, Claimant and Appellant. John Sweet, Commander of the Brigatine, or Private Ship of War the Defiance, Captor and Respondent. The Respondent's Case. 7 p. fol.

NN(2)

Ford Briefs p. 99

(4) The William Galley, 1752

(a) Lords Commissioners of Prizes. The William Galley. Peter Cowenhoven and other Dutch Subjects, Appellants, James Allen and others, Respondents. The Appellants Case. To be Heard before the Right Honourable the Lords Commissioners for Hearing Prize-Appeals, at the Council Chamber of Whitehall. [Signed] Wm. Murray, Rob Jenner. 3 p. fol.

NN

Ford Briefs p. 99

(b) The William Galley. Peter Cowenhoven, Claimant and Appellant. James Allen, Commander of the Privateer the Revenge, and Peter Marshall, Commander of the Privateer the Success, Captors and Respondents. The Respondents Case. To be Heard before the Right Honourable the Lords Commissioners of Prize-Appeals, in the Council-Chamber at the Cockpit, Whitehall, on Thursday the 30th. day of November, 1752, at Six of the Clock in the Afternoon. [Signed] A. Hume-Campbell, Geo. Hay. 3 p. fol.

NN

Ford Briefs p. 99

(5) Stanton v. Thompson, 1759

(a) Rhode Island. Daniel Stanton, of Philadelphia in Pensilvania, Son and Heir of Daniel Stanton, late of Philadelphia aforesaid, deceased, Appellant. Elias Thompson, of Rhode Island, Son and Heir of Isaac Thompson, deceased, Respondent. The Appellant's Case. 3 p.

BLM (Add. Ms. 36,218, f. 1)

(b) Rhode Island. Daniel Stanton, originally, Plaintiff below, and now, Appellant. Elias Thompson, originally, Defendant below, and now, Respondent. The Respondent's Case. 7 p.

BLM (Add. Ms. 36,218, f. 3)

(6) Larkin v. York, 1761

(a) Rhode Island. John Larkin of Westerly, in King's County, Yeoman, Appellant. Edward York of North Kingstown, in King's County, Mariner, Respondent. The Appellant's Case. 3 p.

BLM (Add. Ms. 36,218, f. 103)

(b) Rhode Island. John Larkin, of Westerly, in the Colony of Rhode Island, Yeoman, Appellant. Edward York, of North Kings Town, in the said Colony, Yeoman, Respondent. Upon an appeal to the King in Council, from a Judgment of the Superior Court of Judicature of Rhode Island. The Respondent's Case. 3 p.

BLM (Add. Ms. 36,218, f. 103)

(7) Potter v. Hazard, 1763

(a) Rhode Island. John Potter, of South Kingston, in the Colony of Rhode Island, in America, Appellant. George Hazard, of Newport, in said Colony, Respondent. The Appellant's Case. 6 p.

BLM (Add. Ms. 36,218, f. 240)

(b) Rhode Island. John Potter, Appellant. George Hazard, Respondent. Appendix to the Appellant's Case. 3 p.

BLM (Add. Ms. 36,218, f. 242)

(c) Rhode Island. John Potter, of South Kingstown, in King's County, Yeoman, Appellant. George Hazard, of Newport, Merchant, Respondent. The Respondent's Case. 7 p.

BLM (Add. Ms. 36,218, f. 244)

(8) Freebody v. Brenton, 1764

(a) Rhode Island. John Freebody, Thomas Freebody, and Samuel Freebody, Sons and Executors of the late Appellant John Freebody now deceased, by Order of Revivor, Appellants. Jahleel Brenton, Benjamin Wickham, and George Gardner, Assignees of the Estates and Effects of Joseph Whipple, late of Middletown, in the County of Newport in the said Colony, Esquire, Respondents. The Appellants Case. 4 p.

BLM(2) (Add. Ms. 36,219, ff. 75, 77)

(b) Rhode Island. John Freebody, Appellant. Jahleel Brenton, Esq. Benjamin Wickham, Merchant, and George Gardner, Distiller, Assignees of the Estate and Effects of Joseph Whipple, an Insolvent Person, in Nature of a Bankrupt, Respondent. The Respondents Case. 5 p.

BLM(2) (Add. Ms. 36,219, ff. 79, 82)

(c) Rhode Island. Freebody v. Brenton, 1769. Second Appeal. In Two Appeals Between John Freebody, Thomas Freebody, and Samuel Freebody, Sons, Executors, and Devisees of John Freebody, deceased. Appellants. And Jahleel Brenton, Benjamin Wickham, and George Gardner, Assignees of the Estate and Effects of Joseph Whipple, late of Middletown in the County of Newport, in the said Colony, Esquire Respondents. The Appellants Case. 5 p.

BLM (Add. Ms. 36,219, f. 218)

(d) Rhode Island. Between John Freebody, Thomas Freebody, and Samuel Freebody, the Sons and Executors of John Freebody, late of Newport, in Rhode Island, their late Father, deceased, Appellant. Jahleel Brenton, Esquire, Benjamin Wickham, and George Gardner, Assignees of the Estate and Effects of Joseph Whipple, an insolvent Person, Respondents. And in a Cross-Appeal Between The said Jahleel Brenton, Benjamin Wickham, and George Gardner, Appellants. The said John Freebody, Thomas Freebody, and Samuel Freebody, Respondents. The Case of the said Jahleel Brenton, Benjamin Wickham, and George Gardner. 5 p.

BLM (Add. Ms. 36,219, f. 221)

(9) Shearman v. Cornell, 1766

(a) Rhode Island. Thomas Shearman of Portsmouth, in the Colony of Rhode-Island, Esquire, Appellant. Gideon Cornell of Newport, in the said Colony, Esquire, Respondent. The Appellant's Case. 4 p.

BLM (Add. Ms. 36,220, f. 115)

(10) Lewis v. Wilkinson, 1766

(a) Rhode Island. Robert Lewis and Ellis Lewis, of the City of Philadelphia, Merchants, Appellants. Benjamin Wilkinson, Respondent. The Appellants Case. 7 p.

BLM (Add. Ms. 36,220, f. 127)

(b) Rhode Island. Robert and Ellis Lewis of Philadelphia, in the Province of Pennsylvania, Merchants, Appellants. Benjamin Wilkinson, of Gloucester, in the Colony of Rhode Island, Respondent. The Respondents's Case.

BLM (Add. Ms. 36,220, f. 131)

(c) Robert and Ellis Lewis, Appellants. Benjamin Wilkinson Respondent. Brief State of the Dispute and Observations of the Cases on both sides. 1 p. Ms.

BLM (Add. Ms. 36,220, f. 134)

10.05 New York

(1) Victory, 1736

(a) Solomon de Medina Mosesson, Moses de Medina, and Abraham de Medina of London, Merchants; and Rodrigo Pacheco, of New York, Merchant. Appellants. Matthew Norris, Esq; late Commander of his Majesty's Ship the Lowestoff; and Edward Greenly, Esq; his Majesty's Proctor Respondents. The Appellant's Case. 4 p. fol.

NN

Ford Briefs p. 86

(b) New York. Solomon Medina Mosesson, Moses and Abraham Medina, and Rodrigo Pacheco, Appellants. Matthew Norris, Esq; Respondent. The Respondents Case. 4 p. fol.

NN

Ford Briefs p. 86

(c) Solomon Medina, and others . . . Appellants. Capt. Matthew Norris . . . Respondent. The Appellants Case. 4 p. fol.

NN

Ford Briefs p. 86

(2) Morris's Case, 1735

(a) See above 1.05(8)(m).

10.07 Pennsylvania

(1) Penn v. Baltimore, 1737

(a) See above 9.00(2) and particularly (e) and (f)

(2) McMurterie (or McMurtrie) v. Brown (or Browne), 1765

(a) Pensilvania. Between David McMurterie and William McMurterie, of Philadelphia County in Pensilvania, Merchants, Insurers of the Brigantine called the Providence, John Randall, Master, Appellants. And John Browne, the surviving Owner of the said Brigantine called the Providence, Respondent. The Appellants Case. 4 p.

BLM (Add. Ms. 36,219, f. 227)

(b) Pensilvania. Between David McMurterie & William McMurterie, of Philadelphia County in Pensilvania, Merchants, Insurers of the Brigantine called the Providence, John Randall, Master, Appellants. And John Browne, the surviving Owner of the said Brigantine called the Providence Respondent. Appendix to the Appellants printed Case. 8 p.

BLM (Add. Ms. 36,219, f. 229).

(c) Pensylvania. David M'Murtrie and William M'Murtrie of Philadelphia County, Merchants, Appellants. John Brown of Providence, in the Colony of Rhode Island, Respondent. The Respondent's Case. 3 p.

BLM (Add. Ms. 36,219, f. 234).

(3) Pennsylvania Land Co. v. Stover, 1766

(a) Pennsylvania. John Fothergill, M.D. Daniel Zachary, Thomas How, Devereaux Bowley, Luke Hind, Jacob Hagen, Silvanus Grove, and William Heron, the surviving Trustees nominated and appointed by an Act of Parliament, passed in the Thirty-third Year of the Reign of his late Majesty King George the Second, intituled, "An Act for Vesting Certain Estates in Pennsylvania, New-Jersey, and Maryland, belonging to the Proprietors of a Partnership, commonly called The Pennsylvania Land Company in London, in Trustees, to be sold, and for other Purposes therein mentioned," Appellants. Christian Stover, Respondent. The Appellant's Case. 3 p.

BLM (Add. Ms. 36,220, f. 73)

(b) Pennsylvania. John Fothergill, M.D. and others, the surviving Trustees for the Pennsylvania Land Company in London, Appellants. Christian Stover, Respondent. Appendix to the Appellants Case. 3 p.

BLM (Add. Ms. 36,220, f. 75)

(c) Pennsylvania. Between Timothy Peaceable (upon the Demise of John Fothergill, Daniel Zachery, Thomas Howe, Devereux Bowley, Luke Hind, Richard Howe, Jacob Hagan, Silvanus Grove, and William Heron) And Christian Stover, Respondent. The Respondent's Case. 5 p.

BLM (Add. Ms. 36,220, f. 77)

(4) Long v. Harper, 1766

(a) Pennsylvania. Between John Long and William Plumstead of Philadelphia, in the Province of Pennsylvania, Merchants, Appellants. And Thomas Harper, John Nixon, and Company, Owners of the Ship called, the Molly of Philadelphia aforesaid, Respondents. The Appellants Case. 7 p.

BLM (Add. Ms. 36,220, f. 105)

(b) Pensylvania. Between John Long and William Plumstead of Philadelphia, in the Province of Pensylvania, Merchants, Appellants. And Thomas Harper, John Nixon, and Company, Owners of the Ship called, the Molly of Philadelphia aforesaid, Respondents. Appendix to The Appellants printed Case. 4 p.

BLM (Add. Ms. 36,220, f. 107)

(c) Pensilvania. Between John Long and William Plumstead, of the City of Philadelphia, Merchants, Appellants. And Thomas Harper and John Nixon, & Co., Respondents. The Respondents Case. 4 p.

BLM (Add. Ms. 36,220, f. 109)

(d) Between John Long and William Plumstead, of the City of Philadelphia, Merchants, Appellants. And Thomas Harper and John Nixon, & Co., Respondents. Appendix to the Respondents printed Case. 7 p.

BLM (Add. Ms. 36,220, f. 111)

10.10 Virginia

(1) Burges v. Hack, 1737

(a) Virginia SS. Pleas at the Capitol in Williamsburgh, before the Honorable William Gooch Esq; Lieutenant-Governour, and Commander in Chief of the Colony and Dominion of Virginia, and the rest of the Judges of the General Court of our Lord the King in the said Colony and Dominion, the 15th Day of April, in the Eighth Year of the Reign of our Sovereign Lord George the Second, by the Grace of God of Great Britain, France, and Ireland King, Defender of the Faith, &c. 4 p. fol.

NN

Clayton-Torrence 139

(b) Lemuel Gulliver, on the Demise of Frances Burgess, Plaintiff and Appellant, versus John Hack, Respondent. The Appellant's Case.

BLM (Add. Ms. 36,216, ff. 103-105)
VCRP 125

(2) Fairfax v. Virginia, 1739

(a) Virginia. The Right Honourable Thomas Lord Fairfax, Petitioner. Against the Governor and Council of Virginia, in Right of the Crown, Defendants. The Case of the Petitioner the Lord Fairfax.

DLC, ViU (film)

Sabin 99,894 Clayton-Torrence 155

(b) The Right Honourable Thomas Lord Fairfax, Petitioner, the governor and Council of Virginia, in Right of the Crown, Defendants. The Case on behalf of the Crown. [London 1745]

PHi

(c) See 1.10(1) above for later proceedings and commentary.

(3) Dunbar v. Custis, 1757

(a) Virginia. Charles Dunbar, of the Islands of Antigua, Esquire, only surviving acting Executor of Thomas Dunbar Parke, late of the said Island, Esq; deceased, Appellant. Daniel Parke Custis, Esquire, Son and Heir, and also sole Executor of the last Will and Testament of John Custis, Esquire, of Virginia, Esq; deceased. The Appellant's Case. 7 p.

BLM (Add. Ms. 36,217, ff. 161-64)
NN

Clayton-Torrence 250 VCRP 121-a

(b) Virginia. Charles Dunbar, Esquire, One of the Executors of Thomas Dunbar Parke, Esquire, deceased, Appellant. Daniel Parke Custis, of Virginia, Esquire, Respondent. The Case of the Respondent. 7 p. and Ms. pages

BLM (Add. Ms. 36,217, ff. 165-71)
VCRP 121-a

(4) Lidderdale and Harmer v. Chiswell, 1758

(a) Virginia. Between John Lidderdale and John Harmer, of the City of Bristol, Merchants, and surviving Partners of Thomas Chamberlayne, of the same City, Merchant, deceased, Appellants, and John Chiswell, of the Colony of Virginia, Planter, Respondent. The Appellants Case. 3 p.

BLM (Add. Ms. 36,217, ff. 199-201)
VCRP 121-b

(b) Virginia. John Lidderdale and John Harmer, of Bristol, Merchants, and surviving Partners of Thomas Chamberlayne, of the same City, Merchant, deceased, Plaintiff below, And now Appellants. John Chiswell, of Virginia, Esquire, Defendant below, and now Respondent. The Respondent's Case, On the Appellants Appeal, from a Judgment at Law, founded on a General Verdict. 3 p. and Ms. p.

BLM (Add. Ms. 36,217, ff. 201-05)
VCRP 121-b

(5) Burwell v. Johnson, 1762

(a) Virginia. Lewis Burwell, Esq; and Frances, now his Wife, but who was formerly the Wife, and afterwards the Widow, one of the Executors, and the sole Residuary Devisee, of James Bray the Grandson, were the Plaintiffs below, and are now the Appellants. Philip Johnson, and Elizabeth his Wife, Heiress of the Body of Thomas Bray her late Father deceased, were the Defendants below, and are now the Respondents. The Appellant's Case. 8 p.

BLM (Add. Ms. 36,218, ff. 138-41)
VCRP 122-a

(b) Virginia. Lewis Burwell, Gentleman, in Right of Frances his late Wife, deceased, who was the Widow and One of the Executors and Residuary Devisee of the Will of James Bray, her former Husband, deceased, Appellant. Philip Johnson, and Elizabeth his Wife, Daughter and only Child and Heir of the Body of Thomas Bray, her late Father, deceased, Respondents. The Respondents Case. 3 p.

BLM (Add. Ms. 36,218, ff. 142-43)
VCRP 122-a

(6) Rickards v. Hudson, 1762

(a) Virginia. Samuel Rickards, Archibald MacLane, Israel Mauduit , Edmund Lardner, and William Cook, Assignees of the Estate and Effects of George Buchanan and William Hamilton, late of London, Merchants and Bankrupts, Executors of the last Will and Testament of Neil Buchanan, late of London Merchant, deceased; Francis Jerdone and Robert Duncanson, of the Colony of Virginia, Merchants and Factors, as well for the said Neil Buchanan in his Life, as for his said Executors after his Decease, and for the said Assignees since the said Bankruptcy; and Anne Buchanan Widow, and another of the Executors of the said Neil Buchanan deceased, Appellants.

John Hudson and Anne his Wife, William Johnson, and Martha his wife, Roger Gregory, Executor of Lane Jones, Orlando Jones, Rolling Jones, and Francis Barber Jones, all of Virginia foresaid which said Anne Hudson, Martha Johnson, Lane Jones deceased, Orlando, Rolling and Francis-Barber Jones, were the Children of Lane Jones deceased. The appellants Case. 6 p.

BLM(2) (Add Ms. 36,218, ff. 199-204)
VCRP 122-b

(b) At the Committee of the Lords of the Privy Council. Samuel Rickards, Archibald Maclane, Israel Mauduit, Edmund Lardner, and William Cooke, of London, Merchants, Assignees of George Buchanan and William Hamilton, late of London, Merchants and Bankrupts, Executors of Neil Buchanan, late of London, Esq; Francis Jerdone and Robert Dundanson, of Virginia, Merchants, and Anne Buchanan, of Glasgow, in North Britain, Widow Appellants, John Hudson and Ann his Wife, William Johnson and Martha his Wife, Roger Gregory, Executors of Lane Jones, Orlando Jones, Rolling Jones, and Francis Barber Jones, all of Virginia aforesaid, which said Ann Hudson, Martha Jones, Lane Jones, deceased, Orlando Rolling and Francis Barber Jones, were the children of Lane Jones, Deceased Respondents. The Case of the Respondents. 4 p.

BLM (Add. Ms. 36,218, ff. 205-06)
VCRP 122-b

(7) Camm v. William and Mary College, 1763

(a) Between John Camm, Clerk, Appellant. And The Rector, Visitors, and Governors of William and Mary College in Virginia, Respondents. The Case of the Appellant. 3 p.

BLM (Add. Ms. 36,218, ff. 223-24)
VCRP 122-c

(b) Virginia. John Camm, Clerk, late Professor of Divinity in the College of William and Mary, in the Colony of Virginia, Appellant. The Visitors and Governors of the said College of William and Mary, Respondents. The Respondents Case. 4 p.

BLM (Add. Ms. 36,218, ff. 225-26)
VCRP 122-c

(8) Graham v. William and Mary College, 1763

(a) Virginia. Between Richard Graham, Clerk, Appellant, and the Rector, Visitors, and Governors of the College of William and Mary in Virginia, Respondents. The Case of the Appellant. 3 p.

BLM (Add. Ms. 36,218, ff. 227-28)
VCRP 122-d

(b) Virginia. Richard Graham, Clerk, late Professor of Divinity and Natural Philosophy, in the College of William and Mary, the Colony of Virginia, Appellant. The Visitors and Governors of the said College of William and Mary, Respondents. The Respondents Case. 4 p.

BLM (Add. Ms. 36,218, ff. 229-30)
VCRP 122-c

(9) Tabb v. Edmundson, 1763

(a) Virginia. William Tabb and Humphry Toy Tabb and Martha Tabb, of the Province of Virginia, Infants, by the said William Tabb, their next Friend, Appellants. Thomas Edmundson and John Edmundson, of the said Province of Virginia, Respondents. Et e Contra The Respondents having presented a Petition of Appeal also, although it does not appear that they ever offered to appeal below. The Appellants Case. 3 p.

BLM (Add. Ms. 36,218, ff. 248-49)
VCRP 122-e

(b) Virginia. Lords of the Committee for hearing Appeals from the Plantations. John Edmundson and Thomas Edmundson, of the County of Essex, in the Colony of Virginia, Merchants, Appellants. William Tabb, Humphrey Toy Tabb, and Martha Tabb, of Virginia aforesaid, Respondents, And the aforesaid William Tabb, Humphrey Toy Tabb, and Martha Tabb, Appellants. The said John and Thomas Edmundson, Repondents. The Case of the Appellants, John and Thomas Edmundson. 3 p.

BLM (Add. Ms. 36,218, ff. 250-51)
VCRP 122-e

(10) Cleeve and Hinde v. Mills, 1764

(a) Virginia. Richard Cleeve and John Hinde, the Two surviving Assignees of the Estate and Effects of Pearson Pettit, late of London, Merchant, a Bankrupt, Appellants. And James Mills Merchant, William Bird Esquire, John Robinson Esquire, Richard Bland Gentleman, William Jordan Merchant, Presley Thornton Gentleman, and James Power Gentleman, Respondents. The Appelants Case. 7 p.

BLM (Add. Ms. 36,219, ff. 85-88)
VCRP 123-a

(b) Virginia. Richard Cleeve and John Hinde, Surviving Assignees of Pearson Pettit, a Bankrupt, Appellants. James Mills, Merchant, William Byrd, and John Robinson, Esqrs. Richard Bland, Gent. William Jordan, Merchant, Presley Thornton and James Power, Gent. The Respondents Case. 9 p.

BLM (Add. Ms. 36,219, ff. 89-93)
VCRP 123-a

(11) Parsons v. Parsons, 1765

(a) Virginia. John Parsons, Appellant. William Parsons, Respondent. The Appellant's Case. The Single Question upon this Appeal is, Whether William Ap Thomas devised his Lands in Virginia in Fee or in Tail? If the latter, the Appellant has a clear Title. 3 p.

BLM (Add. Ms. 36,219, ff. 269-70)

(b) Virginia. John Parsons, by John Doe his Lessee, Appellant. Thomas Parsons, a Minor, Son and Heir of William Parsons, Respondent. In Ejectment to try the Title to an Estate in Virginia, and a Special Verdict found therein. The Respondent's Case. 3 p.

BLM (Add. Ms. 36,219, ff. 271-72)
VCRP 123-b

(12) Howlett v. Osburn, 1765

(a) Virginia. Thomas Howlett, Appellant. Thomas Osburn, Respondent. The Appellant's Case. 7 p.

BLM (Add. Ms. 36,219, ff. 273-76)
VCRP 123-c

(b) Virginia. Thomas Howlett, Appellant. Thomas Osburn, Respondent. The Respondent's Case. 3 p.

BLM (Add. Ms. 36,219, ff. 277-78)
VCRP 123-c

(13) Camm v. Hansford and Moss, 1766

(a) Virginia. Between John Cam, Clerk, Appellant, and Charles Hansford, jun. and William Moss, Respondents. The Appellant's Case. 5 p.

VCRP 124-a

(b) Virginia. Between John Camm Clerk, Plaintiff and Appellant, against Charles Hansford, Junior, and William Moss, late Collectors of York Hampton Parish Levy, Defendants and Respondents. The Respondents Case. 7 p. and Ms. pages

BLM (Add. Ms. 36,220, ff. 55-64)
VCRP 124-a

(14) Corbin v. Lomax, 1766

(a) Virginia. Gawin Corbin, an Infant, by his Guardian, Appellant. Lunsford Lomax, Gentleman, by Aminadab Seekright his Lessee, Respondent. In Two Ejectments, and a Case, in Nature of a Special Verdict, made for the Opinion of the Court, which being alike in both Causes, without any material

Variation, the Judgment in One will determine both. The Appellant's Case. 5 p.

BLM (Add. Ms. 36,220, ff. 117-19)
VCRP 124-b

(b) Virginia. Between Gawin Corbin, an Infant, by his Guardian, Appellant. Lunsford Lomax, Respondent. The Respondent's Case. 3 p.

BLM (Add. Ms. 36,220, ff. 120-21)
VCRP 124-b

11.00

Rules of Court

11.05 New York

(1) Supreme Court of Judicature, 1797

(a) Rules respecting the Admission of Attornies and Counsellors in the Supreme Court of Judicature of the State of New-York. At a Supreme Court of Judicature held for the State of New York at the City-Hall of the City of New-York, the 28th day of October, 1797, Ordered, 1st . . . . Jas. Fairlie, Clk. [New York 1797] Broadside 33.5 x 20 cm.

MH*

mp. 48,196 Bristol B10,029

(2) Supreme Court and Circuit Courts, 1799

(a) Rules of the Supreme Court of the State of New-York. To Which Are Added, The Circuit Courts, and Copies of Bills of Costs, To Serve As Precedents. Albany: Printed By Charles R. & George Webster, At their Bookstore in the White-House, corner of State and Pearl-streets. -- 1799. 38 p. 16mo.

MH*

Evans 35,931

11.06 New Jersey

(1) Courts of Law and Equity, 1799.

(a) The Practice of the Courts of Law and Equity, In the State of New-Jersey. As comprised in The Act relative to the Supreme and Circuit Courts; the Act to regulate the Pracitce of the Courts of Law; the Act respecting the Court of Chancery, and the Act to regulate Fees. Printed and published for the convenience of the Judges, gentlemen of the Bar, Clerks of Courts, Sheriffs, &c. By G. Craft, Trenton. [1799]
47 p. 22 cm.

NjR

Bristol 10,878

11.07 Pennsylvania

(1) Supreme Court, 1788

(a) Rules and Order for Regulating the Practice of the Supreme Court of the State of Pennsylvania, and Expediting the Determination of Suits within the same. Made and established By the Chief Justice And His Associates the Justices Of The Said Court, of January term, in the twelfth year of the sovereignty and independence of the said State, and in the year of our Lord One Thousand Seven Hundred and Eighty-Eight, In pursuance of an Act of Assembly, intitled, "An Act for the more speedy and effectual Administration of Justice," Passed the Twenty-fifth Day of September, MDCCLXXXI. Philadelphia: Printed by Zachariah Poulson, Junr. in Fourth-Street, between Market and Arch-Streets. M DCC LXXXVIII.
29 p. 17.5 cm.

MWA*, PPAmP

Evans 20,633 (erroneously dated 1787)
mp. 45,334 Bristol B6,776

(2) County Courts of Common Pleas, 1792

(a) Rules and Orders, for Regulating the Practice of the County Courts of Common Pleas, in the State of Pennsylvania. Lancaster, Printed by J. Bailey and W. Dickson in Kingstreet, M,DCC,XCII. 11 p. 17 cm.

MWA*

mp. 46,539 Bristol B8,101

11.12 South Carolina

(1) Courts of Sessions and Common Pleas, and Court of Equity, 1796

(a) The Rules And Orders of the Courts Of Sessions and Common Pleas, of the Court Of Equity and the Federal Court, in South-Carolina. New York: Printed by T. and J. Swords, No. 99 Pearl-street. -- 1796. -- 48 p. 8vo.

MBAt, NHi*, NN

Evans 31,220 Sabin 87,466 Morgan 1,049 and 1,087 Turnbull p. 330

(2) Superior Courts, 1798

(a) Rules of the Superior Courts of the State of South Carolina

Morgan 1,123 (citing South Carolina State Gazette, January 8, 1798)

(3) Courts of Sessions and Common Pleas, and Court of Equity, 1800

(a) Rules and Orders of the Courts of Sessions and Common Pleas, as made July 1, 1800. Also the Rules and Orders of the Court of Equity, up to May Term, 1800. Charleston: W.P. Young. 1800

No copy located ("this day published" City Gazette July 8, 1800

Evans 38,535 Morgan 1,213

11.20 Federal

(1) Federal Court in South Carolina, 1796

(a) Rules and Orders, above 11.12(1)(a).

ADDENDUM

The bibliography prepared by Donald S. Sinclair, "Murders in Print," published in Murder Did Pay in 1982 by the New Jersey Historical Society lists one imprint not included in this bibliography.

5.06(2a) William Smart, 1772

(a) The dying words and confession of William Smart, who was tried for and found guilty of burglary. He was executed at Burlington, pursuant to his sentence, on Saturday the 4th of July, 1772. Containing the history of his life, and a particular account of the murder of Elizabeth Knight. To which is added the judgment hymn. [Philadelphia?] Printed in the year 1772. 8 p. 19 cm.

NjHi

The American Antiquarian Society reports in 93 Proceedings, Part 1 25 (1983) that it has acquired the following unrecorded broadsides:

5.03(5) Thomas Hickey

(a.2) Concord, Mass: Nathaniel Coverly. 1776

MWA Broadside

8.20(9) Captain James

(a.6) n.p. 1799

MWA

The Society also reports at page 197 that it has acquired two printed legal blanks, both completed in manuscript, probably printed in Boston in 1694 and 1696 by Bartholomew Green and John Allen.

Index of Parallel Entries

Entry or page numbers in Bibliographical Sources cross-referenced to Entry Numbers in this Bibliography

Table	Bibliographical Sources
I	Evans, Bristol, Short-Title Evans, and Shaw-Shoemaker
II	Sabin
III	Parrish, Shoemaker, and Wing
IV	State and Privy Council Bibliographies
V	Subject Bibliographies: Murder, Negroes, Old Frontier, Patriotic Printers, Plays, and Poetry and Verse
VI	Collections

TABLE I: EVANS, BRISTOL, SHORT-TITLE EVANS, AND SHAW-SHOEMAKER

Evans and Bristol numbers are listed in the first column. The Evans number is the same as the mp. number used in Short-Title Evans and and on the microcards. For Bristol numbers a second column is added to list the mp. numbers. Although the mp. numbers are a continuation of the Evans numbers, the easiest way to find an mp. number is to use the Bristol number and refer to Bristol's Supplement.

The Entry or Classification Number used in this Bibliography is given in the second column for Evans numbers and the third column for Bristol numbers.

Evans	Bibliography
51	3.02(2)(a)
61 Ghost	3.02(2)
186	6.02(1)(a)
210	6.02(2)(a)
313	8.02(1)(a)
394	6.02(2)(a.2)
413	5.02(1)(b)
417	5.02(1)(a.2)
432	5.02(1)(c)
539	6.02(4)(a)
588	1.06(1)(a)
613	1.02(1)(a)
642	1.07(1)(a)
643	1.02(1)(b)
655	6.02(6)(a)
657	1.02(1)(c)
730	1.02(2)(a)
801	1.02(2)(b)
822	1.06(2)(a)
823	1.05(1)(c)
824	1.05(1)(d)
856	6.02(7)(a)
865	1.06(2)(b)
877	6.09(2)(a)
879	6.02(8)(a)
902	6.02(10)(a)
911	3.02(2)(j)
1,020	5.02(2)(a)
1,038	1.05(2)(b)
1,079	1.05(2)(a)
1,102	1.05(2)(c)
1,137	1.05(2)(d)
1,138	1.05(2)(d)
1,175	1.02(3)(a)
1,300	1.05(3)(a)
1,431	1.06(3)(a)
1,452	6.02(13)(a)
1,601	5.02(3)(b)
1,619	5.02(3)(a)
1,626	5.02(3)(a)
1,728	5.03(1)(c)
1,729	5.03(1)(a)
1,764	6.02(15)(a)
1,901	1.02(4)(a)
1,910	6.02(16)(a)
2,003	1.02(4)(b)
2,150	1.02(5)(a)
2,151	1.02(5)(b)
2,251	6.02(17)(a)
2,252 Ghost	6.02(17)(a)
2,409	1.03(1)(a)
2,441	4.07(1)(a)
2,451	1.03(1)(b)
2,482	1.09(1)(a)
2,502	1.07(2)(a)
2,551	6.02(18)(a)
2,606	1.04(1)(a)
2,726	1.04(1)(b)
2,735	3.07(1)(a)
2,737	1.02(7)(c)
2,753	3.07(1)(b)
2,754	3.07(1)(b.2)
2,759	3.07(1)(c)
2,779	1.02(7)(b)
2,782	5.02(4)(a)
2,808	3.07(1)(d)
2,818	1.02(6)(a)
2,819	1.02(7)(a)
2,890	4.07(2)(b)
2,933	4.05(1)(a)
2,937	4.07(2)(a)
2,938	4.07(2)(c)
2,940	1.05(5)(a)
3,019	1.05(6)(a)
3,370	4.10(1)(a)
3,639	5.02(7)(a)
3,641	6.02(20)(a)
3,642	6.02(20)(a)

Evans		Bibliography
3,643		6.02(20)(a)
3,655		5.02(7)(b)
3,696		4.05(2)(a)
3,700		1.05(8)(f)
3,701		1.05(8)(f.2)
3,702		1.05(8)(f.3)
3,710		9.00(2)(b)
3,711		4.07(3)(a)
3,727		1.05(8)(a)
		1.05(8)(b)
3,799		1.05(8)(k)
3,811		4.05(3)(a)
3,812		4.05(4)(a)
3,816		1.05(8)(g)
3,817		1.05(8)(h)
3,834		1.05(8)(j)
3,835		4.05(2)(b)
3,845		1.05(8)(c)
3,846		1.05(8)(d)
3,847		1.05(8)(i)
3,848		1.05(8)(l)
		1.05(7)(a.2)
3,851		5.02(8)(b)
3,864		1.05(9)(a)
3,890		5.02(10)(a)
3,893		1.02(8)(a)
4,030		1.05(8)(p)
4,046		4.06(1)(a)
4,052		1.05(8)(q)
4,061		4.07(4)(a)
4,090		1.05(8)(o)
4,091		1.05(8)(n)
4,092	Ghost	1.05(8)
4,093		1.05(8)(e)
4,107		1.05(9)(b)
4,118		1.05(9)(c)
4,119	Ghost	1.05(9)
4,120	Ghost	1.05(9)
4,144		5.02(11)(a)
4,182		9.00(2)(d)
4,185		1.05(9)(c.2)
4,215		6.04(1)(a)
4,230		5.02(11)(b)
4,245		5.02(10)(b)
4,258		5.02(12)(a)
4,326		5.02(12)(c)
4,330		1.05(9)(b.2)
4,379		1.03(2)(c)
4,478		6.01(1)(a)
4,582		7.11(1)(a)
4,599		6.01(1)(b)
4,681	Ghost	8.02(3)
4,708		4.08(1)(a)
4,709	Ghost	4.08(1)

Evans		Bibliography
4,809		8.02(3)(a)
4,812		4.12(1)(a)
4,930		4.08(2)(a)
5,413		1.05(10)(c)
5,507		5.05(1)(a)
5,518		8.02(4)(a)
5,571		5.02(14)(a)
5,792		1.06(5)(a)
5,901		1.06(5)(c)
6,021		1.06(5)(b)
6,022		1.06(5)(b)
6,023		1.06(5)(b)
6,024		1.06(5)(b)
6,624		5.07(1)(a)
6,635		1.02(9)(a)
6,647		6.02(25)(a)
6,808		1.06(5)(d)
6,832		1.04(2)(a)
6,864		1.06(5)(e)
6,886		8.07((1)(a)
7,001		1.02(10)(a)
7,063		8.07(1)(b)
7,168		5.02(16)(a)
7,333		5.02(15)(a)
7,404		5.07(2)(a)
7,414		1.07(4)(a)
7,415		5.02(17)(b)
7,418		1.02(11)(a)
7,455		1.05(3)(a.3)
7,481		1.02(11)(b)
7,494		5.07(3)(a)
7,508		1.06(5)(f)
7,664		1.02(11)(c)
7,796		5.05(2)(a)
7,824		1.05(9)(b.4)
7,837		1.02(12)(b)
7,865		8.20(1)(a)
7,890		8.20(1)(c)
7,891		8.20(1)(b)
7,892		8.20(1)(a)
7,927		8.20(1)(d)
8,356		6.05(1)(a)
8,550		1.06(6)(a)
8,638		5.07(4)(a)
8,829		8.02(5)(a)
9,116		5.03(2)(a)
9,120		5.07(4)(b)
		6.12(1)(a)
9,144		5.02(19)(c)
9,157		5.07(4)(b)
9,197		5.06(1)(a)
9,355	Ghost	6.02(27)
9,494		1.03(4)(a)
9,542		8.20(2)(a)

Evans	Bibliography
9,543	8.20(2)(a.2)
9,544 Ghost	8.20(2)
9,616	6.02(27)(a)
9,660	1.05(11)(a)
9,705	3.02(1)(c)
9,889	1.05(12)(a)
9,920	1.04(3)(a)
9,970	3.06(1)(c)
	3.06(1)(d)
9,973	1.06(7)(a)
9,996	5.07(5)(a)
10,036	5.06(2)(a)
10,190 Ghost	1.05(11)(c)
10,435	1.06(8)(a)
10,437	1.05(13)(a)
10,438	1.05(13)(b)
10,582	1.05(11)(b)
	1.05(11)(b.2)
10,614	1.02(13)(d)
10,622 Ghost	1.02(13)
10,623	1.02(13)(a)
10,624	1.02(13)(e)
10,625 Ghost	1.02(13)
10,626	1.02(13)(c)
10,627	1.02(13)(b)
10,654	1.06(10)(a)
10,658	3.02(1)(d)
10,720	1.06(9)(a)
10,808	5.04(1)(a)
	5.04(1)(b)
10,822	5.02(22)(a)
10,919	8.02(6)(a)
10,926	5.04(1)(c)
10,945	1.12(1)(a)
10,952	5.02(22)(b)
10,958	8.05(1)(a)
11,045	6.04(3)(a)
11,053	1.07(5)(a)
11,129	1.03(1)(c)
11,149	5.05(3)(a)
11,150	5.05(3)(b)
11,151	5.05(3)(c)
11,152	5.05(3)(d)
11,303	5.05(4)(a)
11,307	1.12(1)(b.2)
11,308	1.12(1)(c)
11,463	5.05(5)(a)
11,543	1.02(15)(e.2)
11,573	1.05(9)(c.4)
11,580	1.02(15)(i.2)
11,581	1.02(15)(i.3)
11,582 Ghost	1.02(15)(i)
11,583	1.02(15)(j)
11,597	1.02(16)(a)
11,602	5.05(6)(a)
11,614	1.02(14)(a)
11,683	1.02(15)(n)
11,689	1.11(1)(a)
11,707	5.02(25)(b)
11,737	1.02(15)(l)
11,765	1.06(10)(b)
11,839	5.07(6)(a)
11,898	8.07(2)(a)
11,952	1.05(9)(b.5)
11,973	5.02(26)(b)
11,974	5.02(26)(b.2)
11,975	5.02(26)(b.3)
12,081	1.11(1)(c)
12,094	1.02(15)(m.2)
12,099	1.02(15)(p)
12,159	1.06(11)(a)
12,200	5.02(26)(a)
12,301	1.02(15)(s)
12,302	1.02(17)(b)
12,375	5.02(27)(c)
12,493	5.04(3)(b)
12,494	5.04(3)(b.2)
12,495	5.04(3)(b.3)
12,496	5.04(3)(b.4)
12,559	5.02(27)(a)
12,600	1.02(15)(r)
12,601	1.02(15)(r.2)
12,634	5.04(3)(c)
12,641	5.02(32)(e.2)
12,642	5.02(32)(e)
12,721	1.02(15)(t)
12,722	1.02(15)(t)
12,723	1.02(15)(t.2)
12,724	1.02(15)(t.3)
12,725	5.02(28)(b)
12,759	5.02(32)(l)
12,862	5.02(32)(m)
12,863	5.02(32)(m.2)
12,882	1.06(13)(a)
12,907	5.04(3)(b.5)
12,908	5.04(3)(b.8)
12,909	5.04(3)(b.9)
12,910	5.04(3)(b.10)
12,911	5.04(3)(d.2)
12,914	5.05(10)(a)
12,915	5.05(10)(b)
12,936	5.05(9)(a)
13,019	5.05(7)(a)
13,020	5.05(7)(a.2)
13,021	5.05(7)(a.3)
13,030	5.02(32)(k)
13,031	5.02(32)(k.2)
13,047	8.02(7)(a)

Evans		Bibliography
13,269		5.07(7)(a)
13,314		1.02(15)(u)
13,315		1.02(15)(u.3)
13,316		1.02(15)(u.4)
13,317		1.02(15)(u.2)
13,318		8.02(8)(a)
13,369		5.07(8)(a)
13,426		1.02(18)(a)
13,436		5.07(7)(b)
13,508		5.04(3)(b.11)
13,774		5.03(4)(a)
13,791		5.02(6)(b)
13,840		1.02(15)(w)
13,867		4.08(1)(a.2)
13,868		1.09(3)(a)
14,097		1.02(15)(u.6)
14,352		1.02(15)(x)
14,608		1.02(15)(v)
14,609		1.02(15)(v.2)
14,610		1.02(15)(v.3)
14,655		1.04(4)(a)
14,741		4.12(2)(a)
		4.12(2)(a.2)
14,898	Serial	4.12(2)(a.2)
15,095		5.05(11)(a)
15,101		1.02(15)(z)
15,219		2.04(5)(a.3)
15,363		1.02(15)(aa)
15,376		4.05(5)(a)
15,383		1.13(1)(a)
15,384		1.13(1)(b)
15,385		1.13(1)(d)
15,605		1.13(1)(c)
15,607		5.04(5)(b)
15,725		1.02(15)(bb)
15,752		2.01(1)(a)
15,793		5.02(34)(i)
15,866		1.02(15)(cc)
15,872		5.02(34)(g)
15,873		5.02(34)(g.2)
15,876		4.07(5)(a)
16,139		2.01(1)(c)
16,140		2.01(2)(a)
16,141		2.01(3)(a)
16,142		2.01(4)(a)
16,220		2.02(1)(a)
16,334		2.01(5)(a)
16,439		2.01(6)(a)
16,448		2.01(6)(b)
16,550		1.02(15)(dd)
16,626	Ghost	2.01(1)(c)
16,688		5.02(35)(a.2)
16,697		2.01(7)(g)
16,701		2.01(6)(d)
16,731		2.01(7)(d)
16,752		5.04(7)(c)
16,756		5.04(7)(a)
16,836		1.02(15)(ee)
16,985		2.01(6)(d.2)
17,043		2.01(7)(a)
17,044		2.01(7)(a.2)
17,045		2.01(7)(a.3)
17,046		2.01(7)(b)
17,047		2.01(6)(c)
17,048		2.01(8)(a)
17,132		1.02(15)(ff)
17,368		2.01(6)(f.3)
17,606		1.02(15)(gg)
17,719		2.01(7)(f.4)
17,772		2.01(9)(a)
17,828		5.04(8)(c)
17,903		5.04(8)(e)
17,994		5.02(36)(a)
18,009		5.04(8)(d)
18,302		1.02(15)(hh)
18,320		1.05(14)(b)
18,324		5.02(39)(a)
		5.02(40)(d)
18,470	Ghost	6.02(37)
18,549		2.01(10)(a)
18,559		5.02(39)(b)
		5.02(40)(d)
18,560	Serial	1.05(14)(b.2)
18,640		1.06(14)(a)
18,741		8.07(3)(a)
18,773		1.05(14)(a)
18,886		5.02(40)(a)
18,955		1.02(15)(ii)
18,976		1.06(14)(b)
18,997		1.02(15)(ii)
19,037		5.02(40)(c)
19,056		2.01(10)(b)
19,126		1.06(14)(a.2)
19,164		1.07(6)(a)
19,246		1.05(15)(a)
19,407		6.02(37)(a)
19,431		5.04(8)(b)
19,448		5.02(35)(a)
19,547		6.04(7)(a)
19,635		5.07(9)(a.2)
19,636		5.07(9)(a)
19,637	Ghost	5.07(9)
19,638	Ghost	5.07(9)
19,639	Ghost	5.07(9)
19,693		5.02(42)(a)
19,794		1.02(12)(c)
20,193	Serial	4.12(4)(a)
20,194	Serial	1.07(9)(a)

Evans		Bibliography
24,324		2.04(2)(b)
24,353		2.03(1)(a)
24,407		1.07(29)(b)
24,530		1.02(22)(a)
24,540		6.02(41)(a)
24,782		2.01(7)(f.6)
24,836		5.05(13)(a.5)
24,837	Ghost	5.05(13)
24,838		5.05(13)(a.6)
25,101	Serial	1.07(11)(a.2)
		1.07(12)(a.2)
25,137		5.02(49)(d)
25,296		1.14(1)(a)
25,317		8.20(5)(f)
25,370		2.04(2)(f)
25,371		2.04(2)(f.2)
25,423	Serial	2.04(2)(c)
25,451		8.11(2)(a)
25,456		8.20(4)(a)
25,457	Ghost	8.20(4)
25,458	Ghost	8.20(4)
25,497		8.20(3)(a)
25,499		8.20(5)(b)
25,500	Ghost	8.20(5)
25,521		5.02(49)(a)
25,522	Ghost	5.02(49)
25,532	Serial	2.04(2)(e)
25,603		1.02(23)(a)
25,657		4.20(8)(a)
25,702		8.11(2)(a)
25,906		5.05(15)(a)
26,013		5.02(49)(b)
26,053		2.03(3)(a)
26,118		5.05(15)(b)
26,237		5.05(13)(a.7)
26,238		5.05(13)(b)
26,271		8.20(5)(d.2)
26,272		8.20(5)(d.3)
26,273		8.20(5)(d.4)
26,274	Ghost	8.20(5)
26,280		8.20(4)(b)
26,281		8.20(4)(c)
26,391		2.04(2)(g)
26,513		1.05(19)(a)
26,534		8.20(7)(a)
26,629		5.04(8)(c.2)
26,762		1.09(5)(a)
26,280		8.20(7)(b)
26,915		2.03(4)(a)
26,926	Ghost	5.20(1)(a)
26,930		8.05(7)(a.2)
26,931		8.05(7)(a)
26,996		8.20(3)(b)
27,076		8.07(5)(a)

Evans		Bibliography
27,132		7.07(1)(b)
		7.07(2)(a)
27,261		2.01(7)(k)
27,354		1.12(8)(a)
27,391		1.06(16)(a)
27,552		8.07(3)(a.2)
27,591		8.05(6)(a)
27,592	Ghost	8.20(6)
27,593	Ghost	8.20(6)
27,594		8.20(6)(a)
27,595	Ghost	8.20(6)
27,596		8.20(6)(b)
27,633		8.05(4)(a)
27,634		8.05(4)(a.3)
27,635		8.05(4)(a.4)
27,643		8.05(5)(a)
27,767		5.05(13)(a.8)
27,768		5.05(13)(b.2)
		5.05(13)(b.3)
27,777		1.10(2)(a)
27,815		8.20(8)(a)
27,816		8.20(8)(a.2)
27,819		5.20(1)(a)
28,246		5.04(8)(c.3)
28,622		1.03(7)(a)
28,636		8.09(2)(a)
28,788		2.04(3)(b)
28,878		3.02(1)(c.3)
28,879		3.02(1)(d.3)
28,928	Serial	1.15(1)(b)
28,941		8.07(6)(a)
28,960		8.07(4)(b)
29,024		1.15(1)(e)
29,284		2.04(3)(a)
29,329		5.02(52)(a)
29,598	Ghost	5.05(13)
29,606		2.03(5)(b)
29,667		8.07(7)(a)
29,889		2.03(5)(a)
29,930		1.10(3)(a)
30,042		5.04(8)(g)
30,149		1.02(1)(g.2)
30,424		6.02(43)(a)
30,607		6.06(1)(a)
30,743		1.11(3)(a)
30,821		1.05(16)(b)
30,962		2.03(6)(a)
31,034	Ghost	5.01(3)
31,035	Ghost	5.01(3)
31,036	Ghost	5.01(3)
31,037		5.01(3)(a)
31,173		8.20(6)(c)
31,220		11.12(1)(a)
31,315		2.03(10)(a)

Evans	Bibliography
31,354	7.20(1)(b)
31,364	7.20(1)(a)
31,657	5.01(3)(b)
31,667	1.10(6)(a)
31,668	1.10(8)(a)
31,669	1.10(14)(a)
31,670	1.10(11)(a)
31,671	1.10(7)(a)
31,672	1.10(4)(a)
31,694	4.07(8)(a)
31,795	1.14(2)(a)
31,951	5.10(1)(a)
31,995 Ghost	8.20(7)
32,092	8.20(4)(d)
32,093	8.20(4)(e)
32,116	1.05(21)(d)
32,133	1.05(21)(b)
32,223	2.03(7)(b)
32,292	6.04(10)(a)
32,293	6.04(10)(b)
32,308	8.02(10)(a)
32,320	5.06(4)(a)
32,369	1.05(22)(a)
32,426	1.11(4)(b.2)
	1.11(2)(b)
32,712	1.05(20)(a)
32,837	8.02(9)(a)
32,852	5.02(54)(a)
32,879	5.02(53)(a)
32,880 Ghost	5.02(53)
32,888	6.04(9)(a)
32,889	6.04(9)(a.2)
32,899	5.05(13)(a.9)
32,940	2.03(10)(a.2)
33,255	1.05(21)(c)
33,266	4.07(9)(a.2)
33,267	4.07(9)(a)
33,290	2.01(7)(f.8)
33,360	1.05(23)(a)
33,382	1.12(10)(a)
33,447	1.12(11)(a)
33,523	1.07(30)(a)
33,584	8.02(10)
33,585	8.02(11)(a)
33,598	1.07(33)(a)
	2.03(1)(c)
	2.03(2)(a)
	2.03(3)(b)
	2.03(6)(b)
	2.04(1)(b)
	2.04(2)(f.3)
	2.04(7)(a)
33,652	2.01(7)(e)
33,698	8.20(4)(f)
33,748	2.01(7)(f.9)
33,824	4.12(6)(a)
33,979	6.04(11)(a)
34,028	2.03(9)(a)
34,038	1.07(31)(a)
34,040	1.07(32)(a)
34,080	1.02(25)(a)
34,082 Serial	1.02(1)(h)
	1.02(24)(a)
	2.03(8)(a)
34,220	1.05(22)(f)
34,281	8.07(8)(a)
34,485	1.04(6)(a)
34,498	4.07(10)(a)
34,498n	4.07(10)(a.2)
34,533	2.01(7)(f.7)
34,785	7.20(2)(b)
34,786	7.20(2)(h)
34,787 Ghost	7.20(2)
34,788	7.20(2)(e)
34,789	7.20(2)(i)
34,790	7.20(2)(j)
34,791	7.20(2)(k)
34,792	7.20(2)(f)
34,793	7.20(2)(d)
34,798 Ghost	7.20(2)
34,906	2.05(1)(a)
	2.05(1)(b)
34,908	2.04(8)(a)
34,958	1.10(9)(a)
	1.10(7)(b)
35,047 Ghost	1.02(1)(g)
35,077	4.07(11)(a)
35,078	4.07(11)(b)
35,281 Ghost	2.03(12)
35,282 Ghost	2.03(12)
35,323	4.07(9)(a.4)
35,355	8.08(1)(a)
35,374	1.07(35)(a)
	2.03(1)(c)
	2.03(5)(c)
	2.03(12)(c)
	2.04(3)(c)
	2.04(5)(e)
	2.04(6)(b)
	2.04(8)(b)
	2.04(9)(a)
35,424	1.07(34)(a)
35,607	1.11(5)(a)
35,931	11.05(2)
36,065	7.07(3)(a)
36,121	2.03(11)(b)
36,122	2.03(11)(c)
36,123 Ghost	2.03(11)

Bristol 1,180

Evans	Bibliography
36,124	2.03(11)(a)
36,321	5.02(55)(a)
36,396	1.06(17)(a)
36,503	2.05(3)(a)
36,504	2.05(2)(d)
36,513	2.03(10)(b)
36,558	7.20(2)(k)
36,561	7.20(2)(m)
36,670	1.10(10)(a)
36,749	1.05(9)(b.6)
36,762	4.07(9)(a.2)
36,763	1.07(36)(a)
36,764	1.07(36)(a)
36,873	5.20(2)(a)
37,039	1.05(27)(b)
37,086	1.11(6)(a)
37,094	8.20(9)(a.5)
37,103	1.07(37)(a)
37,104	2.03(12)(a)
37,249	2.03(13(a)
37,376	8.05(8)(a)
37,514	8.05(8)(a)
37,576	1.05(27)(c)
37,763	1.07(36)(a)
	4.07(8)(a.2)
	4.07(9)(a.6)
	4.07(11)(a.2)
	4.07(13)(a)
37,764	1.07(36)(a)
37,781	5.20(2)(b)
37,811	1.10(13)(a)
37,887	2.03(11)(d)
38,079	1.05(29)(a)
38,080	1.05(22)(g)
38,083	1.05(30)(a)
38,321	4.07(12)(a)
38,328	2.04(10)(c)
38,371	1.07(37)(a)
38,372	1.05(27)(a)
38,373	1.05(28)(a)
38,410	5.02(55)(b)
38,414	8.07(9)(a)
38,433	1.07(37)(a)
38,517	4.06(3)(a)
38,535	11.12(3)(a)
38,723	2.03(14)(a)
38,733	2.03(10)(d)
38,814	2.03(10)(c)
38,957	1.10(13)(b)
38,963	1.10(12)(a)
39,087	5.20(2)(c)

Bristol	mp.	Bibliography
75	39,232	5.02(1)(a)
139	39,293	1.05(1)(b)
251	39,402	1.02(3)(b)
464	39,607	5.03(1)(b)
528	39,668	1.05(4)(a)
642	39,779	1.09(1)(a)
648	39,785	1.03(1)(a)
886	40,005	8.02(2)(a)
893	40,012	5.02(5)(a)
902	40,021	5.02(6)(c)
903	40,022	5.02(6)(a)
916	40,033	1.05(7)(a)
925	40,042	5.02(8)(a)
927	40,044	5.02(8)(c)
930	40,049	1.09(2)(a)
935	40,054	5.02(8)(d)
939	40,058	5.02(9)(a)
1,026	40,143	5.02(12)(b)
1,041	40,156	1.03(2)(b)
1,064	40,177	1.03(2)(a)
1,098	40,208	1.06(4)(a)
1,159	40,262	1.05(10)(a)
	40,263	1.05(10)(b)
1,180	40,280	1.03(3)(a)

Bristol	mp.	Bibliography
1,219	40,315	1.07(3)(a)
1,226	40,320	9.00(2)(i)
1,240	40,330	5.02(13)(a)
1,353	40,421	1.06(5)(b)
1,476	40,534	9.00(2)(j)
1,627	40,669	1.06(5)(f)
1,694	40,730	5.02(16)(b)
1,726	40,760	5.02(17)(a)
1,849	40,872	5.02(18)(a)
1,871	40,889	5.02(18)(b)
1,912	40,928	1.02(12)(a)
2,287	41,274	5.02(19)(a)
2,325	41,309	5.02(19)(b)
2,464	41,438	1.05(11)(a.2)
2,478		5.02(30)(a)
2,515		5.03(3)(a)
2,516	41,487	5.03(3)(b)
2,590	41,556	5.02(20)(a)
2,752	41,706	5.02(21)(a)
2,827	41,778	1.03(5)(a)
2,849		5.01(1)(a)
2,862	41,806	5.12(1)(a)
2,879	41,822	5.04(1)(b.2)
2,880	41,823	5.04(1)(a.2)
3,014	41,949	1.12(1)(d)
3,015	41,950	1.12(1)(b)
3,066	41,994	5.04(2)(a)
3,149		1.02(15)(i.3)
3,150		1.02(15)(i)
3,151		1.02(15)(i.5)
3,156	42,050	1.02(15)(e)
3,167	42,077	5.02(23)(a)
3,168	42,078	5.01(24)(a)
3,203	42,112	1.11(1)(b)
3,205	42,114	5.02(25)(a)
3,239	42,143	1.02(15)(f)
3,241	42,145	1.02(15)(a)
3,242	42,146	1.02(15)(a.2)
3,243	42,147	1.02(13)(f)
3,251	42,156	1.02(15)(g)
3,257	41,161	1.02(15)(c)
3,280	42,179	1.02(15)(h)
3,318	42,212	5.02(26)(b.4)
3,324	42,215	1.06(11)(a)
3,332	42,223	5.02(26)(a.2)
3,369	42,260	4.11(1)(a)
3,419	42,309	5.02(27)(b)
3,431	42,321	5.04(4)(a)
3,453	42,343	5.02(28)(a)
3,468	42,358	5.04(3)(a)
3,473	42,362[a]	5.04(3)(d)
3,486	42,373	1.02(17)(a)
3,495	42,377	1.02(17)(c)
3,513	42,396	5.02(32)(i)

Bristol	mp.	Bibliography
3,517	42,399	5.02(32)(j)
3,518	42,400	5.02(32)(b)
3,519	42,401	5.02(32)(e)
3,545	42,426	1.02(15)(t.4)
3,553	42,502	5.02(31)(a)
3,558	42,436	5.02(32)(c)
3,560	42,438	5.02(32)(d)
3,562	42,475	5.02(29)(a)
3,578	42,454	5.02(30)(a)
3,584	42,531	5.05(8)(a)
3,604a	42,472	1.06(12)(a)
3,610	42,478	5.04(3)(b.6)
3,611	42,479	5.04(3)(b.7)
3,619		5.05(9)(a.3)
3,620	42,483	5.05(9)(a.2)
3,622	42,485	5.02(32)(a)
3,645	42,506	5.02(32)(f)
3,647	42,508	5.02(32)(g)
3,652	42,513	5.02(32)(k.3)
3,653	42,514	5.02(32)(k.4)
3,657	42,518	5.02(32)(h)
3,728	42,589	5.02(33)(a)
4,167	42,983	2.04(5)(a)
4,232	43,046	5.03(5)(a)
4,237	43,049	2.04(5)(b)
4,460	43,245	5.04(5)(a)
4,605	43,376	1.04(4)(a)
4,651	43,422	5.02(34)(b)
4,652	43,423	5.02(34)(b.2)
4,653	43,427	5.02(34)(c)
4,654	43,426	5.02(34)c.2)
4,682	43,453	5.02(34)(i.3)
4,683	43,454	5.02(34)(i.3)
4,688	43,459	5.04(6)(a)
4,714	43,485	5.02(34)(h)
4,730	43,501	5.02(34)(f)
4,792	43,424	5.02(34)(d)
4,793	43,425	5.02(34)(e)
4,993	43,732	2.04(5)(a.2)
4,999	43,738	5.02(35)(b)
5,000	43,739	5.02(35)(b.2)
5,073	43,792	5.04(7)(b)
5,111	43,820	2.01(7)(c)
5,189	43,899	1.02(19)(a)
5,195	43,903	2.01(7)(a.4)
5,196	43,904	2.01(7)(a.5)
5,197	43,905	2.01(7)(a.8)
5,198		2.01(7)(a.6)
5,199		2.01(7)(a.7)
5,302	43,990	1.09(4)(a)
5,411	44,095	4.11(2)(a)
5,571	44,246	5.04(8)(a)
5,590	44,263	1.05(10)(b)
5,787		5.04(8)(f)

Bristol	mp.	Bibliography
5,806	44,457	4.12(3)(a)
5,857		5.02(41)(a)
5,891	44,528	2.04(6)(a)
5,898	44,534	5.02(37)(a)
5,907	44,543	5.02(38)(a)
6,006	44,633	5.02(40)(b)
6,084	44,700	8.09(1)(a)
6,171	44,793	1.05(15)(a)
6,212	44,827	1.10(1)(b)
6,278	44,881	5.07(9)(a.3)
6,279	44,882	5.07(9)(a.4)
6,404	44,999	2.02(2)(a)
6,510	45,086	1.06(15)(a)
6,676		5.02(2)(c)
6,763	45,316	5.04(3)(e)
		5.04(3)(e.2)
6,776	45,334	11.07(1)(a)
6,815	45,371	5.02(46)(a.2)
6,817	45,373	5.01(2)(a)
6,818	45,374	5.01(2)(b)
6,928	45,460	5.02(34)(a)
7,067	45,594	5.07(10)(a)
7,068	45,595	1.07(21)(a)
7,204	45,728	5.05(12)(a)
7,237	45,763	5.04(9)(c)
7,251	45,777	2.04(5)(d)
7,260	45,782	5.14(1)(a)
7,299	45,811	2.01(7)(g.3)
7,305	45,816	5.02(48)(a)
7,349	45,855	5.04(9)(a.3)
7,350	45,856	5.04(9)(a.2)
7,412	45,906	1.02(21)(a)
7,434	45,929	1.05(24)(a)
7,501	45,998	5.02(46)(b)
7,502	45,999	5.02(46)(c)
7,674a		5.04(9)(f)
7,675	46,146	5.04(9)(d)
7,735	46,198	2.04(5)(d)
7,762	46,225	2.04(5)(c)
7,764	46,227	5.03(6)(a.4)
7,835	46,293	5.05(13)(a)
7,850		4.20(3)(a)
7,903	46,359	8.05(3)(b)
8,049	46,494	1.07(28)(a)
8,101	46,539	11.07(2)(a)
8,345	46,757	5.02(49)(c)
8,396	46,808	5.02(50)(a)
8,400	46,811	8.20(5)(e)
8,418	46,827	5.14(1)(a)
8,472		5.05(15)(b.3)
8,473	46,873	5.05(15)(b.2)
8,477	46,877	8.07(4)(a)
8,564		8.20(7)(c)
8,714	47,089	1.14(1)(a)

Bristol	mp.	Bibliography
8,724	47,100	8.20(5)(c)
8,854		8.05(4)(a.5)
9,101	47,425	5.02(51)(a)
9,160	47,476	1.14(1)(d)
9,218	47,528	8.04(1)(a)
9,293a	47,599	8.20(7)(d)
9,460	47,706	1.10(5)(a)
9,526		1.08(4)(a)
9,545	47,782	5.02(51)(a.2)
9,602		1.11(4)(a)
9,715	47,926	5.05(13)(b.4)
9,843	48,042	7.02(2)(c)
9,952		1.05(21)(a)
9,989a		5.02(50)(a.2)
9,995	48,173	1.11(4)(b)
10,008		2.04(4)(a)
10,027		1.05(22)(b)
10,029	48,196	11.05(1)
10,049	48,214	8.02(9)(b)
10,133	48,170	8.04(2)(a)
10,143	48,290	7.20(2)(a)
10,192	48,328	4.07(9)(a.3)
10,214	48,344	5.07(11)(a)
10,268	48,648	2.05(2)(a)
10,402		2.04(4)(b)
10,404	48,519	5.03(7)(a)
10,431		1.05(22)(c)
10,432	48,502	1.05(22)(e)
10,448	48,554	5.10(1)(b)
10,585	48,714	7.20(2)(1)
10,683	48,766	4.07(9)(a.5)
10,731	48,896	8.20(9)(a)
10,732		8.20(9)(a.2)
10,733	48,895	8.20(9)(a.3)
10,734	48,897	8.20(9)(a.4)
10,744	48,822	2.05(2)(b)
10,758a		1.07(26)(a.2)
10,810	48,882	1.05(25)(a)
10,825	48,898	1.05(26)(a)
10,878		11.06(1)(a)
11,044	49,078	2.03(12)(b)
11,070	49,100	8.04(3)(a)
11,094		1.05(22)(d)

Bristol Additions		
4,708a		2.01(2)(a)

Shaw-Shoemaker	Bibliography
935	1.07(34)(b)
1,474	2.03(6)(c)
1,558	2.03(10)(f)
1,600	2.03(10)(f)
2,785	1.05(29)(d)
3,598	1.05(16)(b.2)
4,109	2.03(10)(e)
4,110	2.03(10)(e.2)
4,111	2.03(10)(e.3)
9,532	7.20(2)(p)
11,130	1.07(26)(a.3)
12,301	1.02(15)(ii.2)
13,295	1.02(15)(ii.2)
13,364	1.07(29)(c)
13,739	1.02(15)(n.3)
15,759	1.05(29)(b)
15,801	2.02(1)(d)

Shaw-Shoemaker	Bibliography
17,163	2.02(1)(e)
18,341	2.02(1)(i)
18,342	2.02(1)(g)
18,368	2.02(1)(f)
18,494	2.02(1)(g)
18,495	2.02(1)(h)
18,636	2.01(7)(m.2)
18,637	2.01(7)(m.2)
18,661	1.12(10)(b)
19,230	2.02(1)(f)
20,384	1.05(10)(e)
21,518	2.01(7)(n)
24,001	2.02(1)(j)
39,883	1.05(16)(b.3)
39,985 Serial	2.01(6)(e.2)
40,184	2.01(7)(o)
40,699	2.01(7)(p)

TABLE II: SABIN

Sabin	
376	4.07(11)(a)
377	4.07(9)(a)
	4.07(9)(a.2)
729	1.05(9)(a)
730	1.05(8)(g)
731	1.05(8)(l)
833	1.02(15)(s)
1,066	5.02(39)(a)
1,228	2.02(1)(m)
1,449	2.01(7)(g)
1,450	2.01(7)(g.2)
1,453	2.01(7)(d)
1,454	2.01(7)(a)
	2.01(7)(a.3)
1,455	2.01(7)(a.2)
1,456	2.01(7)(b)
1,457	2.01(7)(u)
1,458	2.01(7)(t)
2,059	2.01(6)(d)
	2.01(6)(d.2)
2,060	2.01(6)(c)
2,061	2.01(6)(e.3)
2,062	2.01(6)(b)
2,346	3.05(1)(a)
2,417	1.02(15)(bb)
3,302	2.01(6)(e)
3,302n	2.01(6)(e.2)
	2.01(6)(e.3)
3,599	1.02(9)(a)

Sabin	
3,625	5.02(39)(b)
4,033	1.05(2)(c)
4,034	1.05(2)(b)
4,102	5.04(8)(c)
	5.04(8)(c.3)
4,448	1.14(2)(a)
4,746	2.01(7)(o)
4,747	2.01(7)(o.2)
4,748	2.01(7)(o.3)
5,378	1.06(5)(b)
5,379	1.06(10)(a)
5,628	3.02(2)(f)
5,629	3.02(2)(f)
5,630	3.02(2)(f)
	3.02(2)(g)
6,000	7.20(2)(f)
6,002	7.20(2)(m)
6,003	7.20(2)(b)
6,106	1.07(2)(a)
	1.07(2)(a.3)
6,249	1.02(15)(w)
6,326	3.12(1)(a)
6,735	1.02(15)(k)
6,736	1.02(15)(i.7)
6,737	1.02(15)(ii)
	1.02(15)(ii.2)
6,738	1.02 (15)
	1.02(15)(ii)
6,739	1.02(15)(i.2)

Sabin	Bibliography
6,740	1.02(15)(i.4)
	1.02(15)(i.5)
	1.02(15)(i.6)
	1.02(15)(i.8)
	1.02(15)(i.9)
6,741	1.02(15)(j)
7,328	2.03(1)(a)
7,882	1.05(27)(b)
7,919	1.06(5)(a)
7,970	2.02(1)(h)
8,497	1.04(3)(a)
9,257	2.01(1)(b)
9,455	3.02(2)(d)
9,926	1.02(1)(g)
9,927	1.02(1)(g.2)
	1.02(1)(g.3)
	1.02(1)(g.4)
11,808	5.02(7)(a)
11,868	1.02(1)(i)
	1.02(2)(c)
	1.02(15)(jj)
	1.02(15)(n.4)
	1.03(6)(b)
	1.05(1)(d)
	1.05(2)(f)
	1.05(9)(h)
	1.05(10)(f)
	1.07(32)(b)
	2.01(1)(f)
	2.01(7)(q)
	3.02(1)(e)
	3.02(2)(1)
	5.02(34)(j)
11,898	6.04(7)(a)
12,365	3.02(3)(b)
12,933	1.09(3)(a)
12,983	1.02(15)(t)
	1.02(15)(t.2)
	1.02(15)(t.3)
13,202	5.03(1)(c)
13,204	5.03(1)(a)
13,697	1.07(7)(a)
13,880	1.07((30)(a)
14,030	1.07(37)(a)
14,053	1.07(30)(b)
14,276	1.05(11)(b)
14,494	1.02(7)(c)
15,092	6.02(27)(a)
15,977	1.02(15)(y)
16,608	2.03(13)(a)
17,642	1.02(8)(a)
18,313	1.07(26)(a)
	1.07(33)(a)
	1.07(35)(a)
18,923	1.02(15)(ff)
19,340	4.05(2)(a)
19,341	4.05(2)(b)
19,342	4.05(2)(c)
20,867	1.02(1)(p)
20,884	1.02(1)(n)
20,914	4.12(2)(a.3)
20,918	4.12(2)(a)
20,982	2.03(4)(a)
20,985	2.03(10)(e)
20,989	2.03(10)(a)
20,994n	1.07(34)(b)
21,002	1.07(34)(a)
21,296	2.01(7)(1)
21,297	2.01(7)(1.2)
22,316a	1.03(7)(a)
22,639	2.04(2)(b)
23,532	1.12(1)(a)
24,081	3.06(1)(a)
24,082	3.06(1)(b)
24,083	3.06(1)(c)
	3.06(1)(d)
24,664	1.05(21)(b)
24,744	1.02(10)(a)
24,932n	6.02(37)(a)
25,053	4.12(2)(a.6)
25,124	1.05(11)(a)
25,296	1.02(11)(a)
25,320	1.02(1)(j)
25,397	5.02(7)(b)
25,595	2.04(5)(a.3)
25,636	1.06(7)(a)
25,961	2.03(12)(a)
26,630a	1.02(13)(a)
	1.02(13)(c)
	1.02(13)(d)
	1.02(13)(e)
27,972	3.05(3)(b)
28,099	3.02(2)(j)
28,147	1.05(22)(f)
28,593n	2.01(7)(i)
29,602	5.07(5)(a)
29,638	2.04(3)(b)
30,048	2.04(7)(a)
30,177	1.02(15)(u)
	1.02(15)(u.2)
	1.02(15)(u.3)
	1.02(15)(u.4)
30,380	1.05(8)(1)
31,252	3.10(2)(a)
31,343	2.01(1)(c)
31,344	2.01(1)(b)
	2.01(1)(d)
31,689	1.02(15)(aa)

Sabin	Bibliography	Sabin	Bibliography
31,842	1.02(23)(a)	39,877n	1.05(22)(a)
32,362	1.02(15)(n)	39,925	1.12(1)(a)
	1.02(15)(n.2)	39,926	1.12(1)(b)
32,418	7.07(1)(b)		1.12(1)(b.2)
32,964	1.02(14)(a)	39,927	1.12(1)(c)
32,976	7.07(2)(a)	40,348	1.20(15)(i.7)
32,979	1.07(29)(b)	40,605	2.03(11)(a)
33,058	1.05(10)(c)	40,699	2.01(7)(m)
33,059	1.05(10)(d)	40,815	5.07(4)(b)
33,060	1.05(10)(e)	41,527	8.02(10)(a)
33,061	1.05(10)(g)	41,793	4.07(1)(a)
33,328	2.01(9)(a)	41,794	4.07(4)(a)
33,696	3.02(2)(c)	41,795	4.07(4)(a.2)
33,874	1.06(10)(a)		4.07(4)(a.3)
34,012	5.07(8)(a)	42,374	1.02(15)(p)
34,075	3.02(1)(c)	42,737	1.06(1)(a)
34,076	3.02(1)(c.2)	42,758	1.05(12)(a)
34,077	3.02(1)(c.3)	42,995	5.02(22)(b)
34,078	3.02(1)(d)		5.02(25)(b)
34,079	3.02(1)(d.2)		5.02(34)(g)
34,080	3.02(1)(d.3)	43,564	1.07(32)(a)
34,081	1.02(15)(ii)	43,663	1.03(2)(c)
34,416	9.00(2)(g)	44,079	1.05(3)(a)
	9.00(2)(h)	44,080	1.05(3)(a.3)
34,579	2.04(5)(a)	44,743	5.04(8)(d)
34,780	2.04(5)(a.3)		5.04(8)(d.2)
35,831	4.05(3)(a)	44,778	1.14(1)(e)
35,832	4.20(8)(a)	44,873	1.11(4)(b.2)
36,048	1.07(1)(c)	45,099	9.00(2)(f)
36,360	7.07(3)(a)	45,468	1.02(15)(ee)
36,390	5.06(4)(a)	45,730	1.02(11)(b)
37,196	1.07(1)(d)	45,852	1.02(22)(a)
37,200	1.07(1)(b)		1.02(22)(a.2)
37,203	1.07(1)(a)	45,929	9.00(1)(b)
37,226	1.07(1)(a.2)	45,940	1.02(15)(l)
37,384	1.02(12)(c)	46,244	5.02(1)(b)
37,712	1.02(15)(n.6)	46,369	1.02(4)(a)
	1.02(15)(kk)	46,392	6.02(9)(a.2)
38,827	2.01(10)(a)	46,393	6.02(9)(a.2.a)
38,828	2.01(10)(b)	46,528	6.02(4)(a)
38,829	2.01(10)(c)	46,563	1.02(1)(f)
39,180	1.02(15)(cc)	46,577	1.02(7)(b)
39,184	1.02(15)(m)	46,603	1.02(1)(c)
	1.02(15)(m.2)	46,604	1.02(1)(d)
39,442	1.02(1)(a)	46,605	1.02(1)(d.2)
	1.02(1)(b)	46,606	1.02(1)(d.3)
39,443	1.02(1)(b.2)	46,607	1.02(1)(l)
	1.02(1)(b.3)	46,687	1.02(1)(e)
39,450	9.00(3)(a)	46,735	5.02(1)(a.2)
39,711	2.01(2)(a)	46,736	6.02(2)(a.2)
39,712	2.01(2)(a.2)	46,758	6.02(2)(a)
39,713	2.01(2)(a.3)	46,875	1.02(5)(b)
39,782	1.10(13)(a)	46,934	1.02(2)(b)
39,877	1.05(22)(f)	46,935	1.02(2)(a)

Sabin	Bibliography
47,349	1.05(6)(a)
49,325	1.02(15)(gg)
49,386	3.05(2)(a)
49,387	3.05(2)(b)
50,303	5.02(4)(a)
50,847	1.05(8)(m)
50,849	1.05(8)(f.2)
51,530	1.05(8)(k)
52,641	9.00(1)(a)
53,066	1.06(5)(d)
53,067	1.06(5)(c)
53,074	1.06(13)(a)
53,075	1.06(6)(a)
53,084	1.06(16)(a)
53,082	1.06(5)(g)
53,153	1.06(5)(f)
53,203	1.06(14)(a)
53,436	1.05(2)(c.2)
53,473	1.05(14)(b)
53,542	1.06(11)(a)
55,226	7.07(1)(a)
55,312	1.02(15)(hh.3)
	4.12(2)(a.4)
55,387	1.02(15)(x)
55,572	1.02(14)(a)
56,084	1.06(16)(a)
56,635	5.04(2)(b)
	5.04(2)(b.2)
	5.04(2)(b.3)
	5.04(2)(b.4)
	5.04(2)(b.5)
	5.04(2)(b.8)
	5.04(2)(b.9)
	5.04(2)(b.10)
	5.04(2)(b.11)
	5.04(2)(b.12)
	5.04(2)(b.13)
	5.04(2)(b.14)
	5.04(2)(b.15)
	5.04(2)(b.16)
56,636	5.04(2)(e)
	5.04(2)(e.2)
	5.04(2)(e.3)
56,800	1.06(8)(a)
56,801	1.06(9)(a)
57,236	2.02(1)(f)
	2.02(1)(j)
57,828	1.07(16)(c)
57,903	1.05(13)(b)
58,366	1.05(5)(a)
59,056	2.03(6)(a)
59,653	2.04(3)(a)
59,685	9.00(2)(e)
59,957	1.09(1)(a)
59,959	3.07(1)(a)
59,962	9.00(2)(e)
60,582	1.07(6)(a)
61,069	5.05(9)(a)
62,298	2.03(11)(a)
62,899	2.03(11)(c)
63,045	4.12(2)(a.5)
65,442	1.05(20)(a)
65,578	1.03(2)(c)
67,085	1.02(3)(c)
67,086	1.02(3)(c.2)
67,979	2.03(3)(a)
68,405	1.02(1)(m)
68,567	1.07(5)(a)
69,914	1.05(19)(a)
71,082	1.07(4)(a)
72,199	3.02(2)(h)
73,132	1.04(6)(a)
74,249	4.07(10)(a)
74,432	1.05(14)(a)
74,433	1.05(14)(c)
74,542	5.05(15)(b)
75,021	2.01(3)(a)
75,736	1.02(1)(k)
	1.02(1)(k.2)
78,059	2.01(4)(a)
79,477	2.01(7)(f)
79,478	2.01(7)(f.2)
79,479	2.01(7)(f.3)
79,480	2.01(7)(f.4)
79,481	2.01(7)(f.4.b)
79,482	2.01(7)(f.5)
79,483	2.01(7)(f.6)
79,484	2.01(7)(f.7)
79,485	2.01(7)(f.10)
79,486	2.01(7)(f.11)
79,487	2.01(7)(f.12)
80,668	1.02(15)(i.2)
80,671	1.02(15)(i.4)
80,672	1.02((15)(i.6)
80,673	1.02(15)(i.9)
81,272	2.01(7)(r)
81,390	1.04(2)(a)
82,356	4.12(1)(a)
84,554	1.05(9)(a)
84,556	1.05(8)(j)
84,557	4.05(2)(b)
84,588	1.05(8)(l)
86,587	8.02(3)(a)
86,794	6.01(1)(b)
86,960	1.06(3)(a)
87,439	1.12(10)(a.2)
87,450	4.12(6)(a)
87,456	1.07(29)(d)

Sabin	Bibliography
	2.03(11)(e)
87,458	1.12(10)(a)
87,466	11.12(1)
87,825	2.04(6)(a)
88,270	1.06(1)(a)
90,433	1.04(4)(a)
91,855	1.06(10)(b)
91,939	5.06(1)(a)
92,970	6.04(9)(a)
	6.04(9)(a.2)
94,043	5.05(13)(a.3)
94,044	5.05(13)(a.4)
94,049	5.05(13)(b)
94,052	5.05(13)(a.8)
94,405	1.06(17)(a)
94,411	1.10(2)(a)
94,466n	1.09(1)(a)
94,485	2.03(5)(b)
94,518	5.02(46)(a)
94,519	5.02(46)(b)
94,520	5.02(46)(c.2)
94,521	5.02(46)(a.2)
95,172	1.02(15)(z)
95,390	3.05(3)(a)
96,298	1.03(2)(a)
96,298n	1.03(2)(b)
96,813	1.05(29)(a)
96,819	1.05(23)(a)
96,837	2.03(14)(a)
96,849	1.07(8)(a)
96,856	1.05(28)(a)
96,907	1.05(16)(a)
96,914	8.20(4)(b)
96,915	8.20(4)(c)
96,930a	2.04(10)(d)
96,935	2.04(10)(c)
96,946	1.02(15)(n.3)
	1.02(15)(n.5)
96,951	1.02(15)(n)
	1.02(15)(n.2)
96,954	1.02(4)(b)
96,955	1.02(6)(a)
96,957	1.02(7)(a)
97,404	1.02(15)(dd)
98,638	1.03(6)(a)
98,039n	1.02(1)(o)
98,185	5.05(12)(a)
98,429	1.05(8)(a)
98,430	1.05(8)(b)
98,431	1.05(8)(c)
98,432	1.05(8)(d)
98,433	1.05(8)(e)
98,434	1.05(8)(o)
98,435	1.05(8)(i)
98,436	1.05(8)(n)
	1.05(8)(q)
98,638	1.03(6)(a)
99,132	1.14(1)(a)
99,584	2.04(5)(a)
	2.04(5)(a.2)
99,894	10.10(2)(a)
99,977	4.10(1)(a)
100,038	1.10(9)(a)
	1.10(10)(a)
100,038n	1.10(9)(a.2)
100,228	1.10(13)(a)
100,229	1.10(13)(b)
100,230	1.10(3)(a)
100,231	1.10(12)(a)
100,546	3.09(1)(b)
101,477	1.02(15)(r)
	1.02(15)(r.2)
101,478	1.02(15)(v)
	1.02(15)(v.2)
	1.02(15)(v.3)
102,461	1.05(27)(a)
	1.05(27)(c)
102,617	1.02(15)(hh)
103,349a	5.02(39)(a)
103,350	5.02(34)(b)
	5.02(40)(a)
103,854	2.03(5)(a)
104,617	5.07(9)(a)
	5.07(9)(a.5)
104,626	4.20(4)(a)
104,848	3.02(1)(a.2)
104,849	3.02(1)(a.3)
105,350	5.02(34)(b)
105,702	1.10(7)(a)
105,703	1.10(4)(a)
106,080	1.05(21)(c)
106,090	5.02(35)(b)
106,091	5.02(35)(b.2)
106,092	5.02(35)(a)
106,093	5.02(35)(a.2)
106,304	1.05(9)(b)
106,305	1.05(9)(b.2)
106,307	1.05(9)(d)
	1.05(9)(d.2)
	1.05(9)(d.3)
	1.05(9)(d.4)
106,308	1.05(9)(d.7)
106,309	1.05(9)(d.8)
106,310	1.05(9)(b.4)
106,311	1.05(9)(d.9)
106,312	1.05(9)(b.5)
106,313	1.05(9)(d.10)
106,314	1.05(9)(b.6)

Sabin	Bibliography		Bibliography
106,314n	1.05(9)(e)		

TABLE III: PARRISH, SHOEMAKER, AND WING

Parrish

91	8.20(1)(a)
	8.20(1)(c)
99	1.07(37)(a)
100	2.03(12)(a)
107	1.14(1)(a)
232	1.02(15)(n)
240	7.07(1)(b)
52 App.	1.06(17)(a)

Shoemaker

2,183	6.02(9)(a.2.a)
5,206	4.12(2)(a.3)
9,178	1.02(15)(hh.3)
12,046	1.02(1)(g.3)
13,859	2.01(2)(a.2)
14,787	1.10(9)(a.2)
18,239	1.02(15)(n.5)
39,985	2.01(6)(e.2)

Wing

B-3,003	3.02(2)(f)
B-3,004	3.02(2)(g)
B-3,585	8.02(1)(a)
B-5,994	3.02(2)(d)
C- 288	1.02(1)(g)
C-1,200	1.06(2)(a)
D- 176	6.02(1)(a)
F-1,457	3.09(1)(b)
G-1,415	3.02(2)(j)
H-3,426	3.02(2)(c)
J- 557	1.06(2)(b)
J-1,173	1.07(1)(b)
K- 170	1.07(1)(d)
K- 186	1.07(1)(a)
L- 702	1.02(1)(a)
L- 703	1.02(1)(b)
L-3,040	3.09(1)(a)
M-1,001	3.02(2)(a.2)
M-1,087	5.02(1)(b)
M-1,140	6.02(9)(a)
M-1,156	6.02(4)(a)
M-1,166	6.02(6)(a)
M-1,172	1.02(1)(c)
M-1,173	1.02(1)(c.2)
M-1,174	1.02(1)(d)
M-1,175	1.02(1)(d.2)
M-1,176	1.02(1)(d.3)
M-1,212	6.02(8)(a)
M-1,213	1.02(1)(e)
M-1,246	5.02(1)(a)
M-1,247	5.02(1)(a.2)
M-1,248	5.02(1)(c)
M-1,249	5.02(1)(a.3)
M-1,250	6.02(2)(a.2)
M-1,260	6.02(2)(a)
M-1,353	1.02(2)(b)
M-1,354	1.02(2)(a)
P-1,166	3.02(2)(e)
R-1,722	3.02(2)(h)
T- 804	3.06(1)(b)
T-2,254	1.07(1)(a.2)
T-3,019	3.02(2)(a.3)
V- 19	3.10(2)(a)
W- 59	9.00(1)(a)
W-1,269	3.02(1)(a.2)
W-1,270	3.02(1)(a.3)
W-1,605	3.02(1)(b)
W-2,281	6.02(7)(a)
W-3,094	3.02(1)(a)

TABLE IV: STATE AND PRIVY COUNCIL BIBLIOGRAPHIES

01 NEW HAMPSHIRE

Whittemore	Bibliography
415	5.02(43)(a)
466	5.01(2)(b)
499	5.02(47)(c)
513	4.20(1)(a)

02 MASSACHUSETTS

Adams Controversy	Bibliography
67-4	1.05(11)(b)
	1.05(11)(b.2)
70-4	1.02(15)(j)
70-5a	1.02(15)(i)
70-5b	1.02(15)(i.2)
70-5c	1.02(15)(i.4)
70-5d	1.02(15)(i.6)
70-11	1.05(15)(k)
70-15	1.05(15)(m)
70-29a	1.05(15)(n)
70-29b	1.05(15)(n.2)
73-1	1.02(15)(i.6.a)
74-35a	1.02(15)(u)
74-35b	1.02(15)(u.5)
75-33	1.02(15)(y)
76-97	3.05(2)(a)
78-44	2.01(1)(d)
80-5a	2.01(7)(g)
80-5b	2.01(7)(g.2)
80-6a	2.01(7)(a)
80-6b	2.01(7)(b.2)
80-6c	2.01(7)(b.3)
81-62	2.01(7)(h)
81-65a	2.01(7)(f)
81-65b	2.01(7)(f.2)
81-70	3.05(3)(a)
82-47	2.01(7)(i)
82-75.1	2.01(7)(j)
83-36	3.05(3)(b)

Adams Independence	Bibliography
48b	1.05(11)(b)
	1.05(11)(b.2)
75a	1.02(15)(i)
75b	1.02(15)(i.2)
75c	1.02(15)(i.3)
75d	1.02(15)(i.3)
75e	1.02(15)(i.5)
75f	1.02(15)(i.4)
75g	1.02(15)(i.6.a)
75g note	1.02(15)(i.6.a)
75h	1.02(15)(i.7)
75i	1.02(15)(j)
77	1.02(15)(k)
79a	1.02(15)(m)
79b	1.02(15)(m.2)
80	1.02(15)(l)
84a	1.02(15)(n)
84b	1.02(15)(n.2)
85	1.02(15)(p)
88a	1.02(15)(r)
88b	1.02(15)(r.2)
94a	1.02(15)(t)
94b	1.02(15)(t.2)
94c	1.02(15)(t.3)
94d	1.02(15)(t.4)
117a	1.02(15)(u)
117b	1.02(15)(u.3)
117c	1.02(15)(u.2)
117d	1.02(15)(u.4)
117e	1.02(15)(t.6)
153	1.02(15)(w)
201a	1.02(15)(v)
201b	1.02(15)(v.3)
201c	1.02(15)(v.2)
229	1.02(15)(z)

Ford	Bibliography
265	1.02(3)(b)
619	5.02(5)(a)
628	5.02(6)(c)
629	5.02(6)(a)
630	5.02(6)(b)
642	5.02(8)(a)
651	5.02(9)(a)
652	5.02(8)(c)
653	5.02(8)(d)
679	5.02(11)(a)
1,003	5.02(16)(b)
1,004	5.02(15)(a)
1,008	5.02(17)(a)
1,074	1.02(12)(b)
1,077	5.02(18)(b)

Ford	Bibliography
1,078	5.02(18)(a)
1,268	5.02(19)(c)
1,269	5.02(19)(a)
1,335	5.03(3)(a)
1,349	5.02(20)(a)
1,407	5.02(21)(a)
1,426	5.02(22)(a)
1,510	1.02(15)(e.2)
1,511	5.02(26)(a)
1,512	5.02(26)(a.2)
1,514	5.02(23)(a)
1,515	5.02(24)(a)
1,525	5.02(25)(a)
1,535	1.02(15)(o)
1,606	1.02(17)(b)
1,613	5.02(28)(a)
1,629	5.04(3)(d.2)
1,630	1.02(17)(a)
1,632	1.02(17)(c)
1,633	5.02(27)(a)
1,634	5.02(27)(b)
1,640	5.02(32)(i)
1,641	5.02(32)(b)
1,642	5.02(32)(c)
1,643	5.02(32)(d)
1,644	5.02(32)(e)
1,645	5.02(32)(e.2)
1,646	5.02(32)(f)
1,647	5.02(32)(g)
1,648	5.02(32)(h)
1,678	5.02(29)(a)
1,686	5.02(30)(a)
1,692	5.02(31)(a)
1,722	5.02(33)(a)
1,780	5.03(4)(a)
2,129	5.02(34)(c.2)
2,211	5.02(35)(b)
2,233	2.01(7)(c)
2,274	1.02(19)(a)
2,360	5.02(36)(a)
2,385	5.02(38)(a)
2,437	5.02(42)(a)
2,500	5.02(44)(a)
2,523	5.01(2)(a)
2,531	1.02(21)(a)
2,555	5.02(47)(a)
2,560a	5.02(48)(a)
2,681	5.02(49)(b)
2,700	8.20(5)(d)
2,701	8.20(5)(d.2)
2,702	8.20(5)(d.4)
2,759	5.02(52)(a)
2,843	5.02(53)(a)
2,903	4.07(9)(a.4)
2,919	8.20(9)(a.5)
2,920	8.20(9)(a)
2,921 Ghost	8.20(9)
2,922	8.20(9)(a)
2,922a	8.20(9)(a.3)
2,939	5.02(55)(a)

Cotton Mather

15-A	1.02(1)(g)
43-A	5.02(1)(b)
125	1.02(3)(a)
185	1.02(4)(a)
213-A	6.02(9)(a.2)
284-A	6.02(9)(a)
339	5.02(3)(a)
367	6.02(15)(a)
373	6.02(4)(a)
407	6.02(17)(a)
417	1.03(1)(b)
421	6.02(16)(a)
426	1.02(7)(b)
440	6.02(6)(a)
454-A	1.02(1)(c)
454-A^{2}	1.02(1)(c.2)
454-B	1.02(1)(d)
454-C	1.02(1)(d.2)
454-D	1.02(1)(d.3)
p. 1,133	1.02(1)(f)

Increase Mather

22-B	1.02(1)(e)
56	6.02(8)(a)
115-A	5.02(1)(b)
115-A^{1}	5.02(1)(a)
115-A^{2}	5.02(1)(a.2)
115-B	5.02(1)(c)
115-C	5.02(1)(a.3)
174-A	6.02(2)(a)
174-B	6.02(2)(a.2)

Tapley (Pages)

310	5.02(27)(b)
	5.02(27)(c)
	5.02(28)(a)
311	5.02(27)(a)
312	5.02(32)(e.2)
313	1.02(15)(t.4)
	5.04(3)(b.10)
332	5.02(34)(i.2)

Tapley (Pages)	Bibliography
359	3.02(1)(c.3)
361	1.02(1)(g.2)
	6.02(43)(a)
363	1.02(1)(g.2)
364	1.02(25)(a)
366	1.02(25)(a)
472	1.02(1)(g.3)

03 RHODE ISLAND

Alden

48	1.03(2)(b)
51	1.03(2)(c)
53	1.03(2)(a)
64	1.03(3)(a)
283	1.03(4)(a)
379	1.03(5)(a)
404	1.03(1)(c)
438	1.02(14)(a)
542	1.02(15)(u.2)
573	5.03(4)(a)
630	1.02(15)(v.3)
634	5.03(5)(a)
718	2.01(1)(a)
815	2.01(7)(b)
1,008	6.02(37)(a)
1,105	1.03(6)(a)
1,259	5.03(6)(a)
1,297	5.05(13)(a.6)
1,391	5.05(13)(a.8)
1,567	5.03(7)(a)
1,598	2.04(8)(a)

Winship (Pages)

19	1.03(4)(a)
22	1.03(5)(a)
23	1.03(1)(c)
30	1.02(15)(u.2)
32	1.02(15)(v.3)
42	2.01(7)(b)
48	6.02(37)(a)
52	1.03(6)(a)
57	5.03(6)(a)
65	1.03(7)(a)
69	2.04(8)(a)

04 CONNECTICUT

Fisher

15	1.04(5)(a)

New London	Bibliography
352	6.04(1)(a)
566	1.04(2)(a)
850	5.04(1)(b)
915	5.02(26)(b.4)
936	5.04(4)(a)
947	5.04(3)(c)
950	5.04(3)(b)
951	5.04(3)(b.3)
952	5.04(3)(b.4)
1,093	5.02(35)(b.2)
1,094	5.02(35)(a.2)
1,371 Ghost	1.02(1)(g)

Trumbull

299	1.04(1)(a)
372	1.04(1)(b)
401	1.04(3)(a)
549	5.04(9)(b)
732	5.04(1)(a.2)
839	5.04(1)(c)
926	5.05(10)(b)
941	1.04(5)(a)
1,035	5.02(34)(g.2)
1,072	5.04(8)(d)
1,131	5.03(6)(a)
1,132	5.04(9)(a)
1,135	5.07(4)(b)
1,274	2.01(7)(a.3)
1,312	1.04(6)(a)
1,349	6.04(3)(a)
1,386	5.05(7)(a.2)
1,405	1.05(12)(a)
1,409	1.04(4)(a)
1,460	5.04(5)(b)
1,466	6.04(9)(a)
1,479	5.05(13)(a.4)
1,480	5.05(13)(a.9)

Trumbull 2d

1,887	5.02(26)(b.4)
1,990	1.04(2)(a)
2,090	5.04(5)(a)
2,117 Ghost	8.20(4)
2,122	5.07(9)(a.4)
2,123 Ghost	5.07(9)
2,124 Ghost	5.07(9)
2,148	5.02(34)(i.3)
2,169	5.04(1)(a)
2,170	5.04(1)(b.2)
2,173 Ghost	5.02(49)
2,296	5.04(3)(c)
2,423	5.04(8)(c)

Trumbull 2d	Bibliography
2,478	5.04(3)(b)
2,479	5.04(3)(b.3)
2,480	5.04(3)(b.4)
2,481	5.04(3)(b.9)
2,498	5.05(9)(b)
2,510	5.01(3)(a)
2,517	2.01(7)(a.5)
2,518	2.01(7)(a.8)
2,519	2.01(8)(a)
2,612	5.02(43)(b)
2,613	5.04(9)(a.3)
2,615	5.05(7)(a.3)
2,622	5.03(6)(a.3)
2,683	8.04(2)(a)
2,698	1.03(1)(b)

Trumbull 3d	
2,389	5.04(1)(b)

05 NEW YORK

Rutherfurd (Page and Number)	Bibliography
139, No. 2	4.05(1)(a)
145, No. 5	1.05(8)(a)
146, No. 1	1.05(8)(b)
147, No. 1	1.05(8)(c)
148, No. 1	1.05(8)(f)
148, No. 2	1.05(8)(f.2)
148, No. 3	1.05(8)(f.3)
148, No. 5	1.05(8)(l)
149, No. 2	4.05(2)(b)
151, No. 3	1.05(8)(d)
	1.05(8)(i)
153, No. 1	1.05(9)(a)
154, No. 2	1.05(8)(n)
154, No. 3	1.05(8)(e)
154, No. 4	1.05(8)(p)
154, No. 5	1.05(8)(o)
155, No. 2	1.05(9)(b)
166, No. 5	1.06(5)(a)
167, No. 2	1.06(5)(c)
249, No. 1	1.05(9)(b)
249, No. 2	1.05(9)(c)
249, No. 2n	1.05(9)(c.2)
250, No. 1	1.05(9)(b.2)
250, No. 2	1.05(9)(d)
250, No. 3	1.05(9)(d.2)
250, No. 4	1.05(9)(d.3)
251, No. 1	1.05(9)(d.4)
251, No. 2	1.05(9)(e)
251, No. 3	1.05(9)(b.3)
251, No. 4	1.05(9)(d.7)
252, No. 1	1.05(9)(d.8)
252, No. 2	1.05(9)(b.4)
252, No. 3	1.05(9)(d.9)
253, No. 1	1.05(9)(b.5)
253, No. 2	1.05(9)(d.10)
253, No. 3	1.05(9)(b.6)
254, No. 1	1.05(9)(c.3)
254, No. 2	1.05(9)(g)

06 NEW JERSEY

Humphrey	
82	5.06(2)(a)
110	1.06(11)(a)
128	1.06(13)(a)
129	1.06(12)(a)

Humphrey Appendix	
33	1.06(5)(b)
40	1.06(5)(d)
44	1.06(5)(f)
60	1.06(6)(a)
	1.06(10)(a)
94	1.06(8)(a)
97	1.06(9)(a)

Morsch	
142	5.06(3)(a)
240	1.06(16)(a)
311	6.06(1)(a)
453	1.06(17)(a)
461	2.03(14)(a)
472	4.06(3)(a)

07 PENNSYLVANIA

Gaines	
37a	1.07(30)(a)
37b	1.07(30)(a)
39a	1.07(30)(b)
39b	1.07(30)(b)
39c	1.07(30)(b)
39d	1.07(30)(b.3)

Gaines	Bibliography
39e	1.07(30)(b.3)
49a	1.07(37)(a)
49b	1.07(37)(a)

Hildeburn	Bibliography
32	1.06(1)(a)
64	1.07(1)(a)
70	1.06(2)(b)
196	1.09(1)(a)
206	4.07(1)(a)
214	1.07(2)(a)
270	3.07(1)(a)
278	3.07(1)(b.2)
279	3.07(1)(b)
283	3.07(1)(c)
288	3.07(1)(d)
309	4.07(2)(b)
310	4.07(2)(c)
311	4.07(2)(a)
394	2.04(5)(a)
463	4.07(3)(a)
540	4.07(4)(a)
549	9.00(2)(d)
551	1.05(9)(c)
695	4.08(1)(a)
756	4.08(2)(a)
815	1.07(3)(a)
1,265	8.07(1)(a)
1,417	5.07(3)(a)
1,442	1.07(4)(a)
1,483	1.05(9)(b.4)
1,687	5.07(4)(a)
1,832	5.06(1)(a)
1,872	8.20(2)(a)
2,125	1.06(7)(a)
2,130	5.07(5)(a)
2,176	3.06(1)(d)
2,279	1.06(10)(a)
2,391	1.07(5)(a)
2,406	8.02(6)(a)
2,554	5.07(6)(a)
2,592 Ghost	1.02(15)(i)
2,610	8.07(2)(a)
3,012	5.07(7)(a)
3,039	5.07(8)(a)
3,059	5.07(7)(b)
3,182	4.08(1)(a.2)
3,217	1.02(15)(u.6)
3,490	2.04(5)(a.3)
3,738	4.07(5)(a)
3,784	2.01(2)(a)
3,785	2.01(4)(a)
3,786	2.01(3)(a)
3,858	2.02(1)(a)
3,889	2.01(6)(a)
3,935	2.01(6)(b)
4,048	2.01(7)(a)
4,049	2.01(6)(c)
4,237	2.01(9)(a)
4,248	2.01(7)(f.4)
4,543	8.07(3)(a)

Metzger	
140	9.00(2)(j)
160	8.07(1)(a.2)
176	5.07(2)(a)

Pearl	
31	1.07(30)(a)
32	1.07(30)(b)

08 DELAWARE

Rink	
321	1.08(3)(a)
499	8.08(1)(a)

09 MARYLAND

Baer	
38	3.09(1)(a)
45	3.09(1)(b)
53	3.02(2)(e)
62	3.02(2)(g)
150	1.07(1)(a)
151	1.07(1)(a.2)

Garrett	
22	3.09(1)(a)
23	3.09(1)(b)
35	3.02(2)(f)

Minick	
233	8.09(2)
425 Ghost	8.02(11)
531	2.03(11)(b)

Wheeler	
371	8.09(1)(a)

10 VIRGINIA

Clayton-Torrence	Bibliography
70	3.09(1)(a)
73	3.09(1)(b)
86	3.10(2)(a)
139	10.10(1)(a)
155	10.10(2)(a)
250	10.10(3)

Swem	
823	1.10(4)(a)
4,538	1.10(6)(a)
5,861	3.10(2)(a)
7,696	1.10(9)(a)
7,697	1.10(9)(a)
7,698	1.10(3)(a)
7,790	1.10(2)(a)
7,806	1.10(10)(a)
7,807	1.10(9)(a.2)
7,855	1.10(8)(a)
7,856	1.10(7)(a)
7,857	1.10(11)(a)
7,858	1.10(4)(a)
7,859	1.10(14)(a)
7,860	1.10(6)(a)
8,003	1.10(13)(a)
8,004	1.10(13)(b)

VCRP	Bibliography
121-a	10.10(3)(a)
	10.10(3)(b)
121-b	10.10(4)(a)
	10.10(4)(b)
122-a	10.10(5)(a)
	10.10(5)(b)
122-b	10.10(6)(a)
	10.10(6)(b)
122-c	10.10(7)(a)
	10.10(7)(b)
122-d	10.10(8)(a)
	10.10(8)(b)
122-e	10.10(9)(a)
	10.10(9)(b)
123-a	10.10(10)(a)
	10.10(10)(b)
123-b	10.10(11)(a)
	10.10(11)(b)
123-c	10.10(12)(a)
	10.10(12)(b)
124-a	10.10(13)(a)
	10.10(13)(b)
124-b	10.10(14)(a)
	10.10(14)(b)
125	10.10(1)(b)

11 NORTH CAROLINA

McMurtrie	
59	1.11(1)(a)
60	1.11(1)(b)
64	4.11(1)(a)
111	4.11(2)(a)
181	2.03(7)(a)
182	8.11(2)(a)
219	1.11(3)(a)
220	1.11(4)(a)
232	1.11(4)(b)
233	1.11(4)(b.2)
238	2.03(7)(a)
265	1.11(5)(a)
D-7	8.11(1)(a)

Thornton Official	
3,250	1.11(6)(a.2)
3,251	1.11(6)(a.2)
3,252	1.11(4)(b.3)
3,254	1.11(4)(b)
	1.11(4)(b.2)
3,257	1.11(5)(a.2)
3,258	1.11(6)(a)

Thornton Unofficial	
5,124	8.11(2)(a)
6,606	1.11(1)(c)
6,607	1.11(1)(a)
12,801	7.11(1)(a)

Tinker (Pages)	
694	1.11(3)(a)
	1.11(4)(b)
694-95	1.11(4)(b.2)

Weeks	
115	1.11(4)(b)
123	1.11(5)(a)

Weeks	Bibliography
129	1.11(5)(a)
130	1.11(6)(a)

12 SOUTH CAROLINA

Adams Independence

57a	1.12(1)(a)
57b	1.12(1)(b)
57c	1.12(1)(b.2)
66	1.12(1)(c)

Morgan

80	4.12(1)(a)
288	1.12(1)(b)
290	1.12(1)(b.2)
291	1.12(1)(c)
292	1.12(1)(d)
435	4.12(2)(a)
551	2.01(7)(a.7)
570	8.12(1)(a)
584	8.12(2)(a)
603	4.12(3)(a)
614	2.04(6)(a)
803	1.12(6)(a)
826	1.12(7)(a)
851	2.04(2)(b)
939	1.12(8)(a)
988	1.12(9)(a)
1,049	11.12(1)(a)
1,087	11.12(1)(a)
1,108	1.12(11)(a)
1,123	11.12(2)(a)
1,124	4.12(6)(a)
1,125	1.12(10)(a)
1,213	11.12(3)(a)
1,241	5.12(1)(a)
1,251	4.12(2) Note

Turnbull (Pages)	Bibliography
57	3.12(1)(a)
97	4.12(1)(a)
166	1.12(1)(a)
169	1.12(1)(d)
170	1.12(1)(b)
	1.12(1)(b.2)
171	1.12(10)(c)
202	4.12(2)(a)
246	2.04(6)(a)
290	2.04(2)(b)
330	11.12(1)(a)
346	1.12(10)(a)
349	4.12(6)(a)
356	1.12(11)(a)
368	2.03(11)(b)
369	2.03(11)(a)
	2.03(11)(c)
375	2.03(13)(a)
400	2.03(10)(e)
448	1.12(8)(a.2)
459	2.03(11)(e)

14 VERMONT

Cooley

150	5.04(9)(d)
203	1.14(1)(a)
240	5.04(8)(c.2)
274	5.04(8)(c.3)
329 Ghost	5.01(4)
361	1.14(2)(a)
367 Ghost	8.20(7)
442	2.03(9)(a)
470	4.07(11)(b)
489	5.14(1)(a)

McCorison

198	5.04(9)(d)
256	1.14(1)(a)
304	5.03(8)(c.2)
351	5.04(8)(c.3)
396 Ghost	5.01(3)(b)
418	1.05(16)(b)
428	1.14(2)(a)
452 Ghost	8.20(7)(d)
498	2.03(9)(a)
512	4.07(11)(b)
671	1.05(16)(b.2)
1,891	1.05(16)(b.3)

15 KENTUCKY

Kentucky Imprints

36	1.14(1)(a)
45	1.14(1)(f)
49	1.14(1)(e)
49n	1.14(1)(d)
70	8.20(4)(f)

PRIVY COUNCIL

Ford Briefs (Pages)	Bibliography	Ford Briefs (Pages)	Bibliography
86	10.05(1)(a)	98	10.03(3)(a)
	10.05(1)(b)	99	10.03(3)(b)
	10.05(1)(c)		10.03(4)(a)
90	10.03(1)(a)		10.03(4)(b)

TABLE V: SUBJECT BIBLIOGRAPHIES:

MURDER, NEGROES, OLD FRONTIER, PATRIOTIC PRINTERS,

PLAYS, AND POETRY AND VERSE

MURDER

McDade	Bibliography	McDade	Bibliography
8	5.05(3)(a)	326	5.02(49)(a)
9	5.05(3)(b)	361	5.02(28)(b)
10	5.05(3)(d)	368	5.04(6)(a)
11	5.05(3)(c)	369	6.06(1)(a)
59	5.07(11)(a)	425	5.07(5)(a)
62	5.20(2)(a)	467	3.10(2)(a)
63	5.20(2)(b)	535	5.06(4)(a)
64	5.20(2)(c)	548	1.06(15)(a)
74	5.04(8)(c)	605	5.07(4)(b)
75	5.04(8)(d)	605n	5.07(4)(a)
76	5.04(8)(d.2)	640	1.06(1)(a)
77	5.04(8)(c.2)	663	1.07(32)(a)
77n	5.04(8)(c.3)	675	5.03(1)(a)
119	1.02(15)(e.2)	676	5.03(1)(b)
120	1.02(15)(i.3)	720	6.04(7)(a)
120n	1.02(15)(i.2)	720n	6.04(7)(a.2)
121	1.02(15)(j)	730	5.04(3)(b)
122	1.02(15)(n)	731	5.04(3)(b.2)
122n	1.02(15)(n.3)	732	5.04(3)(b.3)
	1.02(15)(n.5)	733	5.04(3)(b.4)
123	5.02(10)(b)	733n	5.04(3)(b.5)
130	5.07(7)(b)		5.04(3)(b.8)
130n	5.07(7)(a)		5.04(3)(b.9)
131	6.02(27)(a)		5.04(3)(b.10)
167	5.02(7)(a)		5.04(3)(b.11)
168	5.02(7)(b)		5.04(3)(b.12)
184	1.07(7)(a)		5.04(3)(b.14)
204	5.20(1)(a)		5.04(3)(d.2)
242	5.04(7)(a)	740	5.05(9)(a)
254	6.04(9)(a)	741	5.05(9)(b)
307	5.02(13)(a)	760	5.02(52)(a)
308	1.02(7)(c)	780	5.02(4)(a)
312	5.02(51)(a)	846	5.05(15)(b.2)

McDade	Bibliography
847	5.05(15)(b)
874	6.01(1)(b)
897	5.02(34)(b.2)
898	5.02(34)(b)
899	5.02(34)(g.2)
900	5.02(34)(g)
901	5.02(34)(e)
902	5.02(34)(h)
906	6.04(10)(a)
906n	6.04(10)(b)
926	6.02(4)(a)
960	5.05(13)(a.3)
960a	5.05(13)(a)
960b	5.05(13)(a.2)
960c	5.05(13)(a.4)
960d	5.05(13)(a.5)
960e	5.05(13)(a.6)
960g	5.05(13)(a.7)
960h	5.05(13)(b)
960i	5.05(13)(b.2)
960j	5.05(13)(b.3)
960k	5.05(13)(a.8)
960l Ghost	5.05(13)
960m	5.05(13)(a.9)
1,034	5.02(3)(a)
1,071	1.05(27)(b)
1,072	1.05(27)(c)
1,073	1.05(27)(a)
1,082	5.02(39)(a)
1,083	5.02(40)(a)
1,084	5.02(39)(b)
1,106	5.07(9)(a)
1,106n	5.07(9)(a.2)
1,123	1.05(21)(b)
1,124	1.05(21)(c)
1,125	1.05(21)(d)

NEGROES

Porter

85	5.02(51)(a)
89	5.02(42)(a)
170	5.06(4)(a)
203	5.04(9)(a)
204	5.04(9)(c)

OLD FRONTIER

Vail

Vail	Bibliography
164	3.06(1)(a)
165	3.06(1)(b)
183	3.06(1)(c)
294	6.02(9)(a.2)
560	3.06(1)(d)
652	2.04(5)(a.3)
953	5.05(15)(b.2)
954	5.05(15)(b)

PATRIOTIC PRINTERS

Vail Patriotic Pair (Pages)	
403	4.05(5)(a)
412	2.01(7)(a.4)

PLAYS

Hill

72	2.01(7)(l)
82	2.01(7)(p)

POETRY AND VERSE

Stoddard

142	5.02(50)(a)

Wegelin

2	1.02(15)(s)
3	1.02(15)(ii)
136	1.05(21)(d)
201	5.02(11)(a)
291	5.04(3)(d)
469	5.02(35)(b.2)
470	5.02(35)(b)
473	1.03(1)(c)
477B	5.02(32)(i)
478	5.02(6)(b)
481	5.02(18)(a)
587	5.02(21)(a)
588	5.02(17)(b)
589	5.02(8)(c)
590	5.02(32)(d)
621	5.02(36)(a)
631	2.01(7)(c)
648	5.02(8)(d)
728	5.02(49)(b)
746	5.02(6)(a)
771	5.02(32)(f)
787	5.02(32)(g)
792	5.02(32)(h)
802	8.20(5)(d.4)

Wegelin	Bibliography
818	5.01(2)(d)
826	5.02(5)(a)

Winslow	Bibliography
22	1.02(15)(f)
38	5.02(5)(a)
39	5.02(6)(b)
40	5.02(8)(d)
41	5.02(17)(b)
42	5.02(18)(a)
43	5.02(30)(a)
44	5.02(21)(a)
45	1.02(17)(a)
46	1.02(17)(b)
47	5.04(3)(d.2)
48	5.02(32)(b)
49	5.02(32)(c)
50	5.02(32)(g)
51	5.04(8)(a)
52	5.01(2)(c)
75	2.01(7)(e.2)

TABLE VI: COLLECTIONS

Church	
465	3.02(1)(a)
466	3.02(1)(a.2)
541A	3.09(1)(b)
563	3.02(2)(d)
566	3.02(2)(c)
571	3.02(2)(f)
598	3.02(2)(g)
607	3.02(2)(h)
635	6.02(2)(a)
674	9.02(3)(a)
681	9.02(3)(b)
733	1.02(1)(c)
734	1.02(1)(d)
736	1.02(1)(e)
744	1.07(1)(d)
767	1.02(2)(b)
802	1.05(2)(b)
809	1.05(2)(c.2)
826	1.02(3)(c.2)
951	1.05(10)(c)
954	1.06(5)(a)
961	1.06(5)(b)
982	1.06(5)(d)
988	1.06(5)(f)
1,016	1.05(9)(b.4)
1,032	3.02(1)(c.2)
1,058	1.06(9)(a)
1,076	1.02(15)(i.2)
1,077	1.02(15)(i.3)
1,078	1.02(15)(i.4)
1,080	1.02(15)(1)
1,081A	1.02(15)(c)
1,086	1.02(15)(p)
1,094	1.02(15)(r.2)
1,095	1.02(15)(t.2)
1,104	1.02(15)(u)
1,126	1.02(15)(v)
1,134	3.05(2)(a)
1,140	1.02(15)(z)
1,145	1.02(15)(aa)
1,148	1.02(15)(bb)
1,151	2.01(2)(a)
1,152	2.01(3)(a)
1,154	2.01(4)(a)
1,160	1.02(15)(dd)
1,165	2.01(7)(a)
1,166	2.01(7)(b.2)
1,167	2.01(7)(a.3)
1,168	2.01(7)(b)
1,169	2.01(6)(c)
1,175	1.02(15)(ee)
1,178	2.01(7)(b.3)
1,181	1.02(15)(ff)
1,185	2.01(7)(f)
1,190	1.02(15)(gg)
1,200	1.02(15)(hh)
1,279	2.01(7)(1)

Huntington	
6	6.02(2)(a)
65	1.09(1)(a)
167	1.06(5)(f)
205	8.20(1)(b)
252	1.05(11)(a.2)
272	1.05(13)(a)
273	1.05(13)(b)
289	1.12(1)(b)
297	1.02(15)(i.3)
299	1.11(1)(b)

Huntington	Bibliography
321	5.04(3)(c)
322	3.04(3)(d.2)
327	1.02(15)(t.2)
334	5.04(3)(b.7)
340	5.02(32)(g)
392	1.02(15)(v.2)
394	2.04(5)(a.3)
443	5.02(35)(b.2)
444	5.02(35)(a.2)
728	7.20(2)(b)
New York Public	
53	1.02(3)(b)
130	1.03(1)(a)
172	5.02(5)(a)
176	1.05(7)(a)
179	1.09(2)(a)
186	5.02(12)(b)
187	1.03(2)(b)
188	1.03(2)(a)
204	1.03(3)(a)
249	5.02(16)(b)
385	5.02(21)(a)
391	5.04(1)(a.2)
411	1.12(1)(b)
424	1.02(15)(e)
443	1.02(15)(f)
444	1.02(15)(a)
445	1.02(15)(g)
459	5.02(26)(a)
479	5.02(32)(i)
490	5.02(32)(b)
508	5.05(9)(a.2)
664	5.02(34)(b)
665	5.02(34)(c.2)
669	5.02(34)(i.2)
672	5.04(6)(a)
713	5.02(35)(b)
947	5.05(12)(a)
973	5.02(46)(b)
973	5.02(46)(b)
1,228	2.05(2)(a)
1,260	7.20(2)(1)
Rosenbach	
68	2.04(5)(b)

RPJCB 4th (Pages)	Bibliography
9	6.02(2)(a)
76	3.10(2)(a)
155	6.02(2)(a.2)
167	5.02(1)(a)
	5.02(1)(a.2)
	5.02(1)(b)
168	5.02(1)(c)
268	1.02(1)(e)
271	1.02(1)(c.2)
	1.02(1)(d)
	1.02(1)(d.2)
	1.02(1)(a.2)
272	1.02(1)(e)
278	1.02(1)(f)
286	1.07(1)(c)
287	1.07(1)(b)
315	1.02(2)(a)
352	1.02(2)(b)
407	1.02(1)(g)
413	3.02(2)(j)
508	5.05(9)(a.2)
Sowerby	
451	1.02(1)(g)
1,759	1.10(3)(a)
1,760	1.10(4)(a)
1,761	1.10(6)(a)
1,762	1.10(8)(a)
1,763	1.10(11)(a)
1,764	1.10(7)(a)
1,765	1.10(14)(a)
1,951	1.05(2)(e)
	3.12(1)(d)
2,018	1.03(6)(a)
2,088	1.07(26)(a)
	1.07(33)(a)
	1.07(35)(a)
2,090	1.10(9)(a)
	1.10(10)(a)
2,092	1.10(2)(a)
2,167	2.03(7)(a)
3,171	2.03(3)(a)
3,193	4.20(4)(a)
3,216	2.03(11)(c)
3,294	1.07(34)(b)

Index of Main Entries

An alphabetical index of the headings of Principal Entries. Each person or party referred to in a heading is separately listed, with an appropriate change made in the text of the heading. Surnames only are shown, except that for Chapters 5.00, 6.00 and 7.00 given names are also shown.

-Q-

-R-

-S-

-T-

-U-

About the Compiler

WILFRED J. RITZ is Professor at Washington and Lee Law School, Lexington, Virginia. He is the author of *Automobile Liability Insurance: The Law in Virginia* and *The Uniform Commercial Code and the Commercial Law of Virginia*. In addition, he has contributed articles to *Law Library Journal, University of Richmond Law Review, Washington and Lee Law Review,* and *Virginia Law Review,* among others.

www.ingramcontent.com/pod-product-compliance
Ingram Content Group UK Ltd.
Pitfield, Milton Keynes, MK11 3LW, UK
UKHW020230290926
15470UKWH00002B/463

9 780313 240577